The Legacy of the Soviet Bloc

THE LEGACY OF THE SOVIET BLOC

Edited by
Jane Shapiro Zacek and Ilpyong J. Kim

University Press of Florida
Gainesville/Tallahassee/Tampa/Boca Raton
Pensacola/Orlando/Miami/Jacksonville

Copyright 1997 by the Board of Regents of the State of Florida
Printed in the United States of America on acid-free paper
All rights reserved

02 01 00 99 98 97 6 5 4 3 2 1

Library of Congress Cataloging-in-Publication Data

The legacy of the Soviet bloc / edited by Jane Shapiro Zacek and Ilpyong J. Kim.
   p. cm.
   Includes bibliographical references and index.
   ISBN 0–8130–1475–1 (Cloth)
   1. Europe, Easterm—Politics and government—1945–
   2. Europe, Eastern—Foreign relations—1989– 3. Post-communism—Europe, Eastern.
   I. Zacek, Jane Shapiro. II. Kim, Ilpyong J., 1931– .
DJK50.L437   1997   96–16351
320.947—dc20

The University Press of Florida is the scholarly publishing agency for the State University System of Florida, comprised of Florida A & M University, Florida Atlantic University, Florida International University, Florida State University, University of Central Florida, University of Florida, University of North Florida, University of South Florida, and University of West Florida.

University Press of Florida
15 Northwest 15th Street
Gainesville, FL 32611

CONTENTS

DEDICATION

Almost thirty-five years ago, several of the contributors to this volume participated in a year-long graduate seminar at Columbia University entitled "The Communist Orbit." About a dozen students and five faculty members met each Tuesday afternoon to examine various aspects of the international communist system.

By the 1961–62 academic year, when this particular seminar met, features of the international communist system included the Sino-Soviet rift, Castro's consolidation of power in Cuba, Khrushchev's renewed and vigorous public attacks on Stalin and some features of the Soviet system, and the immediate repercussions of the building of the Berlin Wall.

Zbigniew Brzezinski was one of the faculty members who participated in "The Communist Orbit." No component of the communist-ruled world escaped his attention or expertise. His well-articulated theories on why communist leaders acted as they did continually impressed all of us. Professor Brzezinski had come to Columbia from Harvard a year earlier to join the faculty of political science and the Russian (now Harriman) Institute as a young but already prominent scholar of Soviet and communist affairs. His *The Soviet Bloc: Unity and Conflict* had recently been published by Harvard University Press and for many years was a widely used text in Soviet foreign and international communist affairs. Some of us still routinely assign this book in courses about Soviet foreign policy and international communism/post-communism.

Professor Brzezinski rapidly developed a reputation for encouraging his students' intellectual development. His zest and enthusiasm both for communist studies and for life were contagious. We students found ourselves simultaneously probing into obscure publications and traveling to obscure meetings with representatives of communist-ruled countries to interview them and try to uncover information that could not be found in print. Indeed, this tireless quest to learn more about communist societies, still largely closed to outside observers, stayed with us and became one of our lasting debts to this outstanding scholar.

At the same time, Professor Brzezinski urged us to take intellectual risks, to link scholarship to the real world of politics by developing informed opinions about the future course of communist-ruled societies. He was willing to speculate on policy positions that communist leaders in one or another country were likely to adopt. He was usually right. None of us was surprised, then, when in late 1976 he was selected by President-elect Jimmy Carter to serve as national security adviser. Professor Brzezinski skillfully interwove his scholarly knowledge and his real-world understanding of politics and policy making; he played a major role in the formulation, articulation, and implementation of American foreign policy during the Carter presidency.

In mid-1988, Professor Brzezinski completed a manuscript, *The Grand Failure: The Birth and Death of Communism in the Twentieth Century* (published in 1989), which predicted the disintegration of the communist system. "This is a book," he wrote, "about the terminal crisis of communism." He could not have been more right.

He continues to teach, write, and articulate what he believes America's role in the post–Cold War world ought properly to be. He has also kept in touch with his former Columbia doctoral students.

All of these former students whom we asked to contribute to this volume were delighted to do so. Because of time (and, in a few cases, health) constraints, not everyone we contacted was able to produce a manuscript. They join us, however, in dedicating this volume to our mentor and friend, Zbigniew Brzezinski.

Jane Shapiro Zacek
Ilpyong J. Kim

Introduction

The Transformation of Communist Rule

JANE SHAPIRO ZACEK

The breathtakingly rapid collapse of communist rule in Eastern Europe and the Soviet Union is one of the critical events of our time. Although we are not yet able to assess its impact adequately, clearly it has had and will continue to have profound implications for the citizens of these countries struggling to establish and stabilize postcommunist political, economic, and social systems. It also has and will continue to have an enormous impact on the nature of global affairs, currently labeled "the post–cold war new international order."

The communist system was a grand-scale experiment in social engineering. It failed. As Zbigniew Brzezinski wrote in *The Grand Failure* a year before communism collapsed in East-Central Europe, the failure of the Soviet experience precipitated the "terminal crisis of contemporary communism." Postcommunist regimes' current efforts to build and solidify democratic, market-oriented political and economic systems upon the legacy of a one-party, centralized, totalitarian-authoritarian system is another grand-scale experiment, the success of which is by no means certain. What *is* certain is that the process will be long and zigzagged and that democratic institution-building is likely to alternate with periods of sustained authoritarian rule. The experiences of establishing and stabilizing democracy elsewhere in the world demonstrate that creating, implementing, and sustaining democratic processes are not simple and, typically, are not accomplished quickly.

COMMUNIST REFORM EFFORTS

The essays in this volume focus on themes central to understanding why communist political systems could not be reformed sufficiently so that communist parties could retain political power within an environment of reform.

No Communist Party (CP) was willing to relinquish enough of the control that was necessary to implement broad political and economic reforms. Without extensive reforms, the continued economic decline that each country experienced could be neither stemmed nor reversed. Parties generally were unwilling to eliminate central planning (although in Hungary, for example, there were fewer controls on economic production, distribution, sales, and prices than elsewhere in Eastern Europe). Contradictory policies existed side by side so that reformers were simultaneously encouraged and restrained. Small-scale entrepreneurs were permitted to develop and expand private businesses as long as they hired only a few workers and paid exorbitant taxes on profits. Export and import controls, a centralized state-controlled banking system that granted credits almost exclusively to state-owned rather than private firms, limitations on innovation and risk-taking, and other policies doomed to failure the cautious economic reforms that had been introduced. Unless political leaders were willing to change the economic system drastically by such measures as eliminating short-and long-term planning, decentralizing the purchase, distribution, and supply systems, facilitating and encouraging privatization, holding state-owned enterprises accountable for productivity and profitability, permitting (indeed pushing) continually unprofitable firms into bankruptcy, encouraging private and cooperative farming (and ending the state and collective farm system), taking necessary steps to create a convertible currency, and adopting a host of related measures, the extensive reform essential for improving economic performance could not be instituted.

Further, such large-scale economic reform was closely related to, if not contingent upon, equally large-scale political reform. Political controls had to be lifted if a productive economy were to be created. The CP would need to give up its monopoly of political power and become one of several political parties seeking popular support. Society would need to be less controlled so as to encourage popular expression of ideas. Party leaders, even confirmed reformers, understood correctly that significantly reducing the party's authority and role in society would lead directly to its demise.

When CPs were finally compelled to curtail their authority, they generally were not able to restrain ethnic and regional/local claims to power, nor could they prevent frequent industrial strikes and other demonstrations of mass dissatisfaction. Once some reforms, albeit limited, had been undertaken, popular pressures for more significant reforms could not be contained without extensive military and police action, which most party leaders were unwilling to authorize. As a consequence, communist rule collapsed.

The collapse of communist rule in one country deeply and immediately affected events in neighboring countries. The Polish CP's decision to negotiate with Solidarity and to permit partially free competitive parliamentary elections in June 1989, along with the anticommunist vote and the subsequent installation of the first noncommunist government since the late 1940s, had a direct impact on events in Hungary, where party leaders were being urged to share political authority with noncommunists. Similar events were repeated elsewhere in Eastern Europe. In Yugoslavia, parliamentary elections in the republics were coupled with regional leaders' determination to withdraw from the Yugoslav federation and establish independence. All of these events surely influenced the Baltic states' determination to press for independence despite Soviet resistance. This drive for independence spread to other Soviet republics, including Ukraine, Armenia, Georgia, Moldova, and Russia itself. Baltic independence was ensured by the failed August 1991 coup. Independence for the other republics came a mere four months later with the disintegration of the USSR.

Reemergence of Virulent Nationalism

In those multinational countries where nationalist pride and animosities had generally been held in check under communist rule, not only did the central political structure collapse but the country disintegrated into its constituent parts as well. The eruption of rampant nationalism and the consequent drive for political independence is another theme considered in some of the essays in this volume. The situation in the former Yugoslavia has been the most virulent. Since the early 1990s, both Serbia and Croatia have sought to extend their control to all areas in which Serb and Croat nationals live, resulting in protracted and bloody civil wars. Both countries have worked assiduously not only to dismember Bosnia and Hercegovina but also to murder many Bosnian Moslems in the process. Once Bosnia and Hercegovina are permanently carved up, continual armed conflict is likely between Serbs and Albanians over Kosovo and over Serb efforts to gain control of parts of Macedonia and between Serbia and Croatia over regions within Croatia that both claim.

To the north, Russia is faced with major pressures from nationality groups both internally and externally. Russia itself is a multinational federation, in which the non-Russian-populated republics have yet to gain a meaningful voice in central government policy making. Of special importance, some of these republics (such as Chechnya in the northern Caucasus) have vast natural resources that the Russian economy needs but the republics claim sole control over. The new Russian Federation constitution (1993) stipulates equal representation of Russia's eighty-nine republics and regions in a second, upper chamber of the national parliament.

Some Russian-populated regions of the country have also asserted their autonomy within the Federation. A number of regional governmental leaders have called for a reconfiguration of the Federation, in which constituent units would not be determined primarily by ethnic considerations; rather, these units would be geographically large and multi-ethnic, with shared regional interests and concerns. Regional leaders have called for much greater political autonomy backed by constitutional and legal guarantees than the central government is willing to grant. Intergovernmental relations between the constituent units and the central government in Moscow remain unsettled and unstable.

The Russian government's policy toward the millions of Russians living outside Russia in other post-Soviet countries remains unclear. Large numbers of Russians live in the Baltics, Ukraine, Kazakhstan, and elsewhere in central Asia. Former vice-president Aleksandr Rutskoi (arrested with other anti-Yeltsin leaders during the October 1993 takeover of the Russian parliament building) has spoken frequently of the Russian government's "responsibility" to protect Russian nationals in these new states. The Russian military clearly supports this view, as do right-wing political parties. The potential for armed conflict between Russians and non-Russians both in Russia itself and in other post-Soviet states remains great.

The Soviet Union, Yugoslavia as we knew it since its creation after World War I, and Czechoslovakia have, at least for the present, disappeared as multinational states. In their place are a number of countries, all still multinational, a few large, most small, struggling to establish and maintain their independence. Some have a history of independence before the communist takeover to build upon; most have a historical experience of some political autonomy in earlier multinational empires, but that experience ended almost a century ago.

Postcommunist Transition Strategies

Several of the essays in this volume consider the strategies adopted in seeking to create a democratic, market-based political and economic system. While many of the policies are similar, the pace at which they have been adopted and the extent of popular willingness to accept a sustained decline in the standard of living together with continued political and social instability have differed widely. In almost every postcommunist country, the rate of transforming the economic system from centralized to decentralized, from public to private (or at least mixed), from monopolistic to competitive, has slowed. In recent parliamentary elections, former communist parties under new names have won substantial popular support, in part because they have advocated a slower transition toward a privatized market-based economy. In many countries, the reconstituted CP is the leading party in a governing coalition. In Romania, Croatia, Serbia, Slovakia, Ukraine, Kazakhstan, and several other countries, former CP leaders remain in power, having harnessed the support of the citizenry's nationalist aspirations. Some reformed CP leaders have been voted into office after several years of non-CP leadership, as in Poland and Hungary. Even such reformers as Boris Yeltsin and Eduard Shevardnadze were prominent party leaders less than a decade ago. While they (and others) do not seem as locked into earlier experiences (with ideological and political constraints) as Mikhail Gorbachev was, for instance, impatience with the slowness of the democratic process still results in their insistence on emergency executive rule and law-making by executive decree.

Economic transition strategies have included such policies as demonopolization, decentralization, establishment of a wholesale and retail pricing system based on real production costs, elimination of state subsidies, and reduction of bank credits available to keep unprofitable state-owned enterprises operational despite accumulating debts. Privatization efforts have included the promotion of either domestic or foreign (or joint) private investment, a voucher system to provide the citizenry with a stake in privatization and the emerging economic system, implementation of a tax structure that encourages private investment, and creation of a stable, convertible currency. At the same time, economic reformers have pressed for updating production technology and methods, retraining workers laid off as enterprises have restructured, and dealing with the dislocations that have resulted from increased unemployment and growing poverty.

Thus far, privatization in most countries encompasses that part of the economy that has been developed or expanded since the collapse of communist rule. Most medium and large-scale enterprises have yet to become privatized, and timetables for completing the privatization process have been extended indefinitely.

In addition, requirements have been established by international financial credit institutions such as the International Monetary Fund. Countries seeking loans must first limit budget deficits and control inflation rates. Continuing high rates of inflation have been fueled by industrial strikes; governments generally have responded to strikers' demands by raising wages, leading to further inflationary pressures.

In the political realm, multiparty systems have been established, although many parties have not yet built a solid base of support. Party systems generally are in transition, with too many parties vying for representation, resulting in splintered legislatures. Many party leaders have little or no political experience and show little willingness to negotiate or compromise, essential for building a democratic system. Most of the East European countries and the Baltic states reverted to the parliamentary system they had established after World War I, with some form of proportional representation guiding their electoral processes. The other post-Soviet countries and the post-Yugoslav states mainly have opted for a presidential/parliamentary system patterned after the French, although the authority of the president currently exceeds that of the French chief executive. Presidents frequently request emergency powers (and use them even if parliament has refused to grant them), rule by decree, and call for popular referenda to override the legislature when faced with oppositionist parliaments.

Altogether, there are enormous difficulties in trying to introduce and implement political and economic reforms simultaneously, including creating an appropriate legal framework for a democratic system, a judicial system that protects this legal framework, and a market-based economy that requires revamping or creating a multitude of financial and taxation systems. At the same time, policy makers must contend with rising unemployment, sustained high inflation, growing government debt, and declining living standards. Living standards for pensioners have declined steeply, a consequence of the elimination of price controls and state subsidies for most basic consumer goods, housing, medical care, and other social services. Most reform-minded leaders understand that there are limits to how long material improvements in the standard of living and a restoration of political stability can be postponed. Once those limits are reached, popular interest in continuing to sacrifice in order to build a democracy may well end.

INTERNATIONAL RELATIONS ISSUES

The emergence of newly independent countries poses new questions about the nature of relations among them, particularly among those that formerly were part of a larger entity. In the post–Soviet Union, for example, countries that were economically interdependent and dominated by Russian interests are now struggling to establish economic cooperation without subordination, although that may not prove possible. In Eastern Europe (including the Baltics), countries are in the process of reorienting their economies and their commercial relations from east to west, with mixed results. Producing goods for sale outside of the former Soviet bloc necessitates greater attention to quality and competitiveness. All of the East European countries are obliged to import fuel and other natural resources. Supplier (primarily Russian) price subsidies and the possibility of paying in nonconvertible currencies or with goods, features of communist interstate trade, have been eliminated.

The economies of the Central European countries are likely to be less tied to Russia than to the West, Germany in particular, while the economies of countries of the post–Soviet Union (excluding the Baltics) are more likely to be tied to (and dominated by) Russia. The Commonwealth of Independent States (CIS), created in late 1991 when the USSR was in the final stage of collapse, appears at present to be little more than a loose confederation of former Soviet republics; by the end of 1993, all but the Baltic states had become members. While it is unclear what CIS membership actually entails or what authority this entity has, it *is* clear that Russia dominates the organization. As

Gorbachev called for a "common economic space" in the reconfiguration of the Soviet federal system, so the Commonwealth appears to have established (at least on paper) a customs-free association whose members have advantages that nonmembers do not have.

Initially, in 1992, it seemed that the CIS framework might provide for the common security interests of its members. Because of the unwillingness of some members to commit their military forces to a supranational command, preferring instead to establish and retain national control, the CIS as a security umbrella has been replaced by the Russian military. The latter has been involved through its "peacekeeping activities" in supporting pro-Russian governments in Georgia, Tadzhikistan, and Moldova and in reducing the protracted Armenian-Azerbaijan conflict. By mid-1993, the Russian government was funding almost three-fourths of the Tadzhik national budget, even more than the Soviet government had provided in earlier years.

The newly independent states of the post–Soviet Union remain dependent on Russian military protection. At the same time, Russia is seeking to reestablish its military authority over as much of the territory of the former Soviet Union as it can. Thus Russia reluctantly withdrew its troops from Estonia and Latvia only in mid-1994, despite these countries' earlier repeated requests that it do so. Although Russian troops are no longer stationed in Ukraine, there is continued disagreement about ultimate control of the Black Sea Fleet headquartered in Crimea (Ukraine), currently divided between Ukrainian and Russian control. By 1994, Ukraine had finally declared its intention to deactivate its nuclear arsenal (including the return of nuclear warheads to Russia for dismantling), signed the START agreement, and called for U.S. security guarantees in addition to the several billion dollars it needed to implement nuclear arms transfers. (Belarus and Kazakhstan, the other two nuclear nations created through the collapse of the USSR, had already agreed to relinquish their nuclear capability.) Military clashes between Ukraine and Russia cannot be ruled out, particularly if Ukrainian military independence is bolstered by enhanced political and economic independence.

What kinds of security arrangements among themselves and with the North Atlantic Treaty Organization (NATO) can the countries of East-Central Europe establish during this transitional period? The now-defunct Warsaw Pact and Council on Mutual Economic Assistance facilitated Soviet domination over the region. Poland, Hungary, the Czech Republic, and Slovakia are seeking to gain membership in NATO, although Russia has vigorously opposed such membership. The four countries have been granted European Union (EU) associate membership, and they are looking toward full membership (not likely before the turn of the century at the earliest) as a way of assisting their own economies as well as confirming them as part of "the West."

Russian Foreign Policy Issues

Thus far, Russian foreign policies have not deviated much from those of the late Gorbachev years with respect to strategic and conventional force reductions, improvement of economic and political relations with China (even though the CP continues to rule that country), inability to resolve the Kurile Islands issue with Japan, and collaboration with South Korea while maintaining relations with a dictatorial communist regime still in control in North Korea. Several essays consider the continuity between recent Soviet and current Russian foreign policies.

Russia took on the huge Soviet foreign debt (estimated at $75 to $90 billion in 1992), including those portions of the debt initially parceled out to other post-Soviet states. Despite successful negotiations for a rescheduling of payments and some loan forgiveness, Russian indebtedness will continue to be a substantial brake on the country's ability to move toward a market-based economy, strengthen its productive capabilities, and increase its volume of foreign trade.

Russian relations with Marxist governments in the developing world have changed drastically from Soviet policies in the pre-Gorbachev period. Indeed, as Soviet military and economic support declined for many of these self-styled Marxist regimes during the last years of the Gorbachev period, many of them either changed their domestic priorities or replaced their leaders with non-Marxists. With limited economic resources and revised foreign policy interests, Russia, following the Gorbachev policy line, has dramatically reduced its direct role in much of the developing world. Withdrawal of Soviet assistance to Cuba, for example, has left Castro scrambling to find alternative sources of support and pulling back from formerly Soviet-backed revolutionary activities in Latin America and Africa.

Because the failure of communist rule in the Soviet Union is considered the major root cause of the collapse of communism in most of the world, it is appropriate that all of the essays in this volume focus directly or peripherally on events internal to Russia and other post-Soviet states, on other former communist countries, and on postcommunist international relations, policies, and strategies in which Russia figures prominently.

Soviet and Post-Soviet Internal Developments

William E. Odom looks at the role of the Soviet military during the Gorbachev perestroika era and its response to perestroika's requirements for budgetary reductions as well as popular discontent over a variety of military policies. Use of military force to quell domestic unrest (as, for example, in Georgia and Azerbaijan), as well as peaceful efforts to achieve independence in Lithuania, engendered further difficulties because some commanders refused to participate in these activities. Widespread military disarray was demonstrated during the failed coup of August 1991. Defense Minister Dmitrii Yazov was a member of the coup's Emergency Committee, but many military officials, especially in the Air Force, supported Yeltsin and other coup resisters. Just as the military played a critical role in ensuring the coup's failure, its support for the creation of the Commonwealth (as an alternative to Gorbachev's "renewed federation" proposals) ensured the collapse of the USSR.

In April 1992, a Russian defense capability separate from the CIS was reconstituted fully. During the next year, Russia and a number of CIS members signed a collective security treaty and a variety of associated collective military agreements. These arrangements, together with the reality of Russian troops stationed in some of the post-Soviet states (including those that have not signed any collective security documents), facilitate continued Russian domination over much of the territory of the Soviet empire. Odom points out that the newly published Russian military doctrine calls for Russian military hegemony over the whole CIS. Even the Yeltsin government does not seem opposed to this position.

An early prerequisite for moving toward a less authoritarian political system adopted in the last years of the Gorbachev period was curtailment of the role of the CPSU and its control over the key elements of the Soviet system. Constitutionally ending the party's monopoly of political power in 1990 opened a Pandora's box of pressures from both reformers and conservatives: those who favored more rapid political reform and worked toward this end, and those who believed curtailment of the party spelled the death knell of Soviet-style socialism and were determined to save it.

Barbara Ann Chotiner looks at the impact and implementation of the restricted role of the party on the regional and local levels with specific reference to agricultural policy making, an area in which the party traditionally had maintained a dominant role. She raises the general issue of how well new policies and procedures were accepted and implemented during the last years of the Gorbachev period. Officials on all levels had varied reactions to the myriad of political and other reform measures, some contradictory, others reversing just-instituted policies. Further, some party officials were reluctant to relinquish their "detailed enmeshment" in the agricultural production and distribution systems.

Cynthia S. Kaplan (and Henry E. Brady) inquires into attitudes of party members in the Russian Federation. These members were surveyed on a broad spectrum of issues as part of a larger survey of citizens in that republic (over twelve thousand respondents) conducted in the months just before the failed coup of August 1991. The survey demonstrated substantial differences of opinion on what kind of society Russia should be and the steps that needed to be taken to create appropriate political and economic systems for such a society. Kaplan found that there were substantial differences of opinion between party members and the nonparty public on many issues. There were also generational differences.

The December 1993 parliamentary elections demonstrated that a sizable percentage of the population was opposed to continued rapid reform with its accompanying disruptions. Yeltsin found it difficult in early 1994 to construct a cabinet that included articulate and forceful reformers who earlier had held important cabinet and advisory positions (such as Yegor Gaidar and Boris Fedorov) as well as conservatives who, he believed, also should be represented in the government. Thus Yeltsin found himself forced to attend to conservative demands so as to retain political authority, just as Gorbachev had done during his years in power.

One of the clusters of questions posed in the survey centered on the Gorbachev-sponsored renewed Treaty of Union, which was supposed to redefine the political authority granted to the central government and the powers retained by the constituent republics. The original treaty was signed in 1922, thereby creating the USSR. Jane Shapiro Zacek considers Gorbachev's efforts to revise the treaty, beginning publicly in 1988. Failure to gain republic leaders' agreement on a treaty acceptable to a broad spectrum of central party leaders was one of the precipitating events of the August 1991 coup; this failure also served to promote nationalist aspirations for independence and led directly to the disintegration of the Soviet Union.

Zacek traces the negotiations between central and republic leaders, which produced successive treaty drafts. From the outset, the negotiations were not well founded. Rather than negotiations between central government executive and parliamentary officials on one side and republic officials on the other, the treaty should have been negotiated only among republic officials themselves.

The draft treaty became a victim of the failed coup. Yeltsin's enormous prestige acquired during and after the coup, the independence of the three Baltic states recognized within weeks after the coup, and the impending vote on Ukrainian independence strengthened republic governments' unwillingness to negotiate further with the center about the redistribution of political authority.

Zenovia A. Sochor looks at the August coup and its impact in Russia and Ukraine, focusing on the determination of the republics to extricate themselves from central government domination. Activities in each capital differed substantially. In Moscow, Yeltsin and other reformers sought to break with the communist past rather than try to reform it; in Kiev, Leonid Kravchuk and others took hold of the mounting popular sentiment for independence and made it their cause. Events in Moscow became revolutionary, Sochor writes, when the Russian government under Yeltsin's determined leadership rejected the coup, its leaders, and their decrees. More important, the Russian position prevailed.

While Yeltsin and other Russian republic leaders and big city mayors were pressing for more comprehensive reforms than the central government was willing to accept or support, Ukrainian reformers were focused initially on democratization through the ballot box. In contrast to Yeltsin, Sochor writes, Kravchuk did not make a decisive break with the old system. Yeltsin had resigned from the party in 1990, a year before the coup. Kravchuk, like Gorbachev, did not resign until after the coup when the party was made illegal. Kravchuk's appeal was based on nationalism and the drive for Ukrainian independence; his commitment to genuine political and economic reform within Ukraine was vague at best.

Neither Ukraine's nor Russia's future is clearly charted. (The same holds for virtually all the post-Soviet states.) Nils H. Wessell looks at alternative Russian futures five years after the collapse of the USSR. Among the possibilities are a Gorbachev-like effort to reform (with much backing and filling), which is inherently unstable. A second alternative is a military takeover with reversion to an authoritarian political system, more in the Russian tradition than are current efforts to move toward a democratic system.

A third scenario focuses on the disintegration of the Russian Federation; 18 percent of the Federation's population is non-Russian, but these republics encompass just over 50 percent of the country's geography. The last scenario posits the successful transition to a democratic free-market system. The economy revives, and the path toward a more prosperous future is opened. Coherent national political parties are organized, and the Communist Party or its successor is quashed permanently through the ballot box. Civic participation flourishes, a legal system protecting private property is adopted, and corruption is conquered.

Although this last scenario is most preferable, at least from the Western vantage point, it is by no means the most likely. Wessell suggests that a Gorbachev-like effort—trying to maintain a centrist position while constantly negotiating with persistent reformers and determined conservatives—is the most likely in the short term. It is least likely to succeed because it does not offer a clear program of action.

POSTCOMMUNIST TRANSITIONS IN CENTRAL EUROPE

Among Wessell's scenarios is a mirroring of Yugoslav disintegration and protracted civil war. Lenard J. Cohen reviews the aftermath of Yugoslavia's "violent disintegration," particularly the continuing efforts by both Croatia and

Serbia to acquire additional territory occupied by their respective nationals. In so doing, both have succeeded in carving up Bosnia and killing or forcing into emigration tens of thousands of Bosnian citizens.

Events in postcommunist Yugoslavia attest to the horrors of unbridled nationalism. While nationalist movements contributed to the collapse of communist one-party rule in each republic, their consolidation of power in their respective new states has retarded the further development of pluralism and dimmed the prospects for the transition toward democratic rule. Only Slovenia thus far appears to have embarked seriously and purposefully on that transition.

According to Cohen, Croatia and Serbia may be described as "emergent ethnic democracies" in which the dominant ethnic population has privileged status. Authoritarian in nature, both states have permitted some competitive pluralism, mostly free (and frequent) presidential and parliamentary elections, and restrained government repression.

The ethnic diversity in communist-ruled Yugoslavia was extraordinary; no single ethnic group constituted half or more of Yugoslavia's total population as Russians did in the Soviet Union. Some communist-ruled countries such as Poland were quite homogeneous, however, with ethnic minorities making up only a small percentage of the total population.

Lucja Swiatkowski Cannon reviews Polish transition strategies, beginning in late 1989. Poland was the first postcommunist country to move resolutely and rapidly toward establishing a market-based economy. Among the adverse results of this "shock therapy" plan were high inflation, high unemployment, continued national budget deficits, and a marked decline in production.

The political transition toward building a democratic system has been unsteady. Free elections on the national and local levels have been instituted, a multiparty system established, and principles for a new Western-style constitution adopted, but government officials have refused to condemn the communist legacy and oust former communist bureaucrats and managers from positions of authority.

Economic conditions began to improve in 1993 as the steady decline in production was halted and the gross domestic product began to grow again. Foreign investment also has increased, and the level of exports continues to rise. An economic upsurge may lead to renewed popular support for political reform and a resumption of the transition toward democratization.

INTERSTATE RELATIONS

The decline and collapse of communist rule have had a profound impact on the external relations of countries in these early postcommunist transition years. The rapid collapse of political and economic ties between Eastern Europe and the Soviet Union after 1989 drastically changed interstate relations. Moving quickly to extricate themselves from Soviet domination, East European countries have sought to bolster ties with Western Europe and the United States. The reorientation of trade and economic relations from east to west has not been easy.

Andrzej Korbonski looks at security issues facing Eastern European countries in the postcommunist period in light of the collapse of the USSR and the resulting potential for sustained instability in the region. Despite expectations, leaders of these countries recognized that the Western security umbrella would not extend eastward beyond Germany. Each country sought unilaterally to improve its relations with Western Europe, including early association with the European Union. Continued Soviet security interests in the area encouraged East European leaders to focus on collaboration as a way of strengthening their position vis-à-vis the declining Soviet state as well as seeking to reenter Europe. Clear and sustained Russian opposition to the Visegrad countries' membership in NATO indicates that Russia continues to consider them within its security zone. Bowing to Russian concerns, in early 1994 NATO offered a Partnership for Peace relationship to all former communist countries seeking to establish a democratic system. This affiliation is open to countries that emerged from the Soviet Union as well as to East European states.

Generally, Soviet foreign policy during the last years of the Gorbachev regime and Russian foreign policy since 1992 has not changed significantly. Major policy shifts occurred during the late 1980s; there has been greater continuity between the late Gorbachev period and the first post-Soviet years than there was between the late eighties and a decade earlier.

Thomas W. Robinson considers Soviet-Chinese relations during and since the Gorbachev period within the larger context of China's domestic developments and foreign policy objectives. Thus far, the Chinese CP (CCP) has retained its monopoly of rule despite major economic reforms. Contrary to the Soviet–East European attention to dismantling the centralized single-party dictatorship, which led inevitably to its collapse, the Chinese leadership has focused on decentralizing economic decision making and implementation in an effort to restart the drive toward modernization. China remains the only major country to retain communist domination into the mid-1990s. It is fostering economic pluralism within a nonpluralist political system.

Robinson considers Chinese foreign policy during the Deng Xiaoping period of the 1980s and in response to the extraordinary changes both within the communist-ruled world and the larger international environment from 1989 on. For China, 1989 symbolized the crushing of the prodemocracy efforts at Tiananmen Square as well as the collapse of communism in Eastern Europe.

China sought to improve relations with the Soviets in order to reduce its economic dependence (including military sales assistance) on the United States. The agreements signed with the Soviets during Gorbachev's May 1989 visit to Beijing coincided with the Tiananmen protests, culminating in the June crackdown.

Gorbachev saw improved relations with China as directly beneficial to Soviet economic interests, and Yeltsin has continued this policy. Similarly, Gorbachev was interested in improving relations with noncommunist South Korea because of the advantages of mutual increased trade and Korean investment possibilities. Ilpyong J. Kim reviews recent Soviet/Russian relations with South Korea, including leaders' attitudes toward reunification of the Korean peninsula.

Since 1973, South Korea has worked to improve relations with the USSR, Eastern Europe, and China; the Soviets did not reciprocate until 1988. Soviet interest focused on encouraging South Korean investment and credits for Soviet industrial development. North Korea expressed outrage at Soviet–South Korean rapprochement but did not break off diplomatic relations with Moscow or refuse to renew the long-standing Treaty of Friendship and Mutual Assistance.

Yeltsin has continued the Gorbachev policy of promoting economic relations with South Korea as well as devoting greater attention to relations with Pacific Rim countries. He has proposed a series of development projects that need South Korean assistance and has offered to sell the South Koreans military technology and equipment in return.

Major policy changes toward Israel occurred during the Gorbachev period as well, and the Yeltsin government has continued this policy direction. As Robert O. Freedman demonstrates, Soviet policy toward Israel and toward Jewish emigration evolved slowly during the first several years of the Gorbachev period and was linked to the Soviets' interest in improving relations with the United States. The Soviets sought to become part of the Arab-Israeli peace process and to influence that process as a global player (having been deliberately and effectively left out of the Camp David process almost a decade earlier). Simultaneously, Soviet-Egyptian relations improved substantially as the Soviets called repeatedly for a political (rather than a military) settlement between Arabs and Israelis. After the collapse of the Soviet Union, Russia and other successor states continued the new rapprochement with Israel.

Israel was a major beneficiary of Gorbachev's reassessment of Soviet interests after 1986, the collapse of communism in Eastern and Central Europe, and the disintegration of the USSR. Among those who lost out because of this rapid series of events beginning in 1986 were Marxist regimes in the developing world, many of which were dependent for survival on continuing Soviet and East European military and economic support. David E. Albright considers the fate of eighteen Marxist and Marxist-Leninist regimes that had aligned themselves with the communist-ruled world, including Cuba and the five Asian countries which the USSR had recognized as "truly socialist."

The collapse of communist rule with its clear repudiation of Marxism-Leninism virtually everywhere (except in Asia) meant that Third World countries could not count on future economic or military support for ideological reasons. Loss of this external support resulted in the rapid loss of domestic support, which typically had been weak or superficial. Leaders were either forced out of office or (less frequently) replaced through the ballot box. Albright provides considerable detail on the strategies a number of Marxist leaders adopted as they sought to build "national unity" and provide support for their own political futures.

In several cases (Vietnam and Laos in particular, Cuba to some extent), communist leaders have sought to bolster domestic support through economic reform, reduced central planning, movement toward development of a market-oriented economy, and efforts to attract foreign capital and pursue new trading partners. If the Soviet/East European experience is any guide, it is unlikely that a single authoritarian party will be able to retain sole political power once other groupings and parties have gained a stake in the reform efforts and stand to benefit from them.

The collapse of communist rule in Eastern Europe and the Soviet Union has had an enormous impact worldwide. Postcommunist governments are struggling with political and economic reform measures that, if successful, will transform their countries from one-party, totalitarian-authoritarian, centrally planned systems toward stable, pluralist, market-based systems. The transition will not be easy in any instance and may well prove too difficult in some. Most of the postcommunist countries are now seeking to build a democratic foundation on a long tradition of authoritarian/dictatorial rule; their experience with democratic processes has been fleeting and chaotic. Whether the current effort to embrace democratic principles and practices will be more successful and long-lasting than earlier efforts remains to be seen.

1

The Soviet Military Changes Names

WILLIAM E. ODOM

The Russian military played the key role in the creation of the Russian Empire, and accordingly, it enjoyed a primary place among Russian state institutions. The Red Army played the key role in creating the Soviet Union, and thus it enjoyed a primary place among Soviet state institutions. The Russian Empire ended with the decay and revolt of the Imperial Army. The end of the Soviet Union occurred much the same way, only in "cold war," not actual war, as in 1917. General Lavr Kornilov's troops refused to enter Petrograd and depose the Kerensky regime in August 1917. Marshal Dmitrii Yazov's troops proved little more reliable in August 1991, when they were deployed to support the coup against Gorbachev. Aleksandr Kerensky was saved by his political enemies, the Bolsheviks, just as Gorbachev was rescued by his arch rival, Boris Yeltsin. In both cases, the cooperation of political rivals against the army could not endure for long. As the Bolsheviks soon destroyed Kerensky's Provisional Government, so too the heads of several of the republics soon destroyed Gorbachev's "restructured" Soviet government.

Will the analogies end here? Or will some equivalent struggle and recentralization of the empire follow in the 1990s? To be sure, we cannot answer this question, and we are so close to the events that even speculations are likely to be far off the mark. Nor can one explain the creation and decay of both the Russian and Soviet empires merely as a matter of military institutions, although the military occupied a central position in both Russian and Soviet politics. Understanding its behavior offers a remarkable window into the foundation of the Soviet state, and knowing how a subsequent Russian military evolves will be no less important for understanding the new Russian state.

The story of the role of the Soviet military in the collapse of the Soviet Union and the emergence of a new Russian military will undoubtedly have to be retold as more evidence becomes available and as its importance for political and economic developments is better understood. Here I can only sketch the main outlines of the story as they appeared in late 1993.

THE MILITARY AND PERESTROIKA, 1985–1988

By 1987 Gorbachev had forced the Ministry of Defense to accept a fundamental change in military doctrine.[1] "Reasonable sufficiency" or "defensive sufficiency" were labels attached to what purported to be a new, wholly defensive doctrine. Marshal Sergei Akhromeev, chief of the Soviet General Staff, traveled to the United States, where he sought to convince American audiences of the genuineness of this apparent reversal in Soviet military policy.[2] His ambiguous answers to questions about operational plans, however, occasioned some skepticism in the West, and with good reason. Four years later, General V. N. Lobov, chief of the General Staff, described the declaration of a defensive doctrine in 1987 as a deception, political in nature, that was not reflected in practice: "There has hitherto been no correlation between our officially proclaimed defensive goals and the offensive thrust of operational strategic principles in the . . . combat training of troops and naval forces."[3] Politics, nonetheless, proved more important than the General Staff's operations plans.

A key political change was little noted in the West at the time the new military doctrine was announced. Gorbachev had revised the official ideology concerning class struggle and class interests, relegating them to a much lower priority than "humankind interests," a concept that justified cooperation with capitalist states even at the expense of class interests.[4] "The international class struggle" had been a key concept in the third party program of 1961, and it justified for the military a very large "threat"—that of all nonsocialist states—against which to build military forces. Gorbachev's revision removed this basis for the threat in the new party program, enunciated at the Twenty-seventh Party Congress, and with it the rationale for such large Soviet military forces. Outwardly the military leadership accepted the new ideological line, but their consternation was apparent in tortured articles in which military-political officers tried to salvage something of the international class struggle while accepting Gorbachev's astounding ideological revisions.

Meanwhile, Gorbachev launched a major shake-up in the military command structure, based on the embarrassing episode when the young German Mathias Rust flew unimpeded through Soviet air defenses to land his aircraft in Red Square. The changes involved every senior post down to military district commanders, with two exceptions—the deputy minister of defense for armaments and the commander of the air forces.[5] The turnover of senior military personnel continued throughout 1987–89, exceeding in numbers and scope even Stalin's purges of the Red Army in 1937–38. The renewed Soviet high command was subdued by such sweeping personnel actions but still showed no enthusiasm for "defensive sufficiency."

THE SOVIET MILITARY UNRAVELS, 1989–1991

By late 1988, however, Gorbachev had become sufficiently impatient with the military leaders' reluctance to produce concrete plans for force reductions in accord with the new doctrine that he unilaterally decided on a five-hundred-thousand-man cut in personnel and numerous cuts in weaponry. Announcing these reductions at the United Nations in December 1988 and indicating that a plan for conversion of some of the Soviet military industry to civilian production was afoot, Gorbachev confronted the Ministry of Defense and the Military-Industrial Commission (the Council of Ministers' mechanism for managing the entire defense industrial sector) with a policy fait accompli.

About the same time (fall 1988), a roundtable of military and civilian participants for the journal *XX vek i mir* candidly debated the issues of military conscription and the role of the military in perestroika.[6] Such critical talk about the iconlike Soviet military was unprecedented, ranging from exposing the abusive hazing of first-year soldiers, the poor quality of training, and the privileges of senior officers to mistrust of the military as a potential enemy of perestroika. The civilian participants in particular insisted that no significant military threat to the Soviet Union existed to justify either military conscription or using 25 percent of the gross national product for defense spending. Whether this event was the trigger or merely an early manifestation, whether it was inspired by Gorbachev's reformers or an initiative by the editors of *XX vek i mir*, it marked the beginning of a torrent of public criticism of the Soviet military throughout 1989 and much of 1990.

The national movements in the Baltic republics and in the Caucasus had come into the open in the course of 1988 and, particularly in the Baltic republics, they took up the issue of military conscription, openly campaigning for draft-age youth to resist induction. The semiannual call-ups in the spring and fall of 1989 were strongly resisted in both regions, and by the spring of 1990, draft resistance was also widespread in the Slavic republics and in Central Asia. Numerous public groups—Russian Mothers of Servicemen, Shield (an organization of veterans and active-duty younger officers), and others—began to press the Supreme Soviet for basic military reform, most urgently of the conscription system.[7]

Yet another factor added to the popular discontent over military policies. The withdrawal of Soviet forces from Eastern Europe and Germany in 1990 and 1991 was resulting in terrible living conditions for officers and their families because housing and schools were not available in the Soviet Union to accommodate the large number of military families transferred there. At the same time, the five-hundred-thousand-man force reduction was forcing many officers into civilian life without apartments or jobs. The lower ranks of the officer corps became increasingly alienated from the senior leadership in the Ministry of Defense.

All of these factors combined to stimulate a major public debate about the substance of Gorbachev's new military doctrine. The sluggish response by the Ministry of Defense allowed several civilian specialists in the Moscow institutes for study of foreign policy and security issues to advance their own ideas about military reform. They were joined occasionally by disillusioned young officers, most conspicuously Major Vladimir Lopatin, whom Yeltsin would appoint in 1990 as the deputy chairman of the Russian Committee on Defense and Security, a shadow Russian defense ministry. The civilian reformers sought a fundamental change in virtually all aspects of Soviet military policy—doctrine, force structure, nuclear weapons policy, and manpower policies, including the abolition of the military-political apparatus in the armed forces. Marshal Yazov, the minister of defense, countered with a ten-year plan which proposed only quantitative reductions and changes that would appear to meet Gorbachev's already publicly announced unilateral force reductions. The two approaches were wholly incompatible, one involving a systemic reform, the other a nonsystemic adjustment to somewhat lower force levels.[8]

After the events in Baku in January 1990, where military forces were employed in spite of popular opposition in both Russia and Ukraine, Gorbachev began to moderate his pressure on the Ministry of Defense. He spoke well of the military on Red Army Day, February 23, 1990, and on the eve of May Day he promoted Yazov to marshal of the Soviet Union. Gorbachev was severely criticized by military officers at the Congress of the Russian Communist Party in June, and at the Twenty-eighth Congress of the CPSU that same month, he gave some ground to the senior military. By the fall of 1990, as Major Lopatin described it, Gorbachev had essentially turned over military reform to the Ministry of Defense and neutralized the efforts of the civilian reformers and officers like Lopatin who sided with them.[9]

Boris Yeltsin became a major factor in the fate of the Soviet military when he was elected head of the Russian Supreme Soviet in May 1990 and then quit the Communist Party at its congress the next month. Some of the reformers threw in their lot with Yeltsin, especially the younger disaffected officers like Lopatin. Apparently, Yeltsin was also working behind the scenes for support within the senior military ranks because at the turn of the year, 1990–91, Colonel General Konstantin Kobets, a deputy chief of the General Staff, agreed to become Yeltsin's military adviser. When the army was used to try to repress the Lithuanian secessionists in January 1991, Yeltsin took to the airwaves and pleaded with Soviet soldiers not to accept their political officers' arguments about why they should "bash civilians" in Lithuania. The media elites took a similar line, and Gorbachev backed away from supporting the action.

The episode in Lithuania foreshadowed in several ways the collapse of the Soviet Union and soon thereafter its armed forces. First, confusion and mixed loyalties within the military surfaced sharply when an airborne commander in Vitebsk refused to let his unit participate. The Baltic Military District commander also seems to have warned local nationalist leaders of the impending military action. Black Beret special units proved willing to use their weapons against the civilian populace, but the Soviet high command could not be sure about other units. Second, the voice of a Russian political leader challenging the policy of the Soviet government created dilemmas not only for ordinary troops but also for the predominantly Russian officer corps of the Soviet military. Third, Gorbachev allowed himself to be split away from his conservative supporters, those he had won back to a limited degree in the fall of 1990 after the "leadership crisis" in November with the military. And as he swung back toward the reformers, he found little sympathy because many of the liberals were now going over to Yeltsin. Fourth, failure to crush the secessionist movement in Lithuania signaled clearly to conservatives that the Soviet Union was dangerously close to collapse. If the Soviet regime and its Communist Party could not bring the Lithuanians to heel, they certainly would not be able to do so in other republics where independence movements were strongly manifest.

In light of the events in January 1991, one can only wonder that Gorbachev's conservative associates in the regime believed they had a chance to reverse the course of political developments. The military proved unreliable, disaffected not only in the lower ranks but also split at the command levels about political loyalties and legitimate directions. The growing desperation in military-industrial circles over the breakdown of the command economic apparatus, the chaos of the military "conversion" program, and the dim future prospects for this formerly leading sector of the economy probably influenced their decision to act. The shift to a market economy would eliminate the vast hierarchy of military-industrial bureaucrats. In contrast, a large number of senior officers believed they had a chance for positions in a restructured military, whatever the new system. Growing ill-will between the Ministry of Defense and the Military-Industrial Commission (VPK) surfaced in 1988 and 1989 when Gorbachev promised to cut the military budget.

The key officals in Gorbachev's government decided to bring perestroika to an abrupt end in late August 1991. Perhaps a more determined and active effort by coup-makers could have succeeded in neutralizing Yeltsin and his supporters in Moscow, but the state of decay in the military was too advanced for it to be counted on to put down resistance among the national minorities. By betting on the Soviet army at this point, the so-called Emergency Committee undid the Soviet empire.

THE SOVIET MILITARY SAVES YELTSIN

Yeltsin's victory over the Emergency Committee in August 1991 left the Soviet military formally intact but caused a major turnover in the high command. During the crisis, Yeltsin spent a lot of time on the telephone with senior military figures, particularly Marshal of Aviation Ye. I. Shaposhnikov, commander of the air forces, and Colonel-General Pavel Grachev, commander of the elite airborne forces. Colonel-General Kobets physically participated in the defense of the White House, which took him away from the control centers of the General Staff, but presumably he was in phone communications with them.

Yeltsin's relations with members of the Soviet high command are probably the main reason for his ability to avoid defeat. Certainly many of them held him in contempt for his January 1991 appeal for a veritable mutiny by the troops sent into Lithuania, but others apparently shared his view that the army should not be used against Soviet citizens. Events in the Caucasus (in the spring of 1989 in Tbilisi and in Baku during the winter of 1990) had soured many of them on such use of the military. The military's public image was already poor, and numerous articles had appeared in military publications objecting to an "internal" role for the armed forces. In any event, Yeltsin was able to exploit such feelings within the high command to achieve delays in its response to orders from the Emergency Committee.

The full story will not soon be told, but a glimpse into the high command's behavior was given by Marshal Shaposhnikov less than a month after the events.[10] His account indicates that deeply ingrained fear, a legacy from Stalin's time, prevented him and others from openly resisting Marshal Yazov's initial instructions to support the Emergency Committee. By the end of the second day of the crisis, Shaposhnikov was forced to reveal his own opposition because the mayor of Leningrad, Anatoli Sobchak, announced on the radio that the air force was supporting Yeltsin. Fully expecting to be arrested, he reported to a meek Yazov and recommended that he end all military support for the Emergency Committtee. Shaposhnikov and Grachev established cooperative relations against the coup when an attack on the White House was being planned on the night of August 20. Shaposhnikov offered to launch a bombing attack on the Kremlin to stop the coup if Grachev would not use his paratroopers to arrest the Emergency Committtee. After their heated exchange, both stayed in constant telephone contact with the White House. Thus Yeltsin must have had a realistic picture of the situation within the Defense Ministry.

The next day, at Yazov's second appearance before the Defense Ministry collegium of senior officers, Shaposhnikov spoke openly against the Emergency Committee, winning majority support for his stance and provoking Yazov to confess his own error in siding with the the "alcoholics" in the Emergency Committtee.

Afterward, Shaposhnikov was at pains to make clear that the coup was not a "military" one, that Yazov really did not have his heart in it, that the military came out honorably. How accurately Shaposhnikov reported these events is impossible to know, but they have a ring of truth. They reveal the terrible dilemmas that Yazov saw for himself and the military. They also convey a mood of fear among the members of the high command, which Shaposhnikov said remained from Stalin's time. Most officers retained as much discretion as possible to change sides, depending on how events developed. The same pattern of behavior seems to have characterized regional commands as well. The commander of the Far Eastern Military District said in an interview in early September, just days after the events, that it was difficult to tell whether the officer corps had supported the coup or rallied to Yeltsin. A few took a stand, but most stood aside.[11]

ILLUSIONS OF SURVIVAL, SEPTEMBER–DECEMBER 1991

In the aftermath of the failed coup, Shaposhnikov became minister of defense, and Colonel-General Vladimir Lobov became chief of the General Staff. General Kobets was not immediately rewarded for his service in leading the defense of the Russian White House, keeping his old position as state adviser for the Russian government on defense affairs as well as his office in the old Soviet General Staff, but in late September he was appointed chairman of the Russian Committee on State Defense and Security, making him the de facto Russian defense minister. General Grachev became first deputy Soviet minister of defense, a key post, but his reward would come much later, in the spring of 1992, when he was appointed minister of defense for Russia. At the same time, a fairly large number of senior officers were dismissed, including nine of the seventeen members of the military collegium of the Ministry of Defense.[12]

The purge of the senior officer ranks, however, did not go nearly as far as some of the reformers desired. An inconspicuous lieutenant general, Yurii Rodionov, was appointed chief of the Main Personnel Directorate of the Ministry of Defense by Gorbachev's order on September 13.[13] Rodionov's appointment was apparently the work of General Kobets, who used his influence to capture the personnel post so that he could begin to promote and assign people of his own choosing. Kobets was also able to convince the civilian reformers of his support so that they helped put him in charge of the committee for military reform.[14] Kobets expanded his influence by gathering information from all command levels about who had supported the coup. By preventing action on the information, Kobets made the many officers named in it indebted to him.[15] From this vignette it is easy to imagine the intrigue by other officers competing with Kobets.

The central figures at the top of the Soviet military were now Shaposhnikov and Lobov. They represented the opposite ends of the spectrum of reform alternatives in the Ministry of Defense, not a very wide spectrum. Lobov, who had been commander of the Warsaw Pact, served as first deputy chief of the General Staff in 1989–91. Although he enjoyed a reputation as an intelligent and highly experienced officer, he was hardly a reformer. In fact, his periodic public candor showed him to be against basic reforms. Grudgingly, Lobov yielded to some change such as depoliticization of the military, tolerance of symbolic national militias in the republics, and limited participation of republican representatives in defense policy making.[16] Shaposhnikov, initially quite liberal in the context of the officer corps, reportedly met so much resistance to reform from his fellow generals in the weeks following the abortive coup that he offered his resignation to Gorbachev.[17] Yet even he was not ready to dismember the Soviet armed forces, as his policy positions would soon demonstrate. Not only did he strongly defend central command authority, but he sought to make the republics provide housing, food, and social welfare for all military units. Although he tolerated the idea of national militias in principle, he wanted to retain central appointment authority for their commanders.[18]

Kobets occupied a less central formal position in military policy circles than Shaposhnikov and Lobov, but he was equally if not more ambitious. According to Lopatin, Kobets eagerly played the role of reformer but only when reform was inevitable. His position between the Soviet General Staff and the Russian Committee on State Defense and Security, of course, was inherently ambiguous. Thus he apparently formed an alliance with Shaposhnikov in August, immediately after the coup attempt. In early December, while on a visit in Britain, Lobov learned that he had been relieved of his duties as chief of the General Staff, apparently the victim of the Kobets-Shaposhnikov alliance.

As these machinations among the military leadership played out, political, economic, and social dynamics continued to move far ahead of the most daring ideas of reform within the Ministry of Defense. Shortly after the defeat of the coup, for example, Ukraine declared its intention to build its own army, a notion it had been considering for a year or more but now a serious move that could destroy the old military system throughout the union. Thus the senior Soviet military leaders—who stubbornly refused to make major changes to the system for universal military service, denied most of the charges about mistreatment of enlisted personnel, flatly rejected the idea that national republics possessed military capabilities of their own, insisted that military industries provide even more advanced weaponry, and refused to share information about military programs with the parliament and the media—had to yield on these points in the fall of 1991. As they did, they also tried to improve their images as reformers.

Radical reform, of course, was not on the Ministry of Defense's agenda. Even moderate reform would have seemed to require the disbanding of the old political-military apparatus within the armed forces, but by early September, it had acquired a new name, "Organs of Combat Training and Moral-Psychological Education."[19] One significant change occurred fairly rapidly—a mixed military service system was introduced. The semiannual draft decree for October–December reduced the required term of service to eighteen months and allowed conscripts to shift to a professional contract status after six months of initial training.[20] Other changes, such as large reductions in overall manning and dramatic reductions in the number of general officers and political officers, were discussed, even proclaimed by Shaposhnikov as being on the agenda for action, but none followed.

Throughout the fall, reform plans were neglected while senior military leaders who had sided with Yeltsin spent their energies fighting for the key posts and those who had not strove to avoid retirement. They all behaved as if the Soviet military would survive more or less unchanged, failing to see that the Soviet state was coming to an abrupt end.

Commonwealth of Independent States and the Military Question

When the leaders of the three Slavic republics agreed on December 8 to create the Commonwealth of Independent States (CIS), they effectively destroyed Gorbachev's efforts to save the Soviet Union. Article 6 of the CIS agreement, however, committed them to "preserve and maintain the common strategic-military space under unified command," and it obligated them to pursue "a coordinated policy on questions concerning social protection and pensions for military personnel and their families." This ambiguous approach to the military question facing the CIS helped sustain the illusion among the Soviet officer corps that the Soviet Armed Forces would somehow survive as an institution.

Two days later, on December 10, Gorbachev made a last bid to win the military's support at a military leadership conference in the Ministry of Defense. Early the next morning Yeltsin made a counterbid. The military sided with Yeltsin. Public reports of the meeting give three reasons for their decision.[21] The first was national. The predominantly Slavic officer corps was attracted to the pan-Slavic idea of the CIS. Second, they saw little difference between Gorbachev's concept of a union treaty and a commonwealth because the CIS promised a central military command entity. Finally, as one general put it, only the sign on the old Ministry of Defense would change. Yeltsin reportedly stressed his intention to fight for a unified military, insisting that the CIS was the only way out of the impasse. Moreover, he had no intention of forming a purely Russian defense ministry, a step that would have signaled a willingness to break up the Soviet Armed Forces.[22]

At this critical juncture, Yeltsin supporters were in command and might have lost their jobs if Gorbachev retained power. Moreover, Gorbachev was in poor repute throughout the military. Yet supporting Gorbachev was the only hope for saving the Soviet military because, had the military sided with him, the CIS would have remained a dead letter. As during the August crisis, the military question proved the most critical. A few months later, some officers would complain that had they better understood the implications, they would never have supported the CIS.[23]

In the meantime, the top military leaders continued to compete for the limelight. With Lobov out of the picture, Kobets tried to upstage Shaposhnikov in preparation for the CIS meeting in Minsk on December 30 to deal with the military question. As minister of defense, Shaposhnikov naturally prepared a plan, but Kobets offered a more radical alternative supported by civilian reforms. Following the NATO example, it involved a CIS defense treaty and military alliance, not a unified CIS military organization as Shaposhnikov wanted. In the event, Yeltsin chose Shaposhnikov's approach.[24] Shaposhnikov was now defending the status quo, seeking to save as much of the old military system as possible.

THE CIS ARMED FORCES VERSUS NATIONAL ARMED FORCES

Shaposhnikov's plan had already met opposition at the CIS summit in Alma Ata in mid-December, when the core group of Slavic republics were joined by eight others, all but Georgia and the Baltic states. Ukrainian president Leonid Kravchuk rejected Shaposhnikov's scheme. Although agreement was reached on keeping nuclear weapons under central command with a complicated system of sharing political control over them and Shaposhnikov was temporarily appointed commander of the CIS Armed Forces, failure to achieve a defense union reflected fundamental differences, principally between Moscow and Kiev.[25]

At the CIS summits throughout the winter and spring—at Minsk on December 30, 1991, and February 14, 1992, at Kiev on March 20, and at Tashkent on May 15, the major business in every case was the military question. The complex struggles on all sides throughout this series of meetings are more than a short essay can elaborate, but the general outlines can be summarized.

The old Soviet General Staff and Ministry of Defense came to each meeting with large numbers of draft agreements. At none did more than a few of the drafts receive approval by the CIS heads of state. Those agreed to were rarely signed by all members of the CIS so their application was limited. Some heads of state, by signing agreements, exceeded their powers vis-à-vis their own parliaments. Ambiguities and contradictions abound in virtually all of the signed agreements.[26] How strongly Yeltsin backed Shaposhnikov in these endeavors is not clear, but Shaposhnikov's tactics were transparent. He sought to create a legal basis for simply renaming the old Soviet Armed Forces and obliging the CIS states to pay for them, let him command them, and not interfere with their central administration from Moscow.

Each member state reacted differently, based on its own internal concerns and interests. Moreover, none had its own adequately developed military staff to make counterproposals, and most did not fully understand the technical details in the agreements. Ukraine was the best prepared in this regard, and not surprisingly, was the major stumbling block for the CIS Armed Forces, although other states frequently followed the Ukrainian lead. Since most Soviet officers were Slavs, the Central Asian states had no senior officer cadres to deal with the General Staff's proposals. Moldova and Azerbaijan were not much better off, and Georgia seldom participated. Armenia, too, lacked a competent military staff. Belarus proved undecided or ambiguous much of the time, although it could find ethnic Belarussian senior officers to handle the issues.

Shaposhnikov provoked a crisis immediately after the Minsk meeting on December 30. Agreement was reached to create the CIS Strategic Forces, which were defined in a way that allowed them to include four of the five branches of service, leaving only the Ground Forces apart. The very next day Shaposhnikov appointed himself commander in chief of the CIS Armed Forces, based on a dubious interpretation of the Alma-Ata agreements, and also appointed several deputies subordinate to his command. He could have thrown down no more provocative challenge to Ukraine. Such an arrangement not only disallowed a separate Ukrainian military but also had no legitimate basis in agreements of the Minsk meeting. In fact, it created a unified military without a unified political authority above it. The very idea of the CIS had been to get rid of political authority over its members.

Kravchuk responded swiftly, claiming authority over all military forces on Ukrainian territory, including the Black Sea Fleet and strategic nuclear forces. To buttress this move, he decreed that all the personnel in these forces must take an oath of allegiance to Ukraine. Shaposhnikov countered with a decree that they take an oath to the CIS Armed Forces. Thus began an open struggle that played out through the winter and spring. It made Ukraine's position on strategic nuclear weapons ambiguous, and it made the Black Sea Fleet a pawn for what was really a struggle over the political character of the CIS and Ukrainian sovereignty.

More new draft agreements were presented at the CIS meetings in February and March aimed at defining a legal basis for the CIS Armed Forces. In addition to the Strategic Forces, a CIS General Purpose Forces was created with a separate commander, but Shaposhnikov maintained the fiction of a single CIS Armed Forces although it had no legal basis. Detailed draft agreements on finance, supply, recruiting, weapons procurement, military research and development, and so on were advanced but failed to gain unanimous backing. After the March meeting in Kiev, the failure of Shaposhnikov's approach became more widely recognized in Moscow. Yeltsin gave up on it publicly in his speech to the Sixth Congress of People's Deputies in early April, announcing that Colonel General Dmitri Volkogonov would head a commission to establish a Russian army and navy.[27]

Why Shaposhnikov and the General Staff believed they could force Ukraine and several other states to accept a single armed forces is unclear. Perhaps they thought that as the heads of states began to understand the complexities of the Air Defense Forces, the Navy, the Strategic Rocket Forces, and the Air Forces, they would realize that splitting them up would result in their destruction. The air defense and space surveillance systems were a single entity, requiring the entire former Soviet territory to operate effectively. Perhaps they were so singularly concerned with these military-technical issues that the political dimension was lost on them. Whatever the reason, as long as Russia did not create its own ministry of defense and its own separate military forces, the CIS Armed Forces and command structure were essentially Russian.

Yeltsin's decision, therefore, changed the context for a CIS military, one that took on formal expression at the CIS summit in Tashkent on May 15, 1992. A collective security treaty was proposed, but only six of the CIS members signed it—Russia, Uzbekistan, Kazakhstan, Kyrgyzstan, Tajikistan, and Armenia. For the next year, Shaposhnikov put his main energies into giving substance to this treaty. No agreement was reached, however, on whether it should be modeled on NATO or the Warsaw Pact, the two competing concepts.[28] Moreover, Russia refused to carry all the costs of a CIS military staff either for a joint military or a collective security structure. In June 1993, Shaposhnikov gave up on the CIS armed forces and resigned. In a real sense, this marked the de facto end of the Soviet armed forces, but the plethora of CIS military agreements—well over one hundred documents—and the collective security treaty kept alive under new authorities many of the military linkages among the Commonwealth states, especially those with the Central Asian republics and Armenia.

A RUSSIAN ARMED FORCES

The work of General Volkogonov's commission seemed at first to promise a Russian Ministry of Defense led by reformers, possibly with a civilian minister of defense. Yeltsin himself kept the Defense Ministry portfolio and, on April 3, appointed two deputies, a civilian, Andrei Kokoshin, and General Pavel Grachev. Kokoshin had never been closely associated with such radical reformers as Lopatin and others in the parliamentary committee on defense and security, making him appear as an acceptable candidate for the top post in the new ministry, but on May 18 Grachev was given the post.

Once again, Lopatin, the incorrigible reformer, publicly condemned corruption in the military and set the terms for assessing reform.[29] He accused the senior military officers of pocketing large sums of money from joint-stock companies, charging $800 for a one-hour press interview, and other misuses of their positions. Reflecting views held by some of his Russian parliamentary colleagues, he set three measures for achieving reform. First, the Ministry of Defense had to become a political organ in which the General Staff was merely one of several departments, not its central apparatus as it had been in the Soviet period. Second, an expert evaluation of the military by outsiders, not by the military itself, had to be done. Third, qualitative and quantitative criteria had to be set for determining the size and makeup of the military as well as an upper limit for the military budget and manning level.

Such reforms again lost serious prospects when Yeltsin appointed Grachev and his fellow Afghan war veterans, including as a deputy Colonel General Boris Gromov, whose behavior during the August coup was ambiguous. The team of "Afghantsy" (as these veterans were called) began making plans, drafting policies, and trying to meet the two-month deadline for creating the new ministry.

The Defense Ministry used Vice-President Alexander Rutskoi to foreshadow its new scheme for the transition to a Russian armed forces in an interview in *Krasnaya zvezda* on May 22. Indeed, the Soviet General Staff would become the Russian General Staff, and a three-stage reform plan would be implemented. In the first stage, in 1992, the Russian General Staff would gain control of all military units on Russian soil. The second stage, in 1993–94, would include moving from conscription to a mixed conscription and professional manning system, dropping troop strength from the present 2.8 million to 2.1 million, retaining the old five branches of service, and restoring the military's prestige. Stage three, from 1995 to 2000, would see the completion of troop withdrawals from the Baltics and Europe, the attainment of the CFE and START levels, and continuing decline in manning to 1.5 million by 2000. Even a conservative like General Lobov would have found such a slow schedule of reform acceptable, and it undoubtedly frightened the Baltic leaders about further delays in troop withdrawals.

A conference was held at the General Staff Academy in late May 1992 at which its chief, General Ivan Rodionov (infamous for the massacre in Tbilisi in April 1989), "corrected" the published draft of a new Russian military doctrine.[30] His tone was uncompromising in insisting that Russia must retain the Baltic littoral, predominant influence over the Black Sea, and major interest in the Middle East. Moreover, Russia should renounce its no-first-use nuclear weapons policy. At the same time, it should begin a major modernization of its military forces in light of the new technologies that had so basically changed the nature of warfare. Not everyone present agreed with all of Rodionov's points, and several dissenting voices were not reported in the press because of their provocative and threatening nature. Grachev, however, laid out a vision of reform and force modernization that shared the basic thrust of Rodionov's remarks. Finally, Grachev repeated Rutskoi's earlier elaboration of a three-stage plan.

Grachev dismissed Shaposhnikov's plea to save the CIS's armed forces and instead supported the collective security treaty recently signed with five other CIS countries. Clearly, Grachev now had the upper hand in military affairs in Moscow, and Shaposhnikov was left presiding over a confused and hollow CIS military structure. Although still in command of the Strategic Forces, Shaposhnikov saw those eventually pass to control by the Russian Ministry of Defense.

The creation of a new Russian Ministry of Defense, however, did not essentially change the disposition of the rapidly decaying old Soviet Armed Forces, most of which Russia would struggle to retain. Large deployments still remained in all of the former Soviet republics as well as in Germany and Poland. In Moldova, troops were holding the Dniester Republic and claiming it for Russia. They were entangled in civil wars in the Northern Transcaucasus, as well as in Tajikistan. Nothwithstanding these local conflicts, the Air Forces, the Air Defense Forces, and the Navy would still face major logisitical problems in moving to Russia.

During its first year, the Russian Defense Ministry achieved modest success in putting its house in order. Yeltsin signed the Law on Defense in September 1992 and the Law on Military Service in February 1993, providing much needed legal authority for the ministry's operations. Although General Grachev pleaded for putting the new military doctrine into law, Yeltsin and some members of parliament resisted.

Their reason can be easily inferred. The proposed military doctrine treated the whole of the CIS as "single strategic space," asserting Russian military hegemony over it. That was the only way the air defense system, the military space structure, and other parts of the old Soviet military establishment could be salvaged. Although Grachev was not supportive of Shaposhnikov's efforts to achieve control over these assets, he worked hard at creating linkages through bilateral arrangements and the collective security treaty. The new military doctrine would provide legitimacy for all these endeavors as well as open the way for more binding arrangements with the other CIS countries. Given Yeltsin's cooperative foreign policy toward the West, this military doctrine would raise serious questions about Russia's intentions, not only in military affairs but also toward the sovereignty of the CIS countries because of its expansive definitions of threats to Russia's security.

In the spring of 1993, Yeltsin began to back Grachev's policies toward Russia's "near abroad," that is, the former Soviet territories. In Tajikistan, he committed Russia to protect the border with Afghanistan and to support the Tajik government against its domestic opposition. In the Caucasus, Yeltsin did little to constrain the Russian military from tactics that forced both Georgia and Azerbaijan to join the CIS. Grachev was allowed to demand an agreement from Georgia for Russian military bases on the border with Turkey. Whereas Shaposhnikov had failed with negotiations, Grachev and his field commanders were making progress in putting substance into military linkages among several of the Commonwealth states. Ukraine, Belarus, and Moldova, however, were still outside their reach in the fall of 1993.

THE MILITARY-INDUSTRIAL SECTOR

Dismantling the old Soviet military-industrial structure has proven no less complicated than managing the residual pieces of the Soviet military. Although more than 80 percent of its firms were in Russia, important parts were in Belarus, Ukraine, and the Baltic states. Military-industrial conversion to civilian production was more talked about than implemented in Russia, and military industrialists in other CIS countries sought to keep their links with the Russian components.

In the last three years of the Soviet Union, the traditional, mutually supportive relationship between the military-industrial sector and the Soviet military began to break down. The military's concern for the social welfare of its personnel was more urgent than its concern for procurement of new weaponry. After the collapse of central planning of the economy, the military and the military industrialists became competitors for money and resources to satisfy salary and living standards of their personnel. At the same time, some of the senior military, envious of the U.S. lead in military technology, were not anxious to see the Russian military-industrial base collapse. Thus, by the summer of 1992, common ground began to reappear between the military and the industrialists.

Outlines of a three-way deal—between Yeltsin's government, the military, and the industrialists—appeared in Gaidar's budget message to the Russian parliament in March 1992.[31] He proposed a 70 percent reduction in weapons procurement while keeping research and development sufficiently funded to protect several key programs. Personnel costs were rising because of large pay raises given to the military in the fall of 1991, but they were to be contained by reducing the forces by seven hundred thousand men. An 80 percent increase in investment in housing and social support was included, and the military industrialists were to be compensated for the procurement cuts by 40.6 billion rubles allocated for conversion plus 40 billion rubles in credits for the year. Gaidar noted that the defense budget alone accounted for 37 percent of the total state budget for 1992.

These budgetary policies would have made good sense if they had been enforced. In fact, the military budget continued to exceed allocations through 1992 and 1993.[32] The Defense Ministry, struggling to avoid reducing its manpower, increased costs by hiring more than 150,000 "contract" soldiers. Ill-disciplined military spending was matched in the military-industrial sector. Military industrialists argued for saving most of the research and development and production base to meet the future needs of military modernization being designed by the theorists in the General Staff Academy.

By late fall 1993, Yeltsin's government had shown little capacity to curb the military-industrialists. Market pricing and reduced military procurement were creating havoc in large parts of the defense industries, but the old bureaucrats had by no means surrendered.

FROM THE SOVIET ARMY TO A RUSSIAN IMPERIAL ARMY?

The military's role in closing the parliament on October 3–4, 1993, altered its political position significantly. Although General Grachev apparently proved reluctant to use force against pro-parliament groups in Moscow, military units did act decisively once they were committed.[33] As the military had saved Yeltsin in August 1991, it (along with the Ministry of Security and the Ministry of Internal Affairs) saved him once again in October 1993. Whether from gratitude or from recognition of the changed political realities, Yeltsin shortly thereafter convened the Russian Security Council to give the long-sought approval of the new military doctrine.

Although the version adopted was considerably modified from the original 1992 version, it asserted Russian prerogatives over the military affairs of the CIS countries that left little genuine sovereignty to those states in their own

security matters. It also declared Russian interests in Eastern Europe that likewise denied the states of that region the right to choose their own security
alliances, namely with NATO.[34] Only a few weeks earlier, Yeltsin had told the
leaders of Poland and the Czech Republic that joining NATO was a matter for
them to decide. The new military doctrine probably accounts for Yeltsin's reversal of that position a short time later. To protect these Russian interests, the
new military doctrine would require an imperial Russian military. Not surprisingly, nervousness in Eastern Europe accompanied its promulgation.

It is still too early to predict with confidence what course Russian military
policy will take, although the prospects of imperial reassertion looked strong
in the late fall of 1993. The Central Asian states never really wanted to abandon the military connection to Moscow, and because their new governments
were composed largely of old communists, most were anxious to keep the
Russian security tie. They lack both the officer cadres and the resources to
build new national military establishments. The states of the Transcaucasus
were brought back under the Russian military wing against their will. Caught
up in local military conflicts over borders and political power, they proved
easy for the Russian military and intelligence forces to divide and resubordinate
to the CIS.

Affairs in the other CIS countries differed widely by fall 1993. Belarus was
divided internally between those who desired to retain autonomy from Russia and those who sought to maintain the old command economic links, especially to Russian military industries. Ukraine, most adamantly opposed to
restoring security dependency on Moscow, has thus far failed to pursue economic reforms that might provide the government with adequate popular support to resist Russian imperial pressures indefinitely. Its capacity to resist
reintegration with the Russian military is therefore questionable. And Moldova,
failing to get Russia to withdraw its Fourteenth Army from the Transd-
niester Autonomous Republic, is in a weak position to resist Russian demands
if Ukraine should eventually yield to Moscow.

A new Russian imperialism, however, is not the only possible future. A
new constitution was approved by popular referendum in December 1993, and
although the electoral system has produced (in 1993 and again in 1995) a parliament largely resistant to market reforms, this democratic procedure has
survived and halting market reforms have continued. Yeltsin's monetary stabilization policy has also endured, placing restraint on the military budget.
Neither the quantity of forces the military wants nor the technnological modernization it desires from the military industries can be afforded under such
economic policies. Moreover Ukraine and other major CIS countries prove
surprisingly durable. Finally, the military's costly ventures and poor performance in Tajikistan, the Transcausaus, and elsewhere erode its residual popu-

lar support. All of these factors undercut the political influence of the Defense Ministry and the military industries.

This is the crux of the dilemma that not only continues to confront Russia but also confronted the tsarist government throughout the nineteenth century and will continue to bedevil Russian leaders until they resolve it: liberal economic and political development in Russia inexorably undercuts its imperial control over non-Russian territories both by taking away the military resources necessary for that control and by undermining the political legitimacy of such control. By resisting a hegemonic role over the CIS, Russia today can greatly improve its prospects of achieving a liberal domestic system. If it insists on that role, it will surrender all prospect of liberal reform. As in the past, the military question today remains central to this dilemma, and the last word on the military question has certainly not been spoken.

NOTES

1. See William E. Odom, "Soviet Military Doctrine," *Foreign Affairs* 67 (Winter 1988–89), 114–34.

2. Ibid. Marshal Akhromeev later testified before the House Armed Services Committee on the new military policy.

3. *Krasnaya zvezda*, October 23, 1991.

4. M. S. Gorbachev, *Perestroika i novoe myshlenie* (Moscow: Politizdatel'stvo, 1987), 140-63.

5. See Linda Brewer, "The Soviet Military Elite under Gorbachev," unpublished paper, Air Force Intelligence Agency, August 22, 1989.

6. See William E. Odom, "The Soviet Military in Transition," *Problems of Communism* 39 (May–June 1990), 51–71; also William E. Odom, "Smashing an Icon," *National Interest* 21 (Fall 1990), 62–74.

7. Odom, "The Soviet Military in Transition."

8. See William E. Odom, "The Outlook for the Soviet Military in the 1990s," Hudson Institute Study, 1991, for considerable detail on the struggle over military policy between the radical reformers and the Ministry of Defense up until January 1991.

9. Lopatin, conversation with the author in November 1990.

10. FBIS-SOV-91-180, September 17, 1991, "Shaposhnikov Interview Recounts Coup Attempt," 28–30.

11. FBIS-SOV-91-173, September 6, 1991, "General Says Half of Army Backed Coup Attempt," 59–60.

12. FBIS-SOV-91-180, September 17, 1991, "Rodionov Explains Military Personnel Dismissals," 30.

13. FBIS-SOV-91-179, September 16, 1991, "Gorbachev Decree Dismisses Defense Officials," 46, translation of TASS, September 13, 1991.

14. FBIS-SOV-92-015, January 23, 1992, "Lopatin Views Status of Reform," 50–52, translation of an interview with Lopatin in *Nezavisimaya gazeta,* January 7, 1992.

15. Ibid.

16. See Scott R. McMichael, "Military Reform Plan Begins to Take Shape," *Report on the USSR* 3, 43 (October 25, 1991), 7–11.

17. FBIS-SOV-91-203, October 21, 1991, "Shaposhnikov Reportedly Resigns Defense Post," 41–42, translation of the Swedish *Svenska Dagbladet*, October 17, 1991. Citing several sources in the Ministry of Defense, this report claims that Shaposhnikov met dramatic criticism within the ministry for saying publicly that 80 percent of the officer corps would be dismissed. The Main Political Administration, in charge of military-political officers, was particularly upset because it was a major target for reductions. Shaposhnikov, by tendering his resignation to Gorbachev and having it rejected, was able to regain some strength against these resistant elements in the military.

18. McMichael, "Military Reform Plan."

19. FBIS-SOV-91-176, September 11, 1991, "Yeltsin Advisor Volkogonov Details Army Reform," 47–49.

20. FBIS-SOV-91-195, October 8, 1991, "Gorbachev Decree of Fall Draft, Reserve Ranks," 46–47, translation from *Izvestiia*, October 5, 1991.

21. FBIS-SOV-91-239, December 12, 1991, "Significant Proportion for Yeltsin," 25. This is a transcription of Moscow Radio Rossii Network, December 11, 1991.

22. FBIS-SOV-91-239, December 12, 1991, "More on Yeltsin Address," and "Yeltsin Stresses Military Role," 26.

23. Sergei Rogov et al., *Commonwealth Defense Arrangements and International Security* (Washington, D.C.: Joint Paper, Institute of USA and Canada and the Center for Naval Analysis, June 1992), 3.

24. Ibid.

25. Ibid., 3–4.

26. See Moscow press and TV reporting in FBIS-SOV-92-005, January 8, 1992, 5; FBIS-SOV-92-032, February 18, 1992, 18–21; FBIS-SOV-92-008, March 4, 1992, 15–16; FBIS-SOV-92-055, March 20, 1992, 17–18; FBIS-SOV-92-057, March 24, 1992, 18–23. These include translations of agreements as well as some press commentary on the meetings.

27. FBIS-SOV-92-068, April 8, 1992, "Yeltsin Reports on Economic Reform to Sixth Congress of People's Deputies of RSFSR," 27.

28. For details concerning the collective security treaty, especially in the spring of 1993, see FBIS-SOV-93-039, March 2, 1993, "CIS Defense Ministers Discuss Military Hierarchy," 6; FBIS-SOV-93-040, March 3, 1993, "Shaposhnikov Briefs Media on Collective Security," 7–8; Oleg Falichev, "Kollektivnaya bezopasnost' v SNG," *Krasnaya zvezda*, March 2, 1993; FBIS-SOV-93-098, May 24, 1993, "Red Square Program on Defense Issues," 24–26; RFE/RL Daily Reports No. 145, August 2, 1993 and No. 162, August 25, 1993.

29. JPRS-UMA-92, June 24, 1992, "Russian Defense Committee's Lopatin," 6–9, reported in *Kuranty*, May 23, 1992.

30. FBIS-SOV-92-108, June 4, 1992, "General Staff Academy Discusses Armed Forces," 47–50, reported in *Krasnaya zvezda*, June 2, 1992. Also, unpublished typescript of Rodionov's speech, unofficially distributed in Moscow.

31. FBIS-SOV-92-062, March 31, 1992, "Gaidar Delivers Budget Message to Parliament," 33–38.

32. See JPRS-UMA-92-023, June 24, 1992, "Russian Defense Committee's Lopatin," 6, reported in *Kuranty*, May 23, 1992; FBIS-SOV-92-096, May 18, 1992, "Further Hearings on Defense Security Law," 37.

33. See RFE/RL Daily Report No. 219, November 15, 1993, "Yeltsin Criticizes Grachev Over 4 October Events."

34. These conclusions are drawn from a copy of the doctrine that was passed to Western sources. Although it may not include all parts of the official document, the principles of Russian military hegemony over the CIS are unambiguous. It envisions the direct use of Russian military forces to protect the rights of Russians living in former Soviet republics, and it warns that any security arrangements that CIS or East European states may make with states other than Russia will be seen as direct threats to Russian interests. These officially identified threats also include civil wars and violence within the CIS, which Russia judges to be a threat to its own security. In total, they give the Russian military justification for rather large missions and appropriate military capabilities.

2

Creating Political Capital?

BARBARA ANN CHOTINER

Nondemocratic rulers' decision to surrender control over the polity provides both the opportunity and the resources for systemic transformation.[1] Formal Communist Party acceptance of unfavorable outcomes from some contests in the 1989 elections to the Congress of People's Deputies was the first step in this process of divestiture in the USSR. The alteration in March 1990 of Article 6 of the Soviet Constitution, abolishing its prescription of the Communist Party's supremacy over all other organizations, groups, and even informal activities, further advanced possibilities for democratically oriented change. This reduction of prerogatives and preeminence had been approved by the Central Committee (CC) of the Communist Party of the Soviet Union (CPSU) at its plenum held earlier that month.

While this legislative initiative probably was impelled by the collapse of most East European communist regimes in 1989, Soviet leaders clearly recognized a watershed: reformulating Article 6 changed the nature of the political system, the character of the Communist Party, and its administrative prerogatives. Politburo member G. S. Semenova noted the reduced barriers to the emergence of new political parties, and Kazakh president Nursultan Nazarbayev indicated that competition could take place on a more "equal" basis. In proposing abrogation of the party's "leading role," Mikhail S. Gorbachev argued that the CPSU could neither retain institutional viability nor achieve proclaimed goals without popular consent. He seemed to link the quest for citizen support to a reduced administrative role for the party vis-à-vis government agencies and producers.[2] Repeal of the CPSU's primacy in all social spheres obviated the legal necessity for state agencies, economic organizations, and other social and political entities to follow the party's directives, accept its nominations of personnel, or undergo "verification" procedures. Indeed, the autonomy conferred by recasting Article 6 was quickly recognized by local governments. For example, in L'vov Oblast, the provincial soviet issued a directive characterizing "any interferences of party organs in state, economic, and cultural activity . . . as a violation of the Constitution of the USSR."[3]

The loss of the Communist Party's supervisory powers concerned some officials. A report on the 1990 Ukrainian Party Congress stated that delegates to the meeting "categorically objected [to] . . . recommendations to renounce the intervention of the Party in economic life."[4] Obkom first secretary V. I. Kupratyy cautioned that "the alienation of politics from economics is equivalent to the loss of confidence for the party." He intimated that involvement with economic decision making as well as association with production results had not only been linked to public perceptions about the system's political effectiveness but also yielded resources that could be used for coalition-building.[5] The issue of political effectiveness had been raised when the change of Article 6 had first been broached to the Central Committee. For example, Azeri first secretary A. N. Mutabilov wondered how socioeconomic change was to take place when the CPSU's role was reduced. If it had less ability to reverse the declining conditions, what would be the outcome for the party's dominance?[6]

Because reformulation of Article 6 to eliminate the "leading role of the Party" was recognized as opening possibilities toward creating a system in which the CPSU would be less dominant, the impact of this legal change needs investigation. Did amending the constitution prompt significantly different behavior on the part of local CPSU committees and officials than they had previously displayed? After March 1990, did local party organs and functionaries seem to be using attention to production and development questions to create or obtain political advantages? What were some of the instrumentalities for party pursuit of economic goals below the all-union level?

This chapter examines such questions within the context of agricultural production because CPSU agencies were for decades enmeshed in farming operations as well as efforts at rural modernization. In addition, through the last years of the Soviet regime, the Communist Party seemed to exercise greater control over the countryside than the cities. Thus some assessment of the public record of the party's economic activity may shed light on possible production-related bases of influence. The discussion will proceed under three rubrics. One involves general orientations toward as well as instrumentalities for conducting economic policy below the all-union level. A second comprises local partkoms' and apparatchiks' interactions with Soviets for the same jurisdictions because these governmental bodies were now to play the primary role in making and executing rules. The third heading subsumes the content and methods of CPSU involvement with agricultural affairs—from union-republics to raions. Hence, with greater specificity, the impact of the modified Article 6 may become clearer.

Party leaders and scholars responded to unease over relationships between economic undertakings of the CPSU and its political fate. Too, the commentators discussed the ways economic aims should be advanced under altered constitutional conditions. Behavior by apparatchiks, partkoms, and agricultural specialists, however, did not always correspond to expectations.

Like critics of the modified CPSU role in the Soviet system, CPSU Central Committee secretary Alexander Dzasokhov and Yu. S. Romanov, first secretary of the Nenets okruzhkom, focused on questions of political effectiveness. Linked to this issue was the place of economic issues in the public policy universe. Dzasokhov pointed to the impossibility of ignoring a most basic problem—the availability of food—and indicated that "organizational" measures should be taken to ameliorate the situation. Scholar M. Chemodanov characterized economics as "the most important sphere of . . . society,"[7] and Romanov warned that "failures in the economy most of all defeat the authority of the party."[8] Hence opponents were not the only ones who realized the significance of improved economic performance for the Communist Party's fate.

Perhaps as a result, a stream of instructions went out concerning appropriate ways to ensure that economic aims were met. Some pronouncements emphasized "concreteness" in party work. The all-union Central Committee Secretariat urged that "political approaches" to substantive questions should include "timely setting of tasks [and] practical organization of affairs."[9] Not only was such an orientation toward specificity and practicality advocated in the CPSU Secretariat, but a combined session of the Byelorussian Central Committee and Control Commission also enjoined attention to routine as well as long-term difficulties.[10] Hence Communist Party leaders did not necessarily seem to envisage limited involvement with production and development or abstract consideration of generalities. The officials seemed to expect practices that would place apparatchiks or party bodies in the midst of operational decision making. Were the efforts successful, functionaries might be able to exercise some leverage over or make valued contributions to production, development, and economic reform. The influence gained might, in turn, be parleyed into assent or backing on other issues. If economic performance improved, maybe the Communist Party could gain more generalized support.

So as to interfere in a rather detailed fashion, partkoms and CPSU officials were to make contacts with managers, specialists, and government economic bureaucrats. In February 1991, the Secretariat of the CPSU called attention to the necessity for interaction with economic leaders. Politburo member Oleg Shenin emphasized cooperation with economic administrators who were part of the CPSU *aktiv* so that party organs could concert managers' and regulators' undertakings in support of CPSU aims. Although it no longer had the legal right to order government officials and managers to take particular actions or use specific methods, party subunits seemed expected to exercise a more informal guidance. Shenin, Nazarbayev, and the Ukrainian Party Congress suggested, too, that partkoms become enmeshed in appointments. To the extent that party nominations were implemented, another source of punishment or reward would be available to CPSU functionaries and organizations. Rather differently, in a decree on the Orenburg Obkom, the Secretariat of the CC CPSU encouraged lower-level party organs to engage in business ventures.[11]

Yet such directives seem unlikely to have been entirely successful because they met with resistance from some managers and specialists as well as passivity or disagreement by Communist Party organizations and employees. The head of a "strike committee" representing 247 collective farm chairmen called for the disestablishment of raikoms. Agricultural scholars who discussed management in the journal of the USSR State Commission for Food and Purchases appeared to indicate that CPSU oversight militated against performance in the farming sector. Such remarks seemed to betoken potential unwillingness to negotiate or collaborate with party agencies or officials. Central Committee secretary Shenin confirmed the existence of difficulties in gaining cooperation from members of the *aktiv* who occupied responsible positions.[12] These individuals may have believed that only general policy statements by the Communist Party—rather than continued detailed interference by local CPSU organs—were legitimate once Article 6 had been changed. Economic managers, specialists, and state bureaucrats may thus have tried to use available opportunities to increase the autonomy of institutions[13] outside the party.

Such dispositions were likely to have been complemented either by a restrictive reading of party committees' rights in the areas of management and administration or by degrees of confusion and noncompliance, often by-products of organizational change. Several authoritative statements noted that Communist Party agencies' involvement with economic activity was inadequate and did not necessarily follow issued guidelines. The Agricultural Department of the CC CPSU attributed to respect for the soviets' prerogatives a situation in which "many party committees have withdrawn from questions concerned with the organization of agricultural production and the food supply."[14] General Secretary Gorbachev criticized reduced interactions with members of economic elites. Deputy General Secretary Vladimir Ivashko discussed the results of on-site visits by CPSU Central Committee personnel to "republican and oblast party organizations." He stated that in numerous cases, CPSU work was not "practical."[15] Hence many party officials did not seem inclined or may have been unable to continue patterns of detailed enmeshment with production and distribution of goods. These apparatchiks and elected officers, whether from conviction or forestallment, were contributing to the self-direction of collective and state farms; other productive, distributive, and service entities;

and government agencies. As a result, political advantages from manipulation, patronage, and brokerage were probably lost to the Communist Party. Some economic actors, however, may have been grateful for more independence. They may have developed more positive feelings about local CPSU organs and functionaries—or about the Communist Party as an institution.

Even if partkoms and CPSU bureaucrats wished to help create more free "political space" for other institutions to pursue their proper functions along self-determined lines, democratization presages partisan activity in legislatures. Party members and units discussed strategies for gaining soviet enactment and implementation of desired economic policies, but apparatchiks and local partkoms did not always successfully advance CPSU aims through government organs.

Methods devised for influencing local soviets focused on the accumulation of roles as well as joint party-state activities or CPSU help in the performance of civic responsibilities. Such approaches would not seem aimed at strengthening the institutionalization of dominant government organs. A CPSU first secretary's election as chairman of his local legislature was viewed not only as facilitating adoption of CPSU positions but also as reinforcing policy implementation. The second secretary of the Communist Party of Kazakhstan stated that conclusions by its "socio-economic and agrarian commissions . . . were embodied in state acts—ukases of the President of republic." Of course, this individual was Kazakh party first secretary Nazarbayev.[16] It was argued that district soviet chairmen who simultaneously served as raikom party leaders would be better able to discharge their governmental responsibilities: the soviet heads could deploy the prerogatives and contacts of their CPSU posts to gain compliance with concrete problem-solving efforts. The Uzbek party chief admitted that CPSU first secretaries' possession of the soviet chairmanships in their jurisdictions should secure "preservation of the political influence and control of party organs for the development of socioeconomic and sociopolitical situations."[17]

Some of the more collaborative approaches for obtaining favorable consideration of party initiatives might have opened CPSU organizations more fully to differing viewpoints. Subdivisions of the CPSU Central Committee Secretariat positively mentioned the holding, in Orenburg Province, of combined sessions by obkom and soviet commissions to examine issues faced by both bodies. The Moscow Obkom had either appointed or examined naming deputies to its commissions. The Ukrainian Party Congress enjoined partkoms to provide communists in government with "help . . . in the organization of studies, preparation of legal initiatives, work on drafts of laws and decrees."[18] Technical and research assistance may have resulted from the directive, but it may also have impelled CPSU agencies to try to exert substantive influence over state rule-making. Party "fractions" were also—according to Oleg Shenin—to serve as "a connecting link between the deputy corps and the party organs." But the tie was not to be one of equality because party discipline was to apply to the elected officials.[19]

Realizing expectations of controlling CPSU members in legislatures or co-operation between party bodies and soviets at times seemed to have been thwarted by communists themselves. Ruslan Khasbulatov denied the efficacy and/or appropriateness of party members' taking orders about legislative behavior. The second secretary of the Belorussian Communist Party lamented noncooperation by adherents in attending meetings of communist fractions in soviets.[20]

Efforts by CPSU officials to compete with or undercut the activities of soviets and their leaders perhaps created a more serious problem. The chairman of the Astrakhan Provincial Soviet limned the friction between raikom party chiefs who had lost elections to head district councils and the apparatchiks' successful opponents. Almost half of the representatives to the first Congress of the Russian Communist Party spoke to pollsters of deteriorating linkages between its subunits and the soviets. Although such conflict was unlikely to foster successful realization of CPSU programs, another form of organizational sabotage might engender poor implementation and longer-term refusal to cooperate. The Ukrainian Party Congress censured partkoms for excessively prescriptive behavior and for usurping the functions of local governments.[21]

The mixed picture of Communist Party involvement with local government agencies—ranging from manipulation and displacement of state organs to ineffectiveness—suggests several possible courses for CPSU work in agriculture. Party committees could use traditional methods learned before perestroika was inaugurated, the partkoms could operate with or through other institutions, or the CPSU agencies could be stymied in accomplishing stated goals. An understanding of the spectrum of approaches to economic activity can help to illuminate other developments in the Soviet political system, including the evolution of the Communist Party as an institution. Were CPSU leaders and activists less oriented toward administration and more toward elaborating policies and gaining support for them? Did apparatchiks and party committees address issues of economic change and transition to a market system that would probably reduce the ability of politicians to provide or withhold financially valued rewards and punishments? The diminution of opportunities for controlling such inducements would likely impel party and other politicians toward seeking consent through support for ideas and programs as well as policy trade-offs. Both a switch from detailed involvement in production and distribution operations and facilitation of movement away from centralized planning would increase the autonomy not only of individuals but also of economic and social organizations. Greater independence, in turn, would not just reinforce trends toward competition and coalition-building on a political basis but in addition would strengthen resources for constraining both government authorities and the CPSU.[22]

While continuities and discontinuities in party committees' and members' behavior would help to shape political evolution, the substantive content and success of economically oriented CPSU undertakings would help to determine the chances for the Communist Party to play a major role. Moreover, the importance of judgments about efficacy was magnified by citizens' beliefs about the CPSU as the preeminent political force in Soviet society. A June 1990 poll indicated that 20 percent of the respondents thought that the soviet was the dominant political institution in their district.[23] This result suggests that probably a large majority of those questioned viewed the raikom as more responsible for governance as well as policy outcomes.

The central party organs seemed to envisage both rather traditional tasks for local CPSU agencies and contributions to agricultural reform as well as recasting of the economic system. As in pre-perestroika years, partkoms from the union-republican to the raion echelons were directed to reinforce performance of seasonal tasks: the CPSU organs were to deal with "organizational and material-technical" difficulties, recruit auxiliary labor, and try to ensure the sale of required quotas of commodities for public stocks. Communist Party bodies were also to encourage increases of winter crops, "vegetables [and] potatoes."[24] Yegor Stroev, the Central Committee secretary heading the CPSU Agricultural Commission, met with republican, territorial, and provincial party leaders to discuss raising and/or making animal nutriments.[25]

Local CPSU organs were also oriented toward trying to ameliorate the consequences of reduced direction from higher authorities. It is not clear, however, whether party officials were to do so by issuing orders, making threats, and relying on discipline or by persuading and showing the utility of alternative economic strategies. Central Committee secretary A. N. Girenko stated that both the all-union Politburo and Secretariat had considered President Gorbachev's proposals "for . . . economic . . . stabilization." The latter body issued specific suggestions to party agencies at and above the provincial level. Probably to improve worsening food supplies, the Secretariat of the CC CPSU indicated that obkoms and subordinate agencies should try to facilitate greater parity in farmers' terms of trade with industry.[26]

In June 1991, the Politburo called upon republican, territorial, and provincial partkoms to cooperate with communist representatives to gain passage of legislation on issues such as privatization and rights to land. Several months earlier, the Agricultural Commission of the CC CPSU had elaborated guidelines urging party agencies to endorse new laws on land usage. Such regulations were expected to create the basis for family and individual farming motivated by self-interest. Moreover, at least some Central Committee bureaucrats argued that CPSU secretaries and district committees should promote the successful operation of private farms alongside kolkhozes and sovkhozes.[27]

Thus Communist Party members may have perceived several roles for officials and organizations. They may have been expected to serve not just as champions and facilitators of new approaches but additionally as troubleshooters and ensurers of routine processes. A variety of signals from central authorities, increased rights for individual party organizations, and greater localism in decision making contributed to significant diversity in CPSU work.

Party organizations below the all-union level responded to central agenda-setting with a plethora of meetings. Market-oriented reform and its consequences were on the dockets of at least three republican Central Committees, six reskoms, two kraikoms, and twenty-six obkoms. Consideration of these topics was linked to discussion of the deteriorating economic situation and steps that party authorities could take to ameliorate living conditions. At various levels, party committees examined steps that CPSU members or their organizations could take to combat productive and distributional problems. While CPSU bodies were thus oriented toward major issues of concern to all-union officials, party adherents were not necessarily supportive of the national leaders' policy initiatives. The April 1991 session of the Leningrad Provincial Party Committee, for example, featured criticism of the government plan to arrest economic decline.[28]

The concern with general economic questions of course affected agricultural issues. It permitted partkoms to address not only the refashioning of the Soviet system but also customary dilemmas of providing for the basic needs of the population. Therefore, functionaries and activists could fall back on more habitual concerns as well as deal with policies that might still have seemed unorthodox.

Amid uncertainties generated by efforts at change, CPSU organs dealt concretely with the fulfillment of regular agricultural tasks. Without their satisfactory completion, food supplies and the reputation of the Communist Party would be likely to suffer. In Belorussia, apparatchiks and party agencies continued to be heavily involved in bringing in the harvest. Industrial and white-collar employees were asked to give up their regular jobs as well as weekends to assist in the fields temporarily. Both the appeal and reaction recalled pre-perestroika conventions. The partkom demonstrated that it could continue to provide seasonal labor for farmers and worked toward meeting at least some consumer expectations. When a raikom was unable to effect the seasonal transfer of labor from the nonfarming sector, CPSU functionaries undertook some of the physical work themselves. Perhaps the officials viewed the activity as a demonstration of solidarity with a group they claimed to represent and not just an attempt to fend off productive disaster about which the public could easily draw conclusions. Yet at least one bureaucrat continued the Stalinist practice of telling a farm employee exactly how to do his job in a particular circumstance. (The raikom first secretary did first ascertain that the tractor operator was a party member.)[29]

In other parts of the USSR, similar strategies were followed. The Khabarovsk kraikom tried to define "the immediate tasks . . . of communists . . . for participation in . . . the gathering in of the harvest," as well as the beginning of a new crop cycle.[30] If followed by party members, such indications could allow the CPSU committee to influence undertakings by kolkhozes and sovkhozes, along with their auxiliary work forces. In 1990, all the Communist Party professionals and former apparatchiks in Donetsk Oblast were part of a "force of 100,000 communists of the industrial region" who helped farmers pick vegetables. The obkom first secretary seemed to present these efforts as a tangible sign of goodwill from the party to agriculturists. Formerly employed apparatchiks intended to continue the practice, which was defined as a "concrete" method for the CPSU to gain support.[31]

Partkoms continued other projects that were regarded with approval before Gorbachev's General Secretaryship, but CPSU agencies altered methods and ends to meet changed situations. While such practices may betray officials' fondness for managerial roles, the adaptations may also betoken creativity and incrementalism. This gradualism might have permitted alterations of the Communist Party's functions and place in the political system to be assimilated with greater ease—or may have swamped the attempted transformation. The Kursk obkom engaged in troubleshooting. As all-union party leaders had advised, the provincial CPSU committee initiated a project to remedy declining milk yields and received the cooperation of local government officials in investigating problems on the dairy farms. Study participants worked out proposals that were embodied in a decree of the obkom, followed by state determinations. The Komaricheskiy raikom, in Bryansk Province, collaborated with managers and technical experts to outline appropriate numbers of livestock for state and collective farms as well as the size of a state order. The scheme was submitted to the raion soviet for approval.[32]

Fostering agricultural development had been a significant focus of local Communist Party organizations and leaders since Nikita Khrushchev's time, and partkoms continued to try to promote modernization and economic expansion after March 1990. The Astrakhan obkom seemed interested in prodding rural producers to adopt novel methods and technologies, as its socioeconomic department continued "to study. . . advanced experience." The Cheboksary raikom disseminated its conclusions about potential projects for land improvements so that party adherents could use this information. While the district agency might thus have affected technical outcomes or levels of expenditure, raikoms in Belorussia were involved in implementing schemes to raise farm output while restricting new spending. The end was to be achieved by tying activities on personal plots to larger-scale operations on collective and state farms. In contrast, the Grodno obkom invested two million rubles in commercial mushroom growing after being approached by a scientist who was having difficulty finding capital.[33]

Other changes introduced by Communist Party organizations and functionaries affected personnel recruitment, administrative schemes, and definition of productive units. When requested to approve efforts for attracting Volga Germans to Ul'yanovsk Oblast to increase the number of agricultural workers, the obkom first secretary obliged. In Ukraine, the Uzhgorod raikom, its socioeconomic commission, economists, and technicians proposed a new way of paying administrators and professional employees of kolkhozes and sovkhozes. These staff members were to be compensated according to the volume of crop and livestock output. The Rostov obkom accepted experts' and lower party bodies' recommendations for improving management practices. In addition to suggesting tying farm performance to salaries, the Uzhgorod District Party Committee became concerned about the effect of kolkhoz size on yields and successfully proposed division of two collectives.[34]

Besides the security of carrying out familiar activities, developmental projects may have offered CPSU activists and leaders a vehicle for demonstrating interest in the longer-term welfare of constituents. Moreover, technical upgrading and economic retooling were elements of perestroika so that local party agencies could claim to be using various degrees of initiative to realize policies set by all-union bodies. Like some undertakings to ensure routine operations by farms and related entities, involvement in "modernizing" efforts could allow partkoms to enter specific production-related decision processes. Moreover, the availability of studies permitted Communist Party organs not only to identify public policy issues and recommend solutions but also to reduce coalition-forming efforts on behalf of other alternatives.

Providing alternatives and gaining support for them appear to have been the goals of the Orenburg and Rostov Provincial CPSU Committees. The Orenburg obkom, its *aktiv*, and a number of experts elaborated seven "socioeconomic programs." Of these, one aimed at boosting "the effectiveness of the development of the agro-industrial complex" and may have been introduced for consideration in the local assembly.[35] The Rostov obkom was singled out for emulation in promoting increased land leasing for private farming, in conjunction with the survival of kolkhozes and sovkhozes. Besides trying to elucidate ways the new configuration would function—and perhaps methods by which agricultural entrepreneurship could be made to pay—communists in the Rostov area took more practical steps. A plenary meeting of the oblast committee developed specific measures on agricultural leasing to be considered by the provincial soviet, and two hundred persons serving on gorkoms and raikoms concluded rent agreements.[36] These individuals' examples could encourage others to break away from their kolkhozes and sovkhozes. Endorsing the record compiled by Rostov party adherents, CPSU Central Committee secretary Yegor Stroev noted early in 1991 that partkoms elsewhere had also worked to diversify farm types—encompassing individual, family, collective, and state operations. Yet, a few months later, the CC CPSU Secretariat complained that district party bodies' efforts to convince rural inhabitants that independent crop and livestock raising could be advantageous were inadequate. CPSU agencies were also ineffective in prevailing upon government representatives and bureaucrats to issue the necessary ordinances for "land reform" and perhaps to render tangible assistance to smaller-scale agricultural producers.[37] The picture of local party efforts regarding farm restructuring was a mixed one of implementation and inactivity.

Where CPSU agencies and officials did work to open the agricultural sector to assist private enterprise, militants and bureaucrats may simply have seen "another campaign" in which it was their duty to participate.[38] Nevertheless, facilitation or frustration of individual and small-group husbandry offered politicians opportunities to grant or withhold tangible favors. Apparatchiks could build patronage ties with ordinary citizens and gain supporters for themselves or the CPSU. Those who opposed the Communist Party or participated in activities it did not sanction could be penalized.

Extension and withholding of benefits gained notice in the press, as did avoidance of opportunity for using patronage. *Moscow News,* for example, described the plight of apiarist A. F. Suslov. He apparently had difficulty leasing acreage so that he could grow the plants from which his bees could make honey. When Suslov asked the Lipetsk obkom for permission to rent, he was refused, perhaps because he had attended a Peasant Party meeting. In Bryansk Province, the chairman of a district legislature also headed the raion Communist Party committee. Upon request, he ensured that an independent farmer could obtain cattle feed. The first secretary of the Arkhangel'sk obkom claimed frequently to have assisted those conducting husbandry as leaseholders. In contrast, however, one individual who had been farming as an entrepreneur for about one year averred that the raikom secretary "has never . . . visited me." Perhaps the leaseholder's former position as head of the local soviet[39] allowed him to interact with CPSU functionaries in other ways, or maybe district communists believed that new economic relationships should evolve more autonomously.

Whatever the reasoning, patronage-related activity by CPSU officials and organizations was consistent with patterns of behavior discussed above: communist influentials both usurped other agencies' prerogatives and eschewed any role in an economic sphere. Party leaders may also have persuaded government and economic actors to implement the CPSU's policies to help it gain politically useful resources.

The mixed picture of local Communist Party organs' involvement in agriculture—as well as with production managers and government leaders who were to have gained greater control over economic life—underlines that the CPSU was in a transitional stage. Many party officials and agencies were opposed to modifying and restricting the party's traditional monopolistic, managerial role within society. Some party functionaries and activists withdrew substantially from detailed interaction with representatives of state institutions—whether because of the individuals' particular understanding of party documents and statements or from personal conviction. Other members of local partkoms may have become less involved in specific production questions because of confusion or emotional disengagement. Despite party members' motivation, there was some CPSU disentanglement from direct management over segments of the economy as well as some expansion of the questions that might be settled without party interference.

Likewise, there is some evidence that apparatchiks and partkoms were disposed or forced, at least at times, to allow government bodies to make independent decisions. Chronicled above are instances when CPSU officials and agencies worked somewhat collaboratively with economic and government personnel. Officials and institutions outside the party seemed to be gaining at least marginally greater autonomy. Government bodies in various parts of the country were evolving toward more neutral structures within which divergent political forces could interact. In various locations, direct control of economic resources by the CPSU was somewhat reduced so that workers and managers were becoming less constrained.

Nevertheless, some pre-perestroika patterns continued, some CPSU organs and leaders displayed antagonism to local governments, and there were deliberate economic involvements. These phenomena demonstrate that the transition from authoritarianism and single-party rule was uneven, perhaps not always wholehearted, and only in process by August 1991. Still, a large proportion of politicians and government officials who took the lead after August were bureaucrats of the CPSU or elected members of its deliberative bodies. These individuals expressed views and behaved in ways that place former communists across the post-Soviet political spectrum. Experiences undergone and ideas developed in the Gorbachev era may be among the factors impelling not only some "democrats" and pro-market reformers but also opponents of executive power. Of course, still other politicians and opinion leaders continued to believe that significant regime direction of economic activity was essential for popular welfare and national development. Officials constrained individual and enterprise economic behaviors by rules that changed, at times unpredictably, in the unstable political environments of the former Soviet republics.

As the institutional contexts and organizations inherited from the Soviet past continued to lose legitimacy and break down, politicos in the post-Soviet republics were faced with a broad range of questions about acceptable and effective strategies for creating market economies. Yet shifting political frameworks, changing political cultures, and growing distrust among confreres who had once held similar views on relationships between politics and economics hampered compromise as well as change. Appointed and elected leaders had to determine when good economic decisions were poor political determinations and vice versa. These challenges not only divided "liberals" of the late Gorbachev era from each other after 1991 but also underpinned the Russian constitutional crisis and the Ukrainian governmental crisis of 1993. Proponents of reduced governmental involvement in the economy—as a prerequisite for democracy—often argued that market-oriented reforms could be achieved only by the unilateral actions of a powerful executive. Partisans of a larger role for political authorities in the economy and a slower transition to the market frequently became champions of the separation of powers as well as close attention to constitutional provisions. Thus the confusion that once attended early efforts to withdraw the Communist Party from economic management continued in the uncertainty over means and ends following the demise of both the Communist Party and the Soviet Union.

NOTES

I wish to thank Jane Shapiro Zacek for her helpful comments. An earlier version of this essay was presented at the 1992 Annual Meeting of the American Political Science Association, Chicago, Illinois.

1. Guillermo O'Donnell and Philippe C. Schmitter, *Transitions from Authoritarian Rule: Tentative Conclusions About Uncertain Democracies* (Baltimore: Johns Hopkins University Press, 1986), 40–41; S. N. Eisenstadt, "The Breakdown of the Communist Regimes," *Daedalus* 121 (Spring 1992), 24; Adam Przeworski, *Democracy and the Market* (Cambridge: Cambridge University Press, 1991), 66–79.

2. G. S. Semenova, "Avtoritet utverzhdaetsya delom," *Izvestiya TsK KPSS* 11 (November 1990), 46; N. Nazarbayev, "Osvobozhdayas' ot okov zastoya," *Partiynaya zhizn'* 11 (June 1990), 43; M. S. Gorbachev, "O proekte platformy TsK KPSS k XXVIII s"yezdy partiy," *Materialy Plenuma Tsentral'nogo komiteta KPSS, 5–7 fevralya 1990 goda,* by TsK KPSS (Moscow: Izdatel'stvo politcheskoy literatury, 1990), 9.

3. Vyacheslav Sekretaryuk, "Kto idet sledom? Kommunisty L'vovshchiny v oppozitsii," *Partiynaya zhizn'* 12 (June 1991), 18. The quoted material in the text is extracted by Sekretaryuk from an *ukhvala* of the provincial council.

4. Anatoliy Myalovitskiy, "Taktika v usloviyakh mnogopartiynosti," *Partiynaya zhizn'* 14 (July 1990), 23.

5. V. I. Kupratyy, "Chelovek obrashaetsya v obkom," interview by Ye. P. Kasiychuk and V. F. Teteruk, *Kommunist Ukrainy* 1 (January 1991), 72, 64.

6. TsK KPSS, *Materialy Plenuma 5–7 fevrala,* 109. See also "Vystupleniya v preniyakh," in which Mutabilov's comments are included, ibid.

7. Alexander Sergeevich Dzasokhov, "Sekretariat TsK posle s"yezda: Pervye shagi," *Izvestiya TsK KPSS* 9 (September 1990), 5; M. Chemodanov, "Ne pretenduya na monopoliyu v obshchestve, no ostavayas' pravyashchey partiey," *Partiynaya zhizn'* 8 (April 1990), 27, 30.

8. TsK KPSS, *Materialy plenuma Tsentral'nogo komiteta KPSS, 10–11 dekabrya 1990 g.* (Moscow: Izdatel'stvo politicheskoy literatury, 1991), 24.

9. Sekretariat TsK KPSS, "O rabote partiynykh organizatsiy Rostovskoy oblasti po sodeystviyu v formirovanii mnogokladnoy agrarnoy ekonomiki s uchetom politicheskikh ustanovok XXVIII s"yezda KPSS: Postanovlenie Sekretariata TsK KPSS 8 yanvarya 1991 g.," *Izvestiya TsK KPSS* 4 (April 1991), 17.

10. Igor' Molokanov, "Polmesyatsa: Den' za dnem," *Partiynaya zhizn'* 11 (June 1991), 33; Valeriy Mikheev, "Teper' ya konsul'tant . . .," *Kommunist Belorussii* 5 (May 1991), 5.

11. Sekretariat TsK KPSS, "O rabote Orenburgskogo obkoma partii po vypolneniyu reshenii XXVIII s"yezda KPSS: Postanovlenie Sekretariata TsK KPSS 26 fevralya 1991 g.," *Izvestiya TsK KPSS* 5 (May 1991), 25; Oleg Shenin, "Trevogi nashi i nadezhdy," *Partiynaya zhizn'* 13 (July 1991), 13; Nazarbayev, "Osvobozhdayas' ot okov zastoya," 44; "O tekushchem momente i sotsial'no-ekonomicheskoy politike Kompartii Ukrainy: Rezolyutsiya XXVIII s"yezd Kompartii Ukrainy," *Kommunist Ukrainy* 1 (January 1991), 41.

12. "Farmers Warn: We'll Turn Off the Milk Tap," *Moscow News* 17 (May 6–13, 1990), 10; A. Shut'kov "Chemu otdat' prioritet v upravlenii," *APK: Ekonomika, upravlenie* 8 (1990), 41, 42; V. Gotlober, "Preodolet' ostatki dogm v agrarnoy politike," *APK: Ekonomika, upravlenie* 12 (1990), 13, 15; L. Nikiforov, "Agrarnaya reforma," *APK: Ekonomika, upravlenie* 5 (1991), 7; Shenin, "Trevogi nashi i nadezhdy," 13.

13. In this essay, discussion of institutions and their development is dependent on Samuel P. Huntington, *Political Order in Changing Societies* (New Haven: Yale University Press, 1968), 1–92.

14. Otdel agrarnoy politiki TsK KPSS, "Ob usilenii vnimaniya partiynykh organizatsii voprosam stabilizatsii i uluchsheniya prodovol'stvennogo polozheniya strany v usloviyakh perekhoda k rynochnoy ekonomike," *Izvestiya TsK KPSS* 2 (February 1991), 31.

15. M. S. Gorbachev, "Byt' partiey naroda, partiey perestroiki," *Partiynaya zhizn'* 24 (December 1990), 6; V. A. Ivashko, "O polozhenii v strane i zadachakh KPSS v svyazi s perevodom ekonomiki na rynochnye otnosheniya: Doklad zamestitelya General'nogo sekretarya TsK KPSS V. A. Ivashko 8 oktyabrya 1990 goda," in *Materialy plenuma Tsentral'nogo komiteta KPSS, 8–9 oktyabrya 1990 g.,* by TsK KPSS (Moscow: Izdatel'stvo politicheskoy literatury, 1990), 15–16.

16. Vladislav Anufriyev, "Deystvuyushchie litsa i ispolniteli," interview by Viktor Kuz'min, *Partiynaya zhizn'* 12 (June 1991), 46.

17. Kupratyy, "Chelovek obrashaetsya v obkom," 72; A. I. Karimov, "Ob

obshchestvenno-politicheskoy obstanovke v respublike i zadachakh po organizatsionno-politicheskomu ukrepleniyu Kompartii Uzbekistana i podgotovke k perekhodu ekonomiki na rynochnnye otnosheniya: Doklad TsK XXII s"yezdu Kompartii Uzbekistana (II etap)," *Chelovek i politika* 2 (February 1991), 15.

18. Otdely TsK KPSS, "O rabote Orenburgskogo obkoma partii po vypolneniyu resheniy XXVIII s"yezda KPSS," *Izvestiya TsK KPSS* 5 (May 1991), 26; Viktor Novikov, "Pryamaya liniya koroche zigzaga," *Partiynaya zhizn'* 17 (September 1990), 38; "O tekushchem momente i sotsial'no-ekonomicheskoy politike Kompartii Ukrainy: Rezolutsiya," 38.

19. Shenin, "Trevogi nashi i nadezhdy," 9.

20. Lyudmilla Telen, "Ruling Opposition?" *Moscow News* 29 (July 29–August 5, 1990), 10; Aleksey Kamay, "Po puti sotsialisticheskogo vybora," *Kommunist Belorussii* 5 (May 1991), 4, 9.

21. Ivan D'yakov, "'Vlast'—Sovetam, a shto—sebe?'" interview by Stanislav Sendyukov, *Partiynaya zhizn'* 12 (June 1990), 19, 21–22; Vladimir Boykov and Zhan Toshchenko, "Ne upodobit'sya by Zhurdenu," *Partiynaya zhizn'* 18 (September 1990), 25; "O tekushchem momente: Rezolutsiya," 42.

22. This discussion draws upon and is influenced by discussions by several authors: William H. Riker, *The Theory of Political Coalitions* (New Haven: Yale University Press, 1962); Zbigniew Brzezinski, *The Grand Failure* (New York: Charles Scribner's Sons, 1989); Huntington, *Political Order;* Giovanni Sartori, *The Theory of Democracy Revisited* (Chatham, N.J.: Chatham House Publishers, 1987); and John H. Goldthorpe, "Problems of Political Economy After the Postwar Period," in *Changing Boundaries of the Political,* ed. Charles S. Maier (Cambridge: Cambridge University Press, 1987).

See also Zbigniew Brzezinski, *Between Two Ages* (New York: Viking Press, 1970); Charles E. Lindblom, *Politics and Markets* (New York: Basic Books, 1977); O'Donnell and Schmitter, *Transitions from Authoritarian Rule;* and Przeworski, *Democracy and the Market.*

23. Boykov and Toshchenko, "Ne upodobit'sya by Zhurdenu," 25.

24. Sekretariat TsK KPSS, "Ob usilenii organizatorskaya raboty partiynykh komitetov po politcheskomy obespecheniyu uborki urozhaya: 7 avgusta 1990g.," *Izvestiya TsK KPSS* 9 (September 1990), 8; Sekretariat TsK KPSS, "Ob usilenii vnimaniya partiynykh organizatsiy voprosam stabilizatsii i uluchsheniya prodovol'stvennogo polozheniya strany v usloviyakh perekhoda k rynochnoy ekonomike: Postanovlenie Sekretariata TsK KPSS 14 yanvarya 1991 g.," *Izvestiya TsK KPSS* 2 (February 1991), 27; Sekretariat TsK KPSS, "O rabote Orenburgskogo obkoma," 24.

25. "Khronika marta," *Izvestiya TsK KPSS* 5 (May 1991), 11–12.

26. A. N. Girenko, "Ukreplayaya obratnye svyazi," *Izvestiya TsK KPSS* 12 (December 1990), 3; Sekretariat TsK KPSS, "O rabote Orenburgskogo obkoma," 24.

27. Politbyuro TsK KPSS, "O rabote kommunistov v Sovetakh narodnykh deputatov: Postanovlenie Politbyuro TsK KPSS 3 iyunya 1991," *Izvestiya TsK KPSS* 8 (August 1991), 15; "Khronika marta," 10–11; Ye. Stroev, Yu. Manaenkov, I. Skiba, and N. Stashenkov, "O nekotorykh vyvodakh i predlozheniyakh, vytekayushchikh iz itogov

Vsesoyuznogo seminara-soveshchaniya po politecheskomu obespecheniyu perekhoda k mnogoukladnoy ekonomike v agropromyshlennoy sfere," *Izvestiya TsK KPSS* 5 (May 1991), 34.

28. Sektor organizatsionnykh voprosov Organizatsionnogo otdela TsK KPSS, "Shto obsuzhdayut plenumy partiynykh komitetov, *Izvestiya TsK KPSS* 1 (January 1991), 48, 2 (February 1991), 35, 4 (April 1991), 57, 5 (May 1991), 54, 6 (June 1991), 58–59, 7 (July 1991), 28–29; Igor' Molokanov, "Polmesyatsa: Den' za dnem," *Partiynaya zhizn'* 9 (April 1991), 47.

29. Mikhail Krizhanovskiy, "V zashchite bezzashchitnoy derevni," *Kommunist Belorussii* 8 (August 1991), 29–30.

30. Sektor organizatsionnykh voprosov Organizationnogo otdela TsK KPSS, "Shto obsuzhdayut plenumy partiynykh komitetov," *Izvestiya TsK KPSS* 7 (July 1991), 28.

31. Vasiliy Omel'chenko, "Neobychnyy desant," *Partiynaya zhizn'* 19 (October 1990), 24.

32. Alexander Seleznev "Luchshe odin raz uvidet'," interview by Vyacheslav Zudin, *Partiynaya zhizn'* 7 (April 1991), 25; Stanislav Sendyukov, "Akh oni—'kamarinskie'," *Partiynaya zhizn'* 8 (April 1991), 24.

33. D'yakov, "Vlast'—Sovetam," 23; Igor' Molokanov, "Ne rassypat'sya, kak gorokh po polu," *Partiynaya zhizn'* 14 (July 1991), 62; I. Skiba, "Agrarnaya vopros: Chto tormozit reformy," *Partiynaya zhizn'* 10 (May 1990), 55; Viktor Kotov, "Smotret' pravda v glaza," *Kommunist Belorussii* 8 (August 1991), 23–24.

34. Vladimir Kiselyov, "Some Soviet Germans Choose Ulyanovsk over Frankfort," *Moscow News* 25 (July 1–8, 1990), 11; P. A. Fedikovich, "V sotrudnichestve s Sovetami," *Izvestiya TsK KPSS* 7 (July 1991), 102; V. T. Suslin, "Reskreposhchaya ekonomiku sela," *Izvestiya TsK KPSS* 4 (April 1991), 23.

35. Otdely TsK KPSS, "O rabote Orenburgskogo obkoma," 26.

36. Otdel agrarnoy politiki TsK KPSS, Otdel sotsial'no-ekonomicheskoy politike TsK KPSS, Organizatsionnyy otdel TsK KPSS, "O rabote partiinykh organizatsii Rostovskoy oblasti po sodeystviyu v formirovanii mnogoukladnoy agrarnoy ekonomiki s uchetom politicheskikh ustanovok XXVIII s"yezda KPSS," *Izvestiya TsK KPSS* 4 (April 1991), 22; Ye. S. Stroev, "Zemlya trevogi nashey," *Izvestiya TsK KPSS* 3 (March 1991), 8.

37. Yegor Stroev, "Selo spacet mnogoukladnost'," prepared by Nikolay Zenkovskiy, *Partiynaya zhizn'* 4 (February 1991), 34–35; Sekretariat TsK KPSS, "Ob usilenii raboty po politicheskomu obespecheniyu zemel'noy reformy," *Izvestiya Tsk KPSS* 7 (July 1991):15–16.

38. Vladimir Brovkin, "First Party Secretaries: An Endangered Species?" *Problems of Communism* 39 (January–February 1990), 16.

39. Yuri Chernichenko, "The Internal Colony: Why Call This a Peasants Alliance," *Moscow News* 25 (July 1–8, 1990), 5; Lyudmila Telen, "On Tasty and Healthy Food," *Moscow News* 15 (April 14–21, 1991), 11; Sendyukov, "Akh oni—'kamarinskie'," 22; Anatoliy Gromoglasov, "Aplodismentov ne bydet," *Partiynaya zhizn'* 19 (October 1990), 20, 24.

3

The Communist Party on the Eve of Collapse

CYNTHIA S. KAPLAN AND HENRY E. BRADY

The image of the Communist Party of the Soviet Union as a monolithic organization long ago gave way to a more nuanced view of an organization beset by elite conflict reflecting the historical epochs of Soviet political history. Most frequently, our focus was restricted to particular leaders and their followers or to members of the party elite. Even as the Gorbachev era drew to an end and diverse opinions were espoused, research was based primarily on statements by party leaders or published materials such as platforms sponsored by the party elite.[1] In the aftermath of the Soviet Union's collapse, the attitudes of party members themselves assume much greater importance for our understanding of the dynamics of political and social change. Party members' views on Soviet history and policy issues provide a key to understanding the rapidity of the party's demise, the rise of Boris Yeltsin, and the dimensions of political cleavages found among those most active in the former communist system.

Much of Zbigniew Brzezinski's work touches upon the defining role of the party in the communist system. In such classic articles as "Soviet Politics: From the Future to the Past?" and "The Soviet Political System: Transformation or Degeneration?" and in his recent book, *The Grand Failure,* Brzezinski highlights the party's pivotal role in defining the relationship between society and the party-state.[2] He notes in *The Grand Failure* that in reforming, the party must confront a paradox. At risk of undermining its legitimacy, the party must reject the three formative phases of Soviet history: under Lenin, that of a totalitarian party aiming at the total reconstruction of society; under Stalin, that of a totalitarian state that had totally subordinated society; and under Brezhnev, that of a totally stagnant state dominated by a corrupt totalitarian party.[3]

As the party and the society wrangled with the political past, they had to address the central political, economic, and social issues defining a new spectrum of political life.[4] This chapter explores these issues based on the results of a mass survey on Citizen Participation in Politics in Russia conducted from the end of May through the beginning of August 1991 in which a total of

12,309 people were interviewed, including 1,120 members of the CPSU.[5] Elite attitudes, particularly those of party members, are essential in understanding the nature of transition in Russia during the denouement of the August 1991 coup and later.

ATTITUDES TOWARD THE PAST AND MODELS FOR THE FUTURE

During the pre-coup months of 1991 the optimism of the early Gorbachev years had waned, but the cynicism of the Yeltsin period had yet to arise. The intelligentsia, after first rallying uncritically in support of Gorbachev, appeared increasingly disappointed as he attempted to occupy a more centrist position, which during the spring and summer of 1991 demonstrated a distinct turn toward more conservative positions. Overall, the political atmosphere in 1991 remained one of hope in which political activity was believed capable of making a difference. Although the politics of opposition dominated the Russian political scene at this time, the emerging politics of personalities was growing in importance.

Discussions of what should be done in the USSR and in Russia during 1990–91 revolved around basic questions of what kind of society Russia should be. These discussions included the reevaluation of the formative historical phases previously noted by Brzezinski. They explored the central issues of political life: the nature of the political and economic systems, the need for authority, and the model of Western societies. We attempted to get at this debate by asking the respondents, "Which of the following paths to development for our country appears to you to be most correct?" (see table 3.1).

The table shows the percentages of the population who chose each option or who were undecided. The most striking feature is the extraordinary range of answers across the spectrum. Approximately equal portions (20 percent) of the general population supported a return to Brezhnevism and the adoption of

Table 3.1. What is to be done? (breakdown for entire sample, in percentages)

Stalinism	3.3
Brezhnevism	19.2
Democratic Socialism	14.4
Capitalism and socialism	21.5
Western society	21.9
Monarchy	1.3
Undecided/refused/missing	16.9
Other	1.4

Source: Citizen Participation in Politics in Russia Survey, 12,309 respondents interviewed in May–August 1991.

a Western model, a fact that was frequently overlooked in the enthusiasm of Western analysts and Russian liberals for a transition to democracy. For the first time, by using survey responses from a representative sample of the Russian population, we can assess how widely these views were held and, perhaps most critical for our understanding of the nature of political change in Russia, we can compare how these opinions were distributed in the mass populace and among party members.

As evident above, striking differences existed within the general population as a whole in May–August 1991, but to what extent did they exist among party members or the apparat?[6] This was a period in which old and new options for those politically active arose with dazzling speed. The political scene in Russia, including the role of the Communist Party, dramatically changed from 1989 through 1991. In the course of the Gorbachev era the fundamental principles of party life were questioned and many were abandoned. The abolition of Article 6 of the 1977 USSR Constitution in March 1990 meant that the official and exclusive leading role of the CPSU no longer existed. Indeed, by early 1990, an opposition faction within the CPSU, the Democratic Platform, supported a social-democratic alternative, while another faction, the Marxist Platform, maintained a more orthodox position.[7] In June 1990 the Communist Party of the Russian Soviet Federation of Socialist Republics was created and was dominated by conservatives.[8] By October 1990 a new law on public associations provided a legal basis for new political organizations and thousands of these movements and organizations arose, some seeking to become proto-parties.[9]

Given the speed and unexpected nature of change, what did party members see as desirable models for the future? As expected, table 3.2 shows that members of the apparat, as well as current party members, had distinctly different notions of what should be done to solve the problems of the Soviet Union as of mid-1991. Such differences of opinion within the elite could pave the way for cooperation between members of the old establishment and the new opposition during the process of transition, thereby avoiding widespread violence.[10]

Among party members 14.4 percent favored Stalinism or Brezhnevism, while 31.5 percent preferred Democratic Socialism. A substantial percentage (28.5 percent) of party members also supported adopting the best traits of capitalism and socialism, but only 13.9 percent preferred a totally Western option. These results compare with almost 18 percent of the apparat favoring a return to Stalinism or Brezhnevism and about 28 percent choosing the modest Gorbachev reforms of democratic and humane socialism. To be sure, 31 percent wanted to try a mixture of capitalism and socialism—a more strongly reformist option—but only 11.5 percent wanted the radical option of Westernization. What is interesting here is that party members and the apparat, although more conservative on the whole than the general population and less willing to adopt purely Western solutions, were actually more willing to experiment with aspects of both capitalist and socialist systems than was the general populace. They would provide a base for reform which would be sensitive, however, to violations of socialist principles and what some viewed as the undesirable influence of the West.

GENERATIONAL CHANGE

What explains the diversity of opinion found? As Brzezinski and others noted during the 1970s, social change in the Soviet Union might have political consequences best analyzed in terms of generational change.[11] Figure 3.1 shows that at least some of the differences found in the general populace are purely generational. In this figure, the fraction of the sample giving a particular response is plotted by age.[12] The generational support for Brezhnevism and for democratic socialism are similar, and the generational support for capitalism and socialism and for Western society are similar.

DIFFERENCES WITHIN THE CPSU

Generational differences also exist among CPSU members, but preferences for future paths of development among party cohorts differ in surprising ways from those found in the general population. Greater support existed among young as well as middle-aged party members than in the general population for a model combining capitalist and socialist characteristics. The more purely Western option, however, fares more poorly among all party generations, even the young. Two patterns stand in clear distinction to those found in the general populace. There is relatively strong support for a new democratic-socialist system among early middle-aged members, which significantly increases with age, and there is a low level of support for Brezhnevism and Stalinism. Although the latter alternatives become more attractive to older respondents, there is less support for these options than was found within the general population, especially among those of middle age. What emerges is a party membership that had a commitment to some form of democratic socialism that increased with age. An expected nostalgia for Stalinism or Brezhnevism was not as pronounced, even among somewhat older party cohorts, as in the general population. Here we may begin to discern a split between members of the party and the populace at large. Within the general population there appeared to be more support than among party members for an authoritarianism that could be melded with nationalism.

To explore differences among members of the party and apparat, we examined their attitudes toward party policies and Marxist-Leninist principles. When factions formed within the CPSU by 1990, these were central issues confront-

Table 3.2. What is to be done, by major elite group

	Party and apparat			Local Raion administrators	Professionals and managers		
	Apparat	Now CPSU members	Soviet deputies		Educated	Managers	Professionals
Stalinism or Brezhnevism	17.7	14.4	16.7	22.9	5.0	8.7	5.2
Democratic Socialism	28.3	31.5	22.7	25.7	24.7	18.4	8.9
Capitalism and socialism	31.0	28.5	32.6	25.0	37.9	40.8	39.4
Western	11.5	13.9	12.5	14.3	21.0	21.7	26.3
Other	4.4	3.1	4.9	3.5	2.2	4.2	2.6
Undecided	7.1	8.3	9.7	8.6	9.3	5.8	7.3
N	113	1,120	144	140	377	309	946

	Intelligentsia		Population
	Arts and sciences	Intelligentsia	
Stalinism or Brezhnevism	6.1	3.5	4.6
Democratic Socialism	8.5	12.1	14.5
Capitalism and socialism	43.7	40.4	21.6
Western	27.9	31.2	22.0
Other	6.9	9.2	2.7
Undecided	6.9	2.8	15.9
N	247	141	

Source: Citizen Participation in Politics in Russia Survey, 12,309 respondents interviewed in May–August 1991.

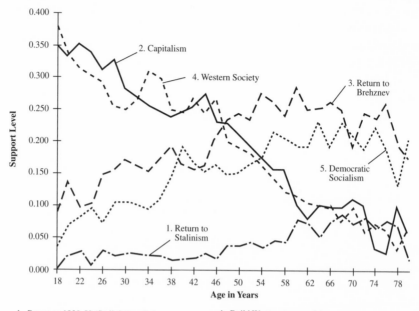

1. Return to 1930-50 (Stalinist) period   4. Build Western-type society
2. Build capitalist system   5. Build new democratic-socialist system
3. Return to 1960-80 (Brehznev) period

Source: Citizen Participation in Politics in Russia Survey; 12,309 Russian citizens interviewed May–August 1991.

Figure 3.1. Generations and politics: What is to be done?

ing members. The Democratic Platform faction supported social-democratic reformism, while the Marxist Platform espoused a more reactionary position. We would expect supporters of Gorbachev to be relatively satisfied with party policy, seeking neither radical democratization within the party nor a return to a more disciplined party life. But how were these attitudes toward party matters among members related to their support for particular models of future development? To explore this relationship we asked those who were members of the CPSU, "What do you personally think of the Communist Party's policies?"

In table 3.3 we summarize the responses to this question broken down by the various options for the country. The 13 percent of CPSU members who stood pat and believed that the Communist Party was correct overwhelmingly chose either the reactionary positions (23.8 percent) or the Gorbachev democratic socialist reforms (47.6 percent). Moreover, 58.8 percent of them chose Gorbachev over Yeltsin. This, the smallest group, was the Gorbachev wing of the CPSU as of May–August 1991.

Of the 18 percent who believed that the CPSU did not strictly adhere to Marxist-Leninist principles, over 28.3 percent wanted to go back to the policies of Stalin and Brezhnev, 28.2 percent supported the Gorbachev reforms, and 20.8 percent wanted stronger reforms. Thus the most reactionary elements were likely to believe that the CPSU did not strictly adhere to Marxist-Leninist principles, but at the same time more people in this group than in the stand-pat group favored Westernization or capitalism and socialism. Although some respondents may have thought that a party critique based on insufficient purity of principle was the safest course of action and others may have been put off by the word "radical" in the reformist response, it is more likely that the question captured a shared belief in the principles of Marxism-Leninism. Those expressing these sentiments probably understood Marxism-Leninism differently, however, suggesting the presence of supporters of both the Democratic Platform and the Marxist Platform factions within this group. We call this group the "True Believers" (including reactionaries).

The 55 percent who believe that the CPSU's policies must become more democratic are, not surprisingly, overwhelmingly reformist. Finally, the 4 percent who gave "other answers" when asked about the policies of the CPSU are the most radical of these factions; 28.6 percent wanted a Western society, 18.4 percent wanted only the Gorbachev reforms, and 16.3 percent wanted the stronger reforms leading to a mixed capitalist-socialist system. Consequently, this group was basically reformist in about the same way as the managers and professionals were shown to be in table 3.2. Indeed, the support of 36.7 percent for Yeltsin versus 20.4 percent for Gorbachev is just about the same as was found for the managers and professionals.

DIFFERENCES BASED UPON "WHAT IS TO BE DONE?"

The above data suggest some substantial differences within the CPSU, but the resultant groups remain relatively heterogenous in their attitudes. Another way to see these differences is to break the CPSU members into groups depending on their answer to the question, "What is to be done?" We do this in table 3.4, which shows that over 58 percent of the reactionary party members who wanted to return to the days of Brezhnev or Stalin chose either to say that the party had not adhered to its Marxist-Leninist principles or that it was basically correct in its policies. Support for Gorbachev and Yeltsin was about evenly matched among members of this group at about 25 percent apiece.

Those who chose the democratic socialism option—the Gorbachev reformers—were, indeed, supporters of Gorbachev (51 percent) and of the Union Treaty (98 percent). They were also most likely (56 percent) to argue that the CPSU needed democratic reform, but a significant fraction also argued that the party was essentially correct (20 percent). Among those who chose the stronger reforms of "capitalism-socialism" almost all (71.6 percent) called for democratic reforms within the CPSU. These were probably supporters of the

Table 3.3. What is to be done by CPSU members' opinions of party policies

	Not Marxist-Leninist enough	Generally correct	Should be democratic	Other response	Undecided
Stalinism or Brezhnevism	23.8	28.3	7.8	10.2	15.9
Democratic Socialism	47.6	28.2	31.3	18.4	23.2
Capitalism and socialism	14.3	20.8	36.3	16.3	26.1
Western	1.4	10.4	17.0	28.6	7.2
Other	3.4	2.5	2.6	12.2	2.8
Undecided	9.5	9.9	5.1	14.3	24.6
Democratic Russia	1.4	2.5	9.8	14.3	2.9
Prefer Yeltsin	8.8	15.3	23.0	36.7	20.0
Prefer Gorbachev	58.8	30.2	30.0	20.4	24.3
N	202	148	621	49	70

Note: CPSU members only.
Source: Citizen Participation in Politics in Russia Survey, 12,309 respondents interviewed in May–August 1991.

Democratic Platform. Finally, those who wanted the Westernization option were most likely to belong to the then new reformist political organization Democratic Russia (17.9 percent), most likely to support Yeltsin (41.7 percent), and least likely to support the Union Treaty (72.5 percent).

At the time of the survey in 1991, the meaning of democracy and its close association with market reform made it particularly important to explore attitudes toward economic policies. In figure 3.2 we explore these attitudes on the basis of answers to some questions. The lines in this diagram show the location of each CPSU faction on these questions. The four top questions come from a battery in which respondents were asked, "What do you think this society should do first to get itself out of the current crisis?" and given alternatives with which they could agree, disagree, or remain undecided.[13]

For all six questions, we have located the lines on figure 3.2 such that the mean (among all CPSU members) is in the middle of the diagram. In addition, we have magnified the scale of the individualism question to spread out the answers, but all other scales have the same units.

The diagram indicates that there is an extraordinary amount of variation across the four factions within the CPSU. Except for the individualism question, on which the means range from only 1.85 to 2.25, the difference between the reactionary faction and the Western faction is typically about a full point. There is also some clustering in the diagram. Two of the factions are always on the left of the mean, and they are often near each other: the reactionary–true believer faction, which wants a return to Stalinism or Brezhnevism, and the Gorbachevites, who want a humane and democratic socialism. The two others, the opposition reformers and the radicals, are always on the right and often near each other as well.

More precisely, the reactionary–true believer group is opposed to privatization, in favor of a planned economy, wants the CPSU back in power, thinks state interests are most important, does not want to lose the gains from socialism, and is in the middle on private property. The Westernizers are in favor of privatization, opposed to a planned economy, do not want the CPSU back in power, are convinced that private property is a good idea (despite a question loaded against such an answer), think individual interests are most important, and are in the middle with respect to protecting the gains from socialism. Overall, the Gorbachev reformers seem much less enthused about a return of the CPSU and a return to the planned economy than the reactionaries–true believers, and the Westernizers seem much more enthusiastic about private property than the opposition reformers and less worried about losing the gains of socialism. The evidence suggests that a desire for reform is often accompanied by belief in socialist principles. Only the smallest group, the Westernizers, appear willing to reject socialism outright.

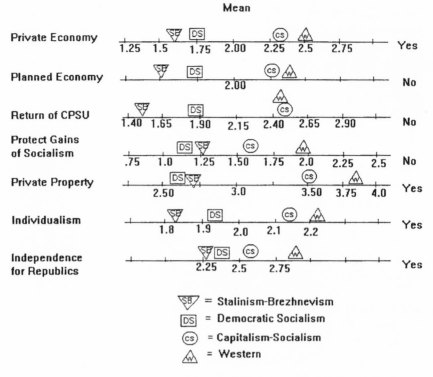

Figure 3.2. Average policy positions of four CPSU factions (CPSU members only)

Factor analyses of these items for just the CPSU members and for the whole population strongly suggest that they form a one-dimensional factor that we call economic reform. Among CPSU members, the items load above .4 on this one dimension and the only problematic item is the individualism question. (In fact, on its face, this seems less fundamentally a question about the economic system.) When we regressed an index of the four groups within the CPSU on the six economic factors above, we discovered that they explain about 25 percent of the variance in CPSU members' choices of what is to be done.[14] This is strong evidence of the influence of economic issues on political and societal preferences.

THE UNION TREATY AND DEMOCRACY WITHIN THE CPSU

At least two other issues defined politics during the 1988–91 period: the politics of democratization and nationalism and the Union Treaty. Unfortunately, we do not have as extensive a battery of questions for each of these issues as we had for the economy, but we do have some questions that provide insight into them.

On the "agree-disagree" battery described earlier in which we asked respondents, "What do you think should be done to get out of the crisis," one option was "Let the republics become independent." A surprising 65.4 percent of the entire sample agreed with this, but even more surprisingly, 66.3 percent of the CPSU members also agreed with it. Perhaps many respondents were thinking of the Baltic republics, whose claims for independence were highly salient at the time of our interview after Gorbachev's crackdown in early 1991. Whatever they were thinking of, this question clearly taps one of a congery of issues related to the Union Treaty. Table 3.4 includes a breakdown of the answers to this question. Only 55.6 percent of the reactionary–true believer groups supported this statement, but 87.2 percent of the Westernizers endorsed it. Once again, the position of the reactionary–true believers foreshadows a nationalist position related to the problematic identity of being a Russian within a new post-Soviet Russia.

The last line on figure 3.2 shows where the four factions stand on the issue of independence for the republics.[15] Clearly, there is much less variation in the responses to this question than to the six economic ones, but the pattern is the same as before. To ensure that we are not simply tapping the economic dimension, we examine whether respondents thought that the Union Treaty should be signed. Of the CPSU members, 88 percent said that the Union Treaty should be signed. Table 3.4 shows the breakdown by each faction. The treaty was opposed by those who favored the maintenance of a unified state as well as those who wanted the dissolution of the union. Our questionnaire also asked people whether they voted in the March 1991 referendum on the union. Table 3.4 reports the percentage who voted for the Gorbachev wording (of those who actually voted).

In addition to these measures of nationalism and opinions on the Union Treaty, we also have the measure of attitudes toward democratization of the CPSU, which was mentioned earlier.[16] To check on the impact of these variables on preferences for future models of development, we use them and all the economic variables in a regression where the dependent variable is the four CPSU factions.[17] Neither of the items on the Union Treaty has any impact, but the other variables do have significant impact. Advocacy of democratizing the CPSU moves a respondent a full one-quarter point on this scale toward Westernization, and going from not wanting the republics to be independent to wanting them to be independent moves a respondent about one-sixth of a point toward Westernization. These are not enormous effects, but given the crudity of the measures, they probably underestimate the impacts of these dimensions.

The Second Major Dimension

It is surprising to find that the items about the Union Treaty have no impact. This was, after all, a major and significant issue which along with the removal

Table 3.4. CPSU members' opinions of party policies, union treaty, and leaders by what is to be done

	Stalinism-Brezhnevism	Democratic Socialism	Captitalism-socialism	Western society
CPSU policies				
CPSU not Marxist/Leninist enough	36.0	16.5	13.4	14.2
CPSU correct in policies	22.4	20.3	6.7	1.4
CPSU should be democratized	31.0	55.9	71.6	70.9
CPSU, other response	3.2	2.6	2.6	9.5
Union Treaty				
Independence for republics	55.6	63.2	72.7	87.2
Sign Union Treaty	89.5	92.6	88.7	79.5
Vote for Union Treaty	94.7	97.9	84.7	72.5
Leader preference				
Prefer Yeltsin	23.5	7.9	22.3	41.7
Prefer Gorbachev	25.9	51.3	26.0	17.9
Opposition party support				
Support democratic Russia	2.4	3.1	9.1	17.9
N	162	353	319	156

Source: Citizen Participation in Politics in Russia Survey. 12,309 respondents interviewed in May–August 1991.

of party representatives from the workplace may have actually provoked the August coup. What is going on? One answer may be that there is a curvilinear relationship between attitudes to the union and the Union Treaty and people's choice of a reactionary, Gorbachev reform, oppositional reform, or radical position. Reactionaries may disapprove of the Union Treaty because it goes too far and Westernizers because it does not go far enough.

Further to probe this complex relationship, we summarize in table 3.5 the answers to a large number of questions by the four basic factions. The responses to all these questions are curvilinear in the four factions—some to an extraordinarily striking degree. The questions fall into four basic categories. At the top are a set of questions about trust in the institutions of the USSR— the Congress of People's Deputies, the Supreme Soviet, the president (Gorbachev), the Council of Ministers, and the prime minister. We asked each respondent whether he or she trusted the institution fully, somewhat, a little, or mistrusted it.[18] The second set of questions is about Russian institutions, including the parliament, the Supreme Soviet, the Supreme Soviet chairman (Yeltsin), the Council of Ministers, and the chairman of the Russian Council of Ministers. The third set of questions is those about the Union Treaty described earlier. Finally, the fourth set of responses comes from a question that asked respondents to choose between Gorbachev and Yeltsin.

None of these variables has any significant impact when it is entered in a regression with the four categories of factions as the dependent variable. Even though many of these variables are curvilinear, this is still surprising because it suggests that these variables represent one or more dimensions of politics that are at right angles—orthogonal—to the economic dimension. A factor analysis confirms this—the USSR trust and Russia trust variables form two dimensions that are distinct from, although somewhat correlated with, the six economic variables described earlier.

What are we to make of this result? Two of the trust variables can be thought of as simply direct ratings of Yeltsin and Gorbachev. Perhaps the other trust measures are just picking this up, particularly given the newness of the institutions. If this is true, then the increasing role of personality must be considered as structuring Russian political life. Figure 3.3 describes a path model with the choice of Gorbachev or Yeltsin as the final variable. In this model we regressed the Yeltsin variable (and the Gorbachev variable) on all the trust measures, the six economic measures, a dummy variable for whether the person voted for the union in the referendum, and the variables for democratization in the CPSU and independence for the republics. All insignificant paths were eliminated, and the figure displays the beta weights for the significant paths.

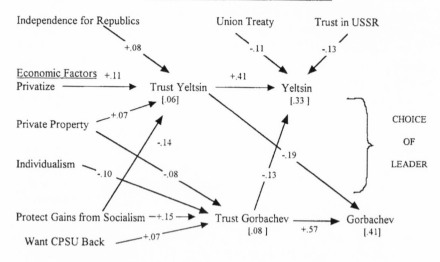

Figure 3.3 Path diagram of support for Yeltsin and Gorbachev
(numbers are beta weights; R² in brackets)

The trust for Yeltsin and trust for Gorbachev variables go a long way toward explaining the choice between Gorbachev and Yeltsin, but a significant role is still played by opinion on the March referendum on the union and by trust in the USSR. This last measure is a combination of all trust questions about USSR institutions except the one involving Gorbachev. Going back in the paths, we find that trust in Gorbachev is strongly positively related to a desire to maintain the gains of socialism and to bring the CPSU back but negatively related to support for individualism and private property. This represents the more conservative elements of the CPSU. Trust in Yeltsin, however, is positively related to support for privatization, for private property, and for independence for the republics. It is negatively related to a desire to maintain the gains of socialism. In this model, the concerns about the union flow in at least two ways toward Yeltsin. On the one hand, being in favor of independence for the republics leads to greater trust in Yeltsin and greater support for him; on the other hand, being supportive of the Union Treaty (or at least Gorbachev's March referendum) leads to less support for Yeltsin.

There may be still a third avenue in which concerns about the nation and the state affect support for Yeltsin. Those who trust the USSR over and above their trust for Gorbachev are less supportive of Yeltsin. We suspect that these trust questions are picking up conservatives' feelings of support for the nation created by Lenin and Stalin.

The model leaves much unexplained. The R-squares (reported in brackets on the figure) are small for the equations for trusting Yeltsin and Gorbachev. Clearly there is much more going on in people's assessments of these two figures than just economic considerations. We wish we had better measures of other factors, but in our short screener we could not get some of the measures we would now like to have.[19]

Two things probably mattered a great deal by mid-1991. First, the politics of opposition allowed the left and right to join in criticizing Gorbachev. Second, this was reinforced by diminishing trust for Gorbachev as a leader. Much of this was driven by the perceptions that Gorbachev was failing and veering first leftward, then rightward in his attempts to placate first one, then another group. Yeltsin was the only credible opposition leader, and discontent solidified around him.

It is true that within the CPSU Gorbachev was still more trusted than Yeltsin (2.77 to 2.64) and more likely to be chosen in a face-off (32.9 percent to 20.5 percent), but in the general population Yeltsin was vastly more trusted (2.86 to 2.31) and more likely to be chosen (35.6 percent to 17.6 percent). Moreover, even within the CPSU, there were substantial variations in support and trust for Gorbachev, as shown in table 3.5. Indeed, if we look separately at those who wanted a return to Stalinism, we find that Gorbachev's trust rating—on the extremely conservative end of the spectrum—was only 2.27.

In summary, there are at least two basic dimensions underlying attitudes among the CPSU members in mid-1991. One dimension was clearly economic. There was a substantial and surprising variation in opinions about the best course of action. The second dimension had a curvilinear relationship to the first one, and it united conservatives who wanted the CPSU back in power, a return to a planned economy, and a strong central government with Westernizers who wanted rapid economic and political change. This curvilinearity and the diversity of the groups with similar positions on this dimension strongly suggest that there was probably more than just one issue underlying this dimension. Indeed, this dimension seems to involve both the political and national issues described earlier: Gorbachev's performance, basic trust in Gorbachev and his program for democratization, and the union referendum and treaty. The diverse nature of support for Yeltsin as suggested by the second dimension and its oppositional character hints at its fragile nature. Although these findings reflect attitudes found among members of the CPSU in 1991, many of the leaders and adherents of new movements and organizations are drawn from among these former party members.[20] As subsequent events were to

Table 3.5. Union Treaty, trust in political institutions, and leader preference by what is to be done

	Stalinism-Brezhnevism	Democratic Socialism	Capitalism-socialism	Western society
Trust in USSR				
Congress of Deputies	2.73	3.10	2.47	2.15
Supreme Soviet	2.80	3.18	2.48	2.17
Gorbachev	2.64	3.24	2.60	2.19
Council of Ministers	2.52	2.84	2.19	1.86
Prime minister	2.30	2.71	2.10	1.77
Trust in Russia				
Parliament	2.70	2.61	2.59	2.72
Supreme Soviet	2.75	2.72	2.70	2.90
Yeltsin	2.57	2.38	2.72	3.08
Council of Ministers	2.64	2.75	2.82	2.98
Chair of council	2.75	2.78	2.92	3.14
Preference				
Gorbachev	25.9	51.3	26.0	17.9
Yeltsin	23.5	7.9	22.3	41.7
Union Treaty				
Sign Union Treaty	89.5	92.6	88.7	79.5
Yes vote, March 1991	94.7	97.9	84.7	72.5

Note: CPSU members only.

Source: Citizen Participation in Politics in Russia Survey, 12,309 respondents interviewed in May–August 1991.

show, Yeltsin was to lose the support of the conservative opposition as he struggled with the Russian parliament. A strategic move away from democratic reform in response to the protest vote of the December 1993 election could further undermine his dwindling sources of support.

ELITE AND MASS DIFFERENCES ALONG THE TWO BASIC DIMENSIONS

It is now a rather simple matter to describe the two central dimensions of Russian politics as of mid-1991—one economic and the other composed of political and national issues—as they are reflected by mass and elite preferences. Figure 3.4 plots the mean of two scales[21] representing the economic and political-national dimensions for the entire population (represented by boxes) and CPSU members (triangles) broken up into those who want Stalinism, Brezhnevism, democratic socialism, capitalism and socialism, and Westernization. Each elite subgroup is joined to its corresponding mass subgroup by a

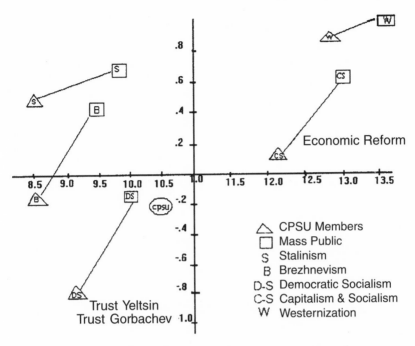

Figure 3.4. Elite and mass positions on economics and trust

solid line. The mass subgroups are always to the northeast of their correspond-ing elite subgroup. The CPSU subgroups, then, tend to be less radical eco-nomically and more favorable toward Gorbachev than the subgroups in the mass public. Both results accord with what we know about mid-1991, and they suggest why events went so quickly after the August coup.

Figure 3.4 reveals substantial differences between the CPSU and the public and significant differences even within the CPSU. Indeed, the Westernization faction of the CPSU is just about in the same place as the intelligentsia, who are at 13.9 on the economic scale and .833 on the trust scale. The figure also shows that there were at least two distinct dimensions driving politics at this time—economics and a dimension we have labeled "trust," although it com-bines a number of factors which we called political and national. The existence of these differences among the elite groups was one of the major reasons why the initial transition away from communism could occur so smoothly within Russia. When the coup occurred in August 1991, there had already been a substantial movement within the CPSU membership and the nomenklatura toward democratization and privatization. Moreover, there was a popular and trusted leader, Boris Yeltsin, who was a natural and logical alternative. The fact that Yeltsin was so strongly supported by the bulk of the population made his task, and that of the other leaders of the opposition to the coup, easier because the opposition leaders did not have to worry about popular outbreaks against them—indeed, they could mobilize public opinion on their behalf. But the most important fact was that even within the CPSU itself, there was strong opposition against reactionaries who plotted the coup.

The diverse sources supporting Yeltsin which evidenced a high degree of trust in him just before the August 1991 coup, however, were to unravel as the pain of reform and political stalemate ensued. Yeltsin had defined himself in opposition to the past and had drawn support from segments of the elite and the general population which did not share a common political outlook. Over time, the politics of opposition to the past gave way to debate over the nature of economic reform. Those favoring reform despite their divergent preferences initially contributed to Yeltsin's strength but ultimately revealed a fragmented public and elite. Thus the defining issues of political life on the eve of the Soviet collapse not only found reflection within the Communist Party and the Russian populace but help us to understand Yeltsin's sources of support and opposition as he embarked upon a policy of transition.

Notes

1. Ronald J. Hill, "The CPSU: From Monolith to Pluralist?" *Soviet Studies* 42 (1991), 217–35. An exception was the Soviet Interview Project. This survey provided interesting information about the CPSU but limited insight into members' attitudes, which, of course, it was not intended to study. See Mark R. Beissinger, "Transformation and Degeneration: The CPSU Under Reform," in *Cracks in the Monolith: Party Power in the Brezhnev Era*, ed. James R. Millar (Armonk, N.Y.: M. E. Sharpe, 1992), 213–35.

2. Zbigniew Brzezinski, "Soviet Politics: From the Future to the Past?," in *The Dynamics of Soviet Politics*, ed. Paul Cocks, Robert V. Daniels, and Nancy Whittier Heer (Cambridge: Harvard University Press, 1976), 337–51; "The Soviet Political System: Transformation or Degeneration," in *Dilemmas of Change in Soviet Politics*, ed. Zbigniew Brzezinski (New York: Columbia University Press, 1969), 1–34; and *The Grand Failure* (New York: Charles Scribner's Sons, 1989).

3. Brzezinski, *Grand Failure*, 41.

4. See, ibid., chap. 6, "The Ten Dynamics of Disunion," 65–94.

5. A representative sample of 12,309 respondents from Russia were interviewed in person. The extraordinarily large size of the sample makes it possible to analyze relatively small groups while maintaining statistical significance. The authors of the survey were Cynthia S. Kaplan, William V. Smirnov, Vladimir G. Andreenkov, and Henry Brady drawing upon the work of Sidney Verba, Henry E. Brady, Kay Schlozman, and Norman Nie on participation in the United States. The first-stage survey from which the data are drawn was supported by the John D. and Catherine T. MacArthur Foundation, the Soviet Academy of Sciences, the Committee on Science and Technology of the Supreme Soviet, USSR, with initial assistance from the International Exchanges

and Research Board and the American Council of Learned Societies. Fieldwork was supervised by Vladimir Andreenkov, the Center for Comparative Social Research, Moscow, Russia. Additional assistance was provided by the Center for Political Studies, Institute of State and Law, Moscow, Russia. Data cleaning and analysis benefited from support by the National Science Foundation (SES-9122389) and the United States Institute of Peace (USIP 049–92F).

6. For purposes of our analysis, membership in the apparatus was defined as people who work in the state sector and whose employer is the state or who work in a political party in the state sector. Party membership is defined as current members of the CPSU at the time of the interview. It is true that during 1989 and 1990 some members had stopped paying dues and even formally resigned, although exact figures on this for Russia were not found. Estimates suggest a decline of 4 percent for the entire CPSU by 1990. Resignations were more likely outside of the Russian Federation because of the influence of nationalism. See Beissinger, "Transformation and Degeneration," 227. Richard Sakwa notes a decline of approximately 4.3 million from the peak of total CPSU membership in October 1988 to August 1991 (*Russian Politics and Society* [London: Routledge, 1993], 134).

7. Beissinger, "Transformation and Degeneration," 229. For a brief summary of the positions of the Democratic Platform and the Marxist Platform in English see Vladimir Pribylovskii, *Dictionary of Political Parties and Organizations in Russia*, ed. Dauphine Sloan and Sarah Helmstadter (Moscow: PostFactum/Interlegal and Washington, D.C.: Center for Strategic and International Studies, 1992), 46–48, 72–74. In Russian, a concise summary is provided in B. I. Koval', ed., *Rossiia segodnia: politicheskii portret v dokumentakh 1985–1991* (Moscow: Mezhdunarodnye otnosheniia, 1991), 21–24.

8. Sakwa, *Russian Politics and Society,* 133.

9. Ibid., 139. For insight into these new organizations see Michael McFaul and Sergei Markov, *The Troubled Birth of Russian Democracy: Parties, Personalities, and Programs* (Stanford: Hoover Institution Press, 1993); Koval', *Rossiia segodnia;* and V. N. Berezovskii and N. I. Krotov, *Neformal'naia Rossiia: O neformal'nykh politizirovannykh dvizheniiakh i gruppakh v RSFSR (opyt spravochnika)* (Moscow: "Molodaia gvardiia," 1990).

10. For a discussion of the importance of elite cleavages in the nature of transition, see Samuel P. Huntington, *The Third Wave: Democratization in the Late Twentieth Century* (Norman: University of Oklahoma Press, 1991).

11. Brzezinski, "Soviet Politics," 345. Also see Donna Bahry, "Politics, Generations, and Change in the USSR," in *Politics, Work, and Daily Life in the USSR*, ed. James R. Millar (Cambridge: Cambridge University Press, 1987), 61–99; and Brian D. Silver, "Political Beliefs of the Soviet Citizen: Sources of Support for Regime Norms," ibid., 100–141.

12. The ages were combined into two-year intervals to "smooth" the data, and proponents of monarchy were omitted.

13. All four questions were scored on three-point (1–3) scales so that the more reformist option had the highest value.

14. We scored the four factions from one to four, with four for the Westernizers and one for the reactionaries, and regressed this scale on the six items.

15. Agreement to this question is coded as three and disagreement as one.

16. We recoded this so that the response advocating "democratization" of the CPSU is one and all others are zero.

17. We added one item on independence for the republics, two measures of attitudes toward the Union Treaty, and one on democratization in the CPSU, to a regression where the dependent variable is the four factions coded as described earlier and all the economic variables are included as well.

18. We coded the result into a five-point scale (with those who were not sure in the middle).

19. A second, much more detailed survey on political participation and attitudes was administered in summer 1993 to a weighted sample drawn from those who were identified as politically active on the screener survey.

20. Beissinger, "Transformation and Degeneration," 228.

21. We define an economic dimension by summing up the answers to five of the six economic questions used earlier. We do not use the individualism question because it does not scale very well with the other ones. We also turn around the questions about gains from socialism, planned economy, and bring the CPSU back so that they conform with the privatization and private property questions. The result is a scale that can run from five to sixteen and has a mean in the population of 11.5 and a standard deviation of 3.3. For the other dimension we simply subtract Gorbachev's trust rating from Yeltsin's trust rating. The resulting scale can go from minus four to plus four, and it has a mean of .559 and a standard deviation of 1.70.

4

Reorganizing Intergovernmental Relations in the USSR

Jane Shapiro Zacek

I firmly came out in favor of the independence of nations and sovereignty for the republics. At the same time, I support the preservation of the union state and the integrity of this country.

Developments took a different course. The policy prevailed of dismembering the country and disuniting the state, which is something I cannot subscribe to."

Mikhail S. Gorbachev, resignation speech, December 25, 1991

The official collapse of the USSR as an integral state came on the heels of the Minsk Declaration creating its successor, the Commonwealth of Independent States, on December 8, 1991. Five days later, in Ashkhabad, Turkmenia, the five Central Asian republics agreed to join the three Slavic republics that had created the Commonwealth. By December 21, three additional republics officially joined and all eleven republics jointly issued a Protocol on the Creation of the Commonwealth of Independent States. Four republics did not join: by December the three Baltic states had already secured their independence, international diplomatic recognition, and membership in the United Nations; Georgia continued to declare its intention to achieve both de facto and de jure independence based on its May 26, 1918, Deed of Independence. In early March 1992, the eight members of the Commonwealth that were not already United Nations members were formally admitted into that organization. To date, the Commonwealth has not emerged as a viable political entity, either for its constituent members or within the international community.

This chapter considers Gorbachev's efforts to create a viable federal system within the USSR by redistributing political authority between the central and republic governments. It was an effort to satisfy republic demands for expanded political and economic authority on the republic level, free from central government constraints. These demands were coupled with the rapid growth and expression of ethnic identity and desire for independence. The central government was unwilling or did not recognize the need to move quickly in negotiations with republic leaders and consistently offered too little until it was too late to continue negotiations. In the end, after the August 1991 coup attempt, republic leaders understood that power had shifted decisively to them from Moscow. Having endured extreme overcentralization for so many decades and having now seized the opportunity to establish themselves as independent entities, they had no incentive to support a continuation of the USSR as an integral state. Whatever advantages there may have been to collaborate (a "common economic space" for production and distribution of goods, a common currency, a shared financial system, joint foreign and defense policies) could be worked out through bilateral or multilateral arrangements among the republic leaders.

Gorbachev initially refused to respond to republic leaders' insistence on greater autonomy and was unwilling to reduce the central government's control substantially in favor of greater political and economic authority for the republics. Apparently, he believed he could hold the union together if he stood firm and slowly negotiated away central authority. Pressed by the conservatives to maintain central control and by the radicals to transfer authority to the republics, he satisfied no one and hastened the disintegration of the country.

The Background in Brief

The USSR was created at the end of 1922 by the X All-Russian Congress of Soviets: its constituent units were Russia, Ukraine, Belorussia, and the Transcaucasian Federation. The creation of a union transformed the All-Russian Congress into the I Congress of Soviets of the USSR. One scholar of the 1917–23 period has written that the "decisive battles" for political control took place "within the Communist Party [CP] organizations." Just as the party was a single centralized organization, with regional CPs (e.g., Ukrainian, Georgian) subordinated to the Russian CP, so the regions were to be incorporated into a single centralized state structure subordinated to Russia.[1]

During 1920 and 1921, the Bolsheviks gained control in those republics that had established their independence after the collapse of the Russian Empire. One by one, each republic signed a treaty with Russia, which in effect subordinated it politically, militarily, and economically to Moscow. In the struggle to create a Russian-dominated federal structure, in which Stalin played a prominent role as commissar of nationalities, Georgia was the most reluctant to go along with the Bolshevik leaders' plans. Georgia insisted on rights equal to those of Ukraine and Belorussia, rather than subordination to a Transcaucasian Federation which would in turn become a single republic in the newly created union. A combination of pressure, threats, and force pushed Georgia into the Federation. Lenin reportedly was "appalled by the coarseness . . . and the connivances" of those Bolshevik leaders (Stalin, Feliks Dzerzhinski, and Grigorii [Sergo] Ordzhonikidze) who had forced the Georgians to submit.[2] Lenin also recognized that the union that had been created would not protect the autonomy of the non-Russian republics, and, he wrote, the "freedom of exit from the union" clause of the Union Treaty would prove worthless, which of course was correct. Nonetheless, Lenin insisted that the union was essential because of the worldwide struggle of socialism against the bourgeoisie.

At the I Congress of Soviets, Ukrainian CP leaders together with other non-Russian party members promoted the formation of a union that would permit real autonomy for its non-Russian republics.[3] The creation of a second chamber in the Congress of Soviets was proposed, which would represent the republics. Khristian Rakovsky, a prominent Ukrainian CP leader, "proposed that no single republic have more than 2/3 of the total votes" in this second chamber. Indeed, the Ukrainians vigorously opposed a centralized state, much to Stalin's openly stated dissatisfaction. In a June 1923 speech to representatives of various republics, Stalin declared, "We are constructing not a confederate but a federal republic, one union state, uniting military and foreign affairs, foreign trade, and other matters." He spoke of the "right of the working class to consolidate its power." The "right of national self-determination is subordinate," he added. The 1922 Union Treaty was included in the new state constitution that was ratified in January 1924 and effective as of that date.[4]

The 1936 "Stalin" constitution declared that the USSR was a federal state and incorporated the statement from the earlier constitution that "each union republic retained the right freely to secede." By 1936, the USSR was composed of eleven republics. The Transcaucasian Federation had been dissolved and three republics (Armenia, Georgia, and Azerbaijan) had been created from it and admitted directly into the union. The Turkmen, Tadzhik, and Uzbek republics had already been demarcated and had entered the union prior to 1936. The Kazakh and Kirgiz republics were newly created and also joined the union.

The description of the "national-state structure" of the country was repeated in the 1977 constitution. Article 70 stated that the USSR was "a unitary, federal and multinational state, formed on the basis of the principle of socialist federalism" (whatever that meant). Articles 74 and 75 reiterated articles from the 1936 constitution that declared the sovereignty of the USSR over all its territory and the primacy of all-union law when there was a conflict between all-union and republic legislation. The short sections on republics' rights (chapters 9 and 10) stated that their responsibilities were "to coordinate and control the activity of enterprises, institutions and organizations of union subordination . . . on questions falling within [their] jurisdiction."[5]

In brief, the USSR was created as a highly centralized system. Politically, the republics were subordinated to the Russian-dominated center through the hierarchical CP structure; economically, they were subordinated through the state planning mechanism. Although there had been cautious experiments with decentralizing economic authority, the USSR in 1985 remained a highly centralized system.

DECENTRALIZING THE SYSTEM

Among the dramatic changes that Gorbachev managed to implement during his first years as CP general secretary was the decisive shift in political power and authority from the Communist Party to state institutions. This historic shift, achieved only after protracted and difficult negotiations, had several critical consequences.

First, the stranglehold of a strictly hierarchical and highly centralized policy-making institution was broken. Second, many party leaders on all levels of government as well as the permanent bureaucracy on each level were tacitly or openly opposed to a structural overhaul of the Soviet system. The history of post-Stalinist reforms in the USSR provides ample proof that the party was incapable of adopting systemic change.

Shifting political authority to state institutions meant a devolution of political power. On the union level, a new state organization was created early in 1989, the 2,250-seat Congress of Peoples' Deputies. A portion of the deputies were elected through a competitive process for the first time in Soviet history; others were selected by various organizations as prescribed by the electoral law. The congress in turn elected some of its deputies to a bicameral working legislature, the Supreme Soviet, with the same name but much smaller in size than its unwieldy and ineffectual predecessor. At the same time, the constitution was amended to provide this new Supreme Soviet with real legislative authority, to be exercised at least six to eight months each year.

On the republic level, supreme soviets also were infused with real legislative authority; the chair of these parliaments (rather than the republic CP's leading official) quickly became the republic's chief spokesperson. (Examples include Vytautas Landsbergis in Lithuania, Zviad Gamsakhurdia in Georgia, Boris Yeltsin in the Russian Federation, and Leonid Kravchuk in Ukraine. Only the latter had earlier been a party leader in his republic, although Yeltsin had been head of the powerful Moscow party organization and member of the CPSU Politburo. The others had never been party leaders; indeed, their popularity stemmed from their opposition to the CP-controlled system.)

Republic supreme soviets did not take orders from the USSR Supreme Soviet and were not subordinate to it. As events unfolded during 1990 and 1991, the republics passed legislation on such issues as state sovereignty, supremacy of republic law within the boundaries of the republic (despite constitutional prohibitions), and republic ownership of land and everything above and below their territorial space—all without regard for the central government's reaction.[6]

There was increasing public discussion about a "renewed federation" during 1989. Gorbachev spoke frequently about a "strong center and strong republics." In late 1988, a Supreme Soviet working group on constitutional reform had been established; the group proposed the principle of "republic precedence" on matters that the central government did not have (or would not be given) specific authority to handle. At the conclusion of the September 1989 Central Committee Plenum devoted to nationality issues, party resolutions called for enhancing the authority of the republics, although this position was by no means unanimous.

Finally, the 1989 revolutions in Eastern Europe (where communist parties collapsed with unimagined rapidity and newly elected governments quickly declared their independence from Soviet hegemony) heavily influenced the Soviet republics. The drive for independence began in the Baltics, where local leaders insisted that the 1940 incorporation of the three countries into the USSR had been done illegally (through secret protocols with Nazi Germany) and against the will of the affected populations, spread to other republics which for short periods after 1917 had established their independence (Ukraine, Georgia, Armenia, Azerbaijan), and finally engulfed all the republics, including the Russian Federation, whose leaders believed that they had been exploited for decades to strengthen and glorify the central government. The road to political decentralization inexorably led to the failure to reach agreement on the distribution of political authority within a new kind of union and to collapse of the union altogether.

The Struggle for a New Federal Compact

In early April 1990, the Supreme Soviet passed legislation titled "On the Principles of Economic Relations between the USSR and the Union and Autonomous Republics," which was signed into law by Gorbachev, now president of the USSR, on April 10.[7] According to this law, economic relations between the center and the republics were "based on the principles of federalism, economic independence, and mutual responsibility." It defined the financial and economic powers of each, described the financial and budgetary relations between the center and the republics (which was to become a major sticking point in the Union Treaty negotiations), and set out the all-union market principle, the "single economic space" of the USSR in which economic activity was to be regulated on a contractual basis rather than simply directed from Moscow.

Fast on the heels of this legislation, on April 26, came a new law defining the distribution of political authority and the "federalness" of the USSR: "The

USSR possesses the powers that the members of the federation jointly assign to its jurisdiction." The law described the union republics as "sovereign states" that "possess full state power on their territory with the exception of the powers they have transferred to USSR jurisdiction." It listed functions exclusively within the authority of the center (Moscow), as well as functions that earlier officially were under joint jurisdiction of Moscow and the republics but henceforth would be under Moscow's sole jurisdiction (including the definition of citizenship, financial and credit policy and price formation, education, health care, exploitation of natural resources, and safeguarding public order). This sweeping grant of authority to the center, while declaring that the republics would have "all that was left," clearly set the stage for the growing confrontation between Moscow and the republic leaders.

For months before the passage of these two major laws, Gorbachev had called publicly for the drafting of a new Union Treaty "that is in keeping with present day realities."[8] By July, at the XXVIII (and last) CPSU Congress, General Secretary Gorbachev emphasized that the "transformation of the union" demanded a wholly new document that recognized a union of sovereign states. The document would be created by agreement of the constituent members of the union and the central government on what authority should be granted the central government and what retained by the republics—a federal compact.

Historically, federal compacts have been reached for the purpose of creating a central government. The Union Treaty framers faced a strong central government of long standing that would need to give up substantial authority in all spheres if a viable federal system were to be created. One leading scholar of federalism describes a federal system as "contractual non-centralization, the structured dispersion of powers among (subnational) centers whose legitimate authority is constitutionally guaranteed."[9] Parties to a treaty or "federal bargain" must see themselves as partners, and the bargain must be voluntarily entered into and based on mutual trust.

The issue of state sovereignty and the preeminence of republic over USSR legislation on the territory of that republic had become central in the discussions over the proposed new treaty. The April 1990 law on the demarcation of (political) power of the USSR and the republics had reaffirmed the principle that USSR laws and decrees were binding throughout the country and that USSR law took precedence.

Nothing in Soviet constitutional history had provided for governmental machinery to settle disputes between republic and USSR legislation, as is typical in federal systems (e.g., the U.S. Supreme Court or the German Federal Constitutional Court). In December 1988, a constitutional supervision committee was proposed; legislation to create this committee was passed the following year.[10] Each republic was to be represented on the committee, although the three Baltic republics from the outset refused to participate. The committee was given authority to suspend unconstitutional legislation, but it was not to be the "court of last resort" because its decisions could be overridden by the Congress of Peoples' Deputies.[11]

Together with issues of republican sovereignty came discussions of a "new type of federalism," in which each republic might establish its own particular relationship with Moscow. The Institute of State and Law, which proffered a framework for the new treaty of union, suggested a "multi-tiered federalism" in which some republics would have a confederal relationship with the union, others a federal one, and still others "closer ties." How this could possibly work within a single political entity, the USSR, was far from clear.

CREATING A "FREE UNION OF SOVEREIGN SOCIALIST STATES"

By June 1990, Gorbachev was speaking frequently about the need to create a new union structure, a "free union of sovereign socialist states." The central government would have authority over "common spheres" such as foreign policy, defense, and "some areas of economic and financial activities." A working group had been created, composed of representatives from each republic as well as some Supreme Soviet deputies, to produce a draft treaty. Rafik Nishanov, chair of the Supreme Soviet's council of nationalities, chaired the group.

In a September 9, 1990, *Izvestiia* interview, Nishanov revealed that the working group had received several draft union treaties from the various republics, four draft treaties "from various public organizations and research institutes," and another twelve independent versions worked out "through efforts of groups within the Supreme Soviet." Additionally, "lots of other draft treaties" were being offered from other sources. At the moment, Nishanov declared, nine groups of experts were working in Moscow on various problems associated with a new treaty and groups within the republics were working on various related issues. Among the major issues were the following:

- How much power should the center have and how much property should it retain?

- How would the union budget be financed? Should union taxes and fees be collected directly by Moscow? Or should the union be dependent on contributions from the republics?

- What areas would the union have exclusive jurisdiction over?

- Should the autonomous republics be members of the union and parties to the treaty or should only the union republics sign?

The issue of dual citizenship (both republic and USSR) for each citizen, considered by a scholar of federalism to be essential, apparently was not raised at this juncture.[12]

On September 19, Nishanov reported to the Supreme Soviet on the work in progress toward a draft treaty. The working group was consulting regularly with a separate Supreme Soviet working group. Discussions with the autonomous republics continued; these republics wanted the right to participate directly in the crafting of a new treaty. Separate consultations were held "on the complex of relations between the USSR and the Baltic SSRs." The Interregional Deputies Group in the Supreme Soviet (composed of outspoken reformers such as Boris Yeltsin, Yuri Afanas'yev, and Anatoli Sobchak) had "done a lot of work conceptualizing the new treaty," Nishanov noted.[13] In all, the working group had received "more than 200 draft treaties." In addition to the issues that he had spoken of in the *Izvestiia* interview, Nishanov listed other important concerns.

- The need to strengthen direct interrepublican ties, especially in economic issues (bypassing Moscow).

- "Ensuring the rights and liberties of citizens regardless of nationality or place of residence." Should the republics ensure such rights? (More than 60 million citizens live outside their "own national-state formation," and the rate of population movement in the country is high, Nishanov noted.)

- Should the "common economic and legal space" be under the joint jurisdiction of the center and the republics?

- The need to create a "real" judicial system: should jurisdiction for this system be split between the center and the republics or shared jointly?[14]

As a way of indicating their importance, the autonomous republics individually declared their sovereignty during the fall months of 1990. Several (Bashkir, Mari, and Chuvash) declared themselves no longer autonomous republics but rather full-fledged union republics.[15]

The First Draft Treaty of Union

In late November, the first draft treaty was issued. It referred to a new Union of Sovereign Soviet Republics. Article 5 listed the powers of the union, which were quite sweeping although some powers were described as "in conjunction with the republics." The draft explicitly recognized Russian as "the state language of the USSR."

The republics would have the right to "independently determine their own state structure," "recognize democracy based on popular representation as a common fundamental principle," and "strive to create a state based on the rule of law." The draft noted that membership in the union was voluntary and that a republic which violated the conditions of the treaty could have its membership terminated. Whether a member could voluntarily withdraw from the union at a later date was not mentioned. Changes in the treaty could be implemented only by unanimous consent of all parties.[16]

During November, too, the Russian Federation was busy signing state treaties with other republics. For example, Yeltsin and Kravchuk signed a "Treaty on the Principles of Relations between the RSFSR and the Ukrainian SSR" on November 20 in Kiev. The treaty proclaimed the "need to build further relations" between the two republics based on their respective declarations of state sovereignty (June 12 for the Russian Federation and July 16 for Ukraine).

In December, at the IV Congress of Peoples' Deputies, Arnold Ruutel, a deputy (and chair of the Estonian Supreme Soviet), spoke of the pressure being put upon Estonia to sign the new Union Treaty. He insisted that creation of the treaty was "premature." How can you talk about delegating rights from the republics to the union until these republics "are in command of their entire economies," have control over their state borders, and so on, Ruutel asked. "Unless truly independent states are formed first," he added, "it is impossible to talk about creating a union."[17] Nobel Peace Prize–winner and outspoken reformer Andrei Sakharov (who had been elected to the congress but had died in late 1989) had also insisted that the republics needed to be strong before they could delegate some of their authority to the center. "The center's strength would derive from the authority and confidence of the sovereign nations," he had stated. Parceling out some of the center's authority would not render the republics sufficiently strong to create a viable federal system.[18]

Shortly after the draft treaty was issued, the Supreme Soviet approved several amendments to the USSR constitution concerning the structure of the central government. The authority of the Council of the Federation (created in spring 1990 as part of the new presidency) was strengthened: no longer was it to have merely a consultative role to the president but was now to "consider all major questions of union significance" and to "coordinate the activities of the union and the republics." Its role, in short, was to guarantee republican representation in the executive branch of the national government, just as the Council of Nationalities was to guarantee such representation in the legislature.

Proposal for a Referendum on the Preservation of the Union

In his report to the IV Congress of Peoples' Deputies in mid-December, Gorbachev proposed a nationwide referendum on the preservation of the union. The results, he said, would be the "final verdict" because they would represent public opinion, not just the highly politicized opinions of republic leaders. The

Supreme Soviet approved the referendum by a 306–44 vote. Fifty percent of the total number of eligible voters nationwide would have to participate in the referendum and 50 percent plus one of those voting would have to approve the proposal for passage. The referendum date was set for March 17, 1991.

Gorbachev had bypassed the republic leaders and appealed directly to the Soviet citizenry, under the banner of increasing democracy. He probably did not anticipate that some republics would refuse to hold the referendum on their territory. The three Baltic republics and Georgia announced that they would not hold the referendum because they "did not regard themselves subject to USSR law." Lithuania, Estonia, and Georgia declared that they would hold "non-binding polls," asking voters to approve or reject independence. Armenia called the proposed referendum "imprecise" because it did not address the issue of whether an autonomous territory had the right to change its subordination within the union (e.g., the Nagorno-Karabakh case).

The referendum question as approved by the Supreme Soviet was, "Do you consider necessary the preservation of the Union of Soviet Socialist Republics as a renewed federation of equal sovereign republics, in which the rights and freedoms of an individual of any nationality will be fully guaranteed?" In the end, only three republics carried the referendum worded in precisely this fashion on the March ballot.

According to the official balloting results, announced on March 25, 80 percent of those entitled to vote throughout the country did so. Of those who voted, 76 percent answered yes. In both Leningrad and Moscow, only 50 percent of those who voted approved the referendum. In Kiev and Sverdlovsk, the referendum was rejected.[19]

THE SECOND DRAFT TREATY OF UNION: A UNION OF SOVEREIGN REPUBLICS

On March 9, just a little more than a week before the referendum, a second draft treaty was published in response to complaints that the electorate was being asked to vote on a "renewed union" without knowing what that term meant. The second draft, which expanded the authority and areas of sole jurisdiction of the republics, was supposed to define what the "renewed union" would consist of. Now the republics were given joint responsibility with the center in such policy-making areas as defense, foreign policy, foreign economic activity, and the union budget. The republics, rather than the center, would also have the responsibility of approving both new members to the union and secession of members from the union. Parties to the treaty would determine the manner of secession, rather than the USSR Supreme Soviet (which, for the first time in Soviet history, had passed detailed legislation on the process of secession in April 1990).

Only eight republics signed the draft. Only nine of them had sent representatives to the drafting meetings during February. Yeltsin, who had sent his first deputy, Ruslan Khasbulatov, to the negotiations, announced that the second draft was unacceptable to the Russian Federation, not least because it was once again being imposed from above.[20]

A continuing sticking point for the Russians was the issue of the autonomous republics: would they be direct parties to the treaty or sign as part of a union republic delegation? The autonomous republics had already won the right to be direct participants in the treaty negotiations and most insisted upon directly signing the treaty. Russia, whose territory contained by far the largest number of autonomous republics, would not accept such equal participation. Gorbachev supported the autonomous republics in these claims. By the end of April, however, he agreed to a "compromise" in which these republics would sign as part of their respective union republics' delegations. TASS reported on May 12 that all of the autonomous republics within the RSFSR except Tatarstan had agreed to the delegation concept. They would sign as "equal subjects simultaneously" both of the USSR and the Russian Federation.

By April, too, the process of drafting the treaty had taken a different turn. Rather than react to center-dominated drafts, republic leaders began to collaborate, after which they would negotiate with Gorbachev. So, for example, the Ukrainian Supreme Soviet invited its counterparts in Russia, Belorussia, Kazakhstan, and Uzbekistan to send "working groups" to Kiev to discuss elements of the March draft treaty that were deemed unacceptable. On April 23, based on positions that the Kiev meetings had hammered out, Gorbachev and the heads of nine republics met in Novo-Ogarevo outside Moscow to discuss the main issues under dispute (including the citizenship question and the autonomous republics' role).

Negotiations between republic leaders and USSR executive and parliamentary leaders continued during the spring and came to be known as "the Novo-Ogarevo process." Before long, this process of consultation and negotiation included issues not directly related to the draft treaty, such as the discussions Gorbachev held with republic leaders before his July meeting with the Group of Seven in London, at which economic and trade issues were considered. Yeltsin described the process as "the cradle of a political process which respects the republics."[21]

By late May, the six republics that had announced that they would not participate in the treaty discussions created a "consultation and coordinating mechanism" in Kishinev, Moldova. Officially called The Assembly of Popular Fronts and Movements from Republics not Joining the Union Treaty, it became known as the Kishinev Forum and was composed of equal representation from each member organization (e.g., the Lithuanian Sajudis, the Georgian Round Table/

Free Georgia coalition, the Moldavian Popular Front). The forum's purpose was to exchange information and to enhance and extend direct economic cooperation among the six republics "independent of the center."[22] These six republics contained only 7 percent of the USSR's total population although their contribution to the country's economy (skilled labor, modernized industries, port facilities, and the like) was considerably greater.

BUDGETARY AND ECONOMIC ISSUES

Negotiations over the text of the new Union Treaty included much more than issues of redistributing political authority between Moscow and the republics. Budgetary and economic issues were central, too. For example, there was the question of how the central government would be financed: would the center have taxation authority or would that power be granted only to the republics? If the latter, how would the central government's activities be financed? What would happen if the republics refused to pay their predetermined share of the center's budget (as in fact the RSFSR refused to do for a short period during the summer of 1991)? Could republics be forced to support the central government financially if they did not approve of Moscow's policies or actions?

A second issue was how to ensure that needed supplies of raw materials from one republic would be transported in a timely fashion to factories in another republic. With the collapse of a central clearinghouse (USSR Gosplan and all-union ministries), factory directors found themselves compelled to negotiate directly with their suppliers as well as with transportation network personnel, frequently in other republics. Although eventually such a system might be made to work (as it does in the United States and other federal countries), it clearly was not yet working in the USSR despite some preliminary efforts at interrepublican economic agreements signed during 1990 and 1991. In a July 1, 1991, *Izvestiia* interview, Kazakh president Nursultan Nazarbayev emphasized the importance of republics dealing directly with one another rather than through the old system of "faceless go-betweens" at Gosplan and the USSR Ministry of Finance.

A third issue centered on the structuring of economic relations between the republics of the new union and those republics that chose not to join the union. Because the USSR had been a single economic unit for so long, there were many plants manufacturing goods not produced elsewhere in the republics that refused to join the new union. For example, a large automobile seat belt factory in Tallinn (Estonia) produced seat belts for the entire Soviet auto industry. Would the Togliatti auto plant in Russia have to negotiate directly with the seat belt factory in Tallinn, would it build a new seat belt capability within the Russian republic, or would it depend on an intergovernmental agreement between Russia and Estonia to ensure the availability of seat belts?

"THE UNION TREATY IS OPEN FOR SIGNING"

Gorbachev announced on August 2 in a nationally televised address that yet another draft treaty had been drawn up and would be "opened for signing on August 20."[23] The text of this latest draft was not published until August 15 in *Izvestiia*, although the paper noted that the treaty had been agreed upon on July 23.

"The Union of Soviet Sovereign States," declared the first of the treaty's basic principles, "is a sovereign federal democratic state formed as a result of the association of equal republics." In this version, the "sphere of jurisdiction" of the USSR was more limited than in earlier versions. The "sphere of joint union and republic jurisdiction" was much greater and included the determination and implementation of military policy and economic and social development. Everything not specifically mentioned as center or joint jurisdiction was to remain "under the jurisdiction of the republics."

The union was granted taxing authority "determined by agreement with the republics," and, in addition, "all-union programs are financed by *pro rata* payments made by the republics affected by the program" with some attention to each republic's ability to pay. The draft did not resolve the issue of whether autonomous republics would join the union directly, but it mentioned that states might enter the union directly or as part of other states.

On August 7, *Izvestiia* reported that only Ukraine of the nine republics that had participated in the latest series of negotiations on the treaty had not approved the draft. Kravchuk announced that his republic's Supreme Soviet could not consider the draft treaty until after direct elections for the presidency and the referendum on the Ukrainian Act of Independence had been held, both of which were scheduled for December 1.

THE "FAILED COUP" AND ITS AFTERMATH

On August 16, Supreme Soviet chair Anatolii Luk'yanov declared that the latest draft of the union treaty, which was scheduled for signature by some republic delegations within a few days, "did not reflect the [March 17] referendum results on preserving the USSR." In particular, he claimed that this draft did not allot the union sufficient property or tax receipts "necessary for its normal functioning as a federal state," and it did not include a "clear statement" about the supremacy of union law.[24]

The coup and its collapse are not the focus of this essay. Rather, I am concerned with the consequences of the coup leaders' actions on the fate of the union, the Union Treaty, and the nature of intergovernmental relations. Yeltsin acted quickly and decisively: his August 19 decree, issued within hours of the State Emergency Committee's announcement that it had taken control of the central government, stated that all decrees of this "so-called Committee" were illegal and invalid on Russian territory (including Moscow) and that no Russian Federation official was to carry out any decision of the state committee. On the same day, Kravchuk declared that he "did not have enough information on what had happened and needed to look into it." By the following day, though, he too had declared the state committee's emergency decrees illegal.[25] Most of the other republics' leaders rejected the State Emergency Committee although Yeltsin boldly and without hesitation took the lead in confronting the coup leaders.

Gorbachev's house arrest at his Crimean vacation home ended just three days after the coup leaders tried to take control in Moscow; he returned to the capital during the night of August 21–22. Among the many changes that had been introduced into the political system during the Gorbachev period had been the dispersal of substantial political power from Moscow to the republics. The coup leaders recognized this dispersal and tried to stem and reverse it. Clearly they did not understand the extent to which power had already flowed out of Moscow and the popular support that elected republic leaders enjoyed. Yeltsin, for example, had been elected Russian Federation president in June 1991 after a highly competitive electoral campaign, the first in Soviet (and Russian) history. Of the 70 percent of eligible voters who had participated in the election, 57 percent had voted for Yeltsin.[26] For the coup to have had a chance to succeed, its leaders would have had to arrest republic leaders and reform spokesmen throughout the USSR, sever their lines of communication, and evict foreign news personnel from the country. Apparently, the coup leaders believed they could pull off a repeat of the October 1964 events that had resulted in a smooth transfer of power from Khrushchev to Brezhnev.

The Union Treaty Compromise Collapses

At the extraordinary session of the USSR Supreme Soviet which convened on August 26, Gorbachev spoke of the need to "resume the process of signing the Union Treaty." But republic leaders were in no mood to continue business as usual. President Nazarbayev of Kazakhstan declared that "the plan that had been worked out was now dangerous. . . . The USSR can no longer be a federation." He called for a "confederative treaty," which would eliminate the central organs of government (USSR Supreme Soviet and Cabinet of Ministers). "An inter-republican economic council is capable of providing leadership for the country during the transitional period" to a confederation, he added. Other republic leaders agreed that the federal system as laid out in the July draft treaty was no longer acceptable.[27]

Together with republic leaders' declarations that the only acceptable "renewed union" would be a loose confederation came the final collapse of the CPSU. Gorbachev resigned from the Central Committee and then the party and called for its dissolution. During the coup, party offices in some of the republics had already been closed on orders of state officials. Within days of the failed coup, CP property was transferred to state authorities. Just as so many CPs had disintegrated seemingly overnight in Eastern Europe less than two years earlier, so now, after almost seventy-four years in power, the Communist Party of the Soviet Union fell apart with remarkable rapidity.

With the party in collapse, the military leadership in disarray (Minister of Defense Dmitrii Yazov had been one of the coup leaders and was under arrest, and many of the local military district leaders had not followed military orders during the coup), the secret police in similar disarray, and the republic leaders calling for the dissolution of central political organs, there was literally nothing to hold the union together. In early September, emergency powers were granted to a newly created State Council, whose membership included Gorbachev and the head of each republic that wished to participate. An Inter-Republican Economic Committee, with similar representation, responsible for economic and social policy, was also created. The Supreme Soviet remained, although its composition would permit greater direct representation for the republics than earlier, and it would be subordinate to the State Council and the Inter-Republican Economic Committee.

The Congress of Peoples' Deputies was dissolved permanently, but Gorbachev refused to give up on a union treaty. In November, he managed to persuade seven republic leaders to come to Novo-Ogarevo and renegotiate yet another draft version of the treaty. Each leader insisted that his respective Supreme Soviet would have to consider and approve any draft version before further steps could be taken. Ukraine did not attend the November meetings. Its overwhelming vote for independence on December 1 sealed the fate of the union. Just one week later, the Minsk Declaration announced the creation of the Commonwealth of Independent States and the end of the USSR.

CONCLUSION

The failed coup effectively ended Gorbachev's three-year effort to create a viable federal system by reducing the authority of the central government, granting new authority to the republics, providing them with a direct role in the central government machinery, and keeping the union together. This effort was doomed from the outset. The treaty negotiation process, in which the central government had the upper hand until mid-1991, could not have produced a working federal arrangement, and it did not. When the republics gained the upper hand at Novo-Ogarevo, it was clear that they were less interested in preserving the union than in asserting their sovereign rights.

Gorbachev had to find support for his treaty efforts among the conservative political leaders in the central government who wanted to slow down the reform process that had gained a momentum of its own. Some of these conservatives led the coup. After they had failed and were under arrest, Gorbachev found virtually no support for preserving the union. He was also left with little credibility.

Political power had shifted decisively to the republics. Yeltsin's heroic and successful defiance of the coup leaders meant that power in Moscow had shifted from the central to the Russian Federation government. If Yeltsin earlier had favored the general concept of a viable federal system, he no longer did.

The power shift to the republics exacerbated potential ethnic conflict and enhanced non-Russians' anti-Russian/anti-Russification sentiments. These non-Russians sought independence not only from the USSR but from a Russian-dominated USSR as well. While Yeltsin and others in the Russian republic government believed that Russia had been exploited by the Soviet government over the years, all of the republics felt they had been subordinated to Russian-dominated interests. Just as the Bolsheviks had called the old Russian Empire the "prisoner of nations," so the non-Russian republics of the USSR felt they had been prisoners of the Russian-dominated Soviet government.

The impact of the East European drive for independence from Soviet hegemony was immense on those western republics of the USSR. The Baltics were the first to work toward independence and based their claim on their illegal incorporation into the USSR in 1940; this claim was validated in 1990 by the USSR Congress of Peoples' Deputies. Other republics that had enjoyed brief periods of independence after the Bolshevik Revolution but had become units of the Russian-dominated union by the early 1920s followed the Baltics' lead. Moldova, too, insisted that its incorporation into the USSR in 1944 had been illegal. When the Baltic states gained their formal independence and were granted broad international diplomatic recognition in September 1991, the precedent was established for other republics to seek independence as well.

The last years of the Gorbachev period were turbulent ones. Rapid change, particularly political and social, was accelerated by often contradictory policies. Policy makers were pressed by rising popular sentiments, demands, and expectations which they could neither control nor direct. An orderly process of decentralizing political authority, restricting the power of the central government, and providing greater authority for the republics could not be put in place. After the republics took the lead in negotiating with Moscow on the reorganization of intergovernmental relations they were no longer interested in retaining the union.

NOTES

1. Richard Pipes, *The Formation of the Soviet Union: Communism and Nationalism 1917–1923*, rev. ed. (Cambridge: Harvard University Press, 1964), 244–45.

2. Ibid., 289.

3. Ninety-five percent of the delegates to the congress were CP members. See Merle Fainsod, *How Russia Is Ruled* (Cambridge: Harvard University Press, 1963), 365–66.

4. Rudolf Schlesinger, *Federalism in Central and Eastern Europe* (New York: Oxford University Press, 1945), 365. See, generally, part IV. See also the useful discussion with accompanying documents of this period in Walter Russell Batsell, *Soviet Rule in Russia* (New York: Macmillan, 1929); and E. H. Carr, *The Bolshevik Revolution, 1917–1923*, Vol. 1 (Baltimore: Penguin, 1966).

5. Robert Sharlet, *The New Soviet Constitution of 1977: Analysis and Text* (Brunswick, Ohio: King's Court Communications, 1978), 97–101.

6. For a historical review of republic rights, see Gregory Gleason, *Federalism and Nationalism: The Struggle for Republican Rights in the USSR* (Boulder: Westview, 1990).

7. *Izvestiia*, April 16, 1990. The previous month, Gorbachev managed to secure the creation of an executive branch of government separate from the legislature, headed by the office of president, to which he was elected by the Congress of Peoples' Deputies. Some observers believe that the creation of the presidency, which was designed to bolster central government authority, strengthened the determination of republic leaders to reduce that authority. See Sergei M. Samuylov, "The Gorbachev Presidency: On the Way to Dictatorship?" *Presidential Studies Quarterly*, 22 (Spring 1992); and, for background, B. A. Lazarev, "The President of the USSR," *Soviet Law and Government* 30 (Summer 1991).

8. *Izvestiia*, March 16, 1990.

9. Daniel J. Elazar, *Exploring Federalism* (Tuscaloosa: University of Alabama Press, 1987), 34. See also the discussion in Stephan Kux, *Soviet Federalism: A Comparative Perspective* (New York: Institute for East-West Security Studies, 1990), esp. chaps. 2, 4.

10. *Pravda*, December 26, 1989.

11. Jane Henderson, "Legal Aspects of the Soviet Federal Structure," paper presented to a conference on Soviet federalism at Leicester University (U.K.), September 11–13, 1990, 23.

12. See, for example, Kenneth C. Wheare, *Federal Government* (New York: Oxford University Press, 1964).

13. In his *For a New Russia* (New York: Free Press, 1992), 28, Sobchak wrote of the Inter-Regional Group's discussions about economics and politics, held just after the group was formed in June 1989; the republics must operate on an "equal but different" principle within a new *confederate* system, the group concluded.

14. *Izvestiia*, September 26, 1990.

15. Ibid., October 13, 17, 23, 28, 1990.

16. Ibid., November 24, 1990; text reprinted in *Current Digest of the Soviet Press* 42, no. 47 (1990).

17. *Izvestiia*, December 18, 1990.

18. Sobchak, *For a New Russia,* 109.

19. For a detailed discussion of the referendum in each of the republics, see Commission on Security and Cooperation in Europe Staff, *Referendum in the Soviet Union* (Washington, D.C., April 1991).

20. See the discussion by Ann Sheehy, "Revised Draft of the Union Treaty," *Report on the USSR* 3, 12 (March 22, 1991).

21. *Izvestiia,* July 9, 1991. See also Roman Solchanyk, "The Draft Union Treaty and the 'Big Five,'" *Report on the USSR* 3, 18 (May 3, 1991).

22. Vladimir Socor, "Political Forces of Six Republics Set Up Coordinating Mechanism," *Report on the USSR* 3, 23 (June 7, 1991).

23. *Izvestiia,* August 3, 1991. The newspaper had reported on July 31 about an evening meeting in Novo-Ogarevo on July 29–30 between Gorbachev, Yeltsin, and Nazarbayev, at which agreement had been hammered out on several articles of a new draft of the treaty.

24. *Izvestiia,* August 20, 1991.

25. *Nezavisimaya gazeta,* August 20, 1991. See also *Kuranty,* August 19, 1991, for details on Yeltsin's position.

26. *Izvestiia,* June 14, 1991.

27. Ibid., August 26, 1991. See also Andrei S. Grachev, *Final Days: The Inside Story of the Collapse of the Soviet Union* (Boulder, Colo.: Westview Press, 1995), esp. chaps. 3–12.

5

August 1991 in Comparative Perspective
Moscow and Kiev

ZENOVIA A. SOCHOR

The meaning and ramifications of the events of August 1991 are open to widely differing, even contradictory, interpretations. Did the coup precipitate a revolution—a sudden, complete overthrow of key institutions (CPSU, KGB, military)? Was it a counterrevolution—an attempt, albeit failed, to halt the significant and substantive changes already under way as a result of perestroika? Or was there no real revolution—only "political decay" on a grand scale, a collapse of the old system with no political institutions or legal arrangements to create a new political community?[1] Underlying these questions is a long-standing debate, initiated by Zbigniew Brzezinski, over whether totalitarian systems can transform themselves or are doomed to degeneration and collapse.[2]

One analyst, Martin Malia, finds the profusion of interpretations exasperating: "Yet almost no one uses the self-evident name, 'revolution' to designate what is so obviously one of the most revolutionary events of 20th century history. For what occurred in August was the end of communism, not just in its East European periphery, but in its heartland and place of origin, the Soviet Union. What more does it take to qualify as a revolution?" He defines revolution thus: "There was a fundamental rupture, a radical break between communism of whatever stripe and Russia's present attempt to build a market economy and democracy."[3]

Another dimension of the events of August 1991, the dissolution of the USSR, evokes little dispute. Once the center buckled, the periphery fell as if the formidable USSR had been built of cards. One republic after another swiftly declared its independence. Less obvious, however, is what role the coup played. Was it the main cause of the disintegration of the USSR? Or was the stage set for collapse well before the coup?

This essay examines the coup from the perspectives of Moscow and Kiev in an attempt to shed light on the nature of the changes that preceded August 1991 and shaped the political choices in its aftermath. A closer examination of

Moscow and Kiev reveals that the political dynamics in the two cities were neither parallel nor identical. In a nutshell, this essay argues that August 1991 precipitated a revolution in Moscow, but in Kiev, a national liberation movement formed as a substitute for revolution. The failed coup also accelerated rather than initiated the demise of the USSR; it culminated a process already under way, dramatized by the declarations of sovereignty, first by Russia, then by Ukraine, in 1990.

Revolution

Certain commonalities come to the fore in any discussion of revolution. A series of crises, such as military defeat or economic failure, precedes a revolutionary situation; despite various efforts at problem solving, the government is not able to cope with or to meet the expectations of a large part of the population. The lack of satisfactory remedies creates internal divisions within the political elite and a faltering sense of legitimacy. To compound the sense of crisis, intellectuals desert the government and counterelites become more assertive. Thereupon arises the most dangerous moment for the government: a situation of "dual power" or "multiple sovereignties." To quote Charles Tilly: "A revolution begins when a government previously under the control of a single, sovereign polity becomes the object of effective, competing, mutually exclusive claims from two or more separate polities."[4]

Any number of events can tip the scales to propel a revolutionary situation into a full-scale revolution: violence in the streets, pell-mell activities of newly mobilized groups, and seizures of power great and small. Within the eye of the storm, nothing is clear; after the takeover, the whole process appears seductively inevitable. Samuel P. Huntington tries to capture the enormity of changes in a revolution: "A full-scale revolution involves the rapid and violent destruction of existing political institutions, the mobilization of new groups into politics, and the creation of new political institutions."[5]

View from Moscow: The Kremlin

Does the general description of revolution apply to what happened in August 1991? Certainly the coup was preceded by significant changes in the system, an impending sense of crisis, and a possible emergence of dual power.

Gorbachev's policy, perestroika, made substantial inroads in dismantling the totalitarian structures. His intent, at a minimum, was to shake up the encrusted bureaucratized system and to signal to the apparatchiki that "standard operating procedures" were not good enough anymore. Once begun, the process yielded far more dramatic results.

Despite numerous restrictions, elections were opened up to multiple candidates for the first time since 1918. A new and enhanced legislative body, the

Congress of Peoples' Deputies, was created, and elections were held to select its 2,250 members; the congress in turn elected a standing Supreme Soviet of 542 members.

Since the elections were skewed and the vast majority of deputies were members of the Communist Party (87 percent), little hope was held out for genuine democratization. Nevertheless, the elections as well as the televised sessions of the congress served to awaken and politicize society; they extended the meaning and content of glasnost considerably (for the first time, cabinet appointments were challenged publicly); they opened the political arena to new actors—especially intellectuals. Most important, the elections and the congress contributed to the decline of the party's leading role. (A number of prominent party apparatchiki who ran unopposed suffered electoral defeat, for example, Yuri Solov'ev, the leader of the powerful Leningrad party organization.) In the end, the Congress of Peoples' Deputies voted, in March 1990, to abolish Article 6 of the Soviet constitution, thereby eliminating the CPSU monopoly of power and clearing the way for a multiparty system.

Gorbachev, ever bent on maintaining a centrist position, first resisted and then accepted the elimination of Article 6. By 1990, however, the political center was fast disappearing as a viable political stake-out. Not only conservative opponents such as Yegor Ligachev (second secretary of the CPSU Central Committee) but also moderate allies such as Prime Minister Nikolai Ryzhkov criticized Gorbachev's policies; they charged that the party had effectively lost control over the formation of policy, cadres, and ideology. Even before the Article 6 debacle, Ryzhkov had argued that Gorbachev should "devote more attention to his Party duties" (as opposed to running the Supreme Soviet).[6] Ryzhkov and the others perceived—and were protesting—a transfer of power away from the party and to the Congress of Peoples' Deputies. Lest there be any mistake about the nature of the threat facing the party, Ligachev began to speak of *dvoevlastie*, that is, dual power.

To be sure, it is debatable whether the congress ever acquired enough power for dual power to be a reality. Before the coup, criticisms were rampant that the Supreme Soviet had become a mere "debating club"; laws were not being implemented; the deputies suffered from "parliamentary fatigue." It is more certain, however, that the power of the party was crumbling. One analyst concluded, "The ruling Party is in a seemingly terminal decline; its popularity, credibility, and numbers are shrinking by the month."[7]

In November 1990, Gorbachev complained that whenever he issued decrees, "The debates begin: What sort of decree is this: Do we have to carry it out, or not?" The result, Gorbachev concluded, was a "paralysis of power" and a "vacuum."[8] Clearly, his own popularity, always more tenuous at home than abroad, had fallen to a new low in the fall of 1990: 21 percent in comparison to

52 percent the previous year. Moreover, Gorbachev's efforts to shore up his executive powers at the expense of the legislature did not gain him greater authority; instead, his actions caused his allies on the left ("democratic re-formers") to break with him. Some of the key intellectuals who developed and espoused the notion of perestroika, Tat'yana Zaslavskaya, Yuri Afanas'yev, and about twenty others, called on Gorbachev, in a letter, either to recommit him-self to genuine economic and political reform or to resign.[9] The most dramatic break came when Foreign Minister Eduard Shevardnadze abruptly resigned in December 1990, protesting the signs of a return to dictatorial rule. These actions were not unlike the "desertion of intellectuals," a phrase used by Crane Brinton to describe one of the preconditions of revolution.

View from Moscow: Russia

Gorbachev's actions—or inactions—were necessary but not sufficient to steer the USSR onto the course of revolution. A variety of scenarios were still con-ceivable, including the ouster of Gorbachev and reimposition of dictatorial rule. What tipped the scale was the nature and method of the opposition. Curi-ously, there was hardly any opposition at the all-union level. As Adam Ulam noted, "Once Gorbachev's popularity began to wane, there should have been some rivals aspiring to the top post. Yet it was a peculiarity of Soviet politics under perestroika that it produced no party seeking power at the all-union level."[10]

Not until July 1, 1991, did nine prominent Soviet politicians, including former Politburo members Eduard Shevardnadze and Aleksandr Yakovlev, an-nounce their intent to organize the Movement for Democratic Reforms. They appealed to democratic and reform-oriented forces throughout the USSR to unite to save the country from anarchy and dictatorship. Moreover, they stress-ed that "the disintegration of the totalitarian system must not lead to the sev-ering of ties that have been naturally established between peoples during the course of history."[11]

July 1991 was too late for a liberal all-union opposition. By and large, demo-crats in non-Russian republics were more interested in securing self-determi-nation than in preserving USSR integrity. Within Russia, both hard-liners and liberals adopted a tactic different from an all-union movement; both chose Russia as a power base; both opposed Gorbachev at the center.

On June 20–23, 1990, the founding congress of the RSFSR Communist Party was held, with a conservative, Ivan Polozkov, elected as first secretary. Speeches at the congress were highly critical of Gorbachev and the reform process as a whole. They blamed the current Politburo leadership—and not the "socialist idea"—for the crisis in the country. The final resolutions reaf-firmed a commitment to socialism, Lenin, and preservation of the Soviet empire. Even though their position had all-union implications, the conservatives chose the Russian Communist Party as their political vehicle. Perhaps hardliners concluded "that they could not challenge Gorbachev at the all-Union level"; hence, they created an organization "that would not come directly under Gorbachev" and chose a leader "who represented a clear alternative to Gorbachev."[12]

At the other end of the political spectrum, at the first session of the RSFSR Congress of Peoples' Deputies, May 16–June 22, 1990, the liberals elected Boris Yeltsin as chairman of the RSFSR Supreme Soviet. Criticisms of Gorbachev were rampant at this congress as well, although they came from the opposite direction. The radical democrats bemoaned the brakes being applied to the reforms by the Ryzhkov government; instead, they urged a rapid shift to a market economy and a reconstitution of the union on the basis of genuinely sovereign republics.

However different their programs, the hard-liners and the liberals combined succeeded in drawing attention to Russia and away from Gorbachev and the center. The political leader who gained most from this "rediscovery" of Russia was Boris Yeltsin; the political loser was Mikhail Gorbachev. Indeed, the Gorbachev-Yeltsin relationship, problematic from the start, proved to be critical to the outcome both of Gorbachev's fortunes and of the USSR. Yeltsin, as one of the leaders of the "democratic opposition" (the Inter-Regional Group) in the Soviet legislature, was a nuisance but not a serious contender for power. His election to the presidency of the RSFSR parliament in May 1990, however, gave him an independent platform. It pitted the leader of Russia (in a fateful move, Yeltsin declared sovereignty for Russia immediately after his election) against the leader of a faltering USSR. His popular election to the presidency, now separated from parliament, in June 1991 further underscored his mass support as opposed to Gorbachev's indirect election to the USSR presidency by the Soviet legislature.

Yeltsin's resignation from the party at the Twenty-Eighth CPSU Congress in July 1990, together with the resignations of several other prominent reformers, was particularly important in radicalizing the political spectrum. In one leap, Yeltsin managed to lump Gorbachev and Polozkov into one category: party apparatchiki. In contrast, Yeltsin took on the mantle of the democrat. With the support of Democratic Russia (the liberal bloc in the Russian parliament and later a broad-based movement), Yeltsin suggested that the party was incapable of reform and that socialism, as a set of guiding principles, was moribund. According to Yeltsin, a revolutionary situation had arisen because of "compromises and half-measures" adopted by the CPSU.[13] It was no longer a question of mild or radical reform of communism but a showdown between communism and anticommunism. An "ideology of opposition" was created, and Democratic Russia, "like other revolutionary movements . . . aimed to destroy, not reform, the ancien regime."[14] This situation resembled "dual power" more than the description Ligachev tried to apply to the tension between party and parliament. It was party versus antiparty.

Despite various efforts at reconciliation between Gorbachev and Yeltsin, their rivalry remained at center stage. By 1991, the situation of dual power, or multiple sovereignties, had two dimensions: Gorbachev versus Yeltsin but also center versus periphery. Gorbachev's repeated attempts in 1991 to rearrange the USSR in a way that would satisfy the republics were rebuffed. Yeltsin's newly found championship of Russian sovereignty also served to up the ante. In short order, Yeltsin acquired for Russia all the trappings of a "normal" republic, such as its own KGB, Ministry of Internal Affairs, Foreign Ministry, and mass media networks. He also signed treaties with other union republics, illustrating in dramatic fashion the sovereignty but also the "foreignness" of the signatories.

When Lithuania was attacked by Soviet forces, Yeltsin sided with the Lithuanians, thus reinforcing the center versus periphery dichotomy. Other republics took their cue from Russia's assertiveness vis-à-vis the center. Where once genuine federation might have been greeted enthusiastically, confederation now would no longer suffice. Having declared their independence, Georgia, Armenia, and Moldavia, in addition to the Baltic states, were not prepared to submerge it into a new Union Treaty, proffered by Gorbachev in the summer of 1991.

However remarkably inept, the coup leaders of August 1991 were nevertheless correct in sensing that a revolutionary situation was afoot. Both the party and the USSR as an entity were seriously threatened. The great historical irony, of course, is that by their bungled coup attempt, they precipitated the very revolution they tried to prevent.

What conclusions can be drawn from the above account? Certainly a revolutionary situation had emerged in August 1991, but if a revolution took place in its wake, it was a peculiar revolution. The arena for revolutionary activity was small: it essentially involved conflict among the elites rather than mass mobilization and violent seizure of power. Rather than psychological or purposive explanations of "why men rebel," or even Marxist theories of economic collapse and class conflict, the more convincing starting point in understanding August 1991 was internal breakdown and state paralysis.

This is not to deny the importance of the miners' strike, the informal associations, or the thousands of Muscovites who demonstrated in support of Yeltsin before and after the coup; it is to say that rising expectations, popular discontent, and street violence did not bring down the communist state. There was more apathy or confusion than political activism among the population in

Russia at large. Despite the seeming omnipotence of the Communist Party, it was weakness at the top rather than strength from below that brought down the government. A kind of "internal secret rot" developed within the political elite, those who experienced a loss of faith in the superiority of socialism over capitalism and were frustrated by the continued backwardness of their country vis-à-vis the "civilized world."[15] Gorbachev may have started as a "born-again socialist," but he pursued his package of reforms with less conviction as new and more radical demands were placed on his table. In the end, he seemed to run out of answers; the dismal lineup of the State Emergency Committee offered only old and discredited answers. Reformers who crossed the line to revolution now took their turn to transform the system.

For these reasons, analysts grope for terms and concepts to explain what happened in August 1991. There was a collapse of the old regime but not really a seizure of power by new elites—only different configurations of the "ruling class," broadly defined (former Communist Party members turned "democrats" and "reformers). To return to Huntington's definition of revolution cited above, old institutions were destroyed but new groups and new political institutions were not yet ready to replace them. Consequently, it was an "incomplete revolution."

View from Kiev

What comparisons can be drawn and insights gained if the perspective switches to Kiev?

Some points are obvious: the initiative for change came from the outside. This is true for perestroika, the declaration of sovereignty, and the coup itself. Gorbachev-type reforms were belated and made fewer inroads in Ukraine because longtime party leader Volodymyr Shcherbitsky's role was to apply brakes to the process. Perestroika was secondhand and resisted by the Ukrainian party establishment.

The founding congress for Rukh, the popular front movement, did not take place until September 1989 (earlier efforts were suppressed). Rukh's initial premise was mostly a "surrogate reform communism," closer in spirit to Prague in 1968 than to Eastern Europe in 1989. Its very name suggested as much: Popular Movement for Restructuring in Ukraine. Leaders of Rukh saw themselves as Gorbachev's allies, seeking to combat the conservative party apparatus. In this spirit, an open letter to Gorbachev was read at the congress, decrying the inflexibility of the top Ukrainian party leadership, which undermined faith in the notion of a "renewal of socialism." Ivan Drach, elected chairman of Rukh and a Communist Party member, stated in an interview in October 1989 that he supported "normal coexistence with the Party leadership" and "victory for the Gorbachev line."[16] In a survey of Rukh delegates to the founding congress, the reformist and moderate stance emerged clearly, even though only about 20 percent of the 1,109 delegates were Communist Party members; 75 percent felt Rukh should support democratization; only 28 percent believed Rukh should compete with the party for leadership.[17]

Despite this moderate position (and perhaps the only politically tenable one at the time), Rukh was embroiled in confrontation from its first tentative steps. Shcherbitsky's knee-jerk reaction was decidedly negative; he attempted to nip in the bud any effort at forming a popular front as had been done in the Baltic states. He unleashed a campaign of harassment and intimidation.

Leonid Kravchuk, head of the ideology department of the Central Committee of the Communist Party of Ukraine, quickly fell in step. When the Initiative Group, formed by members of the Writers' Union of Ukraine, presented a draft program for the Popular Movement for Restructuring in Ukraine in January 1989, the party labeled the program "a manifesto of political demands," aiming to create "an alternative political structure to the CPSU." Kravchuk, who had been present at the plenum meeting when the draft program was submitted, declared that the draft amounted to a "political program," which no party member could support.[18] In May 1989, when the Initiative Group continued undeterred, Shcherbitsky described the Popular Movement as a "new political structure" that would "stand above the organs of Soviet power and, in essence, in opposition to the CPSU."[19]

Perhaps because there were very few reformers, closet or otherwise, within the party, Rukh was automatically viewed as opponent rather than partner. This hard-line position had the dual effect of emphasizing confrontation over co-optation and of radicalizing the more moderately inclined Rukh leaders.

Even when Shcherbitsky resigned, the hard-line position was modulated but not substantially changed. Shcherbitsky announced his resignation on September 28 (about two weeks after the founding congress of Rukh) at the plenum of the Central Committee of the Ukrainian Communist Party. He was replaced by Volodymyr Ivashko, second secretary and member of the Politburo and generally perceived as a moderate. Nevertheless, the potential opening to reform was immediately marked by cautionary signposts. Gorbachev, who was present at the Ukrainian plenum, praised Shcherbitsky rather than criticizing the Brezhnev-era holdover. In almost identical terms, Gorbachev and Ivashko sounded a warning signal to Rukh not to stray from support for perestroika toward "unhealthy" manifestations of nationalism or separatism.

Political initiative, however, was no longer solely in party hands. The political atmosphere in Ukraine was becoming charged, and democratization was being pushed to the top of the agenda. Heated debates, letters, and protests were generated by the draft electoral laws for the upcoming elections to the

Ukrainian parliament. Previous elections to the Congress of Peoples' Deputies had succeeded in ousting party leaders in such key cities as Kiev and Lviv; hence elections now became a focus of political activity. Ukrainian members of the Inter-Regional Group of the Congress of Peoples' Deputies, together with Rukh leaders, proposed alternative election laws, exacting in the process some important changes, including elimination of quotas for reserved seats in parliament for public organizations such as the Communist Party, Komsomol, or trade unions.

In November 1989, Rukh joined with forty smaller groups to form a Democratic Bloc for the upcoming elections to the Ukrainian Supreme Soviet in March 1990. The bloc presented an alternative political platform and fielded political candidates who were antiparty and antisystem. Its manifesto denounced the "old system" of a "dictatorship of the Party apparatus" and called for a multiparty system as well as abolition of Article 6 of the USSR constitution.[20] The Democratic Bloc won 108 of the 450 seats in the Ukrainian legislature.

Once the Ukrainian Supreme Soviet convened, electoral politics seeped into legislative politics. The Democratic Bloc pursued its activities as an opposition bloc called the Peoples' Council (Narodna Rada); its strength was about one-third of the deputies. At the first session of the legislature (May–August 1990), the alignment was clear: on one side, the Peoples' Council; on the other, the so-called Group of 239, that is, the communist majority.

Enhancing the sense of confrontation was Ivashko's replacement by a conservative, Stanislav Hurenko, as first secretary of the Ukrainian party. (Ivashko accepted an appointment to Moscow as Gorbachev's deputy general secretary.)

By the fall of 1990, Hurenko declared that a "brutal political struggle" had emerged. He described Rukh as an openly anticommunist organization; it had "taken off its political masks" and was concentrating its efforts on the seizure of power by any means, not excluding violence.[21] Kravchuk, who had replaced Ivashko as chairman of the Supreme Soviet, echoed a similar tone in an October 22 interview: Rukh has "declared a fight to the finish against Communist ideology and the Communist Party."[22] The press adopted an increasingly alarmist tone; even *Pravda* (September 28) warned that a coup d'état was being hatched by self-styled democrats.

The sense of crisis was heightened and symbolized by the "tent city" set up by students in the main plaza of Kiev in October. Hundreds of students declared a hunger strike and issued a list of distinctly political (and antiparty) demands: resignation of the chairman of the Council of Ministers Vitaly Masol, confiscation of party and Komsomol property, dissolution of parliament and new elections, guarantee of rights of Ukrainian conscripts to perform military service in the republic. About 150,000 people marched on the parliament on

October 16, to be joined, two days later, by workers from Kiev's largest factory, Arsenal. The party, in an unprecedented move, was forced to compromise; Masol resigned.

Just as quickly, however, the party struck back. On November 7, in a move redolent of pre-perestroika tactics, a deputy of the parliament and member of the Democratic Opposition, Stepan Khmara, was arrested on trumped-up charges and imprisoned. The communist majority in the Supreme Soviet stripped him of his parliamentary immunity. Rumors were rife in the capital that a general crackdown would ensue, perhaps followed by the imposition of martial law.

From the account thus far, one might well ask, What was different from the events in Moscow? The situation taking shape seemed to suggest dual power: the party was losing its membership (about 150,000 in 1990 out of 3.3 million members), cohesion, and legitimacy, while Rukh was gaining across the board (over 500,000 members). Since Rukh, as well as the Peoples' Council in parliament, was disproportionately composed of intellectuals, one could argue that a "desertion of intellectuals" was also occurring.[23] Moreover, there were many signs of a general public arousal, with activity "from below." January 1990 had witnessed a "human chain," linking hundreds of thousands of people from Lviv to Kiev in commemoration of the 1918 declaration of independence. About half a million young people in the industrial Dnipro region flocked to Rukh-organized festivals, celebrating "Days of Cossack Glory," in a popular, contemporary, Woodstock style. Coal miners in Donetsk and Dnipropetrovsk held massive strikes, issuing not only economic but also political demands, such as "depoliticization" of coal enterprises in Ukraine.

And yet the revolutionary momentum in Ukraine was diverted. Its energies and passions were channeled into a national liberation movement. The focus shifted away from the recalcitrant party to the subordinate and colonial status of Ukraine. Moscow rather than the party became the center of drama.

Two factors stand out in importance in this transformation. First was the declaration of sovereignty in July 1990. In a stunning turnaround, the Ukrainian legislature voted 355 for sovereignty, 4 against. With this vote, the idea of independence began to edge out antiparty sentiment. Yeltsin had already declared Russia's sovereignty, paving the way for Ukrainians, whether communist or noncommunist, to take a similar brash step. Perhaps inadvertently, the center also contributed to disarming the Group of 239 by taking away the first secretary of the Ukrainian Communist Party, Volodymyr Ivashko, together with sixty-three communist deputies, from the Ukrainian Supreme Soviet to attend the Twenty-Eighth Party Congress in Moscow. When the Ukrainian parliament tried to recall the Moscow-bound deputies for the declaration of sovereignty vote, they refused, thus making clear their allegiance and embarrassing the communist deputies left behind in Kiev.[24] Still another nudge toward sovereignty may have come from USSR prime minister Ryzhkov, who proposed an economic reform package that retained for the center full control over the transition to a "regulated market economy." Ryzhkov was clearly out of step with the overwhelming mood for "economic autonomy." Political leaders as diverse as Vitold Fokin (head of the Ukrainian State Planning Commission and a Communist Party member) and Vyacheslav Chornovil (head of the Helsinki Union, Rukh leader, and a former political prisoner) found themselves on the same side, protesting the exploitative, even "colonial," nature of Ryzhkov's plan.

In a telling move, at its second congress, in October 1990, Rukh dropped the word "restructuring" from its name. Independence had now become its stated goal. Only a year earlier, in October 1989, Drach foresaw Ukraine as a sovereign republic within "a new Union of republics on the basis of a new Union agreement."[25] As 1990 progressed, "restructuring," and even sovereignty, began to seem like overly timid goals.

The second factor was the emergence of Kravchuk as leader of the sovereignty movement. Attitudes toward Gorbachev's proposed Union Treaty showed a significant split within the Ukrainian Communist Party between the "imperialist communists" (for the treaty) and the "sovereignty communists" (against the treaty). Kravchuk identified himself with the latter. As he stated in March 1991, "The president—Gorbachev—when he issues his decrees, forgets that there is our declaration, that there is a republic, that there is a road to sovereignty, that this is now not just a slogan, that it is entering into the consciousness and psychology of the people. And no one can change this, regardless of how much they would like to. . . . When I opted for sovereignty (and I did), I said that I would fight for it to the end. We will not diverge from this path."[26]

In the March 17 all-union referendum on the fate of a "renewed union," Kravchuk tacked his own question on to Gorbachev's, asking if the population in Ukraine supported sovereignty. Although the results were confusing (about 70 percent responded yes to the first question, 80 percent to the second), Kravchuk used the results as a mandate to strengthen Ukrainian sovereignty vis-à-vis the center.

Kravchuk's position fragmented the Group of 239. In the March referendum, about half of the communist members of parliament voted in favor of Kravchuk's question, despite opposition from the party leadership. On June 27, 1991, the Ukrainian parliament made the decision, despite intense pressure from Gorbachev, to postpone signing the Union Treaty until a new republican constitution was in place. The final resolution, worked out by Kravchuk, was adopted by 345 votes; thus the majority of the Group of 239 also supported it. Kravchuk seemed to have made an end run around the "imperialists."

In his role as chairman of the Ukrainian parliament, Kravchuk found himself at the nerve center of political activity. The party, in contrast, appeared to be hesitant and divided. As one analyst noted, "The center of political gravity . . . shifted away from the preeminent all-Union structure—the party—towards the Ukrainian state, whose logic of existence was bound up with an expansion of its prerogatives."[27]

Kravchuk's actions had important consequences. His popularity rating, which had sunk to an all-time low at the time of Khmara's arrest in November 1990, grew to 54 percent among Kievans by June 1991. His stand on the sovereignty issue made the difference. Even more important, the stark dichotomy of the party versus antiparty struggle was dramatically transformed. Kravchuk, Communist Party leader, albeit a "sovereignty communist," was suddenly on the same side of the barricades as Rukh, Levko Lukyanenko, and Chornovil. When the coup occurred in Moscow and precipitated a revolution, there was no coup but also no bona fide revolution in Kiev.

COMPARATIVE PERSPECTIVES

In August 1991, Yeltsin led the "new democrats" in a consciously styled but limited revolution, given that there was barely any violent confrontation or seizure of power by new counterelites, as is the case with classical revolutions. Kravchuk hesitated whether to support the coup or to condemn it, although on August 21, when the State Emergency Committee was already stumbling, he came out with a strong statement against it. At a minimum, the symbolism of Yeltsin heading "democrats" in opposition to the Old Guard was important. Kravchuk did not make the decisive break with the Old Guard that Yeltsin did.

Even before the coup, Yeltsin quit the party and identified it wholesale as the opposition—old-line communism, its Russian reincarnation, as well as its Gorbachev-reform version. Kravchuk straddled the fence on this issue; he did not resign from the party until after the coup. Instead, Kravchuk shifted the focus to national liberation. His commitment, which was made decisively and at some political risk, was to align himself with the sovereignty—and then independence—forces in Ukraine. He identified Moscow as the opposition.

Before the coup, in Moscow, a "revolutionary situation" was emerging in the sense of dual power. In the fall of 1990, this also seemed to be the case in Kiev. Over the ensuing tense months, however, the political situation shifted. Kravchuk and Rukh, originally at opposite ends, formed an uneasy alliance. Even raucous debates over internal political arrangements within Ukraine paled in comparison to the emboldened steps taken to disband the Soviet Union.

The way the revolutionary situation emerged and the decisions made during its course were pivotal for the fate of the USSR as a union. In Russia, a split within the party, between conservatives and liberals, left Gorbachev isolated and increasingly irrelevant in the Kremlin. The political split developed into a center-periphery realignment, as both conservative Polozkov and liberal Yeltsin chose Russia as their power base against a redefined concept of center. Gorbachev tried not to draw a distinction between Russia and the USSR; Polozkov and Yeltsin tried just as hard, and succeeded, in doing the opposite. The power struggle among the elites, punctuated by mass demonstrations, strikes, and organized public activity, led to the simultaneous unraveling of totalitarianism and imperialism.

The national liberation movement in Ukraine made the unraveling of the USSR all but irreversible. Ukrainian independence changed the name of the game from anticommunism to anticolonialism. There was no turning back for Kravchuk; unlike Ivashko, he chose to make Ukraine his power base and quickly moved to shore up Ukraine's independence militarily and diplomatically. The December 1991 referendum resulted in a resoundingly large vote (83 to 90 percent; 54 percent in Crimea) for independence and propelled Kravchuk into power as the first president.

Not surprisingly, the aftermath of 1991 was different in Moscow and in Kiev. In Russia, nationalism became a potent and frequently extremist political force, whether in its "red" or "brown" manifestations. Neither Yeltsin nor the democrats could remain impervious to the shock and the ensuing accusations associated with the rapid demise of the USSR. Nationalism was an issue in the parliamentary elections of 1993, with the right-wing candidate Vladimir Zhirinovsky advocating the restoration of a Great Russia as well as in the presidential elections of 1996, with the communist candidate Gennadii Zyuganov promoting a renewed USSR.

In Ukraine, a tempered nationalism has emerged, based on state-building prerogatives and mindful of the sizable Russian ethnic minority as well as low levels of national consciousness in the southern and eastern regions of Ukraine. Leonid Kuchma, from the Russified city of Dnipropetrovsk, won the presidential elections in 1994 against an incumbent who attempted to play the nationalist card. Ultranationalists have remained on the political margins.

In contrast, efforts to revamp the communist political system have made greater strides in Moscow than in Kiev. The prior existence of a reform-minded elite, the humiliation of the coup leaders, and the stripping of party power immediately after the aborted coup left the Communist Party a much weakened force in Russia. Five years later, in the 1996 presidential elections, the communist candidate enjoyed an upsurge in popularity against a background of economic adversity, crime, corruption, and an unsteady hand at the helm. Nevertheless, Yeltsin won and left the Communist Party in disarray once again.

In contrast, in Kiev, the collapse of communism was not accompanied by the collapse of communists, even though the party was banned. The nomenklatura survived relatively intact under Kravchuk's protective umbrella. Whether reconstituted as the Socialist Party or Agrarian Partya or relegalized as the Communist Party in October 1993, the left bloc remains a force to be reckoned with in Ukrainian politics.

In neither Russia nor Ukraine will a complete revolution—a new political community with new values, groups, and institutions—be easily attained. The way August 1991 was played out in Kiev and in Moscow will continue to influence political developments in both countries.

NOTES

1. George W. Breslauer argues that "the coup accelerated trends and tendencies that were well in train before August 1991." See "Bursting the Dams: Politics and Society in the USSR Since the Coup," *Problems of Communism* 40, no. 6 (November–December 1991):11. See also William E. Odom, "Alternative Perspectives on the August Coup," ibid., 13–19.

2. Zbigniew Brzezinksi, ed., *Dilemmas of Change in Soviet Politics* (New York: Columbia University Press, 1969).

3. Martin Malia, "From Under the Rubble, What?" *Problems of Communism* 41, no. 1 (January–April 1992):90–91.

4. Charles Tilly, "Does Modernization Breed Revolution?" in *Revolutions: Theoretical, Comparative and Historical Studies*, ed. Jack A. Goldstone (New York: Harcourt Brace Jovanovich, 1986), 52–53.

5. Samuel P. Huntington, *Political Order in Changing Societies* (New Haven: Yale University Press, 1968), 266.

6. *Pravda*, July 21, 1989, 3.

7. Aleksandr Meerovich, "The Emergence of Russian Multiparty Politics," *Report on the USSR*, August 24, 1990, 10.

8. *Izvestiia*, November 17, 1990.

9. *Moskovskiie novosti*, November 18, 1990.

10. Adam Ulam, "Looking at the Past: The Unraveling of the Soviet Union," *Current History* 91 (October 1992), 343.

11. See Elizabeth Teague and Vera Tolz, "Prominent Reformers Create Opposition Movement," *Report on the USSR*, July 12, 1991, 1–4.

12. See Alexander Rahr, "The Russian Triangle: Gorbachev—Yeltsin—Polozkov," *Report on the USSR*, July 6, 1990, 4. Also see John Dunlop, "Russia: Confronting a Loss of Empire," in *Nations and Politics in the Soviet Successor States*, ed. Ian Bremmer and Ray Taras (Cambridge: Cambridge University Press, 1993).

13. *Pravda*, July 8, 1990. Also see John Morrison, *Boris Yeltsin: From Bolshevik to Democrat* (New York: Dutton, 1991).

14. Michael McFaul, "The Democrats in Disarray," *Journal of Democracy* 4 (April 1993), 18.

15. See Edgar Morin, "The Anti-Totalitarian Revolution," in *Between Totalitarianism and Post-Modernity*, ed. Peter Beilharz, Gillian Robinson, and John Rundell (Cambridge, Mass.: MIT Press, 1992), 94.

16. "The Current Situation in Ukraine: A Discussion with 'Rukh' Chairman Ivan Drach," in *Ukraine from Chernobyl to Sovereignty: A Collection of Interviews*, ed. Roman Solchanyk (New York: St. Martin's Press, 1992), 40–56.

17. The survey was conducted by sociologist V. Paniotto. See David Marples, "A Sociological Survey of 'Rukh,'" *Report on the USSR*, January 12, 1990, 18–20.

18. *Robitnycha Hazeta*, February 8, 1989, 3; *Radian'ska Ukraina*, February 7, 1989, 2. See also Bohdan Nahaylo, "Confrontation over Creation of Ukrainian Popular Front," *Report on the USSR*, March 3, 1989, 15.

19. *Radian'ska Ukraina*, May 17, 1989.

20. See David Marples, "The Ukrainian Election Campaign: The Opposition," *Report on the USSR*, March 9, 1990, 17.

21. *Radian'ska Ukraina*, November 15 and 17, 1990.

22. Bohdan Nahaylo and Kathleen Mihalisko, "Interview with Ukrainian Supreme Soviet Chairman Leonid Kravchuk," *Report on the USSR*, November 23, 1990, 15.

23. Of the 1,109 founding members of Rukh, 72 percent had a higher education; 11.6 percent were candidates and doctors of science. See Marples, "Sociological Survey," 18. In parliament, 65 percent of the Peoples' Council came from the intelligentsia, as opposed to 5 percent of the Group of 239. See Dominique Arel, "The Parliamentary Blocs in the Ukrainian Supreme Soviet: Who and What Do They Represent?" *Journal of Soviet Nationalities* 1 (Winter 1990–91):111.

24. Kathleen Mihalisko, "Ukraine's Declaration of Sovereignty," *Report on the USSR*, July 27, 1990, 17–19.

25. Drach interview, in Solchanyk, *Ukraine*, 50.

26. *Za Vil'nu Ukrainu*, March 5, 1991. Also see Roman Solchanyk, "Ukraine and the Union Treaty," *Report on the USSR*, July 26, 1991, 22–24.

27. Bohdan Krawchenko, "Ukraine: The Politics of Independence," in *Nations and Politics*, ed. Bremmer and Taras, 81–82. Also see Nadia Diuk and Adrian Karatnycky, *New Nations Rising: The Fall of the Soviets and the Challenge of Independence* (New York: Wiley, 1993), chapter on Ukraine.

6

From Evil Empire to Democratic Capitalism
Alternative Russian Futures

NILS H. WESSELL*

The dramatic events in Eastern Europe and the Soviet Union since 1989 have induced an appropriate humility among specialists in that anachronistic field once known as communist political systems. Who dared in the 1960s to be optimistic about the prospects for communism's collapse in the motherland of socialism? Perhaps only the late Andrei Amalrik, who, in writing the 1969 book *Will the Soviet Union Survive Until 1984?*, was off by only seven years. More typically, Henry Kissinger, justifying the SALT I accords, suggested in 1972 that Western democracies did not have the political stamina to sustain an arms race with the Soviet Union.

Perhaps some specialists had become too specialized. How many times did we not find hopeful implications in still another joint decree of the CPSU Central Committee and USSR Supreme Soviet that purported to expand the role of the raion soviet? How many treatises were produced by Soviet authors titled *Mestnye sovety na sovremennom etape* [Local soviets in the present stage]? Whatever the number—and it must be in the hundreds—overly close reading of them resulted in nearsightedness.

Based on this track record, readers may wish at this juncture to move on. But as a wag once said, the trick to forecasting is to keep forecasting. Expanding on this injunction, what follows is not a single prediction of the future but several alternatives.

Although some commentators warn of the danger of fascism in Russia, I propose to dismiss this scenario at the outset. To be sure, a hurt nationalism and economic chaos, exploited by a populist demagogue widely perceived as a buffoon, are attributes shared in common by both the Weimar Republic and postcommunist Russia. But strictly speaking, fascism in Russia would require a return to the totalitarian model, this time from the right. In the classic definition of Carl J. Friedrich and Zbigniew K. Brzezinski, the triumph of fascism would require an ideologically stimulated transformation of Russian society

*The views presented in this paper represent the views solely of the author and not necessarily of the U.S. Coast Guard Academy, the U.S. Coast Guard, or the U.S. Government.

that, running into obstacles, would prompt the leader of the ruling party to employ violence not just against society but also against internal opposition within the fascist movement. Fascist leaders then complete a revolutionary social transformation, atomizing, as it were, everyone in their way. So the totalitarian model is a demanding standard to meet. Moreover, Russian society differs from Weimar in having already experienced seven decades of totalitarianism, an experience against which it is now reacting.

This essay therefore focuses on four other alternatives. For the sake of clarity, it violates the first rule of forecasting: never give a date to your forecast. The following scenarios are meant to be applicable to a five-year period beginning in 1997: (1) Muddling Through in Permanence; (2) Putsch III Succeeds: Reversion to the Mean; (3) Yugoslavia on a Grand Scale: Disintegration and Civil War; (4) Locke-Smith Breakout: Democratic Capitalist Utopia.

MUDDLING THROUGH IN PERMANENCE

The first alternative future facing Russia is the persistence of the paradigm since 1985: a continuing revolution but a revolution from above.

Yeltsin has initiated more fundamental political change than Gorbachev. Far-reaching decrees are issued, but the reality of social and economic decline scarcely changes. The political realm has seen dramatic change under Yeltsin, but the democratically elected president has powers not so different from those of previous CPSU general secretaries. As characteristically dour Russians lament, it has been "a revolution without change."

Politics

In this scenario, Yeltsin remains in office but, like Gorbachev, must share power with the legislative branch. Despite heavy odds, the communists, nationalists, and even parliament have recovered. Economic privation has revived their reputations as protectors of the comforting safety net of state socialism. Faced with a hostile bloc sometimes coalescing into a majority in the state Duma, Yeltsin in this scenario once again compromises his program to appease his opponents. Yeltsin is committed to more radical free market reforms than Gorbachev the committed socialist could stomach. But over a period of months or years, the red-brown parliament, like its predecessor, ends up in opposition to Yeltsin and stymies reform.

Still, Yeltsin is bolder than Gorbachev. After all, Yeltsin has dared to face popular election, has freed prices, and has legalized private farms, three bones that stuck in Gorbachev's throat. Above all, Yeltsin does not have a reactionary Communist Party apparatus dogging him, and he has not put reactionary enemies in charge of the three pillars of institutional violence: the Ministries of Defense, Internal Affairs, and Security. But Yeltsin is hemmed in. After all, his life and the future of democracy in Russia hung for several hours during the August 1991 putsch on the slender thread of the unwillingness of the Alpha unit to storm the White House. Two years later, with power briefly lying in the streets, he was saved again by military forces. Yeltsin can hardly ignore the concerns of the defense and security apparatus.

Economy

Yeltsin's delay in privatizing the state monopolies and freeing the domestic price of oil mirrored Gorbachev's reluctance to adopt the Shatalin Plan. Under Yeltsin nomenklatura privatization—as management buys up employee vouchers—continues under protection of law. Public monopolies are transformed into private monopolies. Plucky entrepreneurs dare to open only small retail shops. In the countryside state farms find it painless to obey Yeltsin's decree to turn 10 percent of their land over to private farmers. But mimicking the nineteenth-century redistribution of the land after emancipation of the serfs, the state and collective farms keep the arable land and make the gulleys available to the new private farmers. Not that there are many takers. The kolkhozniks elect to stay in the collective farms and avoid the risks of private farming: the vagaries of bad weather, the unavailability of feed on the open market, and price uncertainties. As state farm employees in Nizhny Novgorod shouted at their would-be benefactor when he offered them various options, "We don't want any choice!"[1]

The failure to create competitive private enterprise spells doom for economic performance. The gross domestic product erodes further. Food supplies remain short, and many prices are too high for urban workers. The class consciousness of the working class rises as a privileged bourgeoisie flaunts its wealth, founded on joint ventures with foreign suppliers of capital. Socialism, tarnished by seventy-four years of Leninism, reacquires its luster.

Military

Persistence of the status quo means the failure of attempts by the CIS to maintain or reestablish control of all armed forces of the former Soviet Union. Conventional military assets, if not already lost, slip into the hands of the former republics. Although strategic nuclear weapons have been returned to Russia's control as pledged, strategic delivery systems remain in place.

Ethnic Relations

Political relations between Moscow and the former republics improve but at the expense of the center's authority. Russia grudgingly accepts its lost hegemony, preventing the outbreak of civil war. But internecine strife between non-Russian ethnic groups intensifies as Russian armed forces are withdrawn from hot spots in the Caucasus and Moldova.

Russian relations with the Baltic countries continue to be bedeviled by issues of national sensitivity, including their lobbying of NATO for full membership. Protracted negotiations on the treatment of ethnic Russians in Latvia and Estonia take place against the backdrop of struggling economies, the elimination of cheap Russian energy supplies, and the collapse of the Russian market for exports.

To the extent that its control of territories once part of the Soviet Union permits, Russia ratifies and implements in good faith international arms control agreements, including START II and CFE accords. It is not a tidy world for NATO, but the benefits of Russia's halting transformation far outweigh the nagging doubts and uncertainties.

PUTSCH III SUCCEEDS: REVERSION TO THE MEAN

The situation in 2002 will be no more stable than the value of the ruble. The subversive impulse of reform sets centrifugal forces into a widening gyre of instability. The "parliamentary revolt" of October 1993 was no accident. The center—Yeltsin—cannot hold. Led by a general able to command the loyalty of the armed forces, reactionaries allied with the secret police, whatever their name, coordinate a third putsch. Remedying the technical defects of the August 1991 and October 1993 attempts to seize power, they remove Yeltsin from the scene and create an emergency government of national unity. Russian politics reverts to the mean in Russian history: authoritarian, but not totalitarian, government.

Just as the liberalizing regimes of Catherine the Great, Alexander I, and Alexander II succumbed to reaction, so the fitfully liberal regimes of Gorbachev and Yeltsin will inevitably be followed by a conservative reaction.

As a reformer Yeltsin shares the fate of Aleksandr Kerensky, unable to marshal popular support in behalf of freedom and democracy. His regime will have discredited itself by reintroducing the principle of economic inequality into a society where envy outweighs ambition. Russian workers, subjected to 2,000 percent price hikes in one year, will not rise to Yeltsin's defense any more than they rose to his defense (or Gorbachev's) during the August and October putsches. Few blue-collar workers defended the Russian White House in 1991 or the Kremlin two years later.

Economy

After Putsch III the military-KGB emergency committee acts to reverse the economic decline by reviving central planning. The generals have learned the lesson of the Gorbachev era that economic disintegration is the handmaiden of political disintegration. Moreover, they know that political authority collapsed in communist Poland when the regime lost control of the economy.

The commanding heights of the economy will be easy to seize. Few state monopolies have been truly privatized. Those that have been are in the hands of their former managers, the nomenklatura. A return to the system of state orders, however imperfect, halts economic anarchy. The Russian public, yearning for the security of a return to economic serfdom, applauds the end of chaotic experiments in free market economics.

Slav Federation Restored by Force

In the Putsch III scenario, a general, perhaps in mufti, promises the preservation of the Russian national state, which he defines to include Ukraine and Belorussia (Belarus is a tractor, he notes).

Although the preservation of a Slavic federation may be the maximum territorial objective of this junta, the effort to regather the Russian lands is not a surgical operation. Belarus, on whose territory nearly 1,850 main battle tanks were once deployed, will pose the danger that this skirmish between the Slavs might spill over. Its two Baltic neighbors, Latvia and Lithuania, will harbor Belarusian freedom fighters, not necessarily by choice. In this scenario Russian incursions into Belarusian resistance sanctuaries in the Baltic states succeed with minimal bloodshed. Indignation in Scandinavia is tempered by sighs of relief that the conflict will not spread.

The major uncertainty for the new military junta is whether the newly formed Ukrainian armed forces will mount coordinated and effective resistance. Former St. Petersburg mayor Anatoli Sobchak once warned that independent Ukrainian armed forces would pose "a huge threat to mankind." As one observer remarked, it is a mystery why a Ukrainian army would be more threatening to the world than a Russian or CIS army.[2] But there is no mystery why a Ukrainian army might be a threat to Russian ambitions to reintegrate Ukraine into a Slavic federation. As late as 1994, Ukraine was host to an army of almost five hundred thousand (closer to one million if Border Forces, the National Guard, and security services are included). But a year earlier only 40 percent of the troops were ethnic Ukrainians, according to the CIS General Staff. Still worse from Kiev's standpoint, only 25 percent of the officers stationed in Ukraine were ethnic Ukrainians.[3]

Although it is possible that neither Moscow nor Kiev feels very confident about the loyalty of these forces, the greatest danger is that *both* may feel confident of their loyalty. In the Putsch III scenario Moscow's confidence in the loyalty of the troops is vindicated. Russian dominance of the Slavic federation is implemented by force quickly enough to prevent a prolonged and bloody civil war.

Black Sea Fleet and Shipbuilding Capabilities

Larger than the British, French, or Italian navies, the Black Sea Fleet consists of more than eight hundred ships, of which four hundred are major vessels, including three cruisers carrying guided missiles with nuclear warheads, two aircraft carriers/helicopter cruisers,[4] and at least sixty nuclear-capable Backfire bombers. In addition, the fleet commands a brigade of marines stationed at Sevastopol and a motorized rifle division at Simferopol for coastal defense.

The well-publicized quarrel between Moscow and Kiev over the fleet has already led to a statistics war. Admiral Igor Kasatonov, commander of the Black Sea Fleet until replaced by Vice-Admiral Eduard Baltin in 1993 and a strong advocate of Russian control over it, once insisted that only 30 percent of the sailors under his command were ethnic Ukrainians. A Ukraine spokesmen three days later insisted that 60 percent of Black Sea sailors were Ukrainian. And where Admiral Kasatonov found only 19 percent of his officers to be Ukrainian, Kiev claimed 30 percent.

Demographics aside, speculating on the political loyalties of the sailors who man the fleet will be a high-stakes game. The officers in the fleet have given several indications that they oppose division of the fleet, including the Yeltsin-Kravchuk agreement in June 1993 conceding 50 percent of the fleet to Ukraine. Even Admiral Baltin, jointly appointed by the two presidents and presumably more pliable than Kasatonov, criticized the agreement in principle to divide the fleet evenly. In May 1994 Ukraine agreed to claim only 20 percent of the fleet if Russia would "buy" the balance of its "half."[5]

The stakes are higher than just the existing fleet. Ukrainian territory is home to half the former Soviet Union's capacity for building large ships. Those yards are now under Ukraine's control. The Black Sea Shipyard at Mykolaiv (formerly Nikolaev) is the only yard that has built aircraft carriers/helicopter cruisers.[6] Unfortunately for the Russians, who regard Crimea as Russian territory frivolously given away to Ukraine in 1954, a third large shipyard that mainly builds destroyers is located in the Crimean town of Kerch.

In the Putsch III scenario, the Muscovite junta, reversing Yeltsin's refusal to claim the Crimea, seizes Sevastopol, the headquarters of the Black Sea Fleet, and Simferopol. The naval infantry and motorized rifle division, the latter having reportedly raised the Russian naval ensign on July 1, 1993, declare their loyalty to Moscow. In fact, the junta will probably seize not just the rest of the peninsula, occupied by Catherine the Great in 1770, but the entire Ukrainian coast, including the big naval base in Odessa.

In the Putsch III scenario the Russians will also maintain control of Black Sea Fleet naval facilities on the Georgian coast. After a brief respite under the tutelage of Eduard Shevardnadze, an unusual Georgian for being a democrat, resurgent political chaos in Georgia and the presence of an aggrieved Abkhazian minority on either side of Sukhumi will provide Moscow with the opportunity and leverage it needs to reassert control of Georgia's Black Sea coastline.

Nuclear Weapons

The fate of Soviet strategic nuclear weapons stationed in Ukraine was, of course, the big enchilada for Moscow, Washington, and NATO. Since the stated purpose of the coup will be to reintegrate the eastern Slavs into a single state, the leader of the Moscow junta will be obsessed with the maintenance of the non-nuclear status of Ukraine and Belarus as long as they remain independent. Under Muscovite pressure, they will continue to renounce any intentions to acquire strategic or tactical nuclear weapons but with new provisos that will unsettle Moscow.

Outside the Slavic States

In this spirit, the junta declares a policy of recognizing only the sovereignty, not the independence, of the former Soviet republics. But the generals sense it is far too late to restore the Soviet Union. An already demoralized Russian army seeking to revive the USSR by force will have to fight several small wars on widely scattered fronts in circumstances ideal for guerrilla warfare. Faced with the need to garrison troops in the midst of overwhelmingly hostile indigenous populations in any of the Baltic states, the Caucasus, and much of former Soviet Central Asia, the Muscovite junta will fear intervention by Iran, Turkey, and other states in the Middle East and Central Europe. So the generals limit their territorial objectives to Ukraine, Belarus, the Baltic states, northern Kazakhstan, and probably those districts of Moldova where ethnic Russians predominate.

Without resort to mass violence, the coup leaders will treat Georgian independence as negotiable, that is, subject to subversion by political intrigue and by military assistance to forces friendly to a restored union. The negotiability of Georgian independence was amply demonstrated in October 1993, when a desperate President Shevardnadze applied for membership in the CIS in return for Yeltsin's deploying Russian troops to safeguard key installations while Georgian troops finally suppressed the forces of rebel psychotic democrat Zviad Gamsakhurdia.[7]

In this scenario, the Russian generals, like their Serb counterparts, undertake political-military operations to protect ethnic Russians in the diaspora. Estonia, Latvia, and Lithuania are subjected to a wide range of political and military pressures. Russian forces withdrawn completely from Estonia, Latvia, and eastern Germany in mid-1994 are redeployed to Kaliningrad, alarming the Poles as well as the Baltic states. Moscow demands renewed access to strategic naval and air defense assets in the Baltic.

As a result of these steps, involving some use of force by Moscow but not systemic civil war, a central purpose of the military-KGB coup will have been achieved: to restore the unity of the historic Russian state founded in Kiev one thousand years ago and to reestablish Russian authority over much, but not all, of the territory acquired by later tsars.

Yugoslavia on a Grand Scale: Disintegration and Civil War

Everyone's worst fears are realized in the third alternative future. Modeled after Yugoslavia but on a grander scale, it is a nightmare scenario not only for Russians but also for Western Europe, NATO, the United States, and perhaps the rest of the world. Although the Yugoslav scenario might result from the Putsch III alternative, it could also follow directly from a deterioration of the present situation. Because civil war has broken out, the political leadership of the CIS might best be described as a hydra-headed monster. And whatever the collection of leaders in Ukraine, Belarus, Kazakhstan, Georgia, and Armenia, once civil conflict becomes pandemic, they are unlikely to be democrats, at least for very long.

Economy

In 1995 Prime Minister Viktor Chernomyrdin tolerated a further decline in industrial production so as to rein in the previous year's annual inflation rate of 215 percent. In the Yugoslav scenario, to stem the ruble's free fall, Yeltsin withdraws state subsidies to enterprises. Private employers, unable to survive the padded payrolls that had been bankrupting the Russian state, act on managers' estimates that 25 percent of their workers are redundant.[8] The jobless rate rises from 4 percent to 15 percent.

In conditions of Yugoslavia-like economic and political instability, those foreign investors who began nibbling at Russian assets in 1994 do not walk away from Russia. They run. Since economic backwardness is just another name for capital shortage and Russia desperately needs capital from abroad, this situation suggests that Russia's centuries-long economic backwardness will persist indefinitely into the future.

Ethnic Warfare

Despite the precarious independence such a scenario implies for the newly independent states of the former Soviet Union, the Yugoslav model is not a happy outcome for them either. Independence has been declared by these states, international recognition has followed, but the essential ingredient of statehood is missing: physical control of one's territory. The Muscovite center uses force in an attempt to reconquer the lost lands of the Soviet empire.

In the Putsch III scenario the CIS has fallen apart and disappeared, but a Slavic state has been revived. In the Yugoslav model the Slavic state also falls apart. A glance at a map of the Russian Federation shows the potential geographic scope of its disintegration. If all the ethnic minority political subunits are subtracted, the Russian Federation loses 51 percent of its territory.

The political morass that would be superimposed on top of interethnic conflict is suggested by the demographics. Eighteen percent of the people living in the Russian Federation are non-Russian. Ethnic Russians living in the newly independent states and in the minority regions of the Russian Federation are at once a privileged elite, a threatened minority, and a potential fifth column. They make up 22 percent of Ukraine's population, 38 percent of Kazakhstan's, 34 percent of Latvia's, and 30 percent of Estonia's.

In the Yugoslav scenario, Russian and Ukrainian disputes over minority rights, territory, and military assets spill over into the international arena, igniting a major conflict between Ukraine and Russia. Moscow may or may not be able to exercise effective operational control over tank armies in Ukraine. In 1992 General Konstantin Kobets, deputy minister of defense for the Russian Federation, noted that 30 percent of CIS tanks were deployed in Ukraine and only 28 percent in Russia.[9] Whereas in the Putsch III scenario Russia is able to subdue Ukraine with relative ease as military units rally to Moscow, in this scenario the Ukrainian government wins the allegiance of enough units to force Moscow into a bloody conflict.

Civil conflict is scarcely less dangerous elsewhere in the former CIS. The Russian government exerts military pressure on the Baltic states for strategic reasons: to avoid the Baltic Fleet's being bottled up in the Gulf of Finland, to regain early warning and air defense assets, and to secure a logistical corridor to Kaliningrad (not yet renamed Königsburg). Moreover, Belarusian territory is contested. Even if Moscow shrinks from invading Estonia, Latvia, and Lithuania, incursions by the Russian army into Belarusian resistance sanctuaries along the border with Lithuania motivate Poland and one or more of the Nordic countries to provide financial and clandestine military support to the Baltic states. For the first time in more than fifty years, war casts its shadow across Helsinki, Stockholm, Oslo, and Copenhagen.

Some people will object that this is an unrealistic and alarmist scenario. Some people—many Yugoslavs—objected a decade ago to any speculation that Yugoslavia might disintegrate after Tito. We may expect similar assurances with respect to the unlikely prospect of ethnic civil war between Russians and non-Russians, bolstered by the observation that to date such conflicts have been fought largely between non-Russians and non-Russians. Events in Chechnya already have undermined such assurances. In Moldova, moreover, Russian communists have sought to seize control of the eastern side of the Dnestr River and some territory on the right (or western) side with the tacit support of the Russian Fourteenth Army and with the acquiescence of Yeltsin. Ominously, Romania has reciprocated by providing Moldova with limited amounts of outdated military equipment, raising the specter of a potential interstate conflict.[10]

Soviet nuclear weapons, including several tactical nuclear weapons that escaped inventory controls when the others were returned to Moscow, are likely to command the attention of Western military planners. In the Yugoslav model it may be assumed that unless all nuclear weapons are under effective Russian control, they will be used at least as bargaining chips by nationalists seeking to throw off the Russian yoke. That may be the best case scenario. A worse case is their threatened use, with unknown effect on the calculations of the Russian General Staff. The worst case—actual use—is beyond the comprehension of people not specializing in battlefield use of such weapons.

LOCKE-SMITH BREAKOUT: DEMOCRATIC CAPITALIST UTOPIA

It is a function of Russia's unhappy history that the three scenarios sketched above share pessimism in common. This penchant for pessimism is so characteristic of Russian political culture that it has also infected many Western students of Russia and was partly responsible for the poor forecasting record of Sovietologists on the threshold of the Gorbachev era. Almost to a person we discounted the possibility that a Russian Dubcek could be lurking in the shadows of the Central Committee. Because even pessimism can be overdone, it may be advisable to try to imagine a better future for Russia. We do so even at the risk of sounding like the typically optimistic American whom Andrei Amalrik accused of having a naive faith in history as an unbroken line of progress in which reasonable people act for the common good.

In the Locke-Smith Breakout scenario, democratic capitalism emerges in Russia. John Locke's ideas of natural rights, the consent of the governed, limited government, and the indispensability of private property to political freedom find realization in the practice of the Russian state. Boris Yeltsin remains popular and in power. Yeltsin may not curl up in bed at night with a copy of *Two Treatises on Civil Government* as Catherine the Great was known to do with Montesquieu's *The Spirit of the Laws*, but the political result is the same as if he did. Unlike Catherine, he does not turn sour on the Enlightenment and reempower the lords of the manor to flog the serfs. In fact, the Locke-Smith scenario is Yeltsin's vision of Russia: a united, revitalized Russia, democratic and federal. In the economy, Adam Smith triumphs over both Karl Marx and Eduard Bernstein. The economic bureaucracy of Marxist socialism is dismantled. The transition to genuinely competitive capitalism is accelerated. Although capitalism is loosely regulated by the government and some social safety nets are erected, the invisible hand of economic self-interest is allowed to operate with enough freedom to assure some degree of progress toward a common prosperity.

The political democratization of the country, symbolized by Boris Yeltsin's victory in the July 1996 popular election as Russian president, proceeds apace. Popularly elected local officials committed to grass-roots democracy oust communist holdovers. Just as important, political parties committed to the democratic process bloom in Moscow and in the innumerable cities, towns, and villages thoughout Russia. Social democrats, Christian democrats, constitutional democrats, and conservatives form no more than four coherent parties with substantial public followings. Only the communists are unable to rise from the ashes. In the executive branch the nomenklatura fails to find organizational leverage. In this flowering of self-governing institutions, Alexis de Tocqueville's description of nineteenth-century America moves toward realization in Russia: everywhere Russians take the initiative to create local groups for civic improvement. Peasant distrust of authority yields to a grudging recognition of the benefits of joint action. The cooperative aspects of the *mir* reassert themselves in peasant psychology, but the social control functions of the *kolkhoz* disappear.

Economics

National and local officials create a level playing field for budding Russian entrepreneurs. The street vendors—former *fartsovshchiki* and *mazhery*—capitalize on the privatization of local retailing and daily services. Nomenklatura privatization is forbidden. The former communist regime's economic managers lose their stranglehold on the economy as leveraged buyouts by insiders are replaced by voucher capitalism. The control of the licensing process and enforcement of economic regulations by the mafia of corrupt officials is broken. The motley crew of enforcers in the underground economy is driven out of business by sunshine laws and free competition in the marketplace.

Foreign capital, long poised to enter this immense and undeveloped market, pours in as a result of favorable business conditions and political stability. The McDonald's on Pushkin Square finally turns a profit in rubles freely convertible into dollars for repatriation. McDonald's transfers the Moscow store from the company's public relations budget to the operating budget, and golden arches sprout like mushrooms over the Russian landscape. As Gorky Park gets a facelift, rumors sweep the capital that Mickey, Daffy, and Goofy are on their way to Russia.

In the countryside the peasant has been given the land with no strings attached and with a title to pass on to his heirs. A peasant smallholder class is allowed to develop and is permitted to charge market prices for its agricultural products. A growing class of small farmers prospers, and the cities are bountifully supplied with food at reasonable prices.

Ethnic Relations

The triumph of political and economic laissez-faire has spread to non-Russian lands throughout the CIS. The Georgian government embraces the 1992 slogan of the Georgian Greens, "A Common Caucasus Home." Political instability in Georgia abates, the rights of the aggrieved Abkhazian minority are recognized, and Shevardnadze cements a mutually advantageous economic union and security relationship with Moscow. Moscow becomes a magnet for the former republics of the Soviet Union. They eagerly agree in principle to a common market and, after difficult negotiations on the details, sign economic agreements creating a regime of free trade throughout the CIS.

Russia plays an exemplary role in allowing national self-determination for those who want it. Having been given the freedom to leave Moscow's embrace, few ethnic groups now feel the compulsion to do so. Moscow's authority, though loose, is finally respected.

Military

In this peaceable kingdom of Henri (not Jean-Jacques) Rousseau, the historic Russian need for a large army no longer objectively exists. Military threats from the West, whose values are now widely shared by Russians, have become historical curiosities testifying to the self-fulfilling nature of three decades of Andrei Gromyko's threat analyses. Low morale in the officer corps, housing shortages, and the intractable obstacles to converting the military-industrial complex to civilian production slow the pace of Russian demilitarization but do not alter its fundamental direction.

The easing of East-West tensions is no longer the subject of thoughtful analysis in the West European press. Peace is taken for granted between East and West. The size of the Russian army is not a matter of much international interest. Russian defense minister Andrei Kokoshin, promoted to ensure civilian control of the military after preparatory service as a first deputy defense minister, has adopted a new defensive military doctrine for the Russian state. To this end he has created a rapid deployment force, stationed east of the Urals, to repel external aggression in cases of emergency. The tank armies, "a dinosaur from World War II," according to Kokoshin,[11] have been converted to scrap iron, their engines powering a fleet of heavy trucks exported to the West. The navy is no longer a troublesome issue. Ukraine and Russia agree to subordinate the Black Sea Fleet to the CIS Ministry of Defense. Since the U.S. Navy would appear to be the only force that could interfere with maritime commerce, the rationale for maintaining a large navy dissolves. In a sea of Russo-American goodwill, Russia joins a newly created North Atlantic Eur-Asian Treaty Organization (NEATO).

CONCLUSION

The Locke-Smith Breakout scenario is obviously the scenario Western democracies would most welcome. Moreover, it is the stated policy of the Yeltsin government to move in this direction. But it also requires a fundamental transformation of the Russian state and a profound redefinition of Russian values and national interests. Representing the most dramatic break with the Russian past, it would also require the greatest amount of cooperation and financial support from the West and from Japan.

The dilemma for Western security is that the most desirable outcome is not necessarily the most likely one. Muddling through in permanence is not bad from the Western standpoint. With inflation roaring and the ruble volatile, muddling through implies that the hard decisions—and their consequences—have been merely postponed. So the first scenario is the most likely in the short term, but it is less likely over the five years of the forecast period.

Is, then, a replay of October 1993 or August 1991 the most likely outcome? The State Committee for the State of Emergency (GKChP) was not accidental: the disintegration of order in the country made the August putsch inevitable. Its acceleration after August 1991 strengthened the objective grounds for another coup. Once the residual deterrent effect of the failure of the "October events" and the August putsch has worn off, we may expect further instability. Because the plotters will have learned from the earlier failure, it is more likely that Putsch III will be successful—except that Yeltsin has also learned from experience.

Yeltsin has learned two things, we may speculate. First, not to think he can forestall a coup by putting political opponents into office. While Yeltsin may have violated this principle in elevating Alexander Lebed to the post of secretary of the Security Council, his prompt dismissal after he had served Yeltsin's purposes reinforces the impression of a lesson learned. So Yeltsin, having already picked as his running mate before the August putsch a vice-president with Yanaev-like sympathies, will keep the ministries of defense, security, and internal affairs in friendly hands. During the "October events" Yeltsin relied very publicly on the chiefs of these three ministries. His firing in July 1993 of

Viktor Barannikov as minister of security following his reputed secret meeting with Khasbulatov and Rutskoi seemed rash at the time. But Barannikov's later acceptance of Rutskoi's naming him *his* minister of security confirmed Yeltsin's judgment.

The second lesson Yeltsin is likely to have learned from October 1993 and August 1991 is to strike first. The Duma and Federation Council, forming the bicameral Federal Assembly, may ultimately prove as independent as the Congress of Peoples' Deputies that in 1990 elected Yeltsin its chairman and then authorized the popular vote for president that he won. In any case, the economy is unlikely to stabilize quickly. If discontent in society is matched by rumblings in the military and that boiling resentment coalesces around a program of action, the next round of extraconstitutional struggle will likely be a bloodbath. To forestall it, Yelstin may be tempted to abandon his cacaphonous democratic allies and rule by decree and plebiscite under constitutional provisions for a state of emergency, allowing him to maintain foreign support as a revolutionary democrat in Napoleonic clothing.

And so the single most likely outcome may be a variant of the Putsch III scenario: a replay not of the August putsch or the parliamentary revolt but of the paranoid misinterpretation of those attempted seizures of power that had Gorbachev (August) and Yeltsin (October) masterminding affairs to enhance their own authority.

Would such an outcome lead to Scenario 3 or Scenario 4, a Yugoslav civil war or a democratic capitalist utopia? Yeltsin would likely insist on the continuity of his vision represented by the Locke-Smith Breakout. In this case, the Pinochet model of political authoritarianism and free market economics might be realized. But given the scope of economic, social, and political disintegration that would have to have taken place before Yeltsin would seize the mantle of Bonapartism, it seems probable that by then Russia would be on the brink of civil war. This is an eventuality with which the United States, NATO, and the West are not prepared to deal, a circumstance that underscores the importance of thinking about the unthinkable.

Finally it would be rash to assume that no exogenous event or chance occurrence will upset rational calculations of future alternatives. If the violence of 1991 and 1993 suggested that Russia was only a sniper's bullet away from chaos, Yeltsin's heart bypass operation reminded us that medical uncertainties can themselves create unexpected political tumult.

NOTES

1. Elisabeth Rubinfien, "Russia Moves to Dismantle Collective-Farming System," *Wall Street Journal*, October 27, 1993.

2. Roman Solchanyk, "Ukraine," *RFE/RL Research Report*, February 14, 1992, 4.

3. Stephen Foye, "Civilian-Military Tension in Ukraine," *RFE/RL Research Report*, June 18, 1993, 62; and his "CIS: Kiev and Moscow Clash over Armed Forces," *RFE/RL Research Report*, January 17, 1992, 2.

4. *The Military Balance, 1992–1993* (London: International Institute for Strategic Studies, 1992), 96; and Douglas L. Clarke, "The Saga of the Black Sea Fleet," *RFE/RL Research Report*, January 24, 1992, 45.

5. Ustina Markus, "Stability and Political Turnover," *Transition*, February 15, 1995, 69; John W. R. Lepingwell, "The Black Sea Fleet Agreement: Progress or Empty Promises?," *RFE/RL Research Report*, July 9, 1993, 51–54; Douglas L. Clarke, "Military and Security Notes," *RFE/RL Research Report*, February 28, 1992, 50; FBIS, Daily Report, Central Eurasia, September 20, 1993, 16; and "Ukraine to Cede to Russia Its Part of Black Sea Fleet," *Wall Street Journal*, September 7, 1993.

6. Douglas L. Clarke, "Rusting Fleet Renews Debate on Navy's Mission," *RFE/RL Research Report*, June 18, 1993, 30.

7. Raymond Bonner, "Shevardnadze Enters Stronghold Recaptured from Foes in Georgia," *New York Times*, November 8, 1993; Melor Sturua, "Yeltsin's Newest Proconsul," *New York Times*, October 27, 1993; and Claudia Rosett, "Shevardnadze Finds Fine-Honed Diplomatic Arts Can't Feed His Crumbling and War-Torn Georgia," *Wall Street Journal*, November 2, 1993.

8. *New York Times*, March 31, 1992.

9. Douglas L. Clarke, "Military and Security Notes," *RFE/RL Research Report*, February 28, 1992, 51.

10. Vladimir Socor, "Russia's Fourteenth Army and the Insurgency in Eastern Moldova," *RFE/RL Research Report*, September 11, 1992, 41–48; and his "Creeping Putsch in Eastern Moldova," *RFE/RL Research Report*, January 17, 1992, 8–13.

11. *Krasnaya zvezda*, March 17, 1992.

7

Balkan Politics in Transition
Nationalism and the Emergence of Ethnic Democracies

LENARD J. COHEN

NEW CARTOGRAPHY, NEW CHALLENGES

The violent disintegration of the "Second Yugoslavia," which began in mid-1991 and continued unabated in several regions of the former country through 1994, profoundly altered the political map of the Balkan peninsula. Two of the republics that had formed part of the former federation, Croatia and Slovenia, established their independence through unilateral "disassociation" from the Yugoslav state and, despite armed struggles that ensued on their territories, were soon recognized by the international community. Although military conflict in Slovenia ended rapidly—following the withdrawal of federal armed forces and a cease-fire negotiated by the European Community—protracted fighting in Croatia led to the breakaway of several predominantly Serbian enclaves from the control of the Zagreb government. By the end of 1994, the Croatian government had still not managed to reintegrate these largely non-urban Serbian population areas (which organized themselves into the so-called Republika Srpska Krajina) by either diplomatic or military means.

The former Yugoslav republic of Bosnia-Hercegovina also acquired international recognition as a sovereign state, but that development precipitated a savage war between and among the region's principal ethno-religious groups (first between a Moslem-Croat alliance and the Serbs, then among all three sides with particularly intense Moslem-Croat hostilities, followed by a return to the first pattern), assisted to varying degrees by outside forces. By the second half of 1994 the conflict had resulted in the bifurcation of Bosnia-Hercegovina into a new Moslem-Croat federal entity and a separate Serbian entity (Republika Srpska). Successive internationally mediated plans designed to bring an end to the fighting in Bosnia-Hercegovina and to preserve the state as a loose confederation encompassing its three principal ethnic communities all foundered in the face of the main protagonists' continuing intransigence and mutual mistrust. During the fall of 1994, Bosnian Serb objections blocked acceptance of a peace plan that had been drawn up by the Contact Group (composed of the United States, Russia, France, Germany, and the United

Kingdom), but as 1995 approached the possibilities for a politically negotiated settlement of the conflict improved slightly.*

In Macedonia, which had effectively become independent of the former Yugoslavia with the adoption of a new constitution in November 1991, efforts to establish the new state proved extremely difficult owing to strong opposition from neighboring Greece. Athens's resistance was derived from its fear that the newly proclaimed Republic of Macedonia was likely to have aspirations toward acquiring Greek territory (especially the northern province of Macedonia) and Greek national symbols. Despite such complaints, Macedonia's status as an independent state became somewhat more secure during 1993 and 1994. For example, in April 1993, Macedonia was accepted as a member of the United Nations (UN) under the name Former Yugoslav Republic of Macedonia (FYROM), and by the fall of 1994 the new state had been recognized at some level by more than seventy countries. Macedonian security was also considerably enhanced by the deployment of approximately a thousand UN peacekeeping troops in the country (composed mainly of Nordic personnel but also including a three-hundred-person U.S. military contingent). Brief border incursions into the new country by troops from neighboring Yugoslavia created some alarm during 1994 but did not appear to pose a serious threat to Macedonia's survival.

International acceptance proved rather more difficult for the so-called "rump" or "Third Yugoslavia"—a remodeled two-unit federation composed of Serbia and Montenegro—which endeavored to inherit the diplomatic mantle of the former Yugoslav socialist state. The failure of this new, and much smaller, Yugoslavia to obtain legitimacy from the international community resulted from the widely held judgment that its principal political leader, Serbian president Slobodan Milošević, had masterminded military aggression against both Croatia and Bosnia-Hercegovina. During 1993 and 1994, Milošević worked hard to change his image by demonstrating cooperation with international efforts to resolve the hostilities in Bosnia and to find some solution to the Krajina problem in Croatia. But the Serbian leader, with his strident nationalism and authoritarian political style, remained a pariah to most of the international community.

The aftermath of socialist Yugoslavia's violent disintegration has continued to convulse the Balkan region. Moreover, beyond the battlefield in Bosnia and outside the incessant round of diplomatic negotiations to resolve the conflict, critical issues linked to the long-term establishment of peace and stability in the region remain. For example, within each of the fledgling Balkan

---

*This chapter was completed prior to Croatia's military reintegration of almost all the Krajina in May and August 1995 (only Eastern Slavonia remained outside Zagreb's control) and also before the negotiation of the Dayton Accord, which formally preserved a unified Bosnian state consisting of two "entities," a Moslem-Croat federation and the Republika Srpska.

successor states, the solution of many pressing internal political and socioeconomic problems has been, either directly or indirectly, complicated by the ongoing regional turmoil and disruption. Most significant in this regard have
been the difficulties associated with the two principal sectors of regime transition that preoccupied all the former one-party communist states in Eastern
Europe during the first half of the 1990s, namely, political democratization
and economic transformation.

Ultranationalism and Democratic Consolidation

The most serious threat to the institutionalization of democratic rule in each
of the successor states has been the salience of radical nationalism in political
life. The role of patriotic and nationalist sentiments in relation to democratic
political change throughout the Balkan region was not, of course, entirely re-
gressive. For example, nationalism significantly contributed to the dismantling of one-party monopoly rule in each of the republics during the twilight
of the Yugoslav communist regime and was also a pluralizing factor during
the 1990 multiparty elections. But the onset of armed struggles among various ethno-regional groups after mid-1991 and the consolidation of control by
powerful nationalist parties and elites in several of the successor states tended
to undermine the fuller development of stable competitive politics. In Bosnia,
for example, intense ethno-nationalist warfare precluded any pursuit of democratic development, and the political repercussions of radical nationalism in
both Croatia and Serbia, although less violent, had a similar antipluralist effect. In a formal sense, the nationalist leaders of the latter two states, Franjo
Tudjman and Slobodan Milošević, both operated in a competitive democratic
environment that included opposition party activity and contested elections.
But the authoritarian cast of their leadership styles, and particularly the various measures they employed to intimidate their critics, clearly reflected the
prepluralist environment in which both men had been politically socialized
and had made their early careers. Moreover, the nationalistic rhetoric and policy
initiatives of both leaders proved highly detrimental to intergroup harmony
and democratic evolution in their respective countries.

In the initial period following the collapse of the communist regime, the
prospects for democratic political development appeared more promising in
Croatia than in Serbia. During 1990, members of Croatian communist elite
circles responded to pressures for holding pluralist elections more rapidly than
their comrades in Belgrade, and the political forces that emerged on the Croatian
opposition landscape also appeared more vital and less fragmented than their
counterparts in Serbia. But the imperatives of the Serbian-Croatian war waged
on Croatian soil from July 1991 to January 1992, the subsequent fragile truce
and military preparations by the Zagreb government to reintegrate Croatian
territory remaining under Serbian minority control, and the deployment of

Croatian armed forces in the Bosnian conflict to assist the Bosnian Croats all tended to militarize Croatian society and limit pluralist politics. For example, in view of the prevailing hostilities, the Zagreb government maintained that it was justified in taking legal action against members of the media and opposition who were either critical of the ruling authorities or were regarded as a threat to the constitutional order. Such measures seriously chilled the atmosphere for the development of free political interplay and democratic pluralism.[1]

In presidential and legislative elections in Croatia during August 1992 and February 1993, Tudjman and his ruling political party, the Croatian Democratic Alliance (HDZ), once again emerged victorious in a competitive multiparty contest. The overall situation in the new state, however, could hardly be described as stable or conducive to further democratic evolution. Tudjman's campaign of political pressure against the extreme right-wing leader and member of parliament Dobroslav Paraga—whose Croatian Party of Rights (HSP) took 7 percent of the vote in the August 1992 legislative election—was clearly a punitive measure intended to weaken a political rival's competition for the ultranationalist portion of the electorate (although the extremist behavior of the Paraga forces provided some justification for Tudjman's moves against them). Acts of violence by the Croatian Defense Forces, the aggressively nationalistic and freewheeling paramilitary wing of Paraga's party, ostensibly justified the Tudjman regime's harsh treatment of Paraga as a subversive leader who had violated the country's constitutional norms. After being cleared of various legal charges by a civilian court in 1992, Paraga and a few of his henchmen again faced criminal charges in mid-1993, this time because of "terrorism and anti-constitutional activities," but again they were acquitted by a military court. By the summer of 1994 the Tudjman regime had effectively crippled the HSP, but special police units kept up pressure on the right-wing organization and its leaders.[2]

The most serious examples of illiberalism on the part of the Zagreb authorities was their persistent use of political, economic, and even judicial pressures against independent sectors of the Croatian media which criticized them.[3] The most egregious examples of such behavior (which did not include overt censorship) resulted in serious difficulties for the country's independent media, such as the weekly journal *Danas* and the daily *Slobodna Dalmacija*, and in the legal prosecution of individual journalists, such as the outspoken Jelena Lovrić. In December 1993, when the *Feral Tribune*, a satirical weekly in Split, published controversial "artwork"—the heads of Tudjman and Milošević on the bodies of two men stripped to the waist and snuggling in bed—the tabloid's editor in chief was drafted into the army. Unrepentant, the *Feral* used the same montage in March 1994, this time substituting Alija Izetbegović's head for

Milošević's. The regime's effort later in August 1994 to close down the publication by imposing a heavy "pornography tax" proved equally unsuccessful. The regime was also not reluctant to employ its own media outlets to ostracize journalists who were viewed as having an overly critical view of the authorities or who espoused a "Yugoslav" outlook. Such behavior has clearly been the hallmark of an insecure, thin-skinned regime and its top leader, unaccustomed to broad adherence to the norms of democratic pluralism.[4]

In the early 1990s, Milošević's regime in Belgrade proved even more adept than its counterpart in Zagreb at exploiting the Balkan atmosphere of radical nationalism and militarization to dampen pluralist development. Indeed, the negative impact of radical nationalism on democratic political life in Serbia and in the Third Yugoslavia after the collapse of the former federation in mid-1991 continued a trend that had been set by Milošević during the twilight of the one-party communist regime. Claiming that he was the only person who could ensure the unity of the Serbian people and protect Serbian interests in multi-ethnic settings such as Bosnia, Croatia, and Kosovo, Milošević cleverly mobilized and manipulated the patriotism and anxieties of Serbs both within and without the new borders of the rump Yugoslavia. But Milošević's decision to provide military assistance to the large diasporic Serbian community in neighboring Bosnia engendered international economic sanctions against Serbia that soon resulted in the country's isolation and economic deterioration. Exploiting the largely self-generated conditions of foreign pressure and domestic deprivation to legitimate his regime's survival, Milošević shrewdly appealed to the Serbian people for "patriotic" unity, "ethnic loyalty," and sacrifice. In addition to successfully mobilizing domestic support, such tactics proved to be an extremely effective means of politically marginalizing Serbia's already highly fragmented and weak opposition parties. Thus many moderate opposition leaders attempted to combine a patriotic platform with genuinely democratic beliefs, but their message was portrayed by Milošević as a betrayal of Serbian national interests.[5] Indeed, in efforts to assert their patriotic credentials, Serbian opposition leaders sometimes found themselves in the uncomfortable position of endorsing the minority policies espoused by the Milošević regime.

The weakness of Serbia's squabbling opposition parties was not solely related to their inability effectively to play the nationalist card against Milošević. The Serbian president also benefited enormously from his ruling Socialist Party's organizational experience and control over local power structures outside Belgrade, its access to Serbian governmental resources, and its control over the state-run media. Thus, following his victory in the December 1992 Serbian presidential and legislative elections, Milošević and his ruling party began a widespread purge of oppositionists from the state-controlled television and radio network. As in Croatia, where Tudjman's regime had earlier purged most Serbian personnel from the state media, Milošević used his electoral victory to carry out an ethnic purge of remaining Moslem and Croat employees. In a throwback to the practices of the collapsed single-party system, the regimes in both Belgrade and Zagreb viewed any unconventional expression and strong criticism of the ruling authorities as an abuse of democracy rather than as a crucial pillar of democratic development.[6] Vibrant islands of independent media activity flourished in both capitals, but such critical voices were often subjected to pressure and harassment by the regime.[7]

Democratic change in both Serbia and Croatia was also seriously obstructed by intolerant regime-sponsored policies and practices regarding ethnic minorities. For example, the decision by officials in Belgrade to curtail the political autonomy of Serbia's province of Kosovo and effectively to quash Albanian opposition through military and police rule—a process Milošević had begun in the late 1980s—prompted the Albanian population to boycott the political process in both Serbia and the new Yugoslav state during the 1990s. Employing a policy of passive resistance and noncooperation with the Serbian regime, the Albanians of Kosovo established a parallel or alternative state and societal structure, complete with schools, colleges, hospitals, and political institutions. "We are organizing a separate life outside the Serbian system," declared Albanian leader Ibrahim Rugova in July 1992. "This is our way. We do not want a violent confrontation with Serbia and we will not accept Serbian rule."[8]

Although the Serbian regime claimed that its Albanian citizens (who constitute over 90 percent of the province's population) enjoyed full civil liberties and human rights, Milošević's brand of populist nationalism remained intolerant of the accommodations necessary to satisfy the political aspirations of Kosovo's Albanians peacefully. Milošević viewed the aspirations of Kosovo's Albanians for sovereignty as completely "out of the question" because, in his opinion, such a development would conflict with the Serbian majority's (that is, the Serbs of the entire republic considered as a single unit) right of self-determination.[9] During the first part of 1994, officials of the ruling Socialist Party of Serbia met secretly with Albanian leaders to discuss the situation in Kosovo, but nothing substantial resulted.[10] Discussions between Albanian and Serbian intellectuals also took place, but within the confines of Milošević's restricted pluralist model neither group wielded much political influence. Indeed, Milošević's anxiety about the combustible potential of Albanian nationalist sentiment in Kosovo and his concern that antiregime political protests in Serbia might become unmanageable were important reasons for his regime's increasing reliance on nondemocratic methods and an expanding police force.[11]

An uncompromising and insensitive official attitude toward minority demands for political autonomy and self-determination was also prevalent in

Croatia. Tudjman and his ruling HDZ party in Zagreb viewed the sovereignty of the Croatian state as an expression of the Croatian nation's collective will. When sovereignty is conceived of in this "collectivistic" manner (rather than as an outgrowth of the sovereignty of individuals), it is generally considered legitimate for those who interpret the collective will—often a person or group of individuals with authoritarian pretensions—to accord the dominant ethnic group a privileged status in society.[12] This mind-set, which has aptly been described as "constitutional nationalism" when it becomes the basis of fundamental laws and policies,[13] views the aspirations of minorities for special representation and self-government as inappropriate and even seditious. Actions taken to entrench the sovereignty of the dominant nation within this context naturally tend to alienate large minorities seeking constitutional recognition and political influence. In Croatia, the most deleterious consequences of such constitutional nationalism were manifest in the violent collision between the Croatian majority and the Serbian minority in the Krajina section of Croatia throughout the early 1990s. In late 1992—while a UN truce still prevailed in the area—President Tudjman made it clear that his opposition to Serbian self-determination was specifically related to the activities of those he referred to as "Serbian rebels" in Croatia and not to the new "Third" Yugoslavia established by Slobodan Milošević. "No minority," Tudjman observed, "in any country, including the independent sovereign Croatia, has the right to any kind of self-determination."[14]

Frustrated by the inability of the UN peacekeeping forces to facilitate the reestablishment of the Zagreb government's authority over the predominantly Serbian Krajina or to expedite the return of Croatian residents forced to flee the area during the fighting in 1991, Tudjman broke the year-long truce and launched a military initiative in early 1993, hoping to end Serbian resistance in Croatia.[15] Such military maneuvers, however, and the fresh round of diplomatic discussions that followed had a very limited effect on the status quo (semisecret talks in Norway between the Croatian government and representatives of the Krajina Serbs broke down in November 1993). The continuation of the standoff between the Krajina Serbs and the Zagreb government enhanced the militarization of political life in Croatia and impeded the new state's democratic development. President Tudjman, however, made no apologies for the situation. "We have democracy and in our war conditions we even have too much of it. We are even allowing some anarchy, but of course we will have full freedom and total democracy when we liberate every inch of Croatian land."[16]

The Croatian president frequently expressed his preference for a diplomatic solution to reintegrate the breakaway Serbian areas of Croatia and sought without success to reestablish low-level diplomatic relations with Milošević's Yugoslavia in early 1994. While Tudjman favored a peaceful resolution of the Krajina issue, Croatia was not willing to accept any solution that placed the Serbian minority outside the Croatian constitutional framework. There can be, Tudjman observed, "no talk of a federation let alone a confederation within Croatia."[17] Croatia's domestic ethnic problems and its prospects for developing into a genuine pluralist democracy appeared to be closely linked.[18] For example, during the spring of 1994, Tudjman's semiauthoritarian management style and his policies regarding Bosnia and the Krajina prompted two leading members of the regime, Stejpan Mesić and Josip Manolić, along with several other parliamentary deputies, to break with the ruling HDZ and form their own political party, the Croatian Independent Democrats (HND). Although by this time Tudjman had renewed the Croat-Moslem alliance in Bosnia, he still retained prominent members of the aggressively nationalist "Hercegovinian lobby" in his government—including Minister of Defense Gojko Šušak—and continued to negotiate with Milošević over the future of the Krajina Serbs. Like Tudjman, Manolić and Mesić were ardent Croat nationalists, but they felt that a more subtle approach to the Serbian question, and even more urgently to the Bosnian Moslem issue, was far more prudent than the methods employed by the Croatian president, not to mention those advocated by the "right," "hard," or Hercegovinian lobby in the ruling HDZ.

According to Tudjman, the defection of "turncoats" such as Mesić and Manolić was not surprising because the HDZ was transforming itself from a broad "movement" into a "party" based on the principles of "Christian civilization."[19] The "turncoats," of course, saw matters differently. Mesić, for example, claimed that Tudjman catered to certain "totalitarian" strivings in the HDZ that sometimes resulted in the use of "Bolshevik" methods. Moreover, the HDZ had increasingly hewed, Mesić suggested, to the model of a one-party system, with President Tudjman's office functioning like a "power center" manipulating both parliament and the choice of judges. The party now faced a new challenge: "What kind of state should [Croatia] be?"[20]

Although Croatian politics in the 1990s were strongly influenced by the nationalistic and quasi-authoritarian features of the postcommunist regime and by the difficulties of the ongoing Krajina issue, there were also important signs of a burgeoning civil society in Croatia. Outside the state's formal structure and the newly established multiparty system, many alternative groups devoted to advancing labor grievances or the problems of special sectors began to play an increasingly vocal role in Croatian political life. This group activity, together with the local electoral success in early 1993 of both liberal opposition party forces and regionally based parties, suggested that an enhanced basis for democratic pluralism in Croatia was gradually emerging.

During the first half of the 1990s, Slovenia appeared to be the most successful of the Yugoslav successor states in implementing the difficult transition from authoritarianism to democratic rule. Because of its relative cultural homogeneity, Slovenia was spared the intense internal ethnic conflicts that afflicted the other former Yugoslav republics. Further, following the postcommunist regime's brief and victorious war with units of the Yugoslav People's Army in mid-1991, Slovenia's political development was untroubled by the pressures of military struggle. Finally, civil society and media pluralism in Slovenia had flourished significantly during the five years before the state's independence, largely owing to the relatively liberal policies of Slovenia's reform communists.[21] Moreover, although the center-right parliamentary coalition of Slovenian parties that displaced the communist authorities was not reluctant to employ established procedures and its new legislative authority to exercise influence over the media, the character and success of such efforts were far more moderate than the heavy-handed pattern of formal and informal media restrictions present in Milošević's Serbia and Tudjman's Croatia. Indeed, the willingness of Slovenia's press to publish critical letters from disgruntled and vocal citizens provided an increasingly important outlet for criticism of the Ljubljana regime.[22]

Regime transition in Slovenia was not, however, without its problems. The most apparent defect of political life during the initial period of Slovenian independence was a pattern of chaotic decision making, endless parliamentary disputes, and what was described at one point as "real civil war at the institutional level" among different branches of the government and among various political parties.[23] Personalization of politics connected to an absence of deepseated support for specific parties and party platforms continued. "This is a legacy from the former one-party system in which nobody weighed up the programs, but rather the persons executing them," observed one Slovene editorial commentator. "We have a multiparty system, but we are behaving as in a one-party system. . . . Reflect on how often you can hear that (as a small nation, etc.) we should unite."[24]

During 1993 and 1994, Defense Minister Janez Janša seemed to be at the center of Slovenia's personalized and interinstitutional political conflicts. Janša engaged in a running political battle with various branches of Slovenia's intelligence-security services and the police and also with Slovenia's president Milan Kučan (a former communist). When Janša publicized in mid-1993 that arms were being shipped through Slovenia's Maribor Airport to Bosnia-Hercegovina in violation of the international arms embargo, an embarrassing political scandal erupted. Kučan admitted that he knew about the illegal arms shipments but claimed that Janša and most of Slovenia's political elite were also well aware of them. In March 1994, the tables were turned when Janša was accused of unlawfully ordering eavesdropping on journalists and supporting the assault by military police on a civilian who was allegedly spying on behalf of Kučan (the "Smolnikar affair"). At a dramatic meeting of the State Chamber on March 28, 1994, Janša was removed from his post. There was considerable protest over Janša's removal, and the former defense minister's party, the Social Democrats, subsequently withdrew from their coalition with the Liberal Democrats and Christian Democrats that had been running the country since the multiparty elections at the end of 1992. Despite the short-term crisis, the departure of the freewheeling and intrigue-prone Janša—with his obsession for security and military matters—appeared on balance to be a positive development for the process of democratization in Slovenia.

Ultranationalism's Economic Sources and Consequences

Efforts by socialist Yugoslavia's successor states to manage a smooth transition from authoritarianism to democracy have been seriously complicated by the disastrous economic consequences of continued ethnic conflicts and warfare in the region. In a vicious circle, the violence engendered by assertive and reactive nationalist policies wrecked the economy in many areas, and the resultant economic deprivation fueled destabilizing ultranationalism.

For example, in August 1992 President Tudjman estimated the cost of direct material damage from the war in Croatia at over U.S.$20 billion.[25] Moreover, as a result of the continued warfare there and in Bosnia, the Zagreb government was also burdened with the cost of caring for hundreds of thousands of refugees.[26] Tudjman calculated that Croatia was spending U.S.$3 million per day for their care. The costs associated with the military struggle, as well as the severe disruption of Croatian industry, tourism, and communications, also derailed the postcommunist regime's initial plans for economic transformation and marketization, thereby severing the positive link between political pluralism and economic development that has often proved crucial to the emergence of democratic stability. It was estimated that Croatia's gross national product had shrunk 50 percent from 1990 to 1993 and that production capacity had slipped 40 percent. Because the Zagreb government was forced to print Croatian dinars to pay for military expenses, refugees, and privatization and welfare costs, inflation was approximately 1,000 percent in 1992.

Despite episodic military clashes with Serbian forces in the Krajina, however, during 1993 and 1994 the overall condition of the Croatian economy improved substantially. In October 1993 an anti-inflation program was adopted, and by the spring of 1994 inflation had considerably moderated and unemployment was gradually falling. But the military stand-off and the unresolved interethnic problems with the Serbian minority in Croatia continued. "The war with the Serbs slashed our annual GNP," claimed Croatian foreign minister Mate Granić in October 1993. "Tourism and communications have all been ruined, the Serbs still hold a quarter of our best agricultural land and international aid to Croatia shrinks by the day." Granić estimated that if the Serb-held Krajina were peacefully integrated into Croatia, the economy would take about three years to reach prewar (i.e., mid-1991) levels.[27]

In Serbia and Montenegro (the new Yugoslavia), the pattern of serious economic deterioration in the early 1990s was traceable in large part to the international community's economic sanctions, the general disruption of traditional economic links among the republics of the former Yugoslav federation, and the costs associated with humanitarian and military support for the Serbian communities in Bosnia and Croatia. Serbia's gross domestic product dropped by nearly 45 percent between 1989 and 1992. Exports in 1992 dropped 46 percent from 1991 levels, and imports were down by one-third. Business closures and a steep drop in production also led to a massive increase in the number of people who were unemployed, on welfare, or on paid leave. In 1992, a hyper-inflation of over 20,000 percent exceeded traditional Latin American levels of price fluctuation, which had earlier held the global record. Such depressed conditions in Serbia contributed to rampant currency speculation by powerful money brokers and shady private banks that temporarily offered beleaguered Serbian citizens inflated monthly rates on their dinar accounts. Compounding this situation was the proliferation of private businessmen, war profiteers, and sanction-busting smugglers who manipulated the rapidly growing black market and often acquired a certain celebrity status and political influence in Serbia's vortex of competing nationalist and ultranationalist political groups.

Endeavoring to turn the economically debilitating sanctions to his benefit by urging the Serbian population to assert its "patriotic conscience" in the face of unyielding international pressure against Belgrade, Milošević was still forced to admit that the sanctions had created the basis for "economic pathology" that had "undermined the entire legal system."[28] Yet in his successful bid for reelection in December 1992, Milošević used slick television ads to distract attention from the war, the breakdown of order, and the economic impact of sanctions. His campaign strategy, together with the support of a reservoir of loyal followers and some practiced electoral chicanery on the part of his Socialist Party stalwarts, combined to give Milošević another electoral victory, though by a slimmer margin than in 1990.[29]

Interestingly, a large number of the voters who chose to leave the Milošević fold in December 1992 switched their support to his even more ultranationalist ally of the moment, Vojislav Šešelj, the head of the Serbian Radical Party. The surge of support for Šešelj and his party—attributable to an intense feeling on the part of many Serbs that they were unfairly under siege by both other Balkan ethnic groups and the international community—reflected a powerful undercurrent of ultranationalism in Serbia that had previously been tapped by Milošević and had seriously impaired the emergence of moderate democratic forces. Paradoxically, the Serbian nationalist mind-set celebrated, among other things, the historic Serbian resistance to victimization by foreign powers and the imperative of self-sacrificing Serbian solidarity in the face of losing odds. "If the West's intention was to destroy our economy as a punishment for our political leadership," observed one Serbian economist, "then the sanctions are a success. But if they were designed to bring about multiparty centrist democracy, the sanctions are counter-productive. The election [of December 20, 1992] showed that with the sanctions everything shifted to the far right."[30]

There seemed little doubt that despite the economic hardship caused by the sanctions (a situation considerably ameliorated by sanction-busting and leakage), Milošević had actually exploited the foreign-engineered isolation of Serbia as a means of consolidating his own nationalist support. The limited utility of sanctions as a tool of international politics is frequently acknowledged. Whatever the sanctions' impact, once they were in place the question of how to influence Milošević and Serbian attitudes became far more complicated. Thus, while some Serbian observers urged the lifting of international sanctions as a means of weakening Milošević's appeal to Serbian patriotism and his manipulation of antiforeign and particularly anti-Western feeling, such calls were tempered by the possibility that Milošević would take credit for ending sanctions and Serbia's isolation. Moreover, Milošević was by no means beaten or willing to step aside. "I'm not as confident as I used to be, but I will not resign," Milošević defiantly claimed seven days after being reelected president of Serbia at the end of 1992.[31]

Šešelj's electoral success also signaled a potentially serious political challenge to Slobodan Milosevic's long-standing monopoly over Serbian nationalist sentiment. Throughout the first part of 1993, however, Milošević and Šešelj maintained an informal alliance. For example, they cooperated in January 1993 to engineer the ouster of Milošević's opponent, Milan Panić, from the prime ministership of Yugoslavia (Panić had spearheaded the opposition to Milošević in the December 1992 elections) and also worked together in late May 1993 to push through the unceremonious removal of Dobrica Ćosić, the prominent writer and former Milošević ally who had been serving as the first president of the new Yugoslavia.

Ćosić's removal—which was allegedly precipitated because he had met privately with leading Yugoslav generals without prior notice to Milošević—illustrated the Byzantine character of Serbian political life. After his ouster, Ćosić observed that Yugoslavia had become a "protectorate of Slobodan Milošević," subject to the Serbian president's "tyrannical will" and "passionate love for power."[32] Within hours of his removal, following demonstrations at the federal legislature, Milošević's police brutally assaulted and jailed the major opposition leader, Vuk Drašković, and his wife. Despite their collaboration in removing Ćosić from the post of Yugoslav president, political strain on the Milošević-Šešelj alliance intensified during April and May after Šešelj criticized the Serbian president's support for the Vance-Owen plan (which proposed to divide Bosnia into ten provinces). As Šešelj put it, "A crack has appeared in the patriotic bloc."[33] Milošević clearly realized that any serious effort to cooperate with the international community in bringing genuine peace to Bosnia would require him to abandon his political association with Šešelj.

The president finally broke decisively with Šešelj in the fall of 1993 after the latter threatened that his Radical Party legislators might cooperate with opposition parties in a vote of nonconfidence against the government. Milošević adroitly dissolved the parliament and called for a new election in December. During the campaign, the spectacle of reciprocal verbal abuse and counter-charges between the former allies, as well as the regime's "media demonization" and arbitrary police measures against Šešelj and his followers, hardly offered an edifying portent for Serbian political development.

The grinding economic impact of sanctions against Serbia had played an important role not only in Milošević's decision to break with Šešelj but also in Belgrade's more flexible position (first evident in early 1993) in the negotiations on resolving the war in Bosnia. By the end of 1993, the international response to Belgrade's aggressive nationalist policies had failed to unseat Milošević, but they had seriously damaged the Serbian economy (e.g., roughly 60 percent unemployment; dire shortages of food, fuel, and medicine; record-breaking hyperinflation) in a manner that probably would not be eradicated for several decades. Milorad Unković, the federal minister for foreign trade relations, claimed in May 1994 that during the period since May 1992 Serbia's losses from sanctions amounted to U.S.$35 billion in direct damages and $100 billion in indirect losses.[34] These losses included a "brain drain" of thousands of Serbs that had brought a literal halt to Serbia's scientific and technological development. Meanwhile, the prime minister of Montenegro claimed that sanctions had cost his republic U.S.$5 billion and that "economic life in Montenegro has practically ceased to exist."[35]

Despite the disastrous impact of the sanctions, the fragmented Serbian democratic opposition proved unable to channel popular dissatisfaction to its advantage and equally incapable of tapping the reservoir of patriotic attitudes long monopolized by Milošević and the more radical nationalist forces in Serbia.

In the run-up to the December 1993 legislative elections in Serbia, Milošević formed a new alliance with Željko Ražnjatović, popularly known as "Arkan." The head of the paramilitary group known as the Tigers, Arkan had a history of extremist and criminal activity and was generally believed to have orchestrated war crimes during the fighting in Bosnia. Describing the program of his newly founded Party of Serbian Unity (SSJ), Arkan claimed that he would work for the "unification of all Serbian lands" and "to prevent genocide against the Serbs." Ominously raising the issue of dual loyalty among Serbia's Albanian, Hungarian, and Sandžak Moslem citizens, Arkan threatened that "those who look to Tirana, Budapest and Iran should pack their bags." "Democracy," he told another campaign rally, "was created in Serbia centuries before America was even discovered."[36]

Notwithstanding his nationalist rhetoric, Arkan did not win a single seat in the December 1993 elections. Milošević's SPS also suffered a setback, winning only 123 seats in the 250-seat Serbian legislature, 3 seats short of a working majority. Technically, the president's party had increased its numbers in the Serbian parliament (up from 101 in 1992) but, having broken with Šešelj, the president could no longer count on support from the Serbian Radical Party (whose own standing in the legislature had dropped from 73 to 39 seats). Undaunted by these results and the moderate opposition's increased parliamentary strength, Milošević soon managed to establish a working relationship with a small party faction, the New Democracy Party, and thereby picked up an additional six seats and formed a working majority.

During 1994, Milošević worked unceasingly, together with his self-proclaimed antinationalist and communist spouse, Mirjana Marković, to distance himself even further from what the ruling couple now termed "primitive nationalists," such as Šešelj and various Bosnian Serb leaders, and to seek a new image as a peacemaker. The adoption of a new economic strategy in early 1994, the so-called Super Dinar Program, temporarily halted the country's hyperinflation, put additional consumer goods in the stores, and created an artificial atmosphere of regime vitality that bought Milošević additional breathing space in his increasingly urgent effort to maintain power. By the end of 1994, Milošević's political maneuvering with the Bosnian Serbs had won him a partial and temporary reprieve from the debilitating economic sanctions.

Aspects of nationalist extremism, political illiberalism, and instability stemming from war-related economic disruption and sanctions were most apparent in Croatia, Bosnia-Hercegovina, Serbia, and Montenegro, but the former Yugoslav republics of Macedonia and Slovenia also suffered from the general dislocation of economic life and the breakdown of established trade patterns. Although Macedonia managed to retain its territorial integrity—a proposal by Milošević to dismember the country in 1991 had been rejected by Bulgarian president Zhelyu Zhelev and Greek prime minister Constantine Mitsotakis—Greek and Serbian hostility to the new state seriously hampered economic development.

By the end of 1992, the Macedonian economy was reeling from massive foreign debt and unemployment, hyperinflation, and plunging economic production. Serious economic difficulties continued throughout 1993 and 1994. It has been estimated that during this period Macedonia's per capita gross national product fell from roughly U.S.$1,800 to less than U.S.$760. Such economic deterioration contributed to renewed internal tensions within the country, particularly between the ethnic Macedonian majority and the large Albanian minority, a situation that threatened the political stability and external relations (particularly with Albania) of the fragile fledgling country.

Economic difficulties in Slovenia also tended to fuel discernible aspects of political extremism and nationalism at the fringe of the political spectrum. The wrenching post-Yugoslav and postcommunist economic reorientation and the cost of reconstruction from the short war with the JNA led to an economic depression and a slump in Slovenia's standard of living during the second half of 1991 and the first half of 1992. The situation in Slovenia slowly improved near the end of 1992 as international banks (including the International Monetary Fund) and markets slowly opened, foreign trade was balanced, and the exchange rate of the new state's currency (the tolar) was stabilized. By the middle of 1994, Slovenia was undergoing an economic revival and had built one of the strongest economies in Eastern Europe (per capita gross domestic product in 1993 was approximately U.S.$6,000). Although serious economic problems continued, such as a recession in the industrial sector and a 15 percent unemployment rate, these difficulties had started to abate.[37]

It was the cost of caring for refugees fleeing from the turmoil in Croatia and Bosnia, even more than the general process of postcommunist economic adjustment in Slovenia, however, that appeared to stimulate expressions of xenophobia and nationalism. For example, tapping the anxiety of extreme right-oriented voters who worried that foreign immigrants to Slovenia—some of whom were granted Slovenian citizenship—would become a financial burden and fill Slovenian jobs, the chauvinist Slovene National Party (SNS) won 12 percent of the legislative seats in the election held in December 1992. The SNS was excluded from the newly elected coalition government, but surveys revealed that its controversial leader was quite popular.[38]

Slovenia's political stability and the marginal position of extremist elements were certainly related to the country's relative economic prosperity. The average monthly wage at the end of 1993, for example, was approximately five times higher than in Croatia and more than ten times that in Serbia.[39] Slovenia's continued economic success would be an important factor in determining whether the new state's still fledgling effort to democratize would succeed and remain relatively free of the more virulent ethnically based radicalism troubling its neighbors.

Balkan Futures: The Rise of "Ethnic Democracies"?

In the wake of socialist Yugoslavia's disintegration, the emerging political systems of its successor states have manifested a mixture of democratic and nondemocratic features and can best be described as troubled proto-democratic regimes. The particular nature of incipient democratization in most of these states, however, provides serious cause for concern. Several states, most notably Serbia and Croatia, have exhibited many dimensions of political behavior typical of what has been termed an "ethnic democracy."[40] The defining characteristics of such a regime are the de facto privileged status accorded by the state to one or more of the country's ethnic groups and the correspondingly less advantaged political position of other subcultural or minority groups. In such a regime, government pronouncements and constitutional documents that proclaim a commitment to civic or liberal democracy are generally contradicted by the reality of ethno-political hegemony. The political underrepresentation of minority ethnic communities and other forms of subtle discrimination are rarely the result of formal legal measures but are often incorporated into the "unwritten, but clear rules of the game."

Moreover, although such regimes typically lack a coherent ideology, they generally seek legitimation on the basis of some eclectic program of ethnonationalist principles that are widely disseminated through the state media and the school system and engendered through a panoply of state symbols. Although decidedly favoring a particular ethnic group or coalition of groups at the expense of others, ethnic democracies are typically hybrid regimes that are difficult to classify. Routine policies of the ethnic democracy may borrow unabashedly from capitalist, socialist, and corporatist thought as the regime's leaders endeavor to maintain power and grapple with socioeconomic pressures. Ethnic democracies, with their unusual amalgam of partial political tolerance and self-limiting repression, resemble neither classic liberal democracies nor paradigmatic totalitarian and mature fascist forms of rule. Indeed, depending on the particular admixture of liberal and illiberal practices, a specific ethnic democracy may evolve in either a more democratic or a more authoritarian direction.[41]

Claiming to be committed to competitive pluralism and the highest standards for protecting human rights but markedly unenthusiastic or unschooled about the operation of democratic norms, the ruling elites in such regimes are generally inconsistent and arbitrary in their enforcement of both civil liberties and state-sponsored repression. Superficially, the society appears free. For example, regular competitive elections are conducted, and an opposition media is permitted to function openly, although both such elections and the media often may be subjected to manipulation by the regime. Moreover, even the most innocuous forms of antistate dissent by ethnic and other political minorities may be viewed as potentially dangerous and therefore as warranting harassment or repression. The authorities will tend to tolerate political nonconformism provided that such views remain relatively weak, unthreatening, and uncoordinated. Similarly, the state media and the educational system are likely to be politicized to reflect and expound the regime's nationalist message. Political rights and civil liberties are ostensibly granted to the entire population, but in practice the "collective" rights and interests of the hegemonic ethnic group(s)—as interpreted by the top leaders of the regime—usually take precedence over individual rights. Under such conditions of elite guidance, an ethnic democracy's collective interests become magnified when the state is besieged or involved in warfare.

Many Bosnians, for example, blame the trend toward Islamic militancy and political authoritarianism on the country's president, Alija Izetbegović. "It is time our people matured," Izetbegović told a Moslem party meeting early in 1994. "We can manage on our own, like any other people." He criticized the Bosnian integrationists' practice of symbolizing ethnic unity by displaying different national flags together. "Don't do this. Tying flags together is a romantic folly devoid of meaning." Izetbegović denied charges that he was strengthening Islamic religious influence in Bosnian politics. Indeed, Izetbegović is generally viewed by most Western observers as a moderate nonfundamentalist Moslem leader who, under the pressure of war and ethno-religious polarization in Bosnia, has been pushed toward accepting more militant measures. As Bosnia fragmented into two or three separate states during 1993 and 1994, however, ethno-religious criteria clearly became a more prominent part of political life. "The general trend is toward national states," observed Zdravko Grebo, a prominent Sarajevo liberal. "Everyone now accepts that as the final solution." How to reconcile Moslem religious nationalism with the bi-ethnic orientation of the new Moslem-Croat federation will be a very difficult task, not to mention the more challenging problem of providing fair treatment to that federation's remaining Serb minority. The chances that a broader accommodation of the Moslem-Croat federation with the Republika Srpska of the Bosnian Serbs might be found during the second half of the 1990s appeared extremely remote at the end of 1996.

Considering the elite-led ethnically based conflict and warfare throughout the first half of the 1990s, it is hardly surprising that national states and ethnic democracy, rather than civic states and European-style democracy, have become the norm throughout much of the former Yugoslavia. Whether the majority of successor states will continue to approximate the prototypical model of ethnic democracies, will come to resemble what one Serbian author has described as an "assemblage of little fascisms,"[42] or will gradually develop stronger democratic institutions and more viable pluralist politics remains a very open question. Indeed, at times, Balkan political life in the wake of single-party communist rule appears to be a remarkable throwback to southeastern Europe's experience between the two world wars, with its predominance of highly factionalized nationalistic political parties, control by politically cunning and power-hungry political leaders, frequent violations of human rights and legal norms, and popular cynicism born of rampant corruption.

Under these circumstances, the gradual establishment of more stable and interest-based party systems, law-governed political behavior, and independent judiciaries, not to mention a sharp reduction of corruption in political life, remain major prerequisites for the development of any liberal form of democracy in the Balkans (the question of whether such democracy is appropriate, or likely, in view of Balkan political traditions and preferences is a related but separate subject). Forces supportive of democratic pluralism exist in all of the second Yugoslavia's successor states, but such forces are generally weak and divided. Meanwhile, leaders and constituencies who urge the consolidation of a "national state" or "the people-as-one style of nationalism" continue to exercise a strong antipluralist influence on political development.[43] Until the elites and citizens in the former Yugoslavia's successor states are able to transcend the constraints and intolerance generated by such nationalist ideologies, the Balkan region is likely to remain convulsed by political violence and instability.

NOTES

1. Commenting in 1992 on a problem that has characterized many postcommunist regimes, Tudjman's former adviser, Slaven Letica, described the result of such antidemocratic trends on Croatian political life: "The culture or evil spirit of a single-party system is again present in Croatia. It is the spirit of 'conformism' which holds that any critical opinion has no objective justification, that it is a subjective fallacy, or even high treason ('opposition from within' and 'enemies from without'). . . . The new political elite has inherited and extended the system of the abuse of power . . . the same people being rotated from post to post, from one ministry to another, and there is no professional logic behind these shifts, just like there was none in the old regime. . . . The public is given virtually no explanation as to why somebody is appointed to a post or removed from it" (*Obećana zemlja: Politicki antimemoari* [Zagreb: Globus International, 1992], 491).

2. In October 1993 several other HSP members were found guilty of murdering Paraga's deputy leader, Ante Paradžik. See Jill Irvine, "Nationalism and the Extreme Right in the Former Yugoslavia," forthcoming in *Neofacism in Europe* (Longman).

3. Ken Kasriel, "A Little Bit Pregnant: Degrees of Freedom Jostle with Nationalist Expectations of the Media at War," *Index on Censorship* 2 (1993), 18–19. See also *Human Rights and Democratization in Croatia* (Washington, D.C.: Commission on Security and Cooperation in Europe, 1993), 14–19. For the Zagreb government's view, see *Facts about the Media in Croatia* (Zagreb: Information Department, Ministry of Foreign Affairs, 1993).

4. Tudjman's selection of his son Miroslav to head one of the regime's major security intelligence services—the HIS or Croatian Information Service—also raises doubts about the president's understanding of the appropriate measures to create a law-governed and democratic state.

5. For an excellent discussion of trends in the Serbian opposition, see Aleksandar Pavkovic, "Intellectuals into Politicians: Serbia 1990–92," *Meanjin* 52 (Autumn 1993), 107–16.

6. In early 1993, there was also evidence that political purges in Serbia were expanding from the media and political jobs in state institutions to include nonpolitical jobs in the arts, medicine, and the educational system. See Marcus Tanner, "Serbia Is Swept by 'Political Cleansing,'" *Independent*, February 5, 1993, 10.

7. For example, the internationally well known and highly regarded antigovernment weekly, *Vreme*, has a print issue of only approximately 30,000. The independent news program broadcast by the television station "Studio B" was limited to a Belgrade audience of roughly one hundred thousand people, compared to the three million nationwide audience for state-run television's main news bulletin. See also the comments by Johnathan Sunley and Tira Shubart, "Studio B: A Lone Voice," *Index on Censorship* 4 (1993), 24, 29. In March 1994, journalists who had been fired from the state radio and television network established the Independent Association of Journalists in Serbia.

8. Marcus Tanner, "Albanians in Kosovo Set Up a Shadow State," *Independent*, July 20, 1992, 10.

9. Foreign Broadcast Information Series, Daily Bulletin, Eastern Europe (hereafter FBIS-EEU), October 13, 1992, 40. See also Prvoslav Ralic, *Minority Rights in Serbia* (Belgrade: Ministry of Information of the Republic of Serbia, 1992).

10. In the early fall, Albanian leader Rugova suggested that negotiations with Milosevic might be productive.

11. For example, one Serbian researcher has suggested that fear of a violent takeover by Serbian opposition elements was behind Milošević's creation of a "blue elite," or "truncheon elite," of approximately 70,000 policemen, and that Serbia's ratio of seven police officers for every thousand inhabitants constituted a "new world record" (Gradiša Katić, from *Nedeljna Borba*, June 26–27, 1993, 6, in FBIS-EEU, July 19, 1993, 72). See also Marcus Tanner, "Serbia's Crackdown in Kosovo Raises 'Ethnic Cleansing' Fears," *Independent*, October 15, 1993, 12.

12. For an excellent discussion of the differences between individualistic-libertar-

ian nationalism and collectivistic-authoritarian nationalism, see Liah Greenfeld, *Nationalism: Five Roads to Modernity* (Cambridge: Harvard University Press, 1992), 10–12. On the complex relationship between nationalism and democracy, see also G. Nodie, "Nationalism and Democracy," *Journal of Democracy* 3 (October 1992), 3–23, and Francis Fukuyama, *The End of History and the Last Man* (New York: Free Press, 1992), 266–75.

13. Robert Hayden, "Yugoslavia: Where Self-Determination Meets Ethnic Cleansing," *New Perspectives Quarterly* 9 (Fall 1992), 41–46.

14. FBIS-EEU, October 6, 1992, 31–32. See also Dusan Bilandzic et al., eds., *Croatia between War and Independence* (Zagreb: University of Zagreb, 1991). Tudjman has also been unyielding with regard to claims for regional political autonomy put forward by political forces in Istria, where the Istrian Democratic Alliance (IDS) captured a majority of the votes in the 1992 and 1993 elections. "We are not going to tolerate," Tudjman claimed in August 1992, "either in Istria or elsewhere any regional dismantling of Croatia. . . . We will honor Istria's particularity . . . but we will not allow Croatia to disintegrate in any and especially not in such a delicate area" (BBCSWB, August 2, 1993, Part 2 [Eastern Europe], EE/C1).

15. The Croatian military's initial success against the Serbs probably helped Tudjman's HDZ in winning approximately two-thirds of the vote in the February 7, 1993, election for the upper house of the Croatian legislature.

16. BBCSWB, August 17, 1993, Part 2 (Eastern Europe), EE/1769/C1.

17. Embassy of Croatia Bulletin, October 20, 1994.

18. Domestic opposition to the Tudjman regime increased markedly during the latter half of 1993 in large part because of the Zagreb government's failure to reestablish control over the Krajina or to bring an end to the Croat-Moslem schism in Bosnia. For example, in an open letter to the Croatian president published near the end of September 1993, six prominent Croatian intellectuals accused Tudjman of bringing his country "to the brink of national tragedy and catastrophe" and called upon him to resign. Tudjman's persistent efforts to negotiate a deal with Milošević regarding Bosnia, the letter alleged, had caused both the rift between Moslems and Croats and Zagreb's inability to resolve the problem of Croatia's rebellious Krajina Serbs. The root of the problem, the six intellectuals bluntly informed Tudjman, was his intolerance toward free expression.

19. FBIS-EEU-94-107, June 3, 1994, 26.

20. FBIS-EEU-94-111, June 9, 1994, 46.

21. On this point see Danica Hafner, "Political Modernization in Slovenia in the 1980s and the Early 1990s," *Journal of Communist Studies* 8 (December 1992), 210–26.

22. David Binder, "In Slovenia, Pen Is the Mighty Form of Protest," *New York Times*, November 23, 1993, 11.

23. Darko Strajn, "How Democracy Creates Itself," *IN* 30–31 (July 31, 1992), 1.

24. "Quasi-Government," *IN* 85 (November 11, 1991), 1.

25. BBCSWB, August 29, 1992, Part 2 (Eastern Europe: London Conference on Former Yugoslavia), EE/1472/C2/1.

26. By mid-December 1992, the Croatian government's Office of Displaced Per-

sons and Refugees registered 268,526 persons displaced from their homes in Croatia and 426,852 refugees from Bosnia-Hercegovina who had come to Croatia (*Glasnik ureda za prognanike i izbjeglice* 1 [December 16, 1992]).

27. *Independent*, October 22, 1993, 13.

28. FBIS-EEU, October 8, 1992, 37.

29. In 1990, Milošević had won two-thirds of the votes cast for president of Serbia. In 1992, he took 55.9 percent of the vote in Serbia's presidential election (the majority of votes in 169 of Serbia's 188 municipalities), while his main challenger, Milan Panić, won 34.3 percent of the votes cast. Milosevic's Socialist Party won 101 out of 250 seats in the Serbian Assembly (that is, 40.4 percent of the seats based on 28.8 percent of the vote) and 47 out of 138 seats in the Chamber of Citizens of the Yugoslav Federal Assembly (that is, 34 percent based on 31.4 percent of the vote) (Mijat Suković et al., "Results of the December 1992 Parliamentary and Presidential Elections," *Yugoslav Survey* 34 [1993], 3–50).

30. Cited in Robert Block, "Serbs Fail to Hide Pain of UN Sanctions," *Independent*, January 4, 1993, 6.

31. Dragan Bujošević, "The Time of Unstable Government," *Politika: The International Weekly* 146–47 (January 2–15, 1993), 1.

32. BBCSWB, June 4, 1993, Part 2 (Eastern Europe), EE/1706/C1.

33. FBIS-EEU-93-101, May 27, 1993, 40.

34. FBIS-EEU-94-117, June 17, 1994, 57.

35. FBIS-EEU- 94-105, June 1, 1994, 59.

36. Marcus Tanner, "Serbian Warrior Wins Hearts and Mindless," *Independent*, December 1, 1993, 28.

37. FBIS-EEU-94-113, June 13, 1994, 39.

38. Leon Magdalenc, "Weekly Politics, Popular Slovenians," *IN*, January 22, 1993, 7.

39. Davor Huić, "Slovenia Maintains Diversity, but Nationalist Pressure Rises," *Chicago Sun Times*, October 25, 1993, 50.

40. Sammy Smooha and Theodor Hanf, "The Diverse Modes of Conflict-Regulation in Deeply Divided Societies," *International Journal of Comparative Sociology* 33 (1992), 26–47.

41. For a good discussion of the relationship of ethnic group dominance and the potential for democratization, see Yoav Peled, "Ethnic Democracy and the Legal Construction of Citizenship: Arab Citizens of the Jewish State," *American Political Science Review* 86 (June 1992), 432–40.

42. Stojan Cerovic, as translated in FBIS-EEU, October 6, 1992, 40.

43. For the ideological roots of such antipluralist nationalism see Gale Stokes, "Nationalism, Responsibility, and the People-as-One," *Studies in East European Thought* 46 (June 1994), 91–103.

8

Polish Transition Strategy
Successes and Failures

Lucja Swiatkowski Cannon

In September 1989, Poland established its first government headed by a non-communist as a result of the Roundtable Agreements between the communists and the Solidarity trade union. Poland was hailed as a beacon of freedom in Eastern Europe, which became all the more prophetic when the Polish events were followed by the fall of the Berlin Wall, of the Romanian strongman Nicolae Ceauşescu, the Czechoslovak Velvet Revolution, and free elections in Hungary and Czechoslovakia—all a few months afterward. The Balcerowicz Plan—the Polish strategy for economic reform and establishment of free market economy—was admired for its boldness and comprehensiveness and promised to restore stable growth and prosperity to a population dispirited by decades of irrational communist policies. Poland became the darling of the international community.

Today this promise has diminished. In the parliamentary election of September 19, 1993, two postcommunist parties won 35 percent of the vote and 65 percent of the parliamentary seats. This victory reflects deep popular dissatisfaction with political and economic reforms in Poland. In politics, the refusal to deal with the past left the communists with substantial ideological and economic resources and control of vital institutions and processes crucial to reforms, which they manipulated to their own advantage. That undermined efforts by democratic parties to establish themselves as an alternative in the political process.

In economics, the election constituted a popular judgment that the shock therapy was too costly and unjust to ordinary citizens and was applied in an authoritarian and arrogant manner. The election polarized the Polish electorate into those who benefited from reforms and a majority who suffered a loss of economic security and a collapse of the health, education, and public safety systems. At the same time, the Polish economy showed growth for the third year and the private sector developed explosively to constitute over 50 percent of the gross domestic product.

This chapter analyzes the path of Solidarity from its success in breaking down the communist party monopoly and extending its legitimacy to the reforms, to withdrawing its support from the government of Prime Minister Hanna Suchocka. This struggle to break down the communist party's organizational strength and shape the future was the source of political and economic instability and conflict in Poland. The struggle is not yet over, despite a seeming communist victory, and illustrates the enormous difficulties of the transition.

THE ROUNDTABLE AGREEMENT

In the fall of 1988, the Polish communist party leadership decided to reach a compromise with the Solidarity trade union and started formal Roundtable negotiations with the left wing of Solidarity, the most willing to make a deal. The participants shared a consensus on the need for a solution to a steadily deteriorating economic situation and increasing social unrest.

The result of the Roundtable Agreement was a formal legalization of Solidarity, which was given responsibility for economic reforms, and the retention of power by the communist party in the national security areas. The parliamentary election was held in June 1989, though it was an election in name only. The agreement guaranteed 65 percent of the seats in the Sejm to the communist party and its allies; for the remaining 35 percent, Solidarity put forward its own candidates, who came mostly from left-wing Warsaw dissident circles. In addition, the agreement created the Senate, the upper house of Parliament, but gave it only weak advisory powers. Ninety-nine of its one hundred seats were won by Solidarity.

The presidency was guaranteed to General Wojciech Jaruzelski and key ministries of defense, foreign affairs, and the interior to the communist party. General Czeslaw Kiszczak was to be named prime minister, but because of his unsavory reputation as the interior minister under martial law and political manueuvers by Lech Walesa, he was dropped in favor of a more respectable Solidarity candidate, Tadeusz Mazowiecki. The formation of the government was hailed as a breakthrough abroad, but in Poland it was seen much more cautiously as a creature of the Roundtable Agreement.

The Mazowiecki government interpreted the Roundtable Agreement in a very narrow manner. It excluded Lech Walesa and the rest of Solidarity from participation in the formation of the government and preparation of reform policies. Walesa himself was relegated to the status of a historical figure who was irrelevant to the current situation. The Solidarity revolution was to be very limited.

In view of the changing international situation, in the fall of 1989 demands were made in Poland to pursue a more independent foreign policy. But Mazowiecki repeated tired formulas of the German threat and the alleged necessity of stationing Soviet troops in Poland to defend against it, even in view of increased Soviet flexibility on this issue and the movement toward the reunification of Germany. The retention of martial law personnel in highly visible positions in public life was justified by the Mazowiecki policy of the "thick line," writing off the sins of the past of communist officials. With time, these policies became increasingly controversial.

ECONOMIC SHOCK THERAPY

Under the Roundtable Agreement, the Mazowiecki government had a mandate to make radical changes in economic policy to stabilize the Polish economy, which was collapsing from years of communist mismanagement and repression. The economic reform team was led by Leszek Balcerowicz, deputy prime minister and finance minister. With the assistance of foreign advisers, this team devised an economic reform strategy named "shock therapy," designed to introduce market signals into the Polish economy and to stabilize it on a new level.

The economic shock therapy began in January 1990 and had three main goals: to contain inflation, liberalize prices and markets, and privatize state-owned enterprises. All these measures were to be applied simultaneously to shift the allocation of resources from planners to prices and to contain galloping inflation that had been unleashed by the simultaneous liberalization of almost all prices.

The anti-inflation program consisted of three anchors: a sharply devalued fixed exchange rate, credit ceilings combined with inflation-adjusted real interest rates, and a restrictive wage policy applied to employees in the state sector. The goal was to depress domestic demand, eliminate budget and trade deficits, and lower inflation. This elimination of "empty money" set the stage for a supply response, a strong regeneration of healthy economic activity and growth in the gross domestic product.[1]

The second goal was to introduce market signals into the economy, such as free prices; open trade and investment policies; internal convertibility of the zloty; and mobility of capital, labor, and goods. It was assumed that these market signals would force state-owned enterprises to restructure and make them more efficient and profitable. These restructured enterprises would be natural candidates for privatization because they would have already adjusted to the market economy.

The third goal was to transform the state-dominated Polish economy to a market economy through private sector development and privatization of state enterprises. These independent economic units would make it possible to improve effectiveness, to prevent political interference in the economy, and to make foreign investment easier by allowing either foreign control of Polish firms or the assumption of a passive ownership role through the stock market.

The Balcerowicz team pursued a vision of privatization based on the establishment of a stock market instead of the central bureaucracy as a market mechanism for decisions on investments, an idea introduced in the mid-1980s. Large state enterprises were to be turned into joint stock companies with strong managements and boards of directors, nominated by the supervising ministry. Solidarity-dominated employee councils were to be abolished. Privatization was to be accomplished by cash sales to private, generally foreign, investors or issuing shares on the stock exchange.

These plans produced an outcry because they contradicted a generally accepted view that privatization would lead to a fundamental transformation of the social and economic system, decrease state interference in the economy, create a middle class, and give economic power to ordinary citizens. The preliminary plans in the summer of 1989 included turning Solidarity-dominated employee councils into boards of directors of state-owned enterprises to prevent appropriations of assets and control of strategic decisions by martial law–appointed managers. Later, these enterprises would be privatized with the aid of vouchers given to all citizens to allow their participation despite a lack of investment capital. The strategy that was incorporated in the July 1990 privatization law contradicted virtually all of these expectations.

The results of this privatization strategy were mixed. For a large enterprise, issuing shares on the stock market is a very costly and time-consuming process and unlikely to be applied on a large scale. Individual sales were slow because there were no large domestic investors and foreign investors were wary because of Poland's economic instability, large foreign debt, and recession, as well as restrictive foreign investment laws. These methods were inadequate to the situation in Poland where state property constituted the overwhelming majority of enterprises. Privatization of small retail and service establishments, however, was very successful as was privatization of medium-sized enterprises through employee leases and ownership.

At the end of 1990, the results of the stabilization policy were mixed. Although the inflation rate subsided to 250 percent, when combined with the fixed exchange rate, the zloty became highly overvalued, which had bad repercussions for trade and tourism. Wage controls led to a 30 percent drop in the standard of living in the first six months, which affected mainly blue-collar workers in state-owned enterprises. Unemployment reached 8 percent. Industrial output fell 25 percent and overall gross domestic product 12 percent, an unexpectedly large and unexplainable decline. The simultaneous price liberalization and the depression of wages gave windfall profits to state enterprises and actually reduced pressure for structural adjustment at the same time the state budget improved.[2]

In the spring of 1990, just as the shock therapy program was in full swing, the consensus underlying the Mazowiecki government's program collapsed. The Roundtable Agreement had outlived its purpose and was not followed by greater democratization; the economic reforms, particularly privatization, did not satisfy popular cravings for the just and complete transformation of the system.

Walesa's Challenge

In the political sphere, the Roundtable Agreement stipulated only some liberalization and lifting of censorship. But by the spring of 1990, democratic revolutions were sweeping other East European countries. In Poland, demands were made to move more boldly toward democracy and free elections. But the Mazowiecki government refused to hold an election in early 1990 on the grounds that it might endanger economic reforms and, even more significant, refused to set a date for such an election. As a consequence, demands were made to replace General Jaruzelski, the symbol of martial law, with Lech Walesa, leader of Solidarity, as president of the republic. That too was rejected by Mazowiecki.

In addition, despite Solidarity's initial effort to reform the local administration and municipal elections of May 1990, the Mazowiecki government refused to remove high-level communist bureaucrats or reform other levels of the administration. The result was a breakdown in the implementation of government policy because even Solidarity-controlled ministries did not have the means to carry out government directives when the communist bureaucrats decided to obstruct their edicts.

This determined effort by the Mazowiecki government to abide by the Roundtable Agreement and prevent democratization led Walesa to call for a "war at the top." That translated into an attempt to open up the political process, to remove some of the communist ministers, and to recruit other, less left-wing dissident groups to participate. Walesa accused Mazowiecki of coddling high communist officials and failing to deal with their looting of public property through nomenklatura enterprises. He criticized Poland's lack of an independent foreign policy and the negotiations for Soviet troop withdrawals. Finally, Mazowiecki's efforts to abide by the undemocratic Roundtable Agreement destroyed the consensus in Solidarity. When the communist-dominated Sejm and Mazowiecki refused to nominate Walesa for president as was customary, he decided in June to run for this largely ceremonial office in a free election.

The presidential campaign underscored a very important fact of the Polish electoral process. The rules of the game such as when to hold the election, who can run for office, procedures for voting, and districting were (and continue to be) controlled by the communist constitutional lawyers and used to the advantage of the old nomenklatura. This has been one of the legacies of Mazowiecki's "thick line" policy.

Another "thick line" policy legacy is left-wing control of the public media, which was consolidated by the privatization of many newspapers and journals. The latter were sold for nominal sums to their employees, who were communist propagandists. This control of the media was especially evident during Walesa's presidential campaign. Mazowiecki's smear campaign against Walesa assumed an alarmist and hysterical character. The latter was accused of being an irresponsible populist demagogue, trying to destabilize Poland by fomenting nationalism and religious fanaticism, and an authoritarian plotting a coup d'état. The Europeanness and Westernness of the Mazowiecki group was contrasted with the alleged parochialism, anti-Semitism, and petty obscurantism of Walesa. His image as a national leader was seriously damaged.

Aside from political charges, the economy and its reform became a source of electoral contention. The stabilization policy was deliberately eased in July to help Mazowiecki's candidacy. The interest rate was cut. New credits and expenditures were authorized. Wage indexation was diminished, and the rate of the excess wage tax was lowered. In July, the indexation was 100 percent.[3] Despite the austerity program, between June and November pay rates rose by 57 percent and prices by 23 percent. The level of pay raises threatened the stabilization efforts and contributed to the recession the following year.[4]

Dissatisfaction with the privatization policy led to denunciations of the government program as "propertization" of the nomenklatura officials. In an effort to mollify its critics, the government announced some modifications. Transformation of state-owned enterprises into state joint stock companies, with attendant abolition of employee councils, was limited to enterprises that were about to be privatized. Furthermore, to satisfy demands for popular participation, Balcerowicz announced a plan to distribute privatization vouchers among the general population. But instead of offering individual vouchers, as in Czechoslovakia, the government would organize twenty investment funds, controlling twenty to thirty enterprises each, and exchange vouchers for shares in these funds.[5] This program was very controversial from the beginning.

The presidential election served as a popular assessment of the reforms as well as of Mazowiecki's leadership. He lost support because of his refusal to move toward a democratic political system and to remove from public life those who not so long ago had persecuted Solidarity. While the goals of economic reform were reaffirmed, the methods employed seemed to have lost legitimacy. Mazowiecki received only 18 percent of the vote and was excluded from the second round by Stanislaw Tyminski, a mysterious émigré who gained the support of those who saw no future for themselves in the new economic order: peasants, small town residents, and the hardest hit industrial workers. In the final round, Walesa received 80 percent of the vote.

Results of the presidential election signaled popular disapproval of the methods of economic reform, lack of political and institutional change, lack of democracy, the arrogant and authoritarian style of leadership of the Mazowiecki group, and its symbiotic relationship with the old communists.

THE STRUGGLE FOR FREE ELECTIONS

Walesa's election raised expectations that the disappointing political and economic situation might improve. But the powers of the presidency were largely symbolic, and Walesa had to have a new parliament and government if he were to effect any change in policies. Throughout 1991, public attention was centered on a struggle between Walesa and the de facto coalition of the Democratic Union, organized by Mazowiecki supporters after his defeat, and the postcommunist Democratic Left Alliance to maintain the Roundtable Agreement's political order as long as possible. This coalition enjoyed formidable advantages: control of the Sejm and the constitutional rule-making process and sympathy of the media.

When Walesa assumed the presidency, he named Jan Krzysztof Bielecki, a leader of the Liberal Democratic Congress Party, as interim prime minister with the same cabinet, expecting to hold parliamentary elections in March 1991. But the existing Sejm had to write a new election law and named Bronislaw Geremek, an eminence gris of the Democratic Union, as head of the Constitutional Commission. The proposed law took months to prepare (so that the election was held only in October 1991) and was so convoluted that voters did not understand how to vote, which discouraged participation.

The law was based on unrestrained proportional representation, in which some representatives were chosen in electoral districts while others were selected from national lists with no connection to particular voters; this system was designed to ensure the political survival of postcommunists and well-known personalities, leaders of the Democratic Union. Voting was based on the personal appeals of candidates, not of political parties. The impossibility of voting for parties discouraged their development and muddled ideological differences among candidates. It prevented the emergence of a stable parliamentary majority by fragmenting the Sejm so that it was dominated by its only two organized political forces: Geremek's own Democratic Union and the postcommunist Democratic Left Alliance.

Walesa objected to the proposed election law passed by the Sejm, but ambiguities about his constitutional role as president and fears of plunging Poland into a political crisis that would delay the election beyond the fall of 1991 compelled him to sign the inadequate Sejm version. Thus the first free parliamentary election was held on October 27, 1991, more than two years after the formation of the first Solidarity-led government.

Another contentious issue between Walesa and the old communist-dominated Sejm was the new Polish constitution. Because now it was known that Lech Walesa would occupy the presidency for the next six years, the new constitution was written with him in mind. The chief proposal made by Geremek's Constitutional Commission completely emasculated the office of the president, limiting it to ceremonial duties as nominal head of state.

In Geremek's proposal, the position of the Sejm was paramount and exclusive in all government functions, including the formation, functioning, and control of the cabinet. The president, the prime minister, and the Senate were all deprived of any power. Executive orders of the government could only carry out the legislative acts of the Sejm, which would be enforced by the Supreme Control Council (NIK). Thus the president would have no influence on government programs and no legislative initiative. The prime minister would only coordinate the work of his ministers.[6] Expert opinion held that such a government would be ineffective.

Geremek tried to manipulate the adoption of his proposal by the joint Constitution Commission of the Sejm and the Senate,[7] but it was regarded as improper to have such an important document adopted by a parliamentary commission only. Then he tried to have key parts adopted as part of the "small constitution" in the last weeks before the election. To pressure Walesa further, the Sejm did not pass any legislation from January 1991 (when Walesa assumed office) to July, when it became an issue, so as to paralyze reforms. In addition, the Sejm passed a law[8] essentially preserving communist control of state radio and television on September 13, 1991, which Walesa vetoed.[9]

While the government was preoccupied with these battles, its policy was paralyzed by the expectation of new elections and its ability to deal with new and serious challenges was hampered. The Democratic Union claimed that it did not want to have elections at that time so that it could continue with economic reforms. But throughout 1991 the old communist-dominated Sejm did not pass any reform proposals and the government remained passive in the face of deepening recession and persistent inflation.

Poland's position deteriorated further as a result of external shocks as well as an accumulation of the negative effects of reforms. In 1990, windfall profits collected by banks and enterprises as a result of price liberalization protected them from painful adjustment to the new market environment. The political and economic environment in 1991 worsened when there was a sharp drop in industrial production, the overvaluation of the zloty and a fall in exports, and continuing stagflation. Many state enterprises, cut off from traditional state sources of investment and working capital and unable to sell their products, veered toward bankruptcy and stopped paying their bills, leading to an accumulation of inter-enterprise arrears.

This sharp drop in internal demand was compounded by a drop in external demand, resulting from the collapse of traditional trading relationships, particularly within the Council of Mutual Economic Assistance (CMEA). German reunification cut off Poland from vital export markets in East Germany and from vital industrial inputs. The Persian Gulf War cut off Poland's trade with Iraq, which had served as an alternative source of oil and as a market for industrial products and construction services. It also distracted the attention of the West from Eastern Europe. In October 1990 the Soviet Union started charging its former allies world market prices for oil, to be paid only in hard currency. In January 1991, it cut off barter trade with Poland, and oil deliveries became uncertain. Subsequently, the Soviets stopped paying their bills altogether and owed Poland at least $1 billion.

The deepening recession and erratic budget policy of 1990 were reflected in the deteriorating budget situation. After targets were repeatedly missed, the International Monetary Fund (IMF) suspended disbursements of its adjustment loan to Poland in the summer of 1991 and modified its stabilization policy. It abandoned the fixed exchange rate of the zloty and adopted a "crawling peg" whereby the zloty was devalued 1.8 percent a month in relation to a basket of currencies. This policy was designed to keep Polish exports competitive. The IMF also loosened its tight credit policy. The formula for calculating the excess wage tax was modified; wages and pensions were raised considerably. Furthermore, the IMF allowed the reimposition of tariff protection for agricultural and some industrial goods.[10]

Throughout 1991, the recession continued to take its toll. It was worsened by the lack of internal institutional and systemic reforms.[11] Industrial production declined 12 percent and the gross domestic product 8 percent. Unemployment soared to 12 percent. Inflation continued at 70 percent a year. Despite this dire situation, the government did not feel any need to assist heavily indebted state-owned enterprises in dealing with the recession and emphasized the "creative destruction" of those that failed to adjust. This created more hostility toward the snail-paced privatization policy, and every transaction was contested. In this vacuum, the public was riled by financial scandals in the banks, import and export activities, taxes, and other areas, which underlined the power of postcommunist elites who were using their insider knowledge and ideological contact networks to rob the Polish state of large amounts of funds.

The parliamentary election campaign was somewhat similar to but not as vituperative as the presidential campaign of 1990. The Democratic Union presented itself as the party of general pragmatism, competence, and high-quality leadership, hiding its left-wing core of beliefs. The national independence parties campaigned against the Balcerowicz reform program, advocating anti-recessionary measures and better management of state enterprises that were not in the process of privatization, and demanded the decommunization of the high levels of state bureaucracy and punishment of those who had persecuted dissidents.

The election produced the results engineered by the architects of the election law: the largest numbers of votes—13 percent and 12 percent—were received respectively by the Democratic Union and the postcommunist Democratic Left Alliance. The remainder of the new Sejm was fragmented among twenty-seven other parties with no solid majority on which to base a stable government. After weeks of negotiations, a government was finally put together under the leadership of Jan Olszewski, a respected Solidarity lawyer and Walesa ally. This government was based on the unstable minority coalition of the Center Alliance, the Christian Democratic Union, and the Peasant Alliance, with the tacit support of other parties.

Moreover, Walesa turned against Olszewski, presumably because he feared the appeal of a strong leader who would limit the as yet undefined powers of the presidency. Thus the lack of a democratic constitution set the stage for the institutional conflict between the president and the prime minister that further undermined democracy and reforms.

THE OLSZEWSKI GOVERNMENT'S POLICIES

Olszewski's government represented the views of the national independence parties, whose main platform was decommunization of public life and opposition to the Balcerowicz program. But despite its promises, Olszewski had very little room to maneuver because of dire economic conditions and requirements of international financial institutions. There was a consensus that Poland must avoid renewed hyperinflation so the issue became how to devise a more flexible reflationary policy while not losing control over the size and financing of the state budget deficit. The government persuaded Western financial institutions to accept a budget deficit up to 5 percent of the gross domestic product and the use of a $1 billion stabilization fund for restructuring the debt of state enterprises and banks.[12] Thus the emphasis was on antirecessionary measures with a focus on exports, new investments, tax reduction, debt restructuring, and more flexibility on the budget deficit.

The second aspect of the Olszewski economic program was the interventionist industrial policy, designed to help state-owned enterprises to adjust better to the new market environment. Plans were made to unify and reorganize all economics ministries to coordinate stabilization, privatization, and industrial, trade, and other policies and to establish the state treasury. Long-term industrial restructuring assumed the priority, while previous methods of privatization were continued with attempts to deal with neglected areas such as reprivatization.

Despite this reasonable reassessment of current practices in the face of the economic crisis, Olszewski's policies were continually assaulted by the hostile majority in the Sejm and the media. In March, the Sejm rejected the "outline economic program" for 1992, which led to the resignation of Finance Minister Karol Lutkowski. In May, the Sejm voted to uphold the unreasonable provisions of the old Constitutional Tribunal, driving another finance minister to resign. The ruling declared unconstitutional the laws proposed by the previous Bielecki government that would have rationalized and reduced government spending for wages and pensions.

In politics, the Olszewski government's platform was democratization and decommunization, the removal of high-level communist officials and informers from public life. Work in this area met with great resistance, even though it was being dealt with more successfully elsewhere in Eastern Europe. It was soon overshadowed by the growing conflict between the president and the government over authority in defense and foreign policy areas. Their competing moves to consolidate influence over the Defense, Interior, and Foreign Affairs Ministries led to severe political clashes.

Walesa's conflict with Defense Minister Jan Parys over reorganization of the armed forces and personnel changes in the ministry led to mutual accusations and Parys's eventual resignation. Moreover, during Walesa's visit to Russia, the government made last-minute objections to the proposed terms of the withdrawal of former Soviet troops. On May 26, Walesa announced his withdrawal of support for the Olszewski government. As the formal procedure for dismissal was under way, on June 4, Interior Minister Antoni Macierewicz delivered lists of secret police collaborators to the members of the Sejm. The implication was that some of those seeking the removal of the government were acting out of conspiratorial ulterior motives.

The government was dismissed by 270 votes (out of 460) from three groups most threatened by its activities: postcommunists, post-Mazowiecki supporters, and the maverick nationalist group Confederacy for an Independent Poland, which had insisted on the Defense portfolio in the Olszewski government but had been refused. The main actor in the dismissal was Lech Walesa, who offered the job of prime minister to Waldemar Pawlak, head of the postcommunist Polish Peasant Party (this important historical name was appropriated from the émigré group that returned to Poland and is still in legal contention) that withdrew its support from the government. That act was regarded as illegitimate by many, and the odium of communism that tainted Pawlak led opposition politicians to refuse to serve in his government.

The dismissal of Olszewski polarized political attitudes in Poland. Most significantly, Solidarity identified broadly with the Olszewski program of decommunization and combating recession. It was angry at its attackers and at Walesa for his role in bringing down the government and nominating a postcommunist prime minister. At the June Solidarity Congress, some voices called for the withdrawal of support for the president. Before this motion was voted on, Walesa asked to appear before the congress to defend his record. His appearance turned into a hostile confrontation with the delegates, who expressed outrage over the political crisis. The congress called for immediate decommunization through legislation, antirecessionary policies, the adoption of a democratic constitution and electoral law, and depoliticizing the media. Thus Solidarity's platform resembled the agenda of the Olszewski government, ousted by its former chairman, its former advisers in the Democratic Union, and postcommunists. That signified the disintegration of Solidarity.

THE SUCHOCKA GOVERNMENT

After a period of interregnum and paralysis when Pawlak was unable to form a government, Solidarity played a mediating role and was instrumental in constructing the coalition government under the leadership of Hanna Suchocka, who had an unlikely combination of membership in the Democratic Union and a strong Catholic background. Her coalition of seven parties was divided between the center-right, which favored decommunization, and left-wing social democrats who favored the status quo but reached a consensus to concentrate on economic reforms.

Progress was made in settling outstanding economic issues. The Suchocka government reached an agreement with the IMF about the new standby credits, allowing an 8 percent budget deficit, which had been regarded as unreasonable when demanded by the Olszewski government, and enterprise and bank debt settlements. To break the impasse in privatization in areas where popular dissatisfaction was the highest, the government proposed a Pact on State-Owned Enterprises. It combined elements of industrial restructuring, debt settlements, debt-for-equity swaps, and employee wage restraint and involvement in privatization in a mixture designed to break resistance and define a path to privatization for the hitherto neglected state sector.[13] The legislation on mass privatization was passed by the Sejm in April 1993 in the form of government-controlled, foreign-managed investment funds, whose shares would eventually be exchanged for vouchers.

The most positive development of 1993 was the beginning of an industrial recovery, already noted by a halt in the decline in gross domestic product in 1992,[14] led by exports to the West, largely as a result of the explosive growth of the Polish private sector, which now constitutes over 50 percent of the gross domestic product and 60 percent of total employment. In 1989, 814,000 single proprietorships existed in Poland. That number was doubled three years later. There were 11,700 private incorporated enterprises in 1989; three years later, there were 74,000. Moreover, the success of privatization of small municipal shops and services as well as 800 medium-sized enterprises privatized through employee ownership added to the growing private sector. These private enterprises are in competition with the state sector, forcing better performance and increasing effectiveness of the whole economy.[15]

The outstanding political issues on which there was movement during Suchocka's tenure included the "small constitution" and electoral law, church-state relations, and foreign policy. The key role of Walesa in overthrowing Olszewski and creating the Suchocka government set the precedent for the division of power between the president, the government, and the Sejm in the future Polish constitution. In November 1992, legislation was passed on the "small constitution," an interim set of principles designed to replace the Stalinist constitution of 1952.

This compromise gave the president authority over the army and national security matters and the formation of the government. He could initiate legislation and veto it, and he could dissolve parliament if it did not pass a budget within three months. The executive powers of the government were strengthened. It could rule by decree, which could be vetoed by the president, with exceptions for budget, constitutional issues, personal freedoms, and social security measures. The Sejm was no longer designated as the highest organ of state power.

When the issue of presidential power was resolved, a new controversy arose over the separation between church and state. The left-wing groups argued that modernization of political culture in Poland required a complete secularization of public life. Others claimed that this was exactly the policy pursued by the communists and that Poland must be modernized in harmony with its own national and religious traditions. Former communists and new liberals directed political attacks against the Catholic Church and the Christian Democrat politicians. The accusations of clericalism, interference in the government, censorship, and the abortion debate have been used by left-wing circles to direct widespread public dissatisfaction with social and economic conditions at the time of transition against the Catholic Church. The Vatican did manage, however, to sign the Concordat with the Polish government in the summer of 1993, defining the rules for mutual relations.[16]

In foreign policy, Poland was trying to define its new place between East and West. As a result of the Polish-Russian treaty of friendship signed by Presidents Walesa and Yeltsin in May 1992, Russia withdrew its last combat units from Poland in September 1993.[17] This withdrawal as well as Yeltsin's declaration that Russia had "no objection" to Poland's membership in NATO, later reversed, was seen as a Russian effort to help the postcommunist parties in the 1993 election. About ten thousand troops remained to assist in the final withdrawal of former Soviet troops from Germany. Mutual claims for compensation were canceled.

In the West, Poland signed an association agreement with the European Community, a move which, even though regarded as unfavorable to Poland by many, delineates a path for future economic and political integration with the West. Its desired membership in NATO was postponed by the Clinton administration, which substituted a vague and limited Partnership for Peace, open to all postcommunist countries including Russia.

Despite some achievements of the Suchocka government, it was an inherently unstable and contradictory coalition under the domination of the Democratic Union. Its continuation of many previous policies eventually cost it its political support. After a vote of no confidence led by Solidarity, new elections were called for September 19, 1993. The Sejm rewrote the election law again, purportedly to eliminate the earlier political fragmentation by establishing 5 percent of the vote as a minimum for political parties and 8 percent for coalitions to be represented in the Sejm, but the effective threshold was higher in the smaller districts.

The election campaign was again characterized by strong attacks on the Catholic Church and center-right parties. The postcommunists presented themselves as strong supporters of reforms, but their rhetoric contradicted their methods, particularly in privatization. They appealed to those hurt by reforms and promised to restore economic security by raising wages and pensions and fully funding education, police protection, and medical care. Walesa organized the Non-Party Bloc to Support Reform to drain the votes from the center-right parties. Other parties ran on their old programs.

The final results of the election were 20 percent for the postcommunists and 15 percent for the Peasant Party, which gave them jointly a majority of 65 percent of the seats in the Sejm under the new electoral law. These two parties formed a government under Waldemar Pawlak. Other parties represented in parliament include the Labor Union, Democratic Union, Confederation for an Independent Poland, and Walesa's Bloc.[18] The center-right parties also received 20 percent of the vote but were not represented in the Sejm under the new rules.

CONCLUSION

The victory of postcommunist parties in the 1993 parliamentary elections was a stinging rebuke to the leadership of the Democratic Union that dominated the Polish governments since 1989, except for the short-lived Olszewski government. These governments came to be known as the Roundtable governments and symbolized the lack of democracy as well as a de facto alliance between the postcommunists and the left wing of Solidarity, dominated by the Democratic Union. This alliance undermined its credibility as a democratic reformer.

The Mazowiecki government initially enjoyed a honeymoon for its reform policies, but it needed an able bureaucracy to implement them and strong legislative support to sustain them. By opposing decommunization and removal of high-level communist officials, Mazowiecki kept the communist bureaucracy almost intact and ensured that its own reform policy initiatives were sabotaged at the implementation level.

By opposing free elections, the Mazowiecki government relied on legislative support for reforms from the Sejm, where communist and allied Peasant Party deputies held 65 percent of the seats. In 1990, this group was passive and automatically supported the policy initiatives of the executive. But as time went on, this support severely diminished. Thus a lack of democracy and of institutional reform destroyed the ability to implement and sustain economic reforms and contributed to the recession.

If the Mazowiecki government did not have long-term support in the Sejm or the bureaucracy, it should have been able to count on popular pressure from citizens, particularly Solidarity, which was its political sponsor. But Mazowiecki excluded Walesa from the power circle and did everything possible to prevent him from becoming president. The reform plans also excluded Solidarity initiatives and peasant and small business interests. Thus, at the very beginning, Mazowiecki alienated most of his popular support.

The Roundtable governments achieved notable economic successes in areas where there was a consensus, mainly stabilization and trade liberalization, which were adjusted substantially over time. This created an environment in which the Polish economy could recover from a serious recession and resume growth. Real gross domestic product increased by 3.8 percent in 1993, 4.5 percent in 1994, and 6.5 percent in 1995. The explosive growth of the private sector and the success of small and medium privatization created a "locomotive" for the Polish economy that is leading it out of recession and onto a promising new path.

Serious mistakes of the "shock therapy" undermined support for reforms, however. Too much emphasis was put on macroeconomic stabilization at the expense of privatization policy and institutional reforms. Privatization policy was not seriously pursued, even though it was understood that only privatization and new investment could restructure the Polish economy and allow permanent stabilization. The policy was based mainly on the stock market (which has had a limited capability to privatize companies) and foreign investment that was not forthcoming because of the unstable macroeconomic environment and unpaid foreign debt.

Poland still does not have a mass privatization program that allows ordinary citizens to participate in privatization. The limited program of government-sponsored investment funds proved to be controversial and had only been implemented in 1995, four years after its introduction because it does not allow free choice or a substantial transfer of assets to Polish citizens. Thus a popular consensus that privatization will be the chief means of transforming the system was bitterly disappointed. The policy of destruction of state enterprises was politically unacceptable. Their competitiveness and capacity to accommodate themselves to the new market environment was vastly underestimated, as recent studies have shown.

Furthermore, in a popular judgment, the reforms did not meet social expectations of justice and equity, were instituted in an authoritarian and arrogant manner, and served the interests of political elites. Their costs are high for ordinary citizens with 16 percent unemployed, 40 percent living below the poverty line, and decimation of the social infrastructure. Economic reforms have been disconnected from the political process and from the main force behind them—Solidarity—by the elitism and authoritarianism of reformers.

Overall, the election of the postcommunists signifies an end to the first phase of reforms, carried out under the umbrella of Solidarity. The authoritarian manner in which this reform was carried out, its unanticipated destructive consequences, and its indefinite duration created deep opposition within the population. The current situation of the postcommunist government should be viewed as a period of transition, and those groups that are capable of formulating a more inclusive and participatory reform program will gain political support in the future.

NOTES

1. Timothy Lane, *Inflation Stabilization and Economic Transformation in Poland: The First Year,* IMF Working Paper (Washington: IMF, 1991).

2. Ibid.

3. Ibid.

4. Jan Winiecki, "Zbyt powolna zmiana systemu" [Too slow change of the system], *Gospodarka Narodowa* (Warsaw) 3 (March 1991).

5. David Lipton and Jeffrey Sachs, "Privatization in Eastern Europe: The Case of Poland," *Brookings Papers on Economic Activity,* No. 2 (Washington, D.C., 1990).

6. Komisja Konstytucyjna Sejmu Rzeczpospolitej Polskiej X Kadencju, *Konstytucja: Projekt,* [Constitution Commission of the Sejm of the Polish Republic, *Project of the Constitution*] (Warsaw: Wydawnictwo Sejmowe, 1992).

7. Bronislaw Geremek, "Preface," ibid.

8. Polish Senate, *Law on Radio and Television*, No. 592, Warsaw, September 17, 1991.

9. *Letter from President Lech Walesa to the Sejm of the Polish Republic*, No. 11, Warsaw, November 3, 1991.

10. Guillermo Calvo and Jacob Frenkel, *From Centrally Planned to Market Economy: The Road from CPE to PCPE*, IMF Staff Paper (Washington D.C.: IMF, 1991).

11. Tomasz Telma, "The Polish Economy in 1991," *PlanEcon Report* (Washington, D.C., December 30, 1991), 49–50 .

12. Wojciech Bienkowski, *Roundtable in Systemic Transformation*, RFE/RL Research Report, No. 31, July 31, 1992.

13. Dariusz Grabowski and Janusz Szewczak, "Uwagi o `pakcie o przedsiebiorstwie'" [Comments on the Enterprise Pact], *Tygodnik Solidarnosc* (Warsaw), October 9, 1992.

14. "Poland's Economic Reforms: If It Works, You've Fixed It," *Economist*, January 23, 1993.

15. Michal Zielinski, "Czteroletni Plan Odbudowy—proba bilansu" [Four-year reconstruction plan—a summary], *Tygodnik Powszechny* (Cracow) 44 (November 1, 1993).

16. Anna Sabbat-Swidlicka, "The Catholic Church After Communism," *Catholic World*, January 1994.

17. John Pomfret, "Last Russian Troops Leave Poland," *Washington Post*, September 19, 1993.

18. "Poland: Not as Bad as It Looked—Maybe," *Economist*, September 25, 1993.

9

⸺◆⸺

The Security of East Central Europe and the Visegrad Triangle

ANDRZEJ KORBONSKI

In the "morning after" period since the disintegration of the Soviet bloc and the collapse of communist rule in the *annus mirabilis* 1989, the East Central European countries had to cope with the consequences of the revolutionary changes. These consequences included the legacy of communist rule and of Soviet hegemony in the region and the crises and challenges generated by the process of transition to democracy.

This chapter focuses on a key external challenge to the security of the region, linked to the legacy of more than forty-year-long Soviet domination of the area. First, I will examine the security challenge or dilemma faced by four East Central European states—the Czech Republic, Slovakia, Hungary, and Poland. Then I will focus on ways and means deployed by these countries to deal with the challenge.

SECURITY CONCERNS BEFORE 1989

It may be argued that until 1989 none of the countries under discussion could be viewed as fully sovereign states, and thus their security concerns were largely if not wholly subordinated to the interests of the Soviet Union, which established its hegemony over East Central Europe more than forty years earlier. There is little doubt that throughout this period security has been the key Soviet interest in the region.

If true, this premise raises the question of the meaning of "security" to the Kremlin. Was it comparable to the traditional Western concept of military or physical security, or did it represent something different? I have argued elsewhere that the Soviet notion of security entailed not only the traditional military concept but also political, ideological, and economic aspects.[1] This essay, however, focuses only on the conventional military component of Soviet security interests.

Although in the missile age geography has become a much less important strategic factor than formerly, Soviet security interest in the region could be interpreted to mean that on the eve of the upheaval of 1989 Moscow still viewed

East Central Europe as a valuable piece of real estate that it was prepared to protect against foreign incursions and that, in turn, would resist any attempt either by an external power or by domestic political forces to undermine Soviet military and political hegemony in both the short and long run.

In the eyes of the Kremlin, the Warsaw Pact (which celebrated its thirtieth anniversary in 1985) guaranteed Soviet supremacy in the area. Over the years the pact played three separate albeit interrelated roles: as a security or military alliance; as a diplomatic actor on the international scene; and as an instrument of political integration of East Central Europe. In each case the treaty was a handmaiden of Moscow, which successive Soviet leaders used and manipulated for their own purposes.[2] The most publicized aspect of the latter was the proclamation of the so-called Brezhnev Doctrine, by virtue of which the Soviet Union assumed the role of guardian of the alliance, responsible for its security and integrity.

If the above correctly defines the nature and scope of Soviet security interests in East Central Europe, the question arises whether it was still possible in the late 1980s to identify specific security interests of the individual countries in the region.

There is no doubt that long before the proclamation of the Brezhnev Doctrine Czechoslovakia, Hungary, and Poland viewed the Soviet Union as the principal threat to their security. Two of them—Czechoslovakia and Hungary—fell victim to open Soviet aggression, and Poland, on several occasions in 1980–81, came close to being invaded and escaped its ultimate fate only by imposing martial law in December 1981. Thus, despite the existence of multiple declarations of mutual friendship and support, the principle of limited sovereignty, embodied in the Brezhnev Doctrine, made the USSR rather than the West the chief threat to the physical security and survival of the three countries. Although it is true that until recently Western missiles were targeted on most of East Central Europe, it may be taken for granted that they would have been fired only in response to a Soviet attack on NATO. This scenario, which fortunately was never played out, simply strengthened the view that the Soviet Union and not the West posed the main danger to the security of the region.

There existed other historical threats to the security of Czechoslovakia, Hungary, and Poland, which although forcibly suppressed by the Kremlin, managed to survive more than four decades of communist rule. Thus Poland has continued to harbor fears of German revanchism, which were also shared by Czechoslovakia. Hungary, which did not view Germany as an enemy, considered Romania as its major adversary. Moreover, there was little love lost between Czechoslovakia and Hungary and between Poland and Czechoslovakia, but none of these latent conflicts were likely to develop into genuine threats to each other's security.

Thus, on the eve of the revolutionary changes in 1989, the Warsaw alliance appeared stable, despite growing signs of domestic unrest. In the final analysis, this stability and the security interests of the USSR and of its East Central European allies were protected by close to half a million Soviet troops stationed in Czechoslovakia, East Germany, Hungary, and Poland.

In retrospect, it is difficult to pinpoint the exact moment when the Kremlin decided to unburden itself of East Central Europe.[3] The events of the late 1980s have shown rather conclusively that there was a sea change in the Soviet leadership's style and manner of making policy, especially on the bilateral level, and in the general atmosphere of conducting business in the Warsaw Pact and the Council for Mutual Economic Assistance (CMEA), the other pillar supporting Soviet hegemony in the region.

By mid-1988, the official attitude of the Kremlin strongly suggested that the rapidly worsening economic situation in the region necessitated radical economic reforms, and if the latter required equally striking political reforms, Moscow implicitly promised not to interfere with the process of liberalization.[4] The record shows that the tenor of the message, and especially of its last part, was unmistakable and was not lost on the inhabitants of the area.

Starting with Poland, the dialogue between the government and the opposition led to the so-called Roundtable negotiations, followed by a striking defeat of the communists in the June 1989 elections and the formation of the first noncommunist government in East Central Europe in more than forty years. The crucial decision by the Hungarian government in May 1989 to open the country's border with Austria, resulting in a mass exodus of East Germans—a decision made with tacit Soviet approval—speeded up the process of disintegration of the Hungarian ruling party, which was subsequently badly beaten in the elections of May–June 1990. In Czechoslovakia, the end of the communist regime in November 1989 came so swiftly that there were rumors that the collapse was either engineered by, or orchestrated with, the Soviets.[5]

It may be speculated that while giving a green light to the reforms in individual countries, Mikhail Gorbachev never expected that doing so would amount to issuing a death warrant to the ruling communist parties. Most likely, he assumed that having embraced perestroika, the parties would retain their leading role. This proved to be a fatal mistake from Moscow's point of view, and it opened the door to a democratic transformation of the East Central polities and economies. It also resulted in a striking change in the security relationships within the region.

SECURITY CONCERNS SINCE 1989

Once the demise of communism became an accomplished fact by the end of 1989, the new national leaders of Czechoslovakia, Hungary, and Poland had to face a multitude of formidable tasks, all of which required immediate attention. Not surprisingly, foremost among them was the problem of legitimizing the new political systems, and in the course of 1990 all three countries held either parliamentary or presidential elections to achieve popular approval of the revolutionary transformation. Next on the agenda was the economy, which soon became subject to more or less radical reforms, ranging from "shock therapy" to more gradual reforms. While the governments were preoccupied with political and economic changes, their new rulers seem to have neglected the problem of security.

There were very good reasons for the neglect. To begin with, as pointed out by a Hungarian observer of the East Central European scene, "It is extremely risky to maintain sovereignty and pursue an independent domestic and foreign policy because these countries have not got used to it for at least half a century."[6] Living in constant fear of Soviet intervention, no country in the region has been able either to develop its own notion of security or its own concept of national interest. Their foreign policies and national defense were totally subordinated to the interests of the Kremlin; none of the three countries was allowed to postulate its own military doctrine. They were simply forced to accept the doctrine dictated by Moscow.

Moreover, the new leaders had little if any experience in international relations and foreign policy. In Poland, both President Lech Walesa and Prime Minister Tadeusz Mazowiecki were novices in foreign relations, and they were fortunate that the foreign minister, Krzysztof Skubiszewski, was a professor of international law, who at least was not a total stranger to the field. In Czechoslovakia, neither President Vaclav Havel nor Foreign Minister Jiri Dienstbier—both veteran dissidents—was at home with problems of security and foreign policy, and in Hungary, the only individual who claimed to have some familiarity with key security and foreign policy issues was Foreign Minister Geza Jeszensky, who only a year or so earlier had taught modern European history at the University of California.

This lack of experience, regrettable as it was, would not have been harmful if it had been compensated by the availability of well-trained foreign service and academic specialists. Alas, there were no such specialists, at least during the first two years or so of the transition period. Foreign service in all three countries has been an important part of communist nomenklatura and the same applied in large measure to academic personnel, including those employed in various research institutes attached to the respective ministries or the Academy of Sciences.

Thus when lightning struck in 1989 and the communist debacle was followed within less than two years by the disappearance of the Warsaw Pact and CMEA, a vacuum arose in the region that none of the new rulers knew how to handle. The new leaders were distinguished playwrights, journalists, labor leaders, museum directors, and even university professors, who had courageously resisted communist regimes but who had paid little attention to the future shape of their countries, to their respective place in the European and world order, and, last but not least, to their security concerns and dilemmas. The individuals below the top level tended to be mostly bureaucrats whose training and experience over the past four decades was focused on safeguarding and advancing the interests of the Soviet hegemon.

It is not surprising, therefore, that in the early stages of the transition period, the new policy makers were rather helpless, and in formulating their foreign policies they were often motivated by simple-minded and even naive considerations. As true sons of their respective countries, they were deeply versed in their national histories and strongly influenced by their national political cultures. At the same time, having just signally contributed to the downfall of the despised communist rule, they were driven by a desire to eliminate all its remnants and to destroy all links with the Soviet Union. Finally, in their search for a solution to their security dilemma, they put all their faith in the West, which, they assumed, was ready and willing to take them into its fold. I argue that these three characteristic features of the new leaders explain their attitude and behavior with regard to the security concerns of their respective countries and especially toward creation of a trilateral security arrangement in the region.

In the past, relations between Czechoslovakia, Hungary, and Poland tended to be characterized by hostility and mistrust rather than by friendship and understanding. The relations between Prague and Warsaw, never particularly close in the distant past, became strongly embittered at the end of World War I in the wake of the Czechoslovak incorporation of a part of Silesia, which the Poles considered theirs and which they recovered in October 1938. As a result, the entire interwar period was marred by considerable hostility between the two countries. One glimmer of hope of a possible reconciliation arose during World War II, in the form of a draft agreement on a future Czechoslovak-Polish federation, but within a year the agreement turned out to be null and void and was followed by a return to the traditional enmity. The hostility continued unabated during the entire period of communist rule. Apart from territorial conflicts in Silesia, the Poles could not forget the adversarial Czechoslovak stance during the crises of October 1956 and 1980–81, and the Czechoslovaks could not easily forgive the Poles for their participation in the 1968 Soviet-led Warsaw Pact intervention. Thus, even though seemingly friendly relations were established after 1989, the lingering undercurrent of mistrust remained on both sides.

Czechoslovakia also had traditional problems with Hungary, aggravated by the memories of the interwar Little Entente and the presence of a sizable Hungarian minority in Slovakia. Prague obviously did not endear itself to Budapest because of the former's hostile attitude toward the revolt of October–November 1956, and Hungary's involvement, albeit minor, in suppressing the Prague Spring in August 1968 did not help matters. More recently, the emergence of Slovak nationalism and the issue of the Gabcikovo-Nagyvaros hydroelectric project added more fuel to the conflict.

Only Hungarian-Polish relations could be described as traditionally friendly, helped, no doubt, by both countries' historical hatred of Russia. Poland's warm support of the 1956 Hungarian revolt and Hungary's refusal to join the fierce Soviet-sponsored anti-Polish campaign in 1980–81 cemented the warm friendship.

Turning to the relationship between the Soviet Union and the three countries, Hungary took the lead in calling for the dissolution of both the Warsaw Pact and CMEA and in time gained the support of both Poland and Czechoslovakia. Also, both Czechoslovakia and Hungary from the very beginning insisted on rapid withdrawal of Soviet forces from their territories, which was finally achieved on the basis of bilateral treaties signed in 1990.

No such agreement was signed at that time between Moscow and Warsaw, despite Polish desire to do so. To a large extent, the ensuing impasse was Poland's fault, compounded by West German chancellor Helmut Kohl's erratic behavior in 1990. During the complex negotiations leading to the "Four Plus Two" conference, which was to settle the future of a united Germany and in which Poland was vitally interested, Kohl engaged in several tactical delaying maneuvers, intended to keep Poland from the conference table because of the sensitive nature of the Polish-German frontier and its implications for the domestic political scene in Germany. At some point, giving in to a growing frustration over Germany's behavior, Prime Minister Mazowiecki alluded to the possibility of Soviet troops remaining in Poland for the time being for "defensive purposes."

Finally, the new policy makers, faced with the suddenly emerging security vacuum in their region, put their blind faith in the willingness of the West in the shape of NATO and the European Community (EC) to embrace the newly emancipated countries and to grant them security guarantees and economic aid. They hoped for instant membership in the North Atlantic alliance and the Common Market. Lacking exposure to conventional international relations and inexperienced in conducting an independent foreign policy, they expected the membership process to be relatively quick and simple.

Under these circumstances, not much thought was given in Budapest, Prague, and Warsaw to the necessity of creating a triangular security arrangement in the region. The early hopes of being welcomed with open arms by the West soon proved illusory. At the same time, the expectation that the Soviet Union, having consented to the democratic transformation, would no longer insist on exerting major influence over the region proved equally unrealistic. A major reappraisal of Czechoslovak, Hungarian, and Polish security concerns became necessary.

THE ROAD TO VISEGRAD AND KRAKOW

It may be argued that even before the outbreak of the Persian Gulf crisis in late 1990, the highly touted and promising relationship between East Central and Western Europe had been put largely on hold. One reason was a belief that the early expectations of a much closer political and economic relationship were premature and that both the West and East Central Europeans concluded that a closer rapprochement between the two parts of Europe would have to wait. The cooling off of the initial ardor came from Western Europe, and especially from Germany and France. Although Germany may have initially considered providing major economic aid to East Central Europe, the unexpectedly high cost of integrating the former German Democratic Republic made that impossible. Faced with rapidly diminishing resources, the Federal Republic chose to provide aid to the Soviet Union, which was allowed to station its soldiers on German soil until the end of October 1994.

France appeared to play an even more devious role vis-à-vis East Central Europe. Chagrined over being essentially ignored in the process of German unification, France decided initially to play a major part in the former Soviet bloc, as illustrated by its insistence on dominating the newly formed European Bank for Reconstruction and Development. But it soon became clear to Paris that the cost of restoring the East Central European economies to the level of Western Europe was too staggering, and throughout 1991 France limited its support for the region to verbal encouragement of closer economic cooperation on the ruins of CMEA, and ultimately vetoed an agreement that would have given East Central European countries access to the Common Market.[7]

The key event regarding relations with the Soviet Union was the final dissolution of the Warsaw Pact in March 1991, followed a few months later by the demise of CMEA.[8] Both developments most likely came not too soon for the East Central European states, which were increasingly worried about internal developments in the Soviet Union. They accepted the Kremlin's new thinking on East Central Europe with gratitude and warmly welcomed Moscow's apparent benign neglect of communism's downfall in the area, followed by its agreement to German reunification and its promise to withdraw forces from the region. All this was viewed as inaugurating a new chapter in the East Central European–Soviet relationship.

This rosy picture soon became clouded, however, and optimism gave way to a growing belief that the honeymoon with Moscow was about over. The new perception was caused in part by a rising conviction that Gorbachev was becoming a captive of a conservative alliance composed of the military, the KGB, and the apparat, essentially hostile to the recent emancipation of East Central Europe.[9] The resignation in December 1990 of Foreign Minister Eduard Shevardnadze, viewed as the strongest supporter of the process of East Central European emancipation, was paralleled by continuing attacks by Soviet conservatives accusing Gorbachev of selling out the region. Furthermore, the Kremlin's uncompromising attitude with regard to bilateral treaties of friendship and alliance signaled Moscow's reluctance to restore full sovereignty to its former allies.[10] There was also a fear that the obvious Soviet attempts to hold on to the crumbling empire, as illustrated by the violent encounters in Lithuania and Latvia, might eventually spill over into the neighboring countries. The end of the Council for Mutual Economic Assistance also created serious problems for the region, even though, as described by the London *Economist*, it had been neither mutual, economic, nor of much help to its members.[11]

The main consequence of the disappearance of CMEA was a virtual collapse of Soviet trade with East Central Europe; the USSR greatly reduced the previously guaranteed deliveries of key raw materials, including oil and natural gas. As a result, whole industries in the region, heavily dependent on both Soviet supplies and the Soviet market, were threatened with bankruptcy. The parallel disappearance of the profitable East German market compounded the difficulties.

It is difficult to time exactly the beginning of the trialogue between Czechoslovakia, Hungary, and Poland which led to the signing of the Visegrad accord. Throughout 1990, at least two of the three states appeared to be cool to the idea of regional cooperation. Thus the newly elected president of Czechoslovakia, Vaclav Havel, discounted the possibility of resurrecting the Polish-Czechoslovak federation suggested by Zbigniew Brzezinski.[12] At that time, the Czechoslovaks were totally preoccupied with the desire of "returning to Europe" on their own, not jointly with the Hungarians and the Poles.[13] Even though the latter two were invited to a meeting in Bratislava in April 1990, called to discuss the question of integration with Western Europe, in reality it turned out to be a meeting of the Pentagonale group (Austria, Czechoslovakia, Hungary, Italy, and Yugoslavia), which Prague considered an instrument that would facilitate its entry into Europe.[14]

Hungary also showed little initial interest in a triangular arrangement. On the one hand, the leaders of Hungary viewed their country as the only logical candidate for an early membership in both the EC and NATO and saw no need to be accompanied by Czechoslovakia and Poland. On the other hand, at least two issues hindered closer rapprochement with Czechoslovakia: the presence of the Hungarian minority in Slovakia and the Gabcikovo-Nagyvaros project.

The only country which from the beginning showed strong interest in a possible triangular collaboration was Poland,[15] but its interest was not reciprocated by the other two countries. In addition to Czechoslovakia's historic mistrust of Poland, both Budapest and Prague perceived it as economically the "sick man of East Central Europe" and feared that any closer affiliation with it might force the other two potential partners to assume partial responsibility for Poland's economic plight.[16]

What, then, explains the rather sudden change of heart on the part of Czechoslovakia and Hungary that resulted in the Visegrad agreement?[17] It may be argued that the main reason was the failure of the "revolution of rising expectations" with regard to the Soviet Union and Western Europe. The formal dissolution of the Warsaw Pact, although not unexpected, created a security vacuum in the region that had to be filled somehow. It had become clear that NATO was not prepared to fill it, nor was the Conference on Security and Cooperation in Europe (CSCE) or the Pentagonale group, which was already showing its ineptness in dealing with the escalating conflict in Yugoslavia.

The dissolution of the Warsaw Pact did not, however, put an end to continuing harsh signals from Moscow, strongly suggesting that the Kremlin intended to maintain its hegemonic position in the region even after the pact's dissolution. These signals were significant because they were delivered not only by Soviet foreign policy officials such as Yuri Kvitsinsky, presumably representing the official Soviet government line, but also by well-known academic foreign policy specialists such as Andrei Kokoshin, who, in commenting on the changes in East Central Europe, asserted: "The states involved should respect the USSR's legitimate security interests in international security activities in these countries. This interest requires that the states commit no actions that would threaten the USSR's security on the territory of those countries and that they do not conduct subversive activity intended to overthrow the legally elected bodies of power in the USSR."[18]

The language of the statement is reminiscent of Yalta, and the question could be legitimately raised as to who was to judge actions taken by the East Central European countries that would threaten Soviet security. It was not hard to imagine that the ultimate arbiter would be the Kremlin. Therefore, it was not surprising that the critical comments emanating from Moscow further strengthened the determination of the three countries to reach a trilateral agreement.[19]

There were also other considerations. One was the rapidly growing refugee problem, which was bound to increase further as a result of the progressive disintegration of the USSR and Yugoslavia and the continuing instability of Romania.[20] Also, the persistent decline in trade with the Soviet Union was badly hurting the economic performance of all three countries.

The Visegrad meeting on February 15, 1991, attended by the respective heads of state and government and foreign ministers, was seen by the Czecho-slovak and Hungarian participants above all as an attempt to coordinate the three countries' policies aimed at reentering Europe.[21] Both Budapest and Prague were strongly opposed to any institutionalization of the triangular co-operation which might give an appearance of a bloc that would make it harder for any member to integrate with the West. The same applied to the issue of economic cooperation, which remained vague and was to be confined to con-sultation rather than institutionalization. The signatories of the Visegrad agree-ment took great pains to emphasize that the accord was directed neither at the USSR nor at Germany.[22]

Little progress in tightening the Visegrad triangle occurred over the next five months. Despite declarations of unanimity of views regarding common pursuit of policies aimed at rejoining Europe, each country persisted in its drive to become the first to accomplish this goal, albeit without much success. Still, their efforts resulted in continuing competition, especially in the economic arena, to strike a deal with the EC or its individual members, and any success achieved by one country was resented by the other two.[23] There appeared to be precious little consultation among the three signatories with regard to such issues as obtaining NATO security guarantees or signing bilateral treaties with the Soviet Union.

Domestic considerations also precluded closer collaboration. Prague's at-tention in the second half of 1991 was mainly focused on Slovakia and the future of the Czechoslovak federation. In Hungary, conflict escalated both within and between the legislative and executive branches of the government. In Poland, the seeming failure of the "shock therapy" economic program and the progressive fragmentation of political life on the eve of parliamentary elec-tions scheduled for October diverted attention away from foreign policy and security issues.

The Moscow coup of August 19 strongly reverberated throughout East Central Europe by exposing the security vacuum, which many in the region believed no longer existed.[24] One by-product of the coup was a sudden revival of interest in the Visegrad triangle, whose members decided to present a united front vis-à-vis the Soviet crisis. Following a meeting of foreign and defense experts in Warsaw the day after the coup, the three heads of state planned to call a summit meeting to coordinate their reactions to the events in Moscow. As the crisis petered out, the meeting was called off, but the joint action reaf-firmed the three countries' resolve to pursue trilateral policies, particularly with regard to an affiliation with Western Europe.[25]

The postponed summit took place in Crakow on October 6 and produced two documents.[26] The first one, the "Krakow Summit Statement of the Foreign Ministers on Links with the North Atlantic Alliance," reflected the triangle's disappointment with the proposed North Atlantic Cooperation Council, which called for a vaguely phrased liaison between NATO and the "new democracies of Central and Eastern Europe and the Soviet Union." The second statement, the "Krakow Declaration," essentially restated the arguments contained in the statement of the foreign ministers and called for further trilateral cooperation, mostly in economics.

SECURITY CONCERNS AFTER THE KRAKOW SUMMIT

Despite solemn declarations of continuing commitment to further triangular cooperation, little if any progress was recorded in the fifteen or so months following the Visegrad summit. To be sure, lip service was paid regularly in all three countries to the advantages of the triangle as an instrument safeguarding political stability, transition to democracy, and creation of a market economy, but few concrete measures aimed at further institutionalization of trilateral cooperation have been taken. Another summit meeting was held in Prague in May 1992, at which the three heads of state once again agreed to submit a joint application for membership in the European Community. But an agreement signed in November 1991, establishing a free trade zone among the three countries as of July 1992, was never implemented.[27]

The likely reasons behind the lack of progress can be summarized as follows:

(1) There was a growing perception in all three capitals that outside threats to the security of the region were diminishing. Negative consequences of the breakup of the Soviet Union did not spill over into East Central Europe.

(2) Even though there was still some apprehension of a possible conservative backlash in Moscow, Boris Yeltsin appeared to be in full control of the Kremlin, and nothing in his actions indicated that he might entertain second thoughts about the dissolution of the Soviet empire. The long-delayed signing of bilateral treaties between Russia and the three Visegrad countries strongly implied that Moscow no longer insisted on treating the area as a security buffer zone, protecting Russia from possible incursions from the West.

(3) One of the reasons that motivated Czechoslovakia, Hungary, and Poland to sign the Visegrad agreement was the fear that the worsening economic situation in the Commonwealth of Independent States would unleash a massive flood of refugees descending on East Central Europe on the way to Berlin, Paris, and Rome, worsening an already

difficult economic situation. Despite dire predictions of major popular upheavals in the wake of radical price increases and a drastic decline in living standards of the Soviet population, no mass exodus actually took place.

(4) At least two of the countries—Czechoslovakia and Poland—were facing serious political difficulties at home. Poland, in particular, in the wake of the October 1991 elections, suffered from a progressive fragmentation of its political life, which in July 1992 produced a fourth government in less than three years, reflecting the weakening of domestic consensus and resulting in a progressive paralysis in policy making.

Czechoslovakia also was in a turmoil, generated mostly by the growing intransigence of Slovakia, making the breakup of the Federation almost inevitable. If anything, the result of the parliamentary elections in June 1992 made the situation even more difficult, and to some outside observers the Czechoslovak polity began to resemble that of Poland.

Although Hungary managed to avoid the turmoil suffered by the other two countries, the political situation there was far from stable. Moreover, Hungary was increasingly preoccupied with its minority in Slovakia and Vojvodina, not to mention the perennial problem of Transylvania.

(5) In July 1992 the leaders of the respective countries must finally have realized that their joint effort aimed at speeding up their entry into Europe would not accelerate the rapprochement with the Common Market. All three states succeeded in obtaining the status of associate membership in the European Community, but the cherished goal of full membership continued to elude them and most likely was not going to be granted until the turn of the century. The joint action obviously did not pay off in this respect, and that failure removed one of the key motives behind the signing of the Visegrad, Krakow, and Prague accords.

(6) The same was largely true for the triangle's relations with NATO. It was clear that the Visegrad group was not going to get the desired security guarantee and had to be satisfied, at least for the time being, with membership in the North Atlantic Cooperation Council, the importance of which was greatly diluted by the inclusion of the Central Asian republics, which gave the council a rather bizarre look.

This brief summary shows that a dramatic change occurred in the international arena in the fifteen months or so after the Visegrad summit, which was bound to affect the security concerns of the triangle. There is no doubt that in the second half of 1992, Czechoslovakia, Hungary, and Poland felt more secure than they did two years earlier and no longer feared an outside threat from the East. If anything, the danger to their survival as democratic polities was internal rather than external as the growing pains of transformation proved longer lasting and more complex than anticipated both at home and abroad.

Is the Visegrad Triangle There to Stay?

This essay has discussed the question of who, in the postcommunist period, was going to protect East Central Europe in general, and Czechoslovakia, Hungary, and Poland in particular. The question was far from academic as it concerned the sheer physical survival and the preservation of national sovereignty of the three—now four—countries.

The story of the joint efforts to ensure military security for these countries is a melancholy one. The conditions existing in the region at the time of the collapse of the Warsaw Pact in early 1991 did not inspire much optimism as long as the Soviet Union remained intact, still maintaining an impressive military presence in the area and still being threatened by political instability and haunted by the specter of a conservative coup. This feeling of insecurity in combination with the ambivalent attitude of the West proved strong enough to allow the new leaders in Budapest, Prague, and Warsaw to overcome traditional mistrust and prejudice and to sign the Visegrad agreement. The August 1991 coup reawakened the feeling of insecurity and seemed to propel the signatories toward further trilateral cooperation, symbolized in the Krakow and Prague summits.

Perhaps the most persuasive reason for not abandoning the Visegrad model is that so far at least no substitute has been found to take its place. Even though the Soviet threat may have abated significantly and the START I and START II agreements made that threat even more remote, I would argue that it has not disappeared completely. Unless there is a visible improvement in the well-being of the Russian people, a reactionary backlash cannot be entirely discounted. Although Russian defense minister Pavel Grachev may have been persuaded by Yeltsin that the destruction of SS-18 missiles was in the Russian national interest, the appointment of General Victor Dubynin as the new chief of staff of the Russian armed forces must not have been reassuring to the Poles, who remember him as the arrogant and hard-line commander of Soviet forces in Poland.

Of course, even if a military coup were to succeed, it does not automatically follow that the victorious generals would immediately launch a drive to reestablish Russian hegemony in East Central Europe. The fragility of the current security arrangements in East Central Europe and Russia was sharply under-scored by the reaction to an address by the Russian foreign minister, Andrei Kozyrev, at the CSCE meeting in Stockholm in December 1992. Although the speech turned out to be a ruse, the reaction it generated was a good testimony to the lack of confidence in the permanent character of the present situation in the region.[28] It also meant that insecurity rather than security was likely to characterize the relationship between Russia and the former Soviet satellites in the region.

The disintegration of the USSR, followed by the declarations of indepen-dence by Ukraine, Belarus, and other former Soviet republics, did not increase the feeling of security in East Central Europe. Ukraine, in particular, one of the largest countries in Europe and in possession of nuclear weapons, was viewed as a potential threat at least by Poland, whose historical relations with Ukraine could hardly be described as friendly. The emergence of a vocal Ukrai-nian irredenta, voicing territorial demands against Poland, may have been viewed by some as part of a lunatic fringe, but it was taken seriously by the Poles, who suffered from an anti-Ukrainian irredentist movement of their own. Thus it was not surprising that Poland was the first foreign country to grant diplomatic recognition to the newly independent Ukraine. Although Poland was the most affected country, none of the remaining countries in the tri-angle, for reasons of their own, could remain indifferent to Ukrainian nation-alism, and it can be assumed that they, together with Poland, most likely wel-comed Ukraine's interest in joining the Visegrad group.[29]

The other potential threat to East Central European security was repre-sented by the prolonged civil war in the former Yugoslavia. Here Hungary was the most exposed country because of the presence of the Hungarian mi-nority in Vojvodina, whose autonomy was destroyed by Serbia.[30] Although unlikely, Hungary's decision to protect its nationals oppressed by Belgrade cannot be excluded, especially in light of growing fears that the civil war might be internationalized through the involvement of Albania, Bulgaria, and Mace-donia, also willing to protect their nationals.

The Yugoslav conflict affected the security of the triangle in still another way. The inability of CSCE, EC, and NATO to bring the domestic strife in the former Yugoslavia to some rational conclusion spoke for itself and was bound significantly to discount the value of Western security guarantees, in the un-likely event that they were to be granted to the members of the Visegrad group. Western pronouncements on the subject of East Central Europe could be in-terpreted as largely meaningless teasers that were not credible to the leaders and the people at large.[31] The most recent decision by Germany to put the onus of reducing the flow of asylum seekers on Czechoslovakia and Poland is a case in point.[32]

If the above conclusion is correct, it would appear that despite the less than favorable conditions, there was still no good substitute for the Visegrad group.[33] Interestingly, although the latter did not attract much attention in the closing months of 1992, the West seemed increasingly inclined to treat the three states as a single international actor regarding potential membership in the European Community and the Atlantic alliance.[34]

EPILOGUE

The period since the beginning of 1993 has brought both good and bad news to the Visegrad group. The good news concerned the December 1992 signing of a treaty in Krakow, establishing a free trade zone, the Central European Free Trade Area or CEFTA, embracing the Czech Republic, Hungary, Poland, and Slovakia. The agreement, which took effect in March 1993, anticipated a gradual reduction of tariffs up to the year 2001. The treaty represented a breakthrough on the road to regional cooperation. Until then, memories of CMEA as well as an obsession with an early entry into the European Community were responsible for some countries' reluctance to advance economic collaboration and, as a result, the volume of trade among the four CEFTA participants declined significantly following the dissolution of CMEA. There are indications, however, that the decrease has stopped, which gives some ground for optimism.[35] CEFTA was also viewed as strengthening the Visegrad group's bargaining position vis-à-vis the European Community.[36]

On the negative side of the ledger, the main obstacle on the road to closer multinational cooperation was the confused political and economic situation in the region. One possible roadblock was the dissolution of the Czechoslovak Federation and its foreign policy consequences. The Slovak government, faced with a sizable Hungarian minority in the country, has been increasingly sounding anti-Hungarian notes, accusing Budapest of interfering in Slovak internal affairs and of massing troops on the Slovak-Hungarian border. The quarrel over the Gabcikovo dam has been overshadowed by the escalating conflict regarding the treatment of the Hungarian minority, with the result that Hungary tried to prevent Slovakia's entry into the Council of Europe and Slovakia announced a purchase of arms from Russia, ostensibly for defensive purposes.[37] Neither this nor the March 1994 ouster of the government headed by Vladimir Meciar seemed to have affected Slovakia's positive attitude toward the Visegrad group.

Another problem was presented by Ukraine, which initially appeared strongly interested in joining the Visegrad group. Faced with continuing conflict with Russia and uncertain of Western intentions, however, President Kravchuk in May 1993 floated the idea of an East European security zone stretching from the Baltic to the Black Sea. The new organization, referred to as "NATO II," was to embrace, in addition to the Visegrad group, the three Baltic countries, Belarus, Ukraine, and Moldova, and was clearly intended as a safeguard against the threat emanating from Moscow.[38] The idea was presented to Polish president Walesa during his official visit to Kiev in May. Although earlier on Walesa himself suggested a creation of a similar body, known as "NATO-bis," he rejected Kravchuk's initiative, as did the rest of the group. The political and economic situation in Ukraine continued to deteriorate, necessitating new elections in the spring of 1994, which produced a sharply divided parliament. What impact this will have on Ukraine's future relations with Visegrad remains to be seen.

Undoubtedly, the biggest stumbling block to closer quadrilateral cooperation has been the erratic behavior of Czech prime minister Vaclav Klaus, who has long been known for his less than lukewarm support of Visegrad. During his visit to Germany in March 1993, he stated that the Czech Republic was opposed to further institutionalization of the Visegrad group as an alternative to Czech membership in the European Community. He also rejected the idea of Visegrad as a poor man's club and a buffer zone protecting the EC against the former USSR and the Balkans.[39] To the chagrin of the Poles, Klaus restated his position during a visit to Poland in June.[40] When a meeting of the Visegrad defense ministers took place in Warsaw in January 1994 to discuss the question of NATO membership, Klaus sent only a deputy minister, thereby projecting a strong message that Prague was not interested in joint action. Finally, during President Bill Clinton's visit to Prague in January 1994, Klaus insisted that the four Visegrad presidents meet with Clinton separately rather than as a group, for fear of giving a false impression of collective action.

Consequently, there was no question of a possible all-Visegrad application for membership in the European Union. Instead, Hungary and Poland applied individually for membership in April 1994, and the Czechs decided to wait.

The record of the attitude of the West toward the Visegrad group speaks for itself, and the litany of Western pronouncements, declarations, visits, and promises has bordered on farcical. The Visegrad group's membership in the European Community and in NATO presents a major problem for the West, if only because of the hostile attitude of Russia, and has been reflected in contradictory and confusing statements from Bonn, London, Paris, and Washington. President Clinton decided to cut the Gordian knot by announcing the "Partnership for Peace" program at a NATO summit in Brussels in January 1994. Although it was not their first choice, all the Visegrad members accepted the offer and were among the first countries to sign up.

To conclude, it would appear that at least in the foreseeable future the best option for Visegrad is to strengthen its cooperation at all levels—security, economic, and political—in anticipation of its ultimate entry into both NATO and the European Union, which is not likely to happen until the turn of the century. Thus the next few years are critical, and there is little doubt that a strengthened Visegrad group is bound to be a more attractive partner to the West than heretofore.

NOTES

1. Andrzej Korbonski, "Eastern Europe," in *After Brezhnev: Sources of Soviet Conduct in the 1980s*, ed. Robert F. Byrnes (Bloomington: Indiana University Press, 1983), 304.

2. Ibid., 305–13.

3. Stephen Sestanovich, "What Does He Know and When Will We Know It?" *New York Times*, May 16, 1992.

4. In early July 1988, a group of American and Soviet specialists met in Washington, D.C., to discuss the topic of "the place of Eastern Europe in the relaxation of tensions between the USA and the USSR." A partial summary of the Soviet position can be found in "The Soviet Perspective," *Problems of Communism* 37 (May–August 1988), 60–67.

5. See, R. W. Apple, Jr., "A Soviet Warning on Foot-Dragging Is Given to Prague," *New York Times*, November 16, 1989; and Jim Mann, "Moscow's Push Seen in Prague," *Los Angeles Times*, November 25, 1989.

6. Laszlo Valki, "Security Problems and the New Europe: A Central European Viewpoint" (manuscript, 1992), 1. Professor Valki is a leading Hungarian authority in the area of international security and defense policies.

7. Paul L. Montgomery, "French Sink East Europe Trade Deal," *New York Times*, September 7, 1991. See also William Pfaff, "Keeping the East Europeans Out," *New York Review of Books*, October 24, 1991.

8. See Douglas L. Clarke, "The Warsaw Pact's Finale," *RFE/RL Report on Eastern Europe* 2 (July 19, 1991), 39–42.

9. For an interesting discussion, see Suzanne Crow, "Who Lost Eastern Europe?" *RFE/RL Report on Eastern Europe* 15 (April 12, 1991), 1–15.

10. See Suzanne Crow, "Negotiating New Treaties with Eastern Europe," *RFE/RL Report on the USSR* 3 (July 19, 1991), 3–6.

11. "Comecon: Life after Death," *Economist*, April 20, 1991.

12. Zbigniew Brzezinski, "Post-Communist Nationalism," *Foreign Affairs* 6 (Winter 1989–90), 18. For a summary of Havel's reaction, see Lidia Buczma, "Czecho-Slowacja wobec 'trojkata' Warszawa-Praga-Budapeszt" [Czechoslovakia and the Warsaw-Prague-Budapest triangle], *Sprawy Miedzynarodowe* (Warsaw) 44 (1991), 38–39.

13. Buczma, "Czecho-Slowacja wobec 'trojkata' Warszawa-Praga-Budapeszt," 39–41.

14. Jonathan C. Randal, "Soviet Ex-Satellites Join Neighbors in 'Adriatic-Danubian' Discussions," *Washington Post*, April 10, 1990; Carol J. Williams, "Ex-East Bloc Nations Meet to Forge Regional Alliance," *Los Angeles Times*, April 10, 1990.

15. Jan B. de Weydenthal, "Poland Supports the Triangle as a Means to Reach Other Goals," *RFE/RL Research Report* 1 (June 5, 1992), 15–18.

16. Michael Frank, "Ein Dreierbund ist nicht in Sicht," *Suddeutsche Zeitung,* February 14, 1991.

17. Jan Obrman, "Czechoslovakia Overcomes Its Initial Reluctance," *RFE/RL Research Report* 1 (June 5, 1992), 19–24; Alfred A. Reisch, "Hungary Sees Common Goals and Bilateral Issues," *RFE/RL Research Report* 1 (June 5, 1992), 25–32.

18. Andrei A. Kokoshin, *The Evolving International Security System: A View from Moscow* (Alexandria, Va.: Center for Naval Analysis, 1991), 5.

19. See, for example, "Europa Srodkowa w swietle nowej sytuacji na wschodzie" (Central Europe in the light of a new situation in the East), *Polska w Europie* (Warsaw) 7 (January 1992), 51–64, esp. 53–55.

20. See Vladimir Kusin, "Refugees in Central and Eastern Europe: Problem or Threat?" *RFE/RL Report on Eastern Europe* 2 (January 18, 1991); F. Stephen Larrabee, "Down and Out in Moscow and Budapest: Eastern Europe and East-West Migration," *International Security* 16 (Spring 1992), 5–33.

21. For details, see Vladimir V. Kusin, "Security Concerns in Central Europe," *RFE/RL Report on Eastern Europe* 2 (March 8, 1991), 25–40; Rudolf Tokes, "From Visegrad to Krakow: Cooperation, Competition and Coexistence in Central Europe," *Problems of Communism* 40 (November–December 1991); and Joshua Spero, "The Budapest-Prague-Warsaw Triangle: Central European Security after the Visegrad Summit," *European Security* 1 (Spring 1992), 58–83.

22. Viktor Meier, "Nicht gegen Deutschland gerichtet," *Frankfurter Allgemeine Zeitung,* January 25, 1991.

23. For example, in April 1991, Czechoslovak officials criticized the West for reducing Poland's external debt without offering a similar deal to Czechoslovakia. See Buczma, "Czecho-Slowacja wobec 'trojkata' Warszawa-Praga-Budapeszt," 48–49.

24. "Sense of Vulnerability Chills Former Satellites," *New York Times,* August 22, 1991.

25. Louisa Vinton, "Poland," in "The Attempted Coup in the USSR: East European Reactions," *RFE/RL Report on Eastern Europe* 2 (August 30, 1991), 12.

26. Tokes, "The Budapest-Prague-Warsaw Triangle," 112–13. See also Jan B. de Weydenthal, "The Cracow Summit," *RFE/RL Report on Eastern Europe* 2 (October 25, 1991), 27–29.

27. Andrzej Grajewski, "Kwadratura trojkata wyszehradzkiego" [Squaring the Visegrad triangle), *Polska w Europie* 9 (July–September 1992], 21.

28. Craig R. Whitney, "Russian Carries on Like the Bad Old Days, Then Says It Was All a Ruse," *New York Times,* December 15, 1992.

29. Bohdan Nahaylo, "Ukraine and the Visegrad Triangle," *RFE/RL Research Report* 1 (June 5, 1992), 28–29.

30. Georg Paul Hefty, "Ist Ungarn ein Kern der Stabilitat oder eine Insel in Sturm?" *Frankfurter Allgemeine Zeitung,* August 6, 1992.

31. See, for example, Thomas L. Friedman, "NATO Tries to Ease Military Concerns in Eastern Europe," *New York Times,* June 7, 1991; Patrick E. Tyler, "U.S. Strat-

egy Plan Calls No Rivals Develop," *New York Times*, March 8, 1992; and Craig R. Whitney, "NATO Sees a Peacekeeping Role in Eastern Europe," *New York Times*, June 5, 1992.

32. Joachim Fritz-Vannahme, "Die Gelassenheit des Grenzgangers," *Die Zeit*, December 25, 1992.

33. For a discussion of possible alternatives, see John Orme, "Security in East Central Europe: Seven Futures," *Washington Quarterly* 14 (Summer 1991), 91–105. See also Jan Zielonka, "Security in Central Europe," *Adelphi Papers* 272 (Autumn 1992).

34. Michael Ludwig, "Der Blick von Visegrad nach Westen," *Frankfurter Allgemeine Zeitung*, December 22, 1992.

35. Rick Butler, "Visegrad Four Reap the Rewards of United Front," *European*, February 24–March 3, 1994.

36. Krzysztof J. Ners in *Transition, The Newsletter about Reforming Economies* 4 (June 1993), 8.

37. Berthold Kohler, "Schaukelspiel als Ritual," *Frankfurter Allgemeine Zeitung*, July 29, 1993.

38. Wolfgang Koydl, "Wer fullt das Vakuum in 'Zwischeneuropa'?" *Suddeutsche Zeitung*, May 27, 1993.

39. *RFE/RL News Briefs*, March 22–26, 1993.

40. *Rzeczpospolita* (Warsaw), June 26–27, 1993.

10

Chinese Foreign Policy During and After the Cold War

Thomas W. Robinson

By the late 1980s, Chinese foreign policy had gone through two stages and had entered a third. The first coincided with Mao's rule, 1949–76. The second occupied most of the period of Deng's overlordship, beginning in 1977 and ending in the 1989 Tiananmen incident. The third extended into the 1990s, beginning with the downfall of communism in Eastern Europe and the Soviet Union. There are many differences in Chinese policy that characterize these three periods. Yet each period illustrates, with different "weights," the interrelations between only a small number of causal variables.

THE ERA OF MAOIST DOMINANCE, 1949–1976

As long as China was ruled by Mao Zedong, Beijing's foreign policy was determined largely by three domestic factors: the primacy of politics, the weight of the past, and the importance of ideology. Three international factors—the foreign policies of the superpowers, the structure of the international system, and China's calculation of its relative power and interests—were obviously important but played a relatively minor role. Domestic factors dominated because of the newness of the Chinese revolution and the role of Mao himself.[1]

Revolutionary politics, as structured and symbolized by Mao, set the direction and content of China's approach to its international environment. By 1949, the Chinese Communist Party had long since become a Leninist institution led by a strong group with well-thought-out goals. It also had a mandate to rule from a reasonably pliant Chinese population. It was thus possible to set the country on the course of national unity, socialist revolution, export of communist ideology, anti-Americanism and pro-Sovietism, and restoration of Chinese primacy in Asia. These goals summed up Beijing's foreign policy during the Maoist period. But many specifics also derived from the domestic situation. Thus it was the Mao-induced domestic political cycle that led to similar swings in Chinese foreign policy, from excessive closeness to Moscow during the early revolutionary years, 1949–54, to provoking the Taiwan Straits crisis in 1958 during the Great Leap Forward, to overreaction to alleged Soviet per-fidy during the 1959–62 "lean years," and to the isolationism of the Cultural Revolution after 1965.

Moreover, Mao's own personality—his campaign style, insistence of revo-lution *über alles*, megalomania, and paranoia—informed much of the foreign policy decision making in the pre-1977 era. Economic development did count for something, but politics and Mao occupied center stage. A more rational, national-interest-oriented foreign policy orientation could be perceived only when economic opportunity beckoned, necessity threatened, or when Zhou Enlai was at the foreign policy helm.

The second domestic factor, the weight of the party's past, exerted consider-able pull as well. Particularly influential was the experience of the 1921–49 period of the party's formulation, experimentation, and application of its basic policies and its discovery through trial and error of the "correct" path to revo-lutionary power.[2] Two aspects of this maturation process were important for Chinese foreign policy after 1949. One was the reification of the Maoist strat-egy for revolutionary success into a formula that could be applied to the inter-national as well as the domestic environment.[3] The other involved the early discovery and bitter experience of the balance of power when the party vio-lated the rules. The most elementary and vicious form of the balance is a three-element game in which the weakest member must continually ally and then re-ally itself to the second strongest member to avoid destruction.[4] The party was successful when it pursued such a strategy. When it had to face an enemy with no intervening player, it suffered disaster.[5] The party had learned the lesson well enough by 1949 that Mao's first foreign policy act was to sign an alliance with the Soviet Union against the United States, thus guaranteeing Beijing's security for more than a decade. When it forgot the lessons of trian-gular international relations, as in the 1969 border conflict with the Soviet Union, China found it had no choice but to seek security in the only quarter it could find it, in Washington, D.C.[6] As a result of two-thirds of a century of participation in a three-sided balance of power, therefore, China has become a firm believer in security as a function of power, alliance, and manipulation of friends and enemies.

The third domestic determinant of Maoist foreign policy was ideology. Marxism-Leninism–Mao Zedong Thought clearly influenced the general di-rection of policy. Thus China carried its adulation of the Soviet Union during the early 1950s far beyond requirements of security within the strategic tri-angle and then went to the opposite extreme, totally rejecting Moscow after the break in the 1960s. After going to anti-American ideological extremes in the 1950s and 1960s, China under Mao during the first half of the 1970s could not become as friendly toward Washington as policy necessities dictated. Moreover, it made ideology an important constituent of several important policy departures, including the Taiwan Straits crisis of 1958, the isolationism of the Cultural Revolution, and the attempt to overthrow several African governments in the 1960s. Such ideological blinders also caused Mao to misjudge badly other states' foreign policies and domestic developments, especially that of the United States.

These three domestic determinants of foreign policy explain most of the direction, timing, and specifics of Beijing's international orientation under Mao. Other causative elements remained outside this framework, however, for China existed as a nation in an international system. It was constrained to obey the "laws" of foreign policy behavior common to all nation-states and was therefore influenced by the structure of that system and the foreign policies of the other important actors. During the Maoist period, the most influential of these elements were the power and the policies of the two superpowers, the United States and the Soviet Union. Thus, when the American-Soviet Cold War was at its height in the 1950s and China was comparatively weak, Mao had to incline steeply toward Moscow. When America and Russia were, in Chinese eyes, "contending" among themselves—as in the Cuban missile crisis, the several Berlin crises, and Vietnam—Maoist-led Beijing believed it had the necessary maneuvering room to escape, if only for a while, from the American-Soviet grip.[7]

Maoist China also was constrained to conduct its foreign relations in ways that were not entirely within the confines of, or derived from, the strategic triangle. China was a member of the international system and a constituent of the Asian regional system and hence had to conform to the structure and processes of those systems. For instance, if nuclear weapons were the key to national security and international prestige, China was constrained to acquire them. Mao made that decision early in the 1950s and, after a confrontation with the Soviets on nuclear weapons assistance, acquired an initial nuclear capacity by the mid-1960s. An extraordinary percentage of China's gross national product, heavy industry, and technology was given over to this sphere, while China's relations with the superpowers and its Asian neighbors were markedly affected by its heightening stockpile and its increasingly sophisticated missile-delivery capability.[8]

The normal and inevitable consequence of rapid growth in power such as China experienced is a corresponding increase in the range of national interests. Beijing's international behavior under Mao was a textbook illustration of this central verity of international politics. China began using its new power to involve itself in situations and disputes ever farther from the country's geographical boundaries. China became militarily involved on the territory of all its neighbors for the first time in its history. It participated actively in the diplomacy of Asia, the Middle East, and Africa and the strategic triangle. It moved to the center of the international communist movement and then struggled with Moscow for control over it. It traded with, and sent foreign aid to, distant nations. It attempted, for a while, to exert cultural control over Chinese communities in Asia and elsewhere. In short, it used its new power to pursue the expanded list of national and party goals that such growth in power permitted. Nonetheless, China was acting no differently from any other state in history that, upon significant augmentation of power, discovers new interests and places to apply that power.[9]

As China, obeying this "Iron Law of International Relations,"[10] linked interest to power and thus expanded its foreign policy horizons, its international environment reacted correspondingly. Changes were made in Asia and elsewhere that, while accommodating to a much more activist and interventionist China, set up barriers to unacceptable modifications in Beijing's favor. Most were carried out first by the United States—fighting the Korean War, establishing a series of anti-China alliances in Asia, justifying the entire containment system partly on anti-Chinese grounds, and entering both Vietnam conflicts partly to keep alleged Chinese expansionism within bounds. The Soviet Union also established barriers against Chinese expansionist power and interest. It broke off close economic, military, and ideological relations with Beijing during the late 1950s and early 1960s, competed for the favor of communist parties and nonaligned states across the globe, girded for war after 1969 through massive buildup of forces along the Sino-Soviet frontier, and finally attempted to establish an anti-Chinese alliance system of its own. Moreover, the rapid growth of the export-oriented market economies, together with the rising military power of many Asian states (ranging from India through Southeast Asia to the two Koreas) united to create additional obstacles to untoward Chinese interference. Thus, with sufficient time, international political leadership, and a plentitude of resources, a balance of power was established in Asia and beyond that kept Chinese power and policy expansion under Mao within acceptable limits.

FOREIGN POLICY CHANGES UNDER DENG, 1977–1989

Unlike the Maoist period, Chinese foreign policy under Deng Xiaoping did not coincide neatly with the period of his rule. Both domestic developments and the international environment changed drastically in 1989. Symbolized at home by the tragic and unnecessary Tiananmen incident in June and in the fall by the sundering of the Berlin Wall abroad, a new era began in that year. Major changes in the six determinants occurred, necessitating a new configuration of Chinese policy and a new analysis. During most of the Deng era, however, from Mao's demise to Tiananmen, most of the six determinants remained more or less in place. Chinese foreign policy was still their joint product, although with considerable variation in content. Indeed, major modifications were made and important trends established so that China's foreign relations after Mao were significantly different.

Domestically, the most important change was the replacement of Maoist radicalism by Dengist pragmatic moderation and the corresponding shift from the primacy of politics to that of economics. Beijing's foreign policy reflected whatever appeared good for China's domestic economic development. China gradually turned toward a mixed economy because the path to material betterment was judged to lie through decollectivization; partial return of the profit incentive; price as well as plan as an allocative mechanism; a mixed state, collective, and private pattern of ownership; and access to markets, technology, and goods wherever they might be found. Internationally, this meant opening the door to foreign economic investment, technology transfer, trade, and training. Beijing's foreign policy was summed up by the twin goals of peace and security. Such an atmosphere would be most conducive to rapid growth and modernization while their opposites, war and threat, would destroy China's best and perhaps only chance to catch up with the developed world. And the sole means to that end, given American-Japanese-European economic and technological leadership and Soviet military threat, was to do what was necessary to gain access to the markets, goods, training, and expertise that only the West could offer. It also meant taking out security insurance with the United States against Soviet military threats. These became the cornerstones of China's new foreign policy.[11]

Deng Xiaoping also deradicalized Chinese politics by gradually retiring his revolutionary colleagues, ousting the Maoist radicals, bringing in new leaders with higher educational and technical qualifications, and easing out Cultural Revolution entrants whose only hallmark was Maoist phraseology. He also attempted to install the next generation of successors—led first by Hu Yaobang and later by Zhao Ziyang—composed of like-thinking modernizers who, he thought, would guarantee continuity of his counterrevolution for another decade or two. Finally, he moved fast in instituting reforms and demonstrating their benefits to large percentages of the population and thus built up a support base of technocrats within the party and beneficiaries, including most peasants and increasing numbers of urban dwellers. The tragedy was that his reforms were so successful that they got out of hand; it was Deng himself who felt it necessary forcibly to lead the way at least partly back, in June 1989, to Maoist modes of thought and administration.

The weight of the past continued to be important, but evaluation changed and a heretofore suppressed element, traditional Chinese culture, reemerged. Because Mao had come under a cloud, stress on revolutionary tradition was dampened. The pre-1949 period of formative party history became almost pre-history. Anti-Westernism was deemphasized (campaigns against "spiritual pollution" and "bourgeois influence" were deftly turned aside) and replaced by underlining China's own responsibility for its late start on modernization. Most important, China began rapidly to retraditionalize. Customs, habits, and practices suppressed under Mao made a strong comeback under the rubric of modernization. China thus began to look and act as it had in the late 1920s and early 1930s: variegated, lively, and differentiated, a bewildering mixture of the traditional, the transitional, and the modern.[12]

Maoist ideology was criticized and no longer widely studied.[13] But Leninism (i.e., modern-day Machiavellianism) was retained as the philosophy of party organization and the party's leitmotif. Ideological criteria for membership were relaxed, contested local party elections began to be held, decision making was shifted to government ministries, the raw capacity of the party to influence everyday life and carry out campaigns declined, and pragmatic aspects of Leninism supplanted the dogmatic. These changes allowed the party to justify strong relations with capitalist states, foreign investment and ownership of enterprises within China, and a host of economic, administrative, and legal changes that made it less difficult to do business with China and for outsiders to penetrate the Chinese polity and economy.

Such domestic changes were crucial in propelling China onto an entirely new international course. They continued to explain most of the variance and policy directions in Beijing's foreign policy. But international determinants also changed and thus helped to configure the country's new direction. Within the strategic triangle, Beijing downgraded the Soviet threat after 1978, even though the objective facts of the Sino-Soviet military balance had not changed in China's favor (if anything, the Soviet Union was more powerful militarily than ever before). By adding an evaluation of Soviet intentions to the traditional assessment of Soviet capabilities (why, when Moscow had every opportunity for over a decade to deal a decisive blow to China, had it not done so?), the Chinese leadership concluded that conflict with the Kremlin was significantly less likely.

A second implication was a gradual turn back toward Moscow, testing the waters of Sino-Soviet detente on the way to eventual rapprochement. As in the American case, rhetoric and reality stood mutually opposed. Beijing lumped the Kremlin with the White House as a superpower villain, inveighed against the Russian Bear as a military threat, and refused to improve Sino-Soviet relations unless Moscow would give way on the so-called three obstacles (Afghanistan, Vietnam, and military buildup in the Soviet border regions). Moscow would not (until Gorbachev came to power and instituted the foreign policy aspects of glasnost-perestroika) retreat on any of these. But just as in the

American case, China improved practical (mostly economic) relations with Moscow while at the same time blasting the Soviets verbally and contining to try to settle the border question. Though not as extensive, by any means, as the relationship with the United States, such marginal changes constituted Chinese foreign policy and pointed the way to the future.[14]

Thus, on the basis of "relative equidistance" between Washington and Moscow (with a perceptible leaning to the American side) and of loud cries against alleged superpower attempts at world dominance, China constructed a "new" policy of independence.[15] This roughly balanced policy provided a solid enough basis for the other major variation in Deng's pre-Tiananmen foreign policy: a turn toward the Third World. By the 1980s, the Third World had taken definite shape, substance, and organization (the Group of 77, the Neutral and Non-Aligned Nations Movement, OPEC, and other institutions). At the same time, Beijing's leadership potential had decreased. Self-appointed Third World leaders either rejected Chinese overtures to join them, fearing Chinese overlordship or objecting to China's obvious ideological non-neutrality, or were persuaded by Moscow to keep the Chinese away.[16]

Because of the nature of its economy and the direction of its foreign policy, China was not a member of GATT or of the Group of Seven, new elements in the international arena. The engines of production, invention, finance, and technology were concentrated in the three market-economy centers: Europe, North America, and Northeast Asia. If China wanted what they offered, it would have to buy from them, largely on their terms. Beijing would therefore have to sell to them in equal amounts or reverse its long-standing policy not to take on a massive international debt. Under Deng, China did both. Beijing emphasized exports to earn hard currency, stressed foreign investment in sectors and regions of the economy (mostly consumer goods and the southeast coastal provinces, respectively) that were oriented to export, and took on a foreign debt of several tens of billions of dollars.[17] In sum, to modernize, China would have to, and did become, interdependent.

Another global shift took place in the military sphere. A second revolution in weaponry occurred on the heels of the nuclear missile overturn of the pre-1945 order. As strategic weapons of extraordinary accuracy emerged, with almost no flight time at long distances and total destructive power, new conventional weapons experienced many of the same changes. Precision-guided munitions made possible point destruction in a single shot. High-technology radars, television, and other electronic equipment enabled pilots and ship captains to destroy targets without visually sighting them. Satellite technology and electronic listening devices revealed precisely what the enemy had and where it was located. Conventional (including chemical and biological) explosives so increased their destructive power that they began to approach nuclear levels of lethality. These changes in the nature of warfare, including the enormous increase in pace of the conflict and rapidity of destruction, meant that only those with the proper technological base could hope to win wars or successfully deter conflict with opponents so armed.[18] China's military capabilities were technologically far behind, and the costs of catching up were beyond its reach.

The final post-Mao determinant of Chinese foreign policy was the relation between interest and power, with changes in power as the driving element.[19] This becomes evident by inspecting changes in the four means of national power and how China's interests varied accordingly. The first is diplomacy, defined as steering the ship of state through the difficult waters of international relations, which includes diplomacy and the capability of the nation's leadership to make efficient use of national resources and plan wisely for the future.

The level and pace of economic development is the second element of national power. Here China excelled under Deng, and a breakthrough was made.[20] As domestic administrative reforms began to take hold and the open door international economic policy began to return dividends, growth accelerated, technology spread, confidence grew (along with popular support for Deng's economic pragmatism), and large increases in industrial production and consumer goods were enjoyed. That these same measures were responsible for the economy going out of control in 1988 and 1989, and thus one principal element in the run-up to the Tiananmen incident, should not detract from these achievements.[21]

Cultural policy, backed by relative cultural attractiveness, is a third element. China under Mao hid its culture under a bushel. Under Deng, it was brought out again, refurbished, and shown around. Some comfort was to be derived from China's renewed emphasis on the traditional and the old, even in the midst of modernist transformation. Many saw hope—perhaps unduly—in the Chinese tendency under Deng to adopt some of the latest fads and fashions of the West. That was read, incorrectly, as a sign that China had at last decided to join the world and not to fight it or to isolate itself.[22]

The military is the final element. Changes under Deng enabled Beijing to field a more potent force, defend the country with greater surety, and begin building a modern force that could fend off the Russians and project Chinese power at ever-greater distances from its borders. Military modernization remained last among the Four Modernizations, military budgets stagnated, the People's Liberation Army was under a cloud because of its supposed Cultural Revolution–Lin Biao errors, its leadership was superannuated and tradition-encrusted, its ranks poorly trained and equipped for modern conflict, and its production base allowed to shrink. But China's military budget was the world's third largest; it possessed a large, growing, diverse, dispersed, and rapidly modernizing strategic missile force; its officer and enlisted corps was younger, more highly trained, educated, and better led; it was introducing new tactics; its people's war strategy underwent significant modernization; and it received a flow of new equipment from domestic and foreign sources. With such assets and the promise for continuing improvements as modernization in other areas began to return dividends to the military, China was already on the road to major force augmentation. The military component might in time significantly enhance Chinese power.

Accordingly, changes were apparent. Not even the Soviets thought any more about initiating war. China became a central constituent in the balances of power in Northeast, Southeast, and South Asia, respectively, by helping to deter North Korea, Vietnam, and India. China was thus a security guarantor of regional peace in Asia, along with the United States. Moreover, Beijing became an element in the global nuclear equation, with capability to strike all Soviet territory and an initial capability against the United States. Its views were taken seriously at the American-Soviet arms control talks. The Chinese navy emerged onto the open ocean for the first time since the early Ming Dynasty and cooperated, albeit tacitly, with the Americans against the Soviet Far East Fleet. In addition, China used some of its spare military production capacity to assist distant states, thereby purchasing influence and earning hard currency. It also cooperated with Pakistan in developing nuclear weapons, at least until Washington raised the diplomatic temperature.[23] In sum, for a nation with allegedly manifold military problems, China in reality was in reasonable military shape and was rapidly setting the stage for major expansion.

Further, the international environment, both Asian and global, had changed. Most regional states were modernizing even faster than China and increasing their national power at a correspondingly rapid pace. Their range of interests expanded accordingly, making it relatively more difficult for Beijing to insert itself into arenas, situations, and disputes in which it had not previously maintained an interest. Japan was perhaps the best example. Shorn of a strong military, it put all its energies into the economic sphere. As a result, Tokyo became an economic superpower and expanded its economic interests everywhere. No country in Asia was unaffected by the Japanese drive to export, invest, and obtain raw materials. Chinese salesmen and negotiators constantly found that the Japanese had gotten to neighboring regions first with goods of the highest quality and advanced technology.

Even toward the lower end of the scale, China found that Taiwan, South Korea, Hong Kong, and India, among others, were tough competitors. Beijing's best bet, therefore, was to upgrade its technology by accepting foreign investment, convert an increasing portion of existing capital to service exports, serve as assembler of products at the low end of the production process and then reexport them to earn hard currency, and integrate an increasing percentage of its domestic productive capacity with those of nearby outside entities, especially Hong Kong and Taiwan. Asian international relations tended to focus on questions of tariffs and protection, marketing agreements, large-scale joint ventures versus wholly owned plant investments, and comparative exchange and interest rates. China was just beginning to enter this arena, and in the 1977–89 period was constrained to do so largely on terms offered by others.[24]

Domestically, beginning in 1987, gaining force rapidly in 1988, and finally bursting forth in 1989, first the domestic economic situation and then the political situation went out of control. The multiple causes of the Tiananmen incident of June 4, 1989, are clear in retrospect: economic inflation, political corruption, the regime's fears of the consequences of widespread urban popular dissatisfaction, student demands for political liberalization, decades-long resentment against party misrule and the massive consequences of its mistakes, the many changes resulting from the reforms themselves, the winds of change blowing into China from the outside world, and the disunity among the top party leaders as to how to deal with these matters. Whatever the exact relationship among these causal elements, when brought together they precipitated massive popular demonstrations in the capital and many other cities, followed by imposition of martial law, and finally the tragic and brutal repression of the Beijing demonstrators and other citizens.

Two consequences followed. First, the regime had to concentrate on matters at home and keep out of harm's way abroad. That meant quiescence abroad, as for instance in Beijing's continued cooperation with the superpowers and others regarding North Korean military adventurism and the Cambodian peace process. It also meant negotiating with Moscow for improvement in Sino-Soviet relations (ironically, this came to fruition just before Tiananmen, with the Gorbachev visit in May, which occasioned further demonstrations in Beijing). Second, this period of Chinese foreign policy ended abruptly in the middle of 1989.

Post–Cold War Chinese Foreign Policy, 1989–

The emergence of positively motivated Chinese foreign policy activism and the definitive arrival of Beijing onto the world scene as a global power were decisively interrupted by the shattering events of 1989–91: the Tiananmen incident and its consequences; the downfall of communism in Eastern Europe, the Soviet Union, and Mongolia; trends in post–Cold War international security and economic relations as symbolized by the Gulf War; and the revelation of dysfunctional Chinese foreign policy activities during the entire Deng period. Each had serious effects on China and further delayed its emergence as a relatively equal global power.

The Tiananmen incident was the symbol of the beginning of the end of communist rule. Tiananmen put a stop, if temporarily, to the reformist impetus and brought back the elderly conservative ideologues whom Deng had retired and the neo-Maoist philosophy they espoused. It also precipitated the return of the People's Liberation Army. The political composition of the leadership changed abruptly: economic reformers, led by Zhao Ziyang, were thrown out and the ideological conservatives, symbolized by Yang Shangkun, stepped back in. Foreign policy also changed. The door to the outside world was, until the first half of 1990, mostly closed as fear of outside (particularly American) political and cultural influence overcame the continued desire to import new technology and capital. And since economic recentralization and halting of the economic reforms of the 1980s were the chosen instruments to stop inflation, the consequent precipitous decline in growth rates not only caused the planners to halt or postpone many foreign purchases already contracted for but also induced a beggar-thy-neighbor foreign economic policy to repay the large foreign loans due. Although softened by enhanced Taiwanese investment, such a policy could only cause an economic crisis with many foreign countries, especially the United States.[25]

In sum, Tiananmen led to a near-term foreign policy of circle-the-wagons against an assumedly hostile, America-led Western world. When China attempted to break out of isolation, beginning in the second half of 1990, the causal connection to domestic factors—leadership changes, ideological modification, and renewal of economic reforms—was clear. Symbolized in each sphere, respectively, by the rise of the Shanghai-based reformer Zhu Rongji, the idea that Chinese socialism could include a market-based mode of economic organization, and Deng's visit to Hong Kong's hinterland, a different foreign policy emerged. Renewed diplomatic engagement, support of international organizations, cooperation in addressing international issues, and renewed (if still cautious) emphasis on investment and trade were all indications of a policy to restore the status quo ante Tiananmen.

The regime put into place a policy of step-by-step accommodation with as many states as possible, cautiously reopening the door to foreign investment and resolving trade disputes, and positioning itself as a nation that could normally be counted on to act with others to deal responsibly with international issues. But it also made it clear that Beijing would act to defend its own interests and that it would negotiate solutions to bilateral differences from a position of strength. Its gradual reemergence from isolation in 1991 demonstrated partial success of that policy, as did its resistance to the United States in a series of negotiations over economic relations, security issues, and human rights concerns.[26]

The downfall of communism graphically clarified the true relationship between two major domestic trends of the twentieth century, modernization and revolution. Although revolutionary modernization had been the century's most important political and economic process, beginning with the Bolshevik Revolution, only the 1989–91 East European–Soviet events revealed its full meaning, in general and for China. First, revolution now meant political and economic anticommunism and hence democracy and marketization, precisely the opposite of its earlier meaning of anti-Westernism, anticapitalism, and anticolonialism. Revolution no longer could be equated with Marxism-Leninism and central planning but was now explicitly identified with democracy and capitalism.

Economic and political revolution were clearly linked. In earlier modernizations, political revolution came first because it was necessary to overcome the backwardness of colonialism and traditionalism. Anti-Western nationalism, Leninism/central planning, or authoritarianism/state capitalism naturally emerged, each a reasonably efficient engine of political rule and quantitative economic growth. But with time, these modes of organization became increasingly inefficient. Heavy state, party, personalist, and military control could not bring the benefits of the people's labor directly to them and in fact gave more to the ruling classes and to state-directed military purposes. Modernization thus emerged (measured in Asia approximately by $1,000 per capita national income, 40 percent urbanization, and the appearance of a middle class) in which only democratization, marketization, and substitution of qualitative for quantitative goals could continue modernization. A second revolution thus became inevitable. Events first in Poland, then at Tiananmen, and later in Berlin, Bucharest, and Red Square all indicated that this stage had arrived in these Leninist-dominated societies and would come in all the others.

Although modernization, once begun, could not be stopped, it could be halted temporarily. Smooth modernization can occur when political and economic development keep pace with each other. The impact of arrested or uneven modernization, in either or both spheres, would be heavy in high economic costs, time wasted, and lives expended. Unfortunately, uneven development was the norm. In some countries (e.g., South Korea, Taiwan, East Germany, Hungary), economic development far outran political modernization, causing a crisis as the contradictions between the two spheres required revolutionary resynchronization. In others—China under Deng being the prototypical case—the problem of political succession and the consequent halting of political modernization combined with rapid economic growth and the emergence of a semi-market economy to produce breakdown and violence. Further disorder would be inevitable until the two components of modernization were reconnected to develop in parallel.

Finally, the pace and form of economic and political modernization were directly connected to the cultural tradition, different elements emerging during two stages. In China during the first stage, traditional Confucian virtues of personalism, collectivism, and a rigid social structure fit reasonably well with Marxism-Leninism and party direction of the economy. Once the second stage arrived, these virtues made less sense than other Confucian norms, including egalitarianism, the work ethic, and stress on education, which were congruent with democratization and marketization but not socialist modes of rule and organization. The substitution of the latter set of cultural values for the former would inevitably involve violence and disorder. That is what happened in June 1989 and would undoubtedly occur again until economic and political modernization were resynchronized.[27]

The 1990–91 Gulf War symbolized changes in the international security and economic systems as a result of the end of the Cold War. These changes directly affected China's foreign policy. The Sino-Soviet-American strategic triangle, long the base of global political-military affairs, was replaced with a looser, more informal arrangement among five power centers: North America, Europe (particularly the European Community), Russia, China, and Japan. This new multipolar system possessed several characteristics quite different from its Cold War predecessor.

(1) Although NATO survived and the United States maintained its security tie with Japan, formal ties meant much less than before. An ad hoc approach to common political-security concerns seemed to be emerging, similar to the post-Napoleonic "Concert" system.

(2) Based on advanced economic development and democratic political institutions, a Directory of Developed States also appeared, informally linking North America, Europe, and Japan, informally institutionalized as the Group of Seven.

(3) As a result of the 1991 Soviet events, Russia moved to associate itself with the three giant market democratic regions. If it were to succeed, even as a junior partner, it could add enough strength to the resultant combination to dominate global political-military affairs. China then would be relatively isolated until it too modified its domestic political-economic order in the same direction.

Three massive secular trends continued: democratization, marketization, and interdependence. The globe had become interdependent, thanks to a combination of high technology, rapid communications, lower tariff barriers, and the economic leadership and tolerance of the United States. Although this was evident mostly in trade, it was also true in information flow, technology transfer, inventions, culture, education, and science. As with democracy and marketization, interdependence was first evident in the developed West and then became globalized. No nation, including China, could escape becoming interdependent if it wished to progress.

What were the implications of these trends for Chinese foreign policy?

(1) Cold War alliances were disappearing. The American-Japanese Security Treaty was being called into question. The American-Philippine bases arrangement expired. And even such strong ties as the South Korean–American, the Soviet-Vietnamese, the Soviet-Indian, the Chinese–North Korean treaties, and separate American and Chinese ties with Pakistan were due for modification or existed only in name. Ad hoc, cooperative approaches were likely among the four regional power centers—America, China, Japan, and Russia. These included the North Korean nuclear weapons program, the Korean reunification issue, solution to the Cambodian civil war, and possibly (if they were to come to the edge of violence) the Spratly Islands question and even the China-Taiwan problem.

(2) No new Asian balance-of-power system was likely soon to emerge. The major Asian powers were too busy at home or with extra-Asian problems to develop such a system. All wished to avoid constructing such a system or slipping progressively into one. Nor would an Asia-wide collective security system emerge soon. No country appeared willing to take leadership of such a system. Meanwhile, a rough equality emerged among the four, as America and Russia continued to decline in relative power and Japan and China took on added strength.

(3) Asian affairs would consequently combine Concert-like ad hoc solutions, great power laissez-faireism, and middle power activism. Issues would be addressed as they came up, through an informal committee of the whole mechanism, and not (until late in the decade) lead to a more formal balance of power or a regional collective security mechanism. Russia would be drawn into Asia, and China would be encouraged to participate in solving Asian problems in a peaceful, cooperative manner, the "rules" of which would be drawn up largely by America and Japan. China would probably choose cooperative participation, not isolation.

(4) Presuming that Korean security threats could be settled successfully, the center of Asian activity would shift gradually from security to economic concerns—trade, growth, tariffs, investment, technology transfer, and construction of Asia-based international institutions. The center of new economic growth would also diverge—into Southeast Asia, northwest out of traditional "Asia proper" (the Japan-China-Korea triangle) and into Siberia and the Rus-

sian Far East and eastward across the Pacific as a new trans-Pacific economic community emerged. Nations would order their relative importance more according to rates of growth, levels of gross national product, per capita national income, and technological prowess and less according to traditional measures of power—size of military, population, land extent, and tons of steel.

The Gulf War epitomized for China these post–Cold War trends. That conflict momentarily brought together an overwhelmingly powerful coalition of all major power centers. Victory was inevitable as long as the group remained together. Victory achieved, the coalition automatically fell apart and all returned to their principal concern with domestic affairs. Victory was achieved through a combination of American leadership and the military-technological prowess demonstrated by the coalition's (principally American) armed forces. When the chips were down, the market democracies led the way and attracted the acquiescence of Russia and China, which could join or be isolated. The war could not have been fought or won without all-around security and economic interdependence. The Directory of Developed States reacted instinctively to the Iraqi challenge, considering that if aggression were not met head-on, the United Nations collective security system would fail its first major post–Cold War test and the international system-in-process-of-becoming would decline into a new and crass balance of power. An important opportunity would thus have been wasted and the principles that emerged from the twentieth century's principal conflicts would have been thrown away at century's end.

The Tiananmen incident, the end of the Cold War, the Gulf War, and the collapse of communism in Eastern Europe and the Soviet Union all acted as powerful constraints on the latitude and direction of Chinese foreign policy. Nonetheless, Beijing should have played a larger and more dynamic role than it did in the first years of the 1990s. Its vast increase in absolute power and its great augmentation in relative power should have seen to that. But beginning in early 1991, a succession of revelations revealed highly questionable Chinese international activities that bespoke a style and propensity that were highly disturbing to many nations and called into question whether China was really interested in responsible participation in international relations.

In the national security area, the "offending" activities included:

(1) surreptitious sale of a large nuclear reactor to Algeria for production of nuclear weapons, outside of the rules of the International Atomic Energy Agency;

(2) transfer to Pakistan of technology for production of a nuclear weapon, missile technology, launchers, and missiles;

(3) sale to Iran, Iraq, and Saudi Arabia of various missiles, which served further to destabilize the military equation in the globe's most volatile region;

(4) unwillingness, until put under heavy international pressure, to join the Nuclear Non-Proliferation Treaty, to agree to the rules of the Middle Eastern Missile Technology Control Regime, or to place export of nuclear materials and technology under the inspection rules of the International Atomic Energy Agency.

In the economic realm:

(1) deliberately impeding imports through market-restricting measures and import-substitution strategies while emphasizing exports, thus adopting a beggar-thy-neighbor trade policy to build up a large surplus of hard currency;

(2) imposing a multitude of restrictions on foreign companies in China;

(3) mislabeling textile goods in massive quantities to circumvent import restrictions;

(4) purloining industrial secrets and promising to modify such practices only under extreme trade pressure.

In the human rights area:

(1) continuation and exacerbation of a large number and variety of punishments, arrests, incarcerations, denials of generally accepted procedural safeguards, arbitrary interference in personal affairs, restrictions on travel and emigration, and widespread denial of basic civil liberties accepted by civilized societies;

(2) cracking down on anyone suspected of participating in the Tiananmen incident (in both Beijing and many other cities) or of harboring opinions unfavorable to the regime.

Revelations in all three areas severely constricted China's foreign policy freedom of action. That situation would continue until China became strong enough progressively to ignore other nations' policies and reactions, the international system became more settled, or internal revolutionary changes took hold at home. The result probably would be a combination of all three.

CONCLUSION

Compressing the sweep of forty years and more of Chinese foreign policy into a few generalizations is impossible. Several thoughts nonetheless come to mind.

First, there has clearly been a shift from domestic primacy to a mixture of domestic and international concerns. Indeed, from the beginning, the role of the three international determinants of Chinese foreign policy was greater than commonly realized. And within each cluster, there has also been a change in emphasis from political to economic concerns as well as a decline in the relative importance of the military element. Second, the raw power, in all categories, available to Chinese decision makers has risen exponentially. It is this change that has been at the base of Beijing's greater participation, increased self-confidence, globalization of reach, and hence expanded structure of national interests. But that explosive growth in national power and interest has not, for the most part, been reflected fully in China's being accepted in world councils, its military power projection capability, its strength in the world economy, or its cultural attractiveness.

The result has been a tension between China's greatly expanded potential and the reality of its only modestly enhanced status in global affairs. In an era of rapid transition toward a market democracy and away from Marxism-Leninism, China has become both an anomaly and an anachronism. Instead of becoming a global leader, it has remained both a follower and partially outside—by its own desires as well as others' labeling—the councils of world chieftains. Further, the events of 1989, inside China and throughout the communist world, severely diminished Beijing's ability to take full advantage of the accretion in power produced by the economic advances over the previous decade. Moreover, China's growth in gross national power must always be seen in comparative terms. The country's relative power status entering the fifth decade of existence of the Marxist-Leninist regime, though surely higher than at the beginning, is much attenuated by the even more rapid rise in many of the countries just outside its borders, by the continued American dominance of global affairs, by the resurgence of Europe, and even by the concomitant growth of such Third World rivals as India and the newfound power of many Middle Eastern nations. China thus has had to run fast just to keep up. The question is whether this disjunction will continue and, if so, for how long. Some trends will apparently continue. China's growth in economic power will be no more rapid than that of many other relevant nations. A series of newly emergent nations of consequence will enter the scene, in Asia and elsewhere, further diluting China's power. The Deng succession—in both the generational as well as the personal senses—will sap a portion of China's energies possibly for a considerable period. And finally, some of the elements of national power normally useful for power projection and thus means for demanding a place at the table of the globally influential are less useful in the post–Cold War era or are elements in which China possesses little comparative advantage. The military element, symbolized by the dominance of high-technology weapons systems, is a perfect example, as is the cultural element, symbolized by the global dominance of American popular culture and of English as the primary language of international communication. Combined, they will probably meliorate and attenuate the admittedly large and important gains in Chinese power.

To that list should be added the issue of whether China will choose to pursue a set of policies that will be seen as making it, in the eyes of other nations, a problem, or setting a different course that will lead to its general acceptance as a responsible participant in global affairs. Although many variables enter any such calculation, it would seem that on balance long-term secular trends, both in China and internationally, favor the latter outcome while short- to medium-term forces may favor the former. Until there is a full generational succession in China, until the economic transformation of the country is much more advanced along many dimensions, and until new Asian and international security systems are in place, China could remain largely outside accepted channels and norms of international relations.

There seems little doubt that China will finally emerge as a "great," that is, global, power fully equal to, and accepted by, the other major power centers being constructed during the 1990s. China's task is to manage the transition. Doing so requires China to overcome what could be a very rough path away from communism through authoritarianism and finally to full-fledged market democracy, teaching the Beijing regime the new economic, diplomatic, and national security rules of the international game, coping with such new and possibly commanding variables as environmental issues, avoiding the temptation—in Beijing and in other capitals—to engage in zero-sum policies and thus slipping into the assumption that one or another side is an "opponent" or even an "enemy," and avoiding being overcome by the chance (but inevitable) intervention of unforeseen contingencies of foreign and international affairs.

NOTES

1. For Chinese foreign policy under Mao, see, among others, A. Doak Barnett, *China and the Major Powers in East Asia* (Washington, D.C.: Brookings Institution, 1977); Gordon H. Chang, *Friends and Enemies: The United States, China and the Soviet Union, 1948–1972* (Stanford: Stanford University Press, 1990); Thomas Fingar, ed., *China's Quest for Independence: Policy Evolution in the 1970s* (Boulder: Westview Press, 1980); Stephen Fitzgerald, *China and the World* (Canberra: Australian National University Press, 1978); John Gittings, *The World and China, 1922–1972* (London: Harper & Row, 1974); A. M. Halpern, "The People's Republic of China in the Post-War World" (manuscript) (New York: Council on Foreign Relations, 1972); Han Nianlong et al., eds., *Dangdai Zhongguo Waijiao* [Contemporary Chinese Foreign Relations] (Beijing: Chinese Social Sciences Academy Publishing House, 1987), esp. chaps. 1–19; Harold C. Hinton, *China's Turbulent Quest* (New York: Macmillan, 1972); Robert G. Sutter, *Chinese Foreign Policy after the Cultural Revolution, 1966–1977* (Boulder: Westview Press, 1978); and Michael B. Yahuda, *China's Role in World Affairs* (New York: St. Martin's Press, 1978).

2. See, for example, Jacquez Guillermaz, *A History of the Chinese Communist Party, 1921–1949* (New York: Random House, 1972); Samuel S. Kim, "The Maoist

Image of World Order," in *China, the United Nations, and World Order*, ed. Samuel S. Kim (Princeton: Princeton University Press, 1979), 49–93; James Reardon-Anderson, *Yenan and the Great Powers* (New York: Columbia University Press, 1979); and Stephen Uhatley, Jr., *A History of the Chinese Communist Party* (Stanford: Hoover Institution Press, 1988).

3. See, for example, Wolfgang Bartke, *China's Economic Aid to Developing and Socialist Countries* (New York: Holmes and Meyer, 1975); Lillian Harris and Robert Worden, eds., *China and the Third World* (Dover, Mass.: Arden House, 1979); Lillian Harris, *China's Foreign Policy toward the Third World* (New York: Praeger, 1985); Samuel S. Kim, "China and the Third World: In Search of a Neorealist World Policy," in *China and the World: Chinese Foreign Policy in the Post-Mao Era*, ed. Samuel S. Kim (Boulder: Westview Press, 1984), 178–214; Bruce D. Larkin, *China and Africa, 1949–1976* (Berkeley: University of California Press, 1971); and Charles Neuhauser, *Third World Politics: China and the Afro-Asian People's Solidarity Organization, 1957–1967* (Cambridge: Harvard University Press, 1968).

4. For representative theoretical works, see Scott Boorman, *The Protracted Game: A Wei-ch'i Interpretation of Maoist Revolutionary Strategy* (New York: Oxford University Press, 1969); Theodore Caplow, *Two Against One: Coalitions in Triads* (Englewood Cliffs, N.J.: Prentice-Hall, 1968); Lowell Dittmer, "The Strategic Triangle: An Elementary Game-Theoretic Analysis," *World Politics* (July 1981), 488–515; Thomas W. Robinson, "China in a Tripolar World" (manuscript) (New York: Council on Foreign Relations, 1974); and Peter Kien-hong Yu, *A Strategic Model of Chinese Checkers: Power and Exchange in Beijing's Interactions with Washington and Moscow* (New York: Peter Lang, 1984).

5. See, for example, Dorothy Borg and Waldo Heinrichs, eds., *Uncertain Years: Sino-American Relations, 1947–1949* (New York: Columbia University Press, 1980); Donald A. Jordan, *The Northern Expedition: China's National Revolution of 1926–1928* (Honolulu: University of Hawaii Press, 1976). The exception was the post–World War II period, after the withdrawal of the United States and the Soviet Union as third parties, when Nationalists and communists had to confront one another; see Steven Levine, *Anvil of Victory: The Communist Revolution in Manchuria, 1945–1948* (New York: Columbia University Press, 1987), and the many sources cited therein.

6. Thomas Gottlieb, *Chinese Foreign Policy Factionalism and the Origins of the Strategic Triangle* (Santa Monica: Rand Corporation, 1977); Harry Harding, *A Fragile Relationship: The United States and China since 1972* (Washington, D.C.: Brookings Institution, 1992), 23–66; Jonathan Pollack, *The Sino-Soviet Rivalry and the Chinese Security Debate* (Santa Monica: Rand Corporation, 1982); Thomas W. Robinson, "Restructuring Chinese Foreign Policy, 1963–76: Three Episodes," in *Why Nations Realign: Foreign Policy Restructuring in the Postwar World*, ed. Kai J. Holsti (London: Allen and Unwin, 1982), 134–71; and Robert Ross, "International Bargaining and Domestic Politics: US-China Relations since 1972," *World Politics* (January 1986), 251–87.

7. See, for example, Chang, *Friends and Enemies*, 212–75; John Gittings, *A Survey of the Sino-Soviet Dispute* (Oxford: Oxford University Press, 1967); William Griffith, *The Sino-Soviet Rift and Sino-Soviet Relations, 1964–1965* (Cambridge: MIT Press,

1966); and Francis O. Wilcox, *China and the Great Power Relations with the United States, the Soviet Union and Japan* (New York: Praeger, 1974).

8. See, for example, Harlan Jencks, *From Muskets to Missiles: Politics and Professionalism in the Chinese Army, 1945–1981* (Boulder: Westview Press, 1982); and Gerald Segal and William T. Tow, eds., *Chinese Defense Policy* (Urbana: University of Illinois Press, 1984), 98–113, which lists the relevant literature. For China's nuclear weapons production programs, see John Wilson Lewis and Xue Litai, *China Builds the Bomb* (Stanford: Stanford University Press, 1988).

9. Following is the author's sketch of some of the "rules of the Asian international system" during this period:

> No active military participation by either superpower in Asian regional conflicts. The exceptions, Vietnam and Afghanistan, proved the rule: both were overcome by combined military action of the offended parties and the assistance of the other superpower.

> No direct superpower conflict in Asia. The exceptions—Korea, Vietnam, and the Sino-Soviet border conflict—demonstrate the rule again: each proved too costly.

> Local balances were established and maintained in Northeast, Southeast, and South Asia, and the relevant communist and noncommunist powers were backed as needed by the three members of the strategic triangle.

> Asia was bifurcated economically into Island Asia and Continental Asia, with significantly different characteristics, and with Island Asia leading the way.

10. I know of no exception to this rule. One has only to peruse Arnold Toynbee's *A Study in History* (London: Royal Institute of International Affairs, 1954) to grasp this central fact of international relations, which is constant, regardless of regime type, economic system, or ideological outlook.

11. Thomas W. Robinson, "China's New Dynamism in the Strategic Triangle," *Current History* (September 1983), 241–44 ff.; and Robinson, "The United States and China in the New Asian Balance of Power," *Current History* (September 1985), 231–44 ff.

12. Harry Harding, ed., *China's Foreign Relations in the 1980s* (New Haven: Yale University Press, 1984); Kim, ed., *China and the World*, esp. chaps. 5, 6, 9, and 10; Thomas W. Robinson, "China as an Asia-Pacific Power," in *Changes and Continuities in Chinese Communism*, ed. Yu-ming Shaw (Boulder: Westview Press, 1988): 289–99; and Robert Sutter, *Chinese Foreign Policy: Developments after Mao* (New York: Praeger, 1986).

13. See, inter alia, Stephen Feuchtwang et al., *Transforming China's Economy in the Eighties*, 2 vols. (Boulder: Westview Press, 1988); Edward Friedman et al., *Chinese Village, Socialist State* (New Haven: Yale University Press, 1991); and Andrew G. Walder, *Communist Neo-Traditionalism: Work and Authority in Chinese Industry* (Berkeley: University of California Press, 1986).

14. Commentator, "Theory and Practice," *Renmin Ribao* (December 7, 1984), 1 (translation in Foreign Broadcast Information Service, *Daily Report: China,* December 7, 1984, K1–K2). The famous correction, "We cannot expect the writings of Marx and Lenin of that time to provide solutions to all our current problems," is in *Renmin Ribao* (December 8, 1984), 1 (translation in FBIS-China, December 10, 1984, K21). See also Bill Brugger and David Kelly, *Chinese Marxism in the Post-Mao Era* (Stanford: Stanford University Press, 1990).

15. On the upsurge of Sino-Soviet trade, technology transfer agreements, and exchange of delegations, see Chi Su, "Sino-Soviet Relations of the 1980s," in *China and the World,* ed. Kim, 109–27; and William deB. Mills, "Gorbachev and the Future of Sino-Soviet Relations," *Political Science Quarterly* (December 1986), 535–57 and the sources quoted therein.

16. James C. Hsiung, ed., *Beyond China's Independent Foreign Policy* (New York: Praeger, 1985); Steven Levine, "The Superpowers in Chinese Global Policy," in *Chinese Defense and Foreign Policy,* ed. June T. Dreyer and Ilpyong J. Kim (New York: Paragon House, 1988), 61–86; and Michael Yahuda, *Towards the End of Isolationism: China's Foreign Policy after Mao* (New York: St. Martin's Press, 1983).

17. Richard L. Jackson, *The Non-Aligned, the United States, and the Superpowers* (New York: Praeger, 1983); Samuel S. Kim, "China and the Third World," in *China and the World,* ed. Kim, 148–80; Zhimin Lin, "China's Third World Policy," in *The Chinese View of the World,* ed. Yufan Hao and Guocang Huan (New York: Pantheon Books, 1989): 225–60; and Robert Manning, "The Third World Looks at China," in *China and the Third World,* ed. Harris and Worden, 139–55.

18. Joint Economic Committee, *China's Economic Dilemmas in the 1990s* (Washington, D.C.: U.S. Government Printing Office, 1991), 2:713–17, 741–69; Samuel P. S. Ho and Ralph W. Huenemann, *China's Open Door Policy: The Quest for Technology and Capital* (Vancouver: University of British Columbia Press, 1984); and Wolfgang Klenner and Kurt Wievegart, *The Chinese Economy: Structure and Reform in the Domestic Economy and in Foreign Trade* (Oxford: Transaction Books, 1985).

19. Seymour J. Deitchman, *Military Power and the Advance of Technology* (Boulder: Westview Press, 1983); William H. McNeill, *The Pursuit of Power: Technology, Armed Force, and Society since A.D. 1000* (Chicago: University of Chicago Press, 1982); I. B. Holley, *Ideas and Weapons* (Washington, D.C.: U.S. Government Printing Office, 1983); and Franklin D. Margiotta and Ralph Sanders, eds., *Technology, Strategy, and National Security* (Washington, D.C.: National Defense University Press, 1985).

20. Diplomacy is thus the efficiency with which a nation's leadership manages the country's foreign affairs. The range can be quite wide: through poor management, an otherwise powerful state can squander its resources, leading to needless failures or even defeat in war. A state with relatively few material assets may maximize their utility through superior diplomacy. Such a propensity is usually found among small states. See my "Diplomacy as Political Steersmanship," appendix to my "China in a Tripolar World" (manuscript) (New York: Council on Foreign Relations, 1974). Even such writers as Hans Morgenthau miss this essential point, about which much more work is needed.

21. Joint Economic Committee, *China's Economic Dilemmas in the 1990s*, vol. 1, pt. 2, "Reforms," and pt. 4, "Modernization," 73–225 and 335–525; Joint Economic Committee, *China's Economy Looks toward the Year 2000* (Washington, D.C.: Government Printing Office, 1991), vol. 1; and Elizabeth J. Perry and Christine Wong, eds., *The Political Economy of Reform in Post-Mao China* (Cambridge: Harvard Unviersity Press, 1985).

22. The best statistical way to follow the development of China's economy is through World Bank publications.

23. See Jeffrey C. Kinkley, ed., *After Mao: Chinese Literature and Society, 1978–1981* (Cambridge: Harvard University Press, 1985); Ellen Johnston Laing, *The Winking Owl: Art in the People's Republic of China* (Berkeley: University of California Press, 1988); Perry Link et al., eds., *Unofficial China: Popular Culture and Thought in the People's Republic* (Boulder: Westview Press, 1989); and Orville Schell, *Discos and Democracy: China in the Throes of Reform* (New York: Pantheon Books, 1988).

24. Chinese arms transfer statistics and trends are best (if still imperfectly) captured in the annual U.S. Arms Control and Disarmament Agency's *World Military Expenditures and Arms Transfers* (Washington, D.C.: Superintendent of Documents, 1981–).

25. Wendy Frieman and Thomas W. Robinson, "Costs and Benefits of Interdependence," and John Frankenstein, "China's Asian Trade," in Joint Economic Committee, *China's Economic Dilemmas in the 1990s*, 718–40 and 873–94; Yufan Hao, "China and the Korean Peninsula, in *The Chinese View of the World*, ed. Hao and Huan, 175–200; Harry Harding, *China and Northeast Asia* (Lanham, Md.: University Press of America, 1988); and Robert Scalapino, *Major Power Relations in Northeast Asia* (Lanham, Md.: University Press of America, 1987).

26. For an overview of Chinese foreign policy ca. 1991, see Allen S. Whiting, ed., *China's Foreign Relations, the Annals,* January 1992.

27. These four points follow my "Modernization and Revolution in Post-Cold War Asia," *Problems of Communism* (January–April 1992), 170–79, and the sources cited therein.

11

Russia and the Two Koreas in the Post-Cold War Era

Dynamics of New Relationships

ILPYONG J. KIM

The world has changed dramatically since the beginning of the Gorbachev era in the Soviet Union in March 1985. The Cold War ended after more than four decades of conflict between the United States and the Soviet Union, and the collapse of the Berlin Wall ushered in the reunification of the two Germanys. The Eastern European nations achieved their independence, abandoning the ideology of communism and severing the alliance relationship governed by the Warsaw Pact.

The Union of Soviet Socialist Republics disintegrated after seventy-four years of existence, and the Communist Party of the Soviet Union was disbanded after more than seven decades of control over the Soviet people and society. The fifteen republics of the USSR declared themselves independent (the Baltics had achieved international recognition of their independence in September 1991). But the Commonwealth of Independent States has not achieved its original goal of bringing the republics together in a loose confederation. Under Boris Yeltsin, the Russian Federation has emerged as the great power of the CIS because it has 150 million people, a tremendous industrial base, vast natural resources, and a large share of Soviet military power.

This chapter focuses on the development of relations between the former Soviet Union under Gorbachev and the two Koreas. Diplomatic relations between the former USSR and South Korea were established in 1991, contributing to the strains and stresses in the relations between the former USSR and North Korea. During the Gorbachev era Russian policy toward the Korean peninsula changed fundamentally, resulting in a new international order in East Asia in general and reshaping the relationships between Russia and the two Koreas.

THE SOVIET UNION AND THE TWO KOREAS

Soviet policy toward the Korean peninsula following World War II focused primarily on North Korea in the context of the Cold War. The Korean peninsula was divided into two zones of occupation at the thirty-eighth parallel after the Japanese occupation of Korea from 1910 to 1945. The Soviet Union occupied the North, and the United States moved into the South. The Democratic People's Republic of Korea (DPRK)[1] was established in September 1948 in Pyongyang with Kim Il Sung as its leader under the auspices of the Soviet Union; the Republic of Korea (ROK) under the leadership of Syngman Rhee was created in August 1948 by the U.S. military government in South Korea. Soviet policy in Korea following World War II was designed to create a satellite state on its border as it had done in Eastern Europe.

The Soviet Union was the first to recognize the DPRK and establish diplomatic relations with North Korea as well as create a military alliance system to compete with the American-backed ROK government in the South. Developments in the Korean peninsula in the 1950s were a microcosm of the Cold War in the international arena. The Korean War, which was started by the North, was in a way a proxy war between the two superpowers.[2] After three years of bitter fighting, the war ended on July 27, 1953, when an armistice agreement was signed and the demilitarized zone (DMZ) that has remained intact for more than four decades was established along the thirty-eighth parallel.

Soviet–North Korean relations began to change in the post-Stalin era. Nikita Khrushchev's policy of de-Stalinization at home and peaceful coexistence abroad had repercussions in the domestic politics of North Korea. Kim Il Sung faced challenges to unseat him from his leadership position in the Korean Workers Party (KWP) as well as in the government during the political crisis of 1956. Faced with domestic challenges as well as changes in his relations with Khrushchev and the Soviet Union, Kim Il Sung began to create an independent and self-reliant foreign policy based on the ideology of *juche* (self-identity).

During the height of the Sino-Soviet conflicts in the late 1950s and the 1960s, Kim Il Sung established a balanced and equidistant policy vis-à-vis the two communist-ruled giants by concluding the Treaty of Friendship, Cooperation and Mutual Assistance with Moscow in July 1961 and a week later with the People's Republic of China (PRC). Both were considered security treaties: if North Korea were attacked by a third party, both the Soviet Union and China would automatically dispatch troops to assist it. This military alliance has become a critical issue in the post–Cold War era, and it had to be renegotiated when Gorbachev established diplomatic relations with South Korea.

Until Gorbachev became the Soviet leader and initiated the policies of glasnost and perestroika in the mid-1980s, Soviet policy toward the Korean peninsula had been marked by establishment of a bridgehead in Pyongyang to constrain South Korea's military adventure and counter the expansion of the U.S. sphere of influence in East Asia. Gorbachev's "new thinking" in Soviet foreign policy, however, dramatically changed the structure of the Cold War. The demise of the communist bloc altered the fraternal relations between Moscow and Pyongyang.

During the Gorbachev period, Soviet policy toward Korea had two aims: to maintain military and economic relations with North Korea while initiating new diplomatic relations with South Korea. Hard-liners like the Soviet military establishment continued to pursue a cooperative relationship with Pyongyang, and a five-year cooperation plan signed with the DPRK was implemented according to schedule. While Gorbachev put forward his "historic peace initiatives" with the West during the period 1986–90, Soviet generals provided their ally in Pyongyang with the latest armaments at a total cost of 1.4 billion rubles. The Soviet military establishment supplied Pyongyang with modern ground-to-air missile complexes known as SAM-5s, which were immediately deployed some forty miles north of the DMZ, and MIG 23 and MIG 29 combat fighter planes. Moreover, North Korea had reportedly requested as much as $15–20 billion worth of "special equipment" in 1988 and 1990. This request was not honored.[3] Total Soviet military aid to North Korea, according to unconfirmed sources, was somewhere between two and five billion rubles.

That Soviet policy was influenced by the hard-liners was evident in the Moscow-Pyongyang joint communiqué issued in January 1986 at the end of Soviet foreign minister Eduard A. Shevardnadze's visit to Pyongyang. The communiqué denounced the United States, Japan, and South Korea for their expansion of military hegemony in Asia and their attempt to create a military alliance system. The joint communiqué expressed Moscow's support for North Korea's reunification formula, Pyongyang's demand for replacing the current armistice agreement with a peace treaty with the United States, and the co-hosting of the 1988 Seoul Olympic games. Further, the communiqué stressed that Moscow and Pyongyang opposed the concept of cross recognition—the United States and Japan would recognize North Korea while the USSR and China would recognize South Korea—and opposed the simultaneous entry by South Korea and North Korea into the United Nations. North Korea has persistently opposed cross recognition and simultaneous entry on the ground that such action would perpetuate the division of Korea.

Relations between Moscow and Pyongyang began to deteriorate during the Gorbachev period because Soviet foreign policy priority was beginning to shift from maintenance of the alliance relationship with Pyongyang to a peace initiative in which the Warsaw Pact would be dissolved and negotiations with the United States for nuclear disarmament would be initiated. But the Soviet leadership formally continued to support the course of the Korean Workers Party and the DPRK for the "peaceful and democratic unification" of Korea without any external interference. Any proposal made by Pyongyang to Seoul about unification of the two Koreas was automatically supported by Moscow and endorsed as "constructive." Even the North Korean proposal to establish a Democratic Confederal Republic of Koryo (DCRK) in the 1980s was endorsed by the Soviet leadership as a "constructive proposal" because of the hard-liners' influence in policy making.

The first indication of change in Soviet policy toward Korea was expressed when Gorbachev proposed an Asian-Pacific regional collective security arrangement in his July 1986 Vladivostok speech. Gorbachev emphasized the need to promote dialogue and reconciliation with the West instead of continued ideological confrontation with capitalist countries. He further expanded this proposal in his September 1988 Krasnoyarsk speech and suggested that the USSR was willing to promote economic relations with South Korea. He called for strengthening Soviet security measures in the Asia-Pacific region by starting multilateral arms negotiations. He specifically suggested that the Soviet Union, China, Japan, North Korea, and South Korea hold joint security talks to limit naval and air force activities with a view toward lowering the chance of military confrontation in the region.

Soviet policy toward North Korea began to shift in 1988, when the Soviet Union announced it would participate in the Seoul Olympic games. Pyongyang's recalcitrant attitude toward the cohosting of the Olympics, opposition to simultaneous Korean entry into the United Nations, and objection to Soviet trade with South Korea caused the Soviets to doubt Kim Il Sung and his followers in Pyongyang. Kim and his entourage seemed too rigid in their nationalistic *juche* ideology, opposing every aspect of the Soviet peace initiative. Soviet foreign minister Shevardnadze visited Pyongyang in December 1988 to explain the reasons for Soviet participation in the Seoul Olympics and to pledge that "the USSR would never go beyond trade with its relations with the ROK."[4]

Moreover, the Soviet foreign minister reaffirmed the USSR's military commitment to North Korea, which was included in the joint communiqué issued following Shevardnadze's visit. But the establishment of diplomatic relations between the USSR and the ROK in September 1990, less than two years later, altered USSR-DPRK relations dramatically. Shevardnadze was sent back to Pyongyang to explain, but he was not received by Kim Il Sung or welcomed by the North Korean leadership. North Korean foreign minister Kim Youngnam met Shevardnadze, but, "on hearing an angry tirade, he cut short his visit and went back to Moscow at once."[5]

SOUTH KOREA'S APPROACHES TO THE USSR

For the past half-century, the northern problem, or unification, has been the primary issue of each ROK administration. Successive presidents, from Syngman Rhee of the First Republic in 1948 to Roh Tae Woo of the Sixth Republic in the 1980s, have undertaken to approach the North in an effort to come to terms with unification peacefully. South Koreans yearn for the sense of security that such a resolution would bring. Their uneasiness over the division is caused by the harsh experience of the Korean War.

From the inception of the ROK government in 1948 to President Park Chung Hee's declaration of June 23, 1973, foreign and defense policies of the ROK had been subordinated to the Cold War policy of the United States, which was based on anticommunism and hostility toward the Soviet Union and its allies. In 1973, President Park declared that the ROK government was willing to approach communist nations such as the Soviet Union, China, and those in Eastern Europe regarding the establishment of diplomatic relations.[6] This declaration was the prelude to the "northern policy," or Nordpolitik, that President Roh announced on July 7, 1988.

The development of Soviet–South Korean relations had three phases: the period from June 23, 1973, to 1988, when the ROK government made a series of attempts to open up diplomatic relations with the Soviet bloc countries; the period from 1988, when the Soviet bloc countries—except Cuba and Albania—decided to participate in the Seoul Olympic games, to 1990, when the USSR and South Korea normalized diplomatic relations; and the post-1990 period. The ROK has now established diplomatic relations with every former Soviet bloc country except Cuba.

Notwithstanding Nordpolitik, not much happened during the first phase of Soviet–South Korean relations in the 1970s and early 1980s because of the persisting Cold War and the rigidity of Soviet policy toward the Korean peninsula. The Soviet-U.S. detente and the Sino-U.S. rapprochement in the early 1970s, however, brought about the North-South dialogue and negotiations that yielded the communiqué of July 4, 1972, and the declaration of June 23, 1973. The North-South detente lasted a little over a year; tension escalated in subsequent years.

Despite the June 23 declaration, in which South Korea attempted to approach the Soviet Union and other communist countries in the 1970s, Soviet–South Korean rapprochement did not come about until the change in Soviet leadership in the mid-1980s. Ever since the October 1917 revolution, the Bolsheviks had subscribed to the ideology of Marxism-Leninism, but it is unclear how much of Soviet foreign policy can be ascribed to ideology and how much to cold calculations of how best to advance the interests of the Soviet state. Until Gorbachev initiated the policy of "new thinking" in the late 1980s, Soviet leaders insisted that their foreign policy was scientifically determined and that it sprang directly from the writings of Karl Marx and Vladimir Lenin.

Gorbachev developed a new concept of security, and in *Perestroika: New Thinking for Our Country and the World*, he wrote that "security can no longer be secured through military means. . . . The only way to security is through political decisions and disarmament."[7] During the Gorbachev era of perestroika and glasnost, ideological rhetoric disappeared not only in domestic reform efforts but also in the reformulation of foreign policy because of his pragmatism and realism. Gorbachev's "new thinking" brought about a fundamental reorientation toward international affairs: the USSR would become a cooperative member of the international community. In a historic address to the UN General Assembly on December 7, 1988, Gorbachev said that in de-ideologizing Soviet relations with other states, "we are not abandoning our conviction, our philosophy, or our traditions, but neither do we have any intention to be hemmed in by them."[8]

Soviet policy toward Asia in general and toward South Korea in particular had already shifted when Gorbachev presented a pragmatic economic development strategy for Siberia in his July 1986 Vladivostok address. Gorbachev spoke of improving relations with China and Japan and of having other nations participate in Siberian development projects. He committed himself to withdraw Soviet troops from the Sino-Soviet border areas and agreed to settle the territorial disputes along the main channel of the Amur River. He also called for regional cooperation in security and human rights in Asia consistent with the Helsinki accords. The Soviet approach to the Asia-Pacific region was becoming more pragmatic and increasingly conscious of economic possibilities.

In his Krasnoyarsk speech two years later, Gorbachev offered a seven-point proposal to strengthen the security of the Asia-Pacific region. In the period between these two speeches, he was caught up in the politics of Soviet foreign policy making, particularly regarding rapprochement with South Korea. The turning point came in 1988, when the Soviet government decided its athletes would take part in the twenty-fourth Olympiad, which was to take place in Seoul in September. A separate chapter would be required to analyze the bureaucratic politics of Soviet policy making, but a brief summary of the circumstances surrounding the decision is necessary to understand Soviet policy toward Korea.

George F. Kunadze, director of Japanese research in the Soviet Academy of Sciences (later deputy foreign minister of the Russian Federation), presented a paper in Seoul in June 1991 in which he explained that Soviet policy makers were divided into two camps: the conservatives and the reformers.[9] The traditional bureaucracy in the Foreign Ministry and the International Relations Department of the CPSU Central Committee opposed participation in the Seoul

Olympics because of the possible effects on Soviet relations with North Korea. Kunadze described North Korea's important role in the decision-making process of the Soviet bureaucracy: "But as far as the conventional wisdom of the Soviet bureaucracy was concerned, both Soviet participation in the Seoul Olympics and a trade opening to the ROK were still subject to North Korean approval. Later thanks to the obstinate position of the DPRK, which absolutely refused to approve any Soviet contacts with Seoul whatsoever, this linkage was considerably softened. It happened simply out of necessity: the USSR was determined to take part in the Olympics; hence the Soviet government stopped its futile efforts to get North Korean approval, scaling them down to the search of some reasonable formula, to placate North Korea."[10]

A compromise solution on how to deal with North Korea had to be worked out because the conservatives supported the North Korean position and the pragmatic reformers supported South Korea. "The final decision of this formula suggested that the DPRK was entitled to a certain compensation for not making an open scandal out of the Soviet athletes' voyage to Seoul," Kunadze recalled. "In this vein the Soviet government made a pledge not to establish official-level relations with the ROK. . . . The most important thing is that at the moment of this pledge people in Moscow apparently meant to honor it," Kunadze stressed. "In other words, it was still considered sufficient to maintain low-level private exchanges with the ROK. So once again the issue of the USSR-ROK relations appeared closed for the time being." Why, then, did Soviet policy makers decide to establish diplomatic relations with South Korea?

For several decades, Soviet policy toward Korea had been dominated by conservative experts who had been trained exclusively within the framework of the fraternal relations between the USSR and the DPRK. Many had learned to speak the Korean language, but they had also picked up prejudices against South Korea that limited their grasp of South Korean realities. According to Kunadze, "Unfortunately, the general tendency in Soviet policy towards Korea as well as Soviet Korean research was rather conservative, not to say negative." Soviet research on Korea began to take on a different character in the Gorbachev era, however, and the new thinking brought out "a few Soviet experts somehow miraculously successful in developing an adequate vision of the Korean problem."[11]

The Institute of World Economy and International Relations (IMEMO) emerged as the leading organization devoted to changing Soviet research on Korea and Soviet Korean policy. "As a government think tank responsible mainly for the study of industrially developed countries, IMEMO had had almost nothing to do with Korea," Kunadze asserted. "That exempted us from the lunacy of the ideological stereotypes compiled by the other institutes, traditional contributors to Soviet Korean policy." IMEMO was also "spared the brainwashing instructions from the department of the Central Committee of the CPSU which deals with socialist countries." He concluded, "In short, a newcomer to Korean research, IMEMO ironically found itself adequately equipped for the job with common sense, a good portion of radical ideas, and last but not least a comparatively good understanding of the logic and dynamics of the South Korean state and society."

IMEMO entered Korean policy research with a determination to make a significant contribution to the "traditionally stagnant field of Soviet diplomacy," Kunadze declared. But its scholars did not advocate prompt recognition of the ROK. "Instead we proposed a gradual opening to the ROK in the firm belief that Soviet interests would be better served by taking carefully measured steps forward, one at a time," Kunadze recalled. "We also developed a system of arguments to back this stance up." He explained why IMEMO proposed a gradual approach to the recognition of South Korea: "Although we did not share an orthodox view of the DPRK as a fraternal communist country, we argued that by rushing things through we would be endangering a delicate balance of interests of too many actors, including China, the USA and North Korea. Frankly speaking, China was first on the list of our priorities. Conventional logic suggested that by leaving North Korea no other choice but to retaliate, we would be inviting China to fill the vacuum left after the Soviet departure from Pyongyang. What is more, by doing so, we might have also expected a direct negative reaction on the part of China, with some unclear implications for Sino-Soviet relations."[12]

The bureaucracy advanced two more important arguments against recognition of the ROK. The Soviet military presented a very simple geopolitical argument to the effect that "we should not abandon an alliance without adequate compensation," Kunadze said. "The size and form of the compensation in question was never determined, but nevertheless the argument was considered sound." The second argument was that the Soviet Union had limited tactical reserves. "Everybody agreed that by recognizing the ROK the USSR would not be gaining much in terms of diplomacy or strategy," Kunadze emphasized. "So the only argument in favor of this decision had to be economic benefits. Our choice appeared clear: diplomatic recognition in exchange for economic benefits."[13]

THE ECONOMIC FACTOR IN USSR-ROK RELATIONS

On July 7, 1988, South Korean president Roh Tae Woo issued his "northern policy" (Nordpolitik) declaration in which he called for improved relations with the socialist countries in general and in particular better relations with the Soviet Union and China, the two major powers of the communist bloc. That September, Gorbachev acknowledged the possibility of expanded economic exchange with South Korea. Thus economic relations between the Soviet Union and South Korea received significant attention before diplomatic relations were normalized in September 1990.

According to Kim Hak-Joon, the most astute observer and policy analyst of President Roh's office, the Soviet Union set out to establish diplomatic relations with South Korea in large part because of the altered Soviet perception of Korean economic development and Roh's Nordpolitik.[14] After analyzing articles and research papers by such Soviet experts on East Asia as Oleg Davydov, Mikhail Kapitsa, Dimitry Petrov, Alexander Fedorovsky, V. Martinov, and George Kunadze, Kim concluded that Soviet Korean specialists proposed to start the economic cooperation with South Korea in the fields of light industry, the food processing and pharmaceutical industries, tourism, and trade. Moreover, they proposed to expand the scholarly exchange with South Korea so as to learn from the model of South Korean economic development. The economic overtures were successful: bilateral trade between the Soviet Union and South Korea grew enormously each year after 1986 and was projected to reach $9 billion by 1995.

Gorbachev addressed the Supreme Soviet of the USSR after the third Soviet–South Korean summit in April 1991 and reported that during the ten months since the first summit in San Francisco in June 1990, rapprochement had moved rapidly. "It will enhance the unification of Korea that the Korean people have hoped for," Gorbachev asserted. "In the process of unifying the two Koreas, the two governments should function as sovereign units and we are trying our best to provide an environment in which unification can take place."[15]

Gorbachev also reported on current and future economic and trade relations between the Soviet Union and South Korea, which had been the subject of the summit on Cheju Island. President Roh agreed to provide the Soviet Union with South Korean credit of $3 billion. The two presidents had agreed that the ROK would begin supplying consumer goods in May 1991 to relieve the shortage in the Soviet Union. Gorbachev continued: "It has been promised that the commercial exchange of $1.5 billion this year [1991] and $10 billion in 1995 will be achieved. This is possible since our trade volume has increased 100% each year during the past four years. We have also agreed that investment, especially investment in the petroleum industry, should be increased. . . . We have also discussed the construction of 48 industrial projects, which include exploration of natural gas in Siberia and Far Eastern Russia."[16]

South Korea's overseas investment and markets with the Soviet Union and all East European countries expanded widely as the result of the ROK government's Nordpolitik of approaching the socialist states. Trade volume with the northern states increased by an average of 30 percent after the declaration of July 7, 1988. The $8.1 billion worth of trade with the former socialist countries helped Korea avoid an overall trade deficit. Although Korean investment in the Soviet Union and Eastern Europe and imports of natural resources from the region remained meager, there was indirect investment in 367 projects, and the volume of induced resources reached $500 million by November 1992, according to ROK government sources.[17]

The northern countries, including the former Soviet republics and the countries of Eastern Europe, have an enormous market potential: they account for 24 percent of the global area and 31 percent of the world's population. Hence South Korea's Nordpolitik not only helped those countries in their political and economic ordeals but also brought the Soviet Union into the Asia-Pacific region so that it could contribute to the region's peace and stability. South Korea's annual trade volume with the northern countries is projected to reach $26 billion by 1996 and rise to more than 14 percent of total volume by the year 2000. Thus the Soviet Union and South Korea had a commonality of economic interests in establishing diplomatic relations.

From the perspective of Soviet policy makers, economic benefit was the priority consideration because South Korea was willing to provide a $3 billion loan for economic cooperation. As George Kunadze stressed, however, "The biggest motivation to recognize the ROK grew out of Soviet domestic politics."[18] In his report to the Supreme Soviet about his visit to South Korea, Gorbachev asserted: "We have to pay special attention to the experience of South Korea, which has overcome underdevelopment and reached the stage of industrial development within a short period of time. We all know that South Korea was a dictatorial country not too long ago. If the Soviet Union and South Korea can combine the potential power of each country for beneficial and future-oriented economic development, we can certainly establish a creative and efficient model of economic cooperation. . . . The South Korean leader is preparing to help the Soviet Union to participate in the integration process of the Asia-Pacific economic community. President Roh has invited the Soviet Union to participate in the international body of the Asia-Pacific economic cooperation and in EXPO-93 which will take place in South Korea."[19]

From the South Korean perspective, implementation of Nordpolitik resulted in the state visit of President Roh to Moscow on December 13–17, 1990, the first such visit by the ROK head of state. It was reciprocated by Gorbachev's state visit of April 19–20, 1991. The exchange of visits and the summits not only consolidated Soviet–South Korean relations but also enhanced the environment of peace and stability in East Asia in general and particularly in the Korean peninsula. The improvement in Soviet–South Korean relations also influenced North Korea to open a dialogue with the South and convene meetings of the two Korean prime ministers. After six such meetings in Seoul and Pyongyang alternately, in December the two sides reached an agreement on reconciliation, nonaggression, and exchanges and cooperation that became effective February 19, 1992.

Soviet–South Korean normalization helped bring about the demise of the Yalta system and diminish the Cold War in East Asia. When Gorbachev emerged as the new leader of the Soviet Union and implemented his policies of perestroika and glasnost in the late 1980s, a new international order was shaping up in Western Europe that ultimately brought the end of the Cold War there and the reunification of Germany. Still, the Cold War lingered in Northeast Asia, embodied in the conflict and hostility between the two Koreas. It was hoped the South-North agreement would reduce the tensions and create an atmosphere conducive to reunification.

The CIS was created after the dissolution of the USSR in December 1991, finalizing the dissolution of the USSR. Initially it consisted of nine independent republics, of which the Russian Federation was the largest. For a short period in early 1992, the Russian–South Korean relationship retrogressed because of uncertainty about the future. Economic relations resumed after the state visit of Russian president Boris Yeltsin in November 1992 when he presented twenty-three economic projects for joint development by the Russian Federation and South Korea. The proposed projects covered such fields as exploration of natural resources, cooperation in science and technology, construction of infrastructure such as roads and ports, and tourism. Yeltsin also asked for more active Korean investment to help the troubled Russian economy. He pledged further efforts to expand bilateral relations under the terms of the September 1990 establishment of diplomatic ties as the Russian Federation had become heir to the treaty obligations of the former Soviet Union. Yeltsin spoke of selling military technology and equipment to South Korea, and President Roh was interested in the proposal.[20]

In the November 1992 ROK-Russia treaty, Presidents Roh and Yeltsin affirmed "their conviction that the development of friendly relations and cooperation between the two countries will contribute not only to their mutual benefit but also to the peace, security and prosperity of the Asian and Pacific region and throughout the world." The leaders thus underscored their commitment to the purposes and principles of the charter of the United Nations. They also recognized that "the Moscow Declaration of 14 December 1992 shall continue to govern relations between the two countries." The declaration was incorporated into the treaty between the Russian Federation and the ROK. The text of that treaty and its fifteen articles is similar to what Gorbachev and Roh had signed when diplomatic relations were first established.[21]

The Russian Federation and North Korea

When Boris Yeltsin met South Korean foreign minister Lee Sang-Ock in July 1992 to discuss his planned visit to Seoul four months later, he said, "Kim Il Sung will be awfully jealous when I visit Seoul."[22] The Russian also declared that the ideological bonds between Moscow and Pyongyang no longer existed. North Korea clearly does not figure importantly in the foreign policy calculations of the Russian Federation.

The Soviet Union was first among the nations that recognized the DPRK when it was founded in September 1948, and Joseph Stalin placed Kim Il Sung in a leadership position. The Soviets gave the DPRK economic and military assistance, and during the Korean War (1950–53) Stalin supported North Korea's effort to unify the country by military means. In the post–Korean War period, 1954–60, the Soviet Union provided grants and credits totaling 1.3 billion rubles. (North Korea still owes 2.2 billion rubles to the former Soviet Union; this debt was inherited by the Russian Federation.) The Soviets also dispatched six thousand technicians and experts to help rebuild the North Korean economy, and more than twenty thousand students from North Korea studied in various institutions of higher education in the Soviet Union in the 1950s and 1960s. Many of these students were trained in nuclear physics and nuclear engineering and later helped to develop North Korea's nuclear program. The former Soviet Union was the source of 60 percent of North Korea's electric power, 33 percent of its iron and steel, 60 percent of its petrochemical products, and 40 percent of its textile goods.

The Soviets continued to support Kim Il Sung in the 1960s and 1970s despite North Korea's standing apart from Sino-Soviet disputes regarding influence in the Pyongyang government. After the death of Stalin and the de-Stalinization initiated by Khrushchev in 1956, however, Kim had to face up to factional struggle in North Korean politics. By using Stalin's tactics of setting one faction against another, he was able first to purge the pro-Soviet faction and then to eliminate the Chinese faction, thereby instituting his *juche* ideology. According to a former deputy minister of internal affairs in the North Korean government who was exiled to the Soviet Union, *juche* ideology "has nothing to do with the ideology of Marxism or Leninism; it is Kim's own ideology based on Korean tradition and his own cult of personality."[23] Some Marxist scholars in the West have even charged that North Korea is not a Marxist state but a Korean nationalist state similar to the Yi Dynasty. Thus the ideological bond between the Soviet Union and North Korea disappeared long before Boris Yeltsin declared it dead in 1992.

The policies of perestroika and glasnost of the former Soviet Union fundamentally changed the Soviet–North Korean relationship. Under Gorbachev's "new thinking," Soviet policy toward the Asia-Pacific region in general and the Korean peninsula in particular took on a new coloration. The strategic interest of the Soviet Union during the Cold War years became an economic interest during the Gorbachev era (1985–91). North Korea was important to the Soviets when it served their strategic interests, but now South Korea is important to the Russians because it serves their economic interests. Consequently, Soviet–North Korean relations were downgraded when diplomatic relations between the Soviet Union and South Korea were established in September 1990.

As early as 1988, when the Soviet Union decided to participate in the Seoul Olympic games, North Korea's response was somewhat ambivalent. The Soviets promised not to open diplomatic relations with the South and to continue economic and military aid to the North. When Hungary established diplomatic relations with South Korea in 1989, however, the spokesman for North Korea's Foreign Ministry charged that the way Hungarian officials handled the matter constituted a betrayal and an unjustifiable act for which they should take full responsibility. The attack indicated North Korea's sense that Eastern Europe and the Soviet Union were doublecrossing an erstwhile ally.

The Soviet media began to take a more realistic and pragmatic approach to the Korean problem, as signaled by the suggestion in September 1989 by *Izvestia* that Soviet–South Korean normalization of relations be initiated by recognizing the existence of two independent states on the Korean peninsula. On January 8, 1990, *Pravda* called for normalization. These recommendations were followed by the official statement of Foreign Minister Shevardnadze after the U.S.-Soviet foreign ministers' conference on February 14, 1990, that "the Soviet Union supported the reduction of tensions in the Korean peninsula and the North–South Korea dialogue in which the Soviet Union is willing to serve as a mediator."[24] Thus the Soviet role in the resolution of the Korean question was perceived as that of mediator between the two sides rather than as ally of North Korea.

In the early months of 1990, both the Soviet press and Moscow radio began to criticize the dictatorship and isolation of North Korea. It was reported that more than 8,800 students and technicians, including 500 students in China, were called back to North Korea for ideological reorientation. A weekly magazine of the reformist group, *Issues and Facts*, on April 1, 1990, speculated that if North Korea opposed reform and an opening to the outside world, it might face the fate of Romanian president Nicolae Ceauşescu and his wife: death by execution. The Soviet media were laying the groundwork for the 1990 Soviet–South Korean summit meeting that led to the normalization of relations three months later.

North Korean responses to the Soviet–South Korean rapprochement were not as critical as they had been regarding East European normalization with

South Korea. A commentary in the North Korean party newspaper, *Rodong Sinmun,* on April 4, 1990, stressed that "the Soviet–South Korean normalization of diplomatic relations cannot be tolerated because it perpetuates the division of Korea." The same newspaper emphasized on June 6, 1990, that the summit in San Francisco was "a plot to divide Korea into two halves by the splitists"—they would never be forgiven. In responding to the official announcement of normalization, *Rodong Sinmun,* on October 5, 1990, described "the establishment of Soviet–South Korean relations [as] an act of betrayal" that North Korea found shocking.

When the Soviet Union established diplomatic relations with South Korea, it did not sever its relations with North Korea. Two critical issues remain: the status of the treaty of friendship and mutual assistance that had been concluded in July 1961 and the repayment of the North Korean debt of some 2.7 billion rubles incurred during the Soviet period. The security treaty was automatically renewed in July 1991 for ten more years, but controversy over the treaty arose when Yeltsin said in Seoul during his visit to South Korea in November 1992 that Moscow would consider repealing an article in the treaty that provided for the automatic intervention of Russia in the event of a war involving either North Korea or Russia.[25]

North Korea would like to see the treaty in force until it expires in 1996 without any change (i.e., in the event of war, Russia would enter the conflict on the side of the DPRK). Article 1 of the treaty, which provided for mutual assistance, has been a concern of Seoul and the United States ever since it was concluded in 1961. In February 1992, Igor Rigachev, then Russian deputy minister of foreign affairs, was dispatched to Pyongyang to determine the North Korean leader's attitude toward the 1961 treaty. Rigachev interpreted the military commitment in Article 1 as valid only in the event of an unprovoked attack against the DPRK, not in the event of a North Korean attack on another party.

Russia's first diplomatic representative to North Korea after the breakup of the Soviet Union learned that relations between Moscow and Pyongyang were far from normal over issues in the security treaty. "It was also at this time," Andrew A. Bouchkin stressed, "that representatives of the regime declared for the first time at the official level that they considered the treaty outdated and did not object to it being terminated."[26] It is now clear to Moscow and Pyongyang as well as to Seoul that the treaty's "existence is a pure formality and does not pose any hidden threat whatsoever, although the category of 'unprovoked attack,' as reinterpreted, was rather loose and inconcrete."[27]

During his 1992 visit to Seoul, Yeltsin declared that it was necessary to terminate the treaty with the DPRK, which was a total surprise to everyone; even the Russian Ministry of Foreign Affairs was unprepared for the announcement. The ministry reaffirmed that Russia needed to honor all international commitments of the former USSR. Kunadze, Yeltsin's deputy foreign minister, was dispatched to Pyongyang as a special envoy in January 1993 to negotiate, among other issues, North Korea's stance on the nuclear issue and the new relations between North Korea and the Russian Federation. The negotiations between Kunadze and North Korea's foreign minister Kim Young-nam and deputy foreign minister Kang Seok-choo failed to come to agreement on any of the key diplomatic issues except the mutual assurance of their desire to resume and promote "all-embracing contacts" and get a better understanding of each other's positions. Thus Moscow-Pyongyang relations have been deteriorating since the collapse of the Soviet Union and have improved little despite efforts by the Russian Federation.

Russian deputy foreign minister Aleksandr Panov visited Pyongyang after Kim Il Sung's death in September 1994 but failed to resolve pending diplomatic issues between the two countries, including Pyongyang's repayment of debts to Moscow. As of January 1991, North Korea's debt to the USSR was 2.7 billion rubles, and the two countries agreed that the debt could be paid in commodities. North Korea agreed to repay 2.1 billion rubles between 1991 and 1995, and Pyongyang shipped 501 million rubles worth of commodities in 1991, including computers, their accessories, construction services, shipbuilding and repair services, light industrial products, handicrafts, liquors, furniture, timbers, and iron ore and mineral products.

Economic relations between Moscow and Pyongyang began to tighten up several years before the collapse of the Soviet Union. While the Soviet Union was moving toward a market economy, Moscow insisted that all Soviet–North Korean trade be conducted in hard currency. In the first four months of 1991, trade deliveries were suspended because of difficulties in the hard currency transaction.

Russia, like the USSR in the past, supplied oil and petroleum products, products of iron and steel and chemical industries, coking coal, coke, cotton, and other items. The deliveries from the DPRK included ferrous rolled stock, cement, motor storage batteries, microelectric engines, and consumer goods. Special emphasis was placed on a group of commodities to be supplied by the DPRK as partial repayment of its debt, including the plant for computer manufacturing, light industrial goods, talcum, barite, and other mine products. North Korea also sent construction and timber industry workers to Russia to help repay the debt. Trade turnover for 1991 under the agreement amounted 853 million rubles (or around $1.5 billion). Trade volume for 1992 was $600 million, an increase of 32.3 percent from 1991. North Korea's exports to Russia were up 5.3 percent, amounting to $200 million, while Russia's were up 17.6 percent, reaching a total of $400 million.

In the first six months of 1993, North Korea's imports from Russia amounted to about $200 million, an increase of 45 percent over the same period in 1992. Thus in 1992 the DPRK supplied Russia with $145 million worth of manufactured goods (including $40 million worth of household electric appliances), $30 million worth of food (including fresh and canned fruit), some metal-cutting machine tools, cement, and calcium carbide. North Korea also reexported sugar, canned meat, cigarettes, dry milk, knitwear, household electric appliances, and computers and their accessories to Russia from such countries as Singapore, China, and Hong Kong. In the first six months of 1993, North Korea's imports from Russia amounted to around $200 million, which was an increase of 40 percent over the previous year. In the first quarter of 1994, however, Pyongyang's trade with Russia was only $12.1 million, a decrease of 43.7 percent compared to 1993. The record-breaking trade volume between Russia and North Korea was $1.5 billion in 1989, the last year of the Cold War, and continued to shrink in subsequent years.

The collapse of the Soviet Union and disintegration of socialist governments in Eastern Europe affected North Korea's economy, particularly its trade relations with the former Soviet Union. In the late 1980s, more than 40 percent of North Korea's trade was carried out with the Soviet Union, which exported mainly materials and technical know-how to North Korea. The disintegration of the Soviet Union ended the fraternal spirit and preferential trade and economic relations between Moscow and Pyongyang, damaging North Korea's economy and trade. Thus the DPRK began to explore opening economic relations with the West, particularly the United States and Japan, in the early 1990s.

CONCLUSION

During the Cold War, Soviet foreign policy was preoccupied with Western Europe and the United States. Policies regarding East Asia in general and more specifically the Korean peninsula were subordinated to the strategic interest of the Soviet Union. But that was then and this is now. The Russian Federation is likely to become a major power if not a superpower. Its policy focus is shifting from Europe to the Asian Pacific because "it has become quite clear that the world community is entering a new Pacific era and the Asia-Pacific region is growing into a new center of world civilization," as one Russian expert on Asia declared. In addition, "relations with the Korean states carry a special meaning for Russia because of a century-old community living in Russia and the strategic importance of the Korean peninsula."[28]

The convergence of Soviet interest in economic benefits and South Korean interest in normalization of relations with the Soviet Union under Nordpolitik

resulted in the establishment of diplomatic relations between the two countries. While diplomatic and economic relations between Moscow and Seoul
made a breakthrough in the 1990s, Moscow-Pyongyang relations deteriorated
proportionately. The 1961 treaty of friendship and mutual assistance is intact,
however, and has been renewed to the year 2001. The realities of the international and strategic environment are not reflected in the treaty, especially the
military clause. Hence the Russians expect to renegotiate it to correspond to
the new realities of Russian–North Korean relations.

Russian interests would be best served if Russia can help the two Koreas to
conduct discussions aimed at reducing tensions and fostering stability and peace
in the peninsula. "It is in the Russian national interest," Gennady Chufrin,
deputy director of the Russian Institute of Oriental Studies, asserted, "to promote the unification process even though the unification of Korea is first of
all and above all an internal affair of the Korean people." Further, a unified
Korea "may contribute positively to the state of international relations because Korea is to become a natural ally of Russia in opposing the revival of
Japanese militarism."[29] Such a revival would not only unify the two Koreas
but also contribute to the convergence of the strategic interests of the Russians, Koreans, and Chinese.

Russia would be best served if it continued to coordinate its policies with
the two Korean governments and cooperate with them in promoting regional
security in Asia and the Pacific. One foreign policy issue on which Russians
and North Koreans may see eye to eye is formation of a special economic zone
in Northeast Asia in which Russian natural resources, North Korean labor,
and South Korean capital and technology could be brought together to contribute to the economy of the region. Such a development would include exploration of Russia's Far East and development of the Pacific Rim and the
Tyumen River basin, where the vital interests of Russia, Japan, and the two
Koreas converge. The development of the basin, which borders on Russia, China,
and North Korea, under the auspices of the United Nations (with the support
of the United States) could serve as a model for future cooperation by the
potential beneficiaries.

NOTES

This chapter is a considerably revised and updated version of my "The Soviet Union/
Russia and Korea: Dynamics of New Thinking," in *Korea and the World: Beyond the
Cold War* (Boulder: Westview, 1994).

1. Ilpyong J. Kim, *Historical Dictionary of North Korea* (Metuchen, N.J.: Scarecrow
Press, forthcoming).

2. Ilpyong J. Kim, *Historical Dictionary of the Korean War* (Metuchen, N.J.: Scarecrow Press, forthcoming).

3. Andrew A. Bouchkin, "North Korea and Russia: A Blind Alley?" in *Foreign Relations of North Korea,* ed. Doug Joong Kim (Seoul: Sejong Institute, 1994), 308.

4. Ibid., 310.

5. Ibid.

6. Ilpyong J. Kim, "Policies toward China and the Soviet Union," in *The Foreign Policy of the Republic of Korea,* ed. Youngnok Koo and Sung-Joo Han (New York: Columbia University Press, 1985), 198–218.

7. Mikhail S. Gorbachev, *Perestroika: New Thinking for Our Country and the World* (New York: Harper & Row, 1987), 69.

8. *New York Times,* December 8, 1988.

9. George F. Kunadze, "USSR-ROK: Agenda for the Future," in *ROK-USSR Cooperation in a New International Environment* (Seoul: Institute of Foreign Affairs and National Security, 1991), 81–94.

10. Ibid., 82.

11. Ibid.

12. Ibid., 84.

13. Ibid.

14. Hak-Joon Kim, "South Korean–Soviet Detente and South–North Korean Relations," in *The Korean Peninsula and International Politics in Transition* (Seoul: Publication Committee of Essays for the Commemoration of Kim Ilpyong's Sixtieth Birthday, 1991), 3–19.

15. *Pravda,* April 27, 1991.

16. Ibid.

17. *Korea Times,* November 25, 1992.

18. Kunadze, "USSR-ROK," 86.

19. *Pravda,* November 22, 1991.

20. *Korea Newsreview,* November 28, 1992.

21. *Korea Times,* November 20, 1992.

22. *Korea Newsreview,* November 28, 1992.

23. Kang Sang Ho interview in *Ogonek,* 1, 1991.

24. Sejong Institute, *Source Materials on Soviet Relations with the Korean Peninsula, 1986–1991* (Seoul: Sejong Institute, 1991), 78–79.

25. *Korea Newsreview,* November 28, 1992.

26. Bouchkin, "North Korea and Russia," 314–15.

27. Ibid.

28. Gennady Chufrin, "Russian Policy toward the DPRK: Goals and Uncertainties," paper presented at the International Conference on Four Major Powers' Policies toward the DPRK, Seoul, September 30, 1992.

29. Ibid.

12

Soviet-Israeli Relations in the Gorbachev Era

Robert O. Freedman

Soviet foreign policy toward the State of Israel changed markedly during the Gorbachev era. When Gorbachev came to power in March 1985, there were no diplomatic relations between the two countries (although Moscow did recognize Israel's right to exist) because Brezhnev had broken off relations during the 1967 Six-Day War. During Gorbachev's reign, first consular, then full diplomatic relations were restored. The year before Gorbachev came to power, fewer than 1,000 Soviet Jews were allowed to emigrate, and most of them went to the United States. During Gorbachev's last year in power, 1991, more than 180,000 Soviet Jews were allowed to leave, and the vast majority went to Israel. Moscow's attitude toward the Arab-Israeli conflict also changed dramatically. Before Gorbachev's rule, the USSR had strongly sided with the Arabs and had helped push through the "Zionism Is Racism" resolution in the United Nations General Assembly. Gorbachev adopted a far more evenhanded policy, telling the leaders of Israel's two main Arab enemies, Syria and the Palestine Liberation Organization (PLO), that they would have to settle their conflict with Israel by political means, not by war, and joining the United States in sponsoring the repeal of the "Zionism Is Racism" resolution. The fourth major change in Soviet policy toward Israel in the Gorbachev era involved cultural and people-to-people relations. Almost nonexistent in the pre-Gorbachev era (except for occasional visits of left-wing groups), this relationship blossomed dramatically during the period Gorbachev ruled the USSR. Religious, cultural, and athletic teams participated in exchanges such as the Bolshoi Ballet's visit to Israel and Israel's Habimah Theatre visit to the Soviet Union.[1]

During Gorbachev's first two years in office, however, Soviet-Israeli relations remained cool, although he began to send out diplomatic "feelers" to Israel. This chapter will analyze the evolution of Gorbachev's policy toward Israel, with particular emphasis on how it fit into the larger framework of his policy toward the Middle East and the United States.

A New Relationship: Soviet-Israeli Relations, March 1985– August 1986

During his first year and a half in power, Gorbachev continued many of the policies begun by Leonid Brezhnev, Yuri Andropov, and Konstantin Chernenko (SAM-5s were sold to Libya, the war in Afghanistan was intensified, and emigration of Soviet Jews was at a very low level), but the new Soviet leader was already showing considerably more diplomatic flexibility than his predecessors, as was evident in his policy toward Israel. Gorbachev, unlike his predecessors, did not appear willing to cede the Arab-Israeli peace process to the sole direction of the United States, and at the time he took power, the peace process seemed to be under way again. In February 1985, King Hussein of Jordan (who had just restored diplomatic relations with Egypt) signed an agreement with PLO leader Yasser Arafat on a joint negotiating strategy toward Israel, a move rapidly endorsed by Egyptian president Hosni Mubarak. The new Soviet leader's signals to Israel, therefore, should be understood primarily as an attempt to gain entry in a Middle East peace process by securing Moscow a place in an international peace conference. In addition, Gorbachev very much wanted a summit meeting with the United States in which such key issues as strategic arms agreements and trade and technology exchanges would be discussed. These twin goals, entering into the Arab-Israeli peace process and favorably influencing the United States, were to be at the heart of Gorbachev's policy toward Israel until the collapse of the Soviet Union in 1991.

The signals sent by Moscow to Israel covered two central areas: the reestablishment of diplomatic relations between the Soviet Union and Israel and an increase in the number of Soviet Jews allowed to leave the USSR. The Soviets made gestures to Israel despite a series of Israeli actions that bound the Jewish state even more tightly to the United States, including its signing of strategic cooperation and free trade agreements, its agreement to allow the United States to build a Voice of America transmitter on Israeli territory, and its decision to enter the American Star Wars defense scheme.

The first major Soviet gesture came in mid-May, two months after Gorbachev took power, in the form of *Izvestia*'s publication of Israeli president Chaim Herzog's congratulatory message to the USSR on the fortieth anniversary of the Allied victory over Nazi Germany. The *Izvestia* publication was significant not only because it was the first time such a message from an Israeli leader had been published since relations were broken in 1967 but also because the message itself contained a denunciation of the Nazis. Herzog declared that the Jewish people "will never forget the huge contribution of the Red Army in the final destruction of the Nazi monsters in Europe and her assistance in the freeing of Jews who survived the concentration camps." Because Soviet propaganda media had long equated Israeli and Nazi activities and had even accused Zionists of actively aiding the Nazis, this message seemed to be a major reversal of Soviet policy on this issue.[2]

In mid-July, when Arafat and Hussein called for an Arab summit and the issue of Soviet Jewry was likely to be raised at the upcoming review session commemorating the tenth anniversary of the signing of the Helsinki agreements, Gorbachev apparently decided that a major discussion between Soviet and Israeli diplomats regarding renewed diplomatic relations and increased emigration of Soviet Jews to Israel was in order. The meeting between Israeli ambassador to France Ovadia Sofer and his Soviet counterpart, Yuli Vorontsov, took place in Paris at the home of Israeli-born pianist Daniel Barenboim. Sofer's description of the meeting was leaked to Israeli radio, which promptly broadcast it. During the conversation, Vorontsov seemed to indicate that diplomatic relations could be restored if the Israelis at least partially withdrew from the Golan Heights and that large numbers of Soviet Jews would be allowed to emigrate if they went to Israel, not the United States, and if Israel ended its anti-Soviet propaganda in the United States and Europe.[3]

Yet the Soviet hint of renewed relations, though welcome in Israel, met a highly negative reception among Moscow's Arab allies, especially Syria. Syria, the USSR's main bastion in the Arab world, was incensed that the USSR would consider renewing ties with Israel while even part of the Golan Heights seized during the 1967 war remained in Israeli hands. As a result, the USSR, in both official visits and radio broadcasts to the Arab world, repeated the old Soviet position that diplomatic relations would not be restored until Israel gave up all the land conquered in 1967. Gorbachev made yet another gesture to Israel in October when his (then) close Eastern European ally, Poland, and Israel agreed to establish "interest sections" in foreign embassies in each other's capitals—the first stage in the process of reestablishing diplomatic relations. Although Moscow was not yet resuming diplomatic ties itself, this was a clear gesture that it was prepared to do so, and during his visit to Paris in early October, Gorbachev noted that "so far as reestablishing relations [with Israel] is concerned, I think the faster the situation is normalized in the Middle East, the faster it will be possible to look at this question."[4]

The announced resumption of low-level diplomatic relations with Poland, World Jewish Congress president Edgar Bronfman's visit to Moscow carrying a message from Israeli prime minister Shimon Peres, Peres's meeting with Soviet foreign minister Eduard Shevardnadze at the United Nations in October, and Gorbachev's visit to Paris stimulated rumors in Israel that Moscow was about to release twenty thousand Soviet Jews and allow them to be flown directly to Israel on French planes.

Despite this promising start, the hopes of a rapid restoration of Soviet-Israeli relations soon cooled, in part perhaps because of a falling-out between King Hussein and Yasser Arafat, which torpedoed any chances for the Arab-Israeli peace process to make headway. A second reason may have been Gorbachev's desire not to alienate Moscow's Arab allies at the time of the November

1985 summit with U.S. president Ronald Reagan. Arab leaders, perhaps remembering the 1972 Nixon-Brezhnev summit, seemed concerned that the superpowers might work out a deal at their expense; and Reagan's presummit demand that an arms control agreement be linked with Soviet behavior in the Third World may have heightened Soviet determination to prove that no such deal had taken place. Indeed, in a spate of articles appearing in the Soviet media at the time of the summit, including Arabic-language radio broadcasts and *Novosti* statements distributed in Beirut, the USSR dismissed claims that Arab interests would be compromised at Geneva as "fabrications and lies."[5]

SOVIET-ISRAELI RELATIONS, AUGUST 1986–JANUARY 1989

Soviet-Israeli relations remained on hold during the first half of 1986. Gorbachev, preoccupied first with the CPSU Congress and later with the aftereffects of the Chernobyl nuclear disaster, made no overt moves toward improving ties with Israel until late summer. In a surprise announcement on August 4, the USSR declared that it had agreed to public talks on the reestablishment of consular relations with Israel. There appear to have been three main reasons for the announcement.

First, in the aftermath of the U.S. bombing of Libya in April for its alleged terrorist activities, Moscow could not be certain that the United States would not take action against Syria, another sponsor of terrorism. An American—or an American-backed Israeli—punitive strike against Syria would raise serious questions of Soviet credibility if Moscow did not aid its Middle Eastern ally in such a situation (especially after its failure to aid Libya).[6] Yet if Moscow went to Syria's aid, a superpower confrontation was likely. These unpalatable alternatives apparently made Gorbachev decide to move diplomatically to avert the possibility of such a clash both by publicly cautioning Libya and Syria against terrorism so as not to give the "imperialists" any pretext for attacks and by negotiating seriously with Israel to arrange consular-level talks in Helsinki, Finland, and acceding to Israel's demand that the talks be made public. The USSR's efforts to play a role in the Middle East peace process may also have motivated the decision to initiate public contacts with Israel. Following Jordanian King Hussein's public split with Arafat in February 1986, Moscow sought to exploit the new diplomatic situation by calling for a committee made up of the UN Security Council's five permanent members to prepare for an international conference on the Middle East. When, in late July, Prime Minister Peres of Israel and King Hassan of Morocco held a surprise meeting in Morocco, however, Moscow may have feared that it would once again be left on the diplomatic sidelines while a major peace initiative unfolded.

A third factor contributing to Moscow's request for consular talks may have been the desire to improve ties with the United States. The Soviet announcement of consular talks with Israel on August 4 coincided with the announcement of the scheduling on September 19–20 of a meeting between U.S. secretary of state George Shultz and Soviet foreign minister Eduard Shevardnadze to prepare for a U.S.-Soviet summit. The nuclear disaster in Chernobyl, the precipitous drop in world oil prices (more than 50 percent of Soviet hard currency earnings came from oil and natural gas sales), Gorbachev's initial efforts to restructure the Soviet economy, and the major economic difficulties facing the USSR all moved the Soviet leadership toward an agreement that would prevent another expensive spiraling of the arms race. Thus Gorbachev sought a second summit with the United States, and, overestimating Jewish influence in the United States, he may have felt that the gesture to Israel would help pave the way for the summit. This factor may have been of particular importance because the former Soviet ambassador to the United States, Anatoly Dobrinin, who was personally well acquainted with Jewish influence in Washington, had replaced Boris Ponamarev as head of the then influential International Department of the CPSU Central Committee. In addition, his deputy, Karen Brutents, had long argued for a more pragmatic Soviet foreign policy approach in the Middle East, which may also have influenced the new Soviet approach to Israel.

Nonetheless, the Soviet-Israeli talks in Helsinki, the first such official diplomatic negotiations between the two countries since the 1967 war, did not immediately produce the results either side said it wanted, although the symbolic significance of the talks was probably much more important than their content. While the Soviets stated that they wished to send a team of officials to inventory Soviet property (primarily owned by the Russian Orthodox Church) in Israel, the Israeli delegation, under heavy domestic pressure, raised the issue of Soviet Jewry at the talks, and the meeting ended after ninety minutes.[7] However, the fact that the talks were held and that one month later Peres and Shevardnadze held detailed (and apparently cordial) negotiations at the United Nations, as well as subsequent meetings between the Soviet and Israeli ambassadors to the United States, indicated that the Soviet Union was keeping alive its contacts with Israel.

The Shevardnadze-Peres meeting was followed by the Reykjavik summit between Reagan and Gorbachev, the second such summit in less than two years. Although no arms control agreement was reached, primarily because Gorbachev linked such an agreement to the termination of the American Strategic Defense Initiative, Reagan emphasized the issue of Soviet Jewry, reminding the Soviet leader that Moscow could demonstrate its desire for an improved relationship with the United States by permitting an increased number of Soviet Jews to leave the USSR.

After the summit, Gorbachev moved toward a policy of "new thinking" (*novoye myshleniye*) in foreign policy, and the pace of Soviet-Israeli diplomatic relations picked up considerably. Israeli ambassador Meir Rosenne and Soviet ambassador Yury Dubinin met in Washington in late January 1987, and the Soviet ambassador reiterated the Soviet desire for an international conference and reportedly indicated that Moscow was willing to be more forthcoming on Soviet Jewish emigration. Moscow also sent nondiplomatic delegations to Israel although the report of their trips in the Soviet press indicates that the visits had a political function. *Literaturnaya Gazeta* on January 28 discussed the visit of a Soviet delegation that signed an agreement at the Weizman Research Center for cooperation in genetic and cellular research. In addition, *Izvestia* correspondent Konstantin Geivandov wrote two articles describing his January visit to Israel that were far less negative than previous Soviet reporting about Israel. He said that his meeting with a group of Knesset members had been "constructive and useful" and noted that they had advocated the development of bilateral ties between the Israeli and Soviet publics in the cultural, scientific, and sports areas. Although he also made negative comments about Israel (especially its treatment of the Palestinians), the writing was so different in tone from previous Soviet commentaries on Israel that it might be viewed both as another Soviet signal to Israel of Moscow's interest in improved relations and as a sign to the Soviet public and the international community that Moscow was preparing to upgrade its ties with Israel.[8]

On their visits to Israel, Soviet delegations were always confronted with the question of Soviet Jewish emigration. Any major Soviet move toward increasing the number of Jews allowed to emigrate would be seen as a possible sign of the USSR's intention to improve relations. Soviet Jewish emigration was more than just a bilateral Soviet-Israeli issue, however. At Reykjavik the United States had emphasized human rights questions, especially Soviet Jewry. Consequently, as Gorbachev decided to move rapidly toward nuclear arms agreements with the United States, he must have realized that allowing an increasing number of Soviet Jews to emigrate would reap important political benefits in the United States. At the same time, however, the increase in emigration might produce important political benefits in Israel, at least for the Labor Party. Its leader, Shimon Peres, when prime minister in 1985 (he had stepped down in October 1986 as part of a National Unity agreement with the rival Likud Party, led by Yitzhak Shamir), had cited increased emigration of Soviet Jews as the price for Soviet participation in an international peace conference, something Gorbachev wanted very much.

Thus, although a more restrictive emigration decree went into effect on January 1, 1987, limiting emigration to first-degree relatives (mother, father, sister, brother, child) of people abroad, statements by several Soviet officials indicated that emigration would rise, and indeed after averaging less than 100 per month in 1986, emigration shot up to 470 in March 1987 and 717 in April, and a Novosti official, Sergei Ivanko, predicted an exodus of 10,000 to 12,000 by the end of the year.[9] It was in this context that two major non-Israeli Jewish leaders, Morris Abram, president of both the National Conference on Soviet Jewry and the Conference of Presidents of Major Jewish Organizations, and Edgar Bronfman, president of the World Jewish Congress, journeyed to Moscow in late March and met with Soviet officials, including Anatoly Dobrynin. According to Abram, they received "assurances" from the USSR in several areas pertaining to Soviet Jewry, especially the promised emigration of most "Refuseniks," in return for their willingness to consider changes to the Jackson-Vanik and Stevenson amendments that limited trade with the USSR.[10]

In arranging the meeting with Abram and Bronfman (although subsequently denying that any "deal" had been made), Moscow apparently had two goals. First, with a new summit on the horizon and the Soviet leader now energetically pushing his plan for an intermediate-range nuclear arms agreement, the sharp increase in the number of Soviet Jews allowed to leave the USSR, the promise of a still greater exodus inherent in the Bronfman-Abram visit, and the Soviet decision to free the jailed prisoners of Zion (those imprisoned for wanting to go to Israel) all clearly had major public relations value in the United States. In addition, however, it gave political ammunition to Peres, who saw the increased emigration as the price Moscow was willing to pay to participate in an international conference. Peres's political rival, Yitzhak Shamir, sought to counter this development by formally separating the issues of Soviet-Israeli relations and Soviet Jewry.

In early April, Peres actively supported an international conference; Shamir, who just as actively opposed such a conference, publicly stated that he hoped Peres's efforts to arrange an international peace conference would fail. Peres met in Rome with two high-ranking Soviet officials, Karen Brutents, deputy director of the International Department of the CPSU, and his Middle East adviser Alexander Zotov (who was later to become Soviet ambassador to Syria). Peres described the meeting as "the first serious direct dialogue between the two nations." Although the Israeli leader agreed to keep the details of the six hours of discussions secret, he gave the impression that major progress had been made in the negotiations regarding both the exodus of Soviet Jews and improvement of Soviet-Israeli relations. He declared that the USSR had spoken against any "coercion" by the superpowers in the context of an international peace conference or by the conference itself; that Moscow had agreed to bilateral talks as part of the international conference; and that Palestinian representation at the conference had been discussed in more general terms than just the PLO.[11]

The Soviets made yet another gesture to Israel in late April during a Moscow visit by Syrian president Hafiz Assad—Israel's most implacable foe. Gorbachev warned Assad against going to war against Israel because of the danger of nuclear escalation and advised that the Syrian-Israeli conflict be solved politically. Gorbachev also asserted that the absence of relations between the USSR and Israel "cannot be considered normal."[12]

Despite these gestures from Moscow, Peres proved unable to bring down the Israeli government over the issue of Israel's attendance at an international conference. Immediately after Peres's political failure, the Soviet ambassador to the United States, Yuri Dubinin, met Peres in Washington at the apartment of Edgar Bronfman to discuss the Middle Eastern situation (and the Israeli cabinet debates about the peace process). In July a Soviet consular team arrived in Israel for a three-month stay. Nonetheless, Moscow played down the significance of this development; the head of the eight-member Soviet consular team, Yevgeny Antipov, deputy director of the Consular Directorate of the Soviet Foreign Service, stated, "Our mission is not diplomatic, not political. It is purely a technical task (to inventory the property of the Russian Orthodox church and to handle the updating of passports)."[13] The political nature of the Soviet consular delegation, however, became ever more apparent as the delegation's visas were regularly renewed. Numerous conversations were held between Soviet and Israeli officials (the longest—ten hours—between a Peres adviser, Nimrod Novik, and Vladimir Tarasov of the Soviet Foreign Ministry in mid-August), and the Soviets did not even bother to deny the Soviet-Israeli contacts to the Arabs.

Even the outbreak of the Intifada in December 1987, which in the pre-Gorbachev era would have been the signal for savage Soviet attacks on Israel, did not slow the momentum of improved relations. Indeed, during Yasser Arafat's visit to Moscow in early April 1988, Gorbachev told him that Israel's interests, including its security interests, had to be taken into consideration in any peace settlement, along with those of the Palestinians, and that UN Resolution 242 had to become the legal basis for an international peace conference.[14]

Gorbachev's comments may have been aimed at convincing Israel it had nothing to fear from an international conference, but it would appear that Arafat, despite his assertion that this was "the most successful of all his visits" and that there was "complete unity of views," did not like all that he heard. He may have been especially annoyed by Gorbachev's unwillingness to state that the PLO was the sole legitimate representative of the Palestinian people or to use the term "Palestinian state," limiting himself to the more ambiguous term "self-determination."[15] These may well have been further tactical gestures to the Israeli leadership, which was united on its opposition to the PLO and to a

Palestinian state, if on little else, as well as to the United States, which also opposed the PLO and a Palestinian state. Indeed, in an interview with the Kuwaiti newspaper *al-Siyasah*, a Soviet Foreign Ministry official, Alexander Ivanov-Golitsyn, responded to a question about a Palestinian state, "It was the first time the Soviet leadership did not discuss a Palestinian state. This is not a rescindment of the Soviet stand, but we believe some flexibility should exist." Responding to a question about Palestinians who were dispossessed in 1948, he said, "We as realistic politicians can only discuss the establishment of a state in the West Bank and Gaza. Palestinians living abroad can return to this state. Israel is a fait accompli. Talking about the repatriation of the 1948 Palestinians is something extreme."[16]

Gorbachev's gesture to Israel during Arafat's visit was accompanied by a further low-level improvement in relations between the USSR and Israel. The Soviet Party Youth Organization, Komsomol, invited a group of Mapam (a left-of-center party but noncommunist) youth to visit the USSR; Soviet ham radio operators were permitted to talk to their counterparts in Israel; a famous Soviet singer, Alla Pugachova, gave concerts in Israel; and the Soviet Union even allowed Soviet Jews to visit Israel as tourists.

In June 1988, two months after Arafat's visit to Moscow, during a press conference following another U.S.-Soviet summit, Gorbachev presented the most "evenhanded" statement on the Arab-Israeli conflict made by any Soviet leader since the Arab-Israeli war of 1948–49, when Moscow had supported Israel.

> We stand for a political settlement of all issues, *with due account for the interests of all sides concerned and, of course, for the principled provisions of the relevant U.N. resolutions.* We are talking about the fact *that all the Israeli-occupied lands be returned* and the Palestinian people's rights be restored. We said to President Reagan how we view the role of the United States, but we cannot decide for the Arabs in what form the Palestinians will take part in the international conference. *Let the Arabs themselves decide, while the Americans and we should display respect for their choice.*
>
> Furthermore, *we ought to recognize the right of Israel to security and the right of the Palestinian people to self-determination. In what form—let the Palestinians together with their Arab friends decide that. This opens up prospects for active exchanges, for a real process.*
>
> I will disclose one more thing. We said that *following the start of a conference—a normal, effective conference, rather than a front for separate talks—a forum which would be interrelated with bilateral, tripar-*

tite, and other forms of activity, we will be ready to handle the issue of settling diplomatic relations with Israel.

We are thus introducing one more new element . . . I should reiterate: *We proceed from the premise that the Israeli people and the State of Israel have the right to their security because there can be no security of one at the expense of the other. A solution that would untie this very tight knot should be found.*[17] (Emphasis added.)

In addition to his efforts to project an "evenhanded" image in the Arab-Israeli conflict, Gorbachev was now attempting to be evenhanded in the ongoing political conflict within Israel between Shamir and Peres. Thus he arranged a meeting between Shamir and Soviet foreign minister Shevardnadze in New York in June 1988. In deciding to arrange this meeting, Gorbachev seems to have been motivated by one major consideration. Shamir's Likud Party was gaining in the polls against Labor (in large part because of the Intifada), which meant that there was a good chance that Shamir would form Israel's next government following the November 1988 elections, and Moscow may well have wished to signal its willingness to deal with him. The Soviets sent Shamir a further signal during the talks—which both sides publicly characterized as "useful and constructive"[18]—by announcing that the next Israeli consular visit to Moscow would occur in mid-July. Shamir now could demonstrate to the Israeli public that he too could obtain benefits from Moscow.

Moscow's evenhandedness in Israeli politics was to pay off when Shamir won in the November 1988 elections. Although Gorbachev may not have been happy that the hard-line Likud Party dominated the new National Unity government, relations between the two countries continued to improve. Soviet actions, however, were less responsible for this situation—the Israeli consular mission in Moscow was severely circumscribed in its activities[19]—than were Israeli policies. Thus at the beginning of December, Israel promptly returned a group of four Soviet hijackers who had flown to Israel after seizing a busload of children as hostages and releasing them in return for an aircraft. Moscow warmly praised Israel for its role in the affair. During his UN visit after the hijacking, Gorbachev was photographed by *Agence France Press* shaking hands with Israel's UN ambassador, Yochanan Bein. Gorbachev reportedly told Bein, "I want to thank the Israeli people for the efficient cooperation we received with regard to the hijacked airplane. . . . Please tell the Israeli government and the people of Israel that there is a lot of good will and friendship in the Soviet Union toward Israel."[20] Gorbachev had to cut short his stay in the United States because of a massive earthquake in Armenia, and here again Israel proved helpful to the USSR by sending medical teams and four tons of medical supplies and setting up a field hospital in the city of Kirovakan. Thus by the end of 1988, and despite the Intifada, Soviet-Israeli relations had improved markedly. Consular delegations had been exchanged, Moscow had adopted a much more evenhanded policy on the Arab-Israeli conflict, and the PLO and Syria had been put on notice that Moscow supported a political settlement, not military conflict with Israel. The weakening of the USSR in the 1989–91 period was to lead to a further strengthening of Soviet-Israeli relations.

SOVIET-ISRAELI RELATIONS, 1989–1991: A NEW RELATIONSHIP

The twin Soviet goals of using an improved relationship with Israel to gain entry into the Arab-Israeli peace process and to influence the United States were to dominate Soviet policy toward Israel in the 1989–91 period, although a growing Soviet interest in trade with Israel and even Soviet public opinion were also factors in the relationship. Unfortunately for Gorbachev, however, his diplomacy during this period, despite the Soviet withdrawal from Afghanistan, was increasingly hampered by the USSR's domestic problems, which intensified by the beginning of 1989. Not only had perestroika not proven immediately successful, but the Soviet economy was worsening. Economic issues became increasingly important in Soviet foreign policy, and Moscow sought to expand its trade relations. Thus Soviet trade with Israel suddenly became considerably more attractive to Moscow than it had been previously.

In addition, in an effort to make perestroika work and circumvent the Communist Party bureaucracy that was hampering his economic reform plans, Gorbachev moved ahead with plans for democratic elections for a new Supreme Soviet in 1989. Apparently hoping that popularly elected officials would be his allies in the reform efforts, Gorbachev engineered not only the elections but also the creation of a new powerful post of president of the Soviet Union, to which he had himself elected by the Supreme Soviet.

Trade was uppermost on the minds of Soviet officials at the beginning of 1989, and the USSR's economic problems caused Moscow to take a new look at Soviet émigrés. Meeting with Soviet consular officials at the turn of the year, Shevardnadze set forth a new policy toward Soviet émigrés that had the potential to further improve Soviet-Israeli relations. Instead of viewing them as traitors, they should be treated as potential assets for the improvement of ties between the Soviet Union and their new homelands. Shevardnadze also urged consular officials to encourage business contacts between the USSR and firms owned by these "compatriots."[21] Because more than 170,000 Soviet émigrés were living in Israel, this new policy had major implications for Soviet-Israeli relations.[22] Less than a week after the consular conference, Shevardnadze met Israel's new foreign minister, Moshe Arens, in Paris, where both were attending a conference on the control of chemical weapons. In talks which Arens termed "very friendly, open and sincere," Shevardnadze reportedly promised to upgrade Israel's consular delegation in Moscow and to allow Israeli diplomats to conduct political talks there. The Soviet foreign minister also indicated that the Israeli consular delegation could move from its crowded quarters in the Dutch embassy to the embassy building that had housed the Israeli embassy before relations were severed in 1967. In addition, Shevardnadze, who again urged Israel to participate in the international peace conference as soon as possible because "all parties' interests" would be taken into account there,[23] noted in an interview in *Le Figaro* that he agreed with Arens that Israeli-Soviet contacts should be stepped up in an effort to achieve a settlement in the Middle East.[24] Other signals of an improvement in Soviet-Israeli relations included an end to the jamming of Kol Israel (Radio Israel) broadcasts to the USSR, the granting of visas to 175 Israelis to attend a Soviet-Israeli basketball game in Moscow, and the offer by the Soviet ambassador to Egypt to help establish a dialogue between Israel and the PLO. In addition, in its clearest signal to the Arabs to date, Genadi Tarasov, interviewed in Kuwait's *Al-Anba*, noted that because Israel was a party to the Middle East conflict, it must be included in dialogues. Tarasov then listed three objectives to be obtained from the Soviet-Israeli meetings:[25] (1) Most important, the Israelis must become familiar with the USSR's stand from the original source because it was well-known that some people in Israel and in the West would try to cast doubts on the USSR stand. (2) Another objective was to become familiar with the Israeli stand from the original source. (3) A third objective was to try to influence the Israeli stand as much as possible and encourage Israel to act constructively and realistically with respect to a Middle East settlement.

Moscow's heightened interest in contacts with Israel may have been related to the new diplomatic situation in the Middle East at the start of 1989, which seemed propitious for advancing the Arab-Israeli peace process. The PLO had decided in November 1988 on a two-state solution to the Palestinian-Israeli conflict, and Arafat had clarified PLO recognition of Israel and renunciation of terrorism in a press conference one month later. Shevardnadze, in his tour of the Middle East in February 1989, sought to build on the diplomatic momentum, emphasizing the need for a political settlement of the Arab-Israeli conflict during his visit to Damascus and lavishly praising Egypt during his Cairo visit that capped the Egyptian-Soviet rapprochement that had been under way since 1987. He also proclaimed the new, nonideological and cooperative approach which he said was to be the hallmark of Moscow's new foreign policy: "Traditional and—we'll be blunt—obsolete standards and outlooks are being reviewed. It is indicative that in this common channel the Soviet Union, aspiring to the democratization of interstate communication, is reducing, or even completely excluding from it the previously predominant ideological component. The world can be saved from nuclear, ecological, economic and other catastrophes only by acting together and being guided by the priority of values common to mankind. We have a vital interest in the construction of international relations on innovative designs."[26]

Despite Shevardnadze's optimistic approach, little progress was made in the Middle East peace process until the defeat of Iraq in the 1991 Gulf War. Israel had suggested elections for the West Bank and Gaza Palestinians as part of the peace plan it introduced in May 1989, but the proposal was to collapse—along with Israel's National Unity government in March 1990—both because of conflict between Labor and Likud and conflict within the Likud between Shamir and Ariel Sharon. As the Middle East peace process marked time, formal state-to-state relations between Moscow and Israel also stalled when Gorbachev refused to accede to Israeli and American calls for Moscow to agree to revoke the "Zionism Is Racism" UN resolution, allow direct flights of emigrants to Israel, and reestablish full diplomatic relations with Israel. Nonetheless, ties rapidly developed in cultural, religious, and humanitarian spheres. Thus when disaster again struck the USSR in the form of a train crash on the Trans-Siberian railway, Moscow gratefully accepted Israeli offers of aid for the burn victims of the crash, and a team of Israeli doctors was sent to Moscow. When the medical team returned to Israel, it was met by the head of the Soviet consular delegation in Israel, Georgy Martirosov, who credited it with having saved many lives, including those of two children, and said that its actions had contributed to a "positive atmosphere" between the USSR and Israel.[27]

While diplomatic relations between Israel and the USSR remained chilly, other aspects of the relationship blossomed. The Israeli Habimah Theatre, which had originated in the USSR, returned for a triumphal visit in early January 1990; and Soviet Parliament member Leonid Shkolnik became the first member of the new Supreme Soviet to visit the Knesset. At the same time, Soviet Jewish tourists visited Israel in large numbers (twenty-five thousand in 1989), and a memorial was established in Israel for the two hundred thousand Jewish soldiers of the Soviet army who died in World War II.

Israeli agriculture minister Avraham Katz-Oz, who had been denied a visa in September, arrived in Moscow in December 1989 on an invitation from the Soviet Academy of Sciences. During his visit, he reached agreement with the Soviet Union whereby Israel would sell $30 million in agricultural produce to the USSR and would assist Moscow in water planning, cotton production, and the establishment of dairies and chicken coops. As part of the agreement, one thousand children from each country would exchange visits.[28]

In January 1990, two other Israeli cabinet ministers went to Moscow: Zvulun Hammer, minister of religion, and Ezer Weizman, minister of science. Weizman, who had just been excluded from the inner cabinet by Shamir because of his contacts with the PLO, was certainly persona grata in Moscow, and he had an extended meeting with Shevardnadze in which, according to Weizman, Shevardnadze promised to upgrade relations with Israel from the consular level to that of chargé d'affaires and to talk to Iran about the fate of Israeli soldiers missing in Lebanon. While in Moscow, Weizman also signed a scientific cooperation agreement with the Soviet Academy of Sciences. During Weizman's visit, Gorbachev once again sought to demonstrate the USSR's evenhandedness between Israel and the PLO, as he upgraded the PLO mission in Moscow to full embassy status and appointed an ambassador to the PLO Executive Committee. TASS explained that Moscow's view of the important role of the PLO was the reason for its decision "to turn the PLO mission in Moscow into the Embassy of the State of Palestine."[29]

From the point of view of the PLO, however, the Soviet move may have appeared symbolic. Soviet Jews were now emigrating to Israel in record numbers, and new regimes in East Germany, Czechoslovakia, and Poland had cut off military assistance to the PLO; following Hungary's lead, Poland, Czechoslovakia, and Bulgaria moved to establish diplomatic relations with Israel. The PLO's international position clearly was weakening. As an aide to Arafat noted, "The deep changes in the Eastern bloc, which was our chief international ally for the past twenty-five years, will prevent it from playing any Middle East role for at least another five years. The PLO is now working to build new international bridges as an alternative for the absence of an active East Europe."[30]

Not only the PLO was showing signs of displeasure with Soviet policy. Syria, Moscow's primary ally in the Arab world and Israel's other main enemy, was also increasingly uncomfortable with the changing Soviet policy. In a November 1989 *Washington Post* interview, Soviet ambassador to Syria Alexander Zotov bluntly told the Syrians that "new realities" in the USSR would limit Soviet military assistance to that country. Specifically, he noted the "limits" of Soviet capability to supply sophisticated equipment. "Some of our complicated types of military equipment we prefer to sell for hard currency," he said, and he stressed the need for Syria's "due observance" of the principle of "reasonable defensive sufficiency" so as to "make her potential adversary, supposedly Israel, think twice before planning an offensive action."[31] Essentially, Zotov was rearticulating that Moscow would support neither Syria's long-sought desire for military parity with Israel nor any Syrian attack against Israel.

While Moscow sought to downplay reports of Soviet-Syrian friction, it appeared clear that Assad, facing serious economic problems, his enmity toward Iraqi leader Saddam Hussein as strong as ever, and unsure of Soviet backing, was in a weak diplomatic position. Consequently, Assad agreed in late December 1989 to reestablish diplomatic relations with Egypt, in part to protect his flank against Iraq and in part to position his country for a role in the peace talks if they materialized. Soviet Foreign Ministry spokesman Gennady Gerasimov hailed Syria's action as a step that "will help further consolidate the Arab ranks and exert a positive impact on the situation in the Arab world and in the region as a whole."[32] Nonetheless, Assad's general unhappiness with the turn of events in Eastern Europe and the Soviet Union was clear. In a speech marking the twenty-seventh anniversary of the coup d'état that first brought the Ba'ath to power in Syria in 1963, Assad stated, "Let us now perceive that Israel was the first beneficiary, among all nations of the world, of the international changes that have taken place." Assad criticized the emigration of Soviet Jews to Israel but added that "the relationship between Syria and the Soviet Union is now as firm as ever."[33]

Meanwhile, Soviet Jewish emigration to Israel continued to soar. Speaking in Washington following the U.S.-Soviet summit in early June, Gorbachev made an attempt to assuage Arab concern over this emigration by strongly condemning the settlements in occupied territories and threatening Israel with a possible cutoff of emigration if Soviet Jews were settled there.[34]

Predictably, the Israeli government responded that it was not government policy to direct Soviet Jews to the occupied territories. Avi Pazner, a senior adviser to Shamir, stated: "We will make it clear to Gorbachev our policy that we are not sending, not encouraging and not giving incentives to Soviet Jews to settle in the areas of Judea, Samaria and Gaza. . . . The Jews arriving here have complete freedom of choice and can choose where to live and it is a fact that very few, until now, have chosen to live in these areas." One Israeli official, who did not wish to be named, stated in response to Gorbachev's threat: "I think the comments were meant for Arab consumption. The Soviets are seeking urgent financial and economic cooperation with the West and are too vulnerable on this issue to act on it."[35] Shamir took a more strident tone the next day: "If the Soviet Union or President Gorbachev does not think it can today tell its citizens where to live, it is clear as the sun that we, as followers of freedom and democracy, cannot limit [our citizens]."[36] On June 6, however, Soviet foreign minister Shevardnadze assured U.S. secretary of state James Baker that Moscow would not halt Jewish immigration to Israel despite Gorbachev's threat.[37]

As the summer of 1990 wore on, Shevardnadze's words were borne out as record numbers of Jews, fearing both the collapse of the Soviet Union and growing anti-Semitism there, left the USSR for Israel. In June 1990, the month Gorbachev issued his threat, 11,015 such emigrants arrived in Israel; in July, 15,395; and in August, 17,484. Thus in retrospect, it appears clear that Gorbachev spoke out more in an attempt to propitiate the Arabs than with any real intention of cutting off immigration to Israel.

In any case, by August 1990, Arab attention had been diverted from the issue of Soviet Jewish immigration to the Iraqi invasion of Kuwait, which both divided and paralyzed the Arab world.[38] Unencumbered by Arab pressure, the state interests of the USSR in increasing trade and scientific interchange with Israel took precedence. Israeli hard-line minister of science and technology Yuval Ne'eman, along with Finance Minister Yitzhak Moda'i, held a meeting with Gorbachev in mid-September. According to Ne'eman, Gorbachev never raised the Palestinian issue.[39] Moda'i reported that Gorbachev had said his concerns about Soviet Jewish immigrants moving to the occupied territory had been satisfied. Even Ariel Sharon, Israel's housing minister and a leading hawk, who was responsible not only for housing Soviet Jews but also for building settlements in the occupied territories, made a visit to Moscow to discuss the purchase of prefabricated Soviet housing materials. To be sure, some voices in Moscow opposed the warming of ties with Israel as well as the increasing emigration to Israel. These voices were reflected in outspoken conservative Soviet press organs such as *Sovetskaya Rossiya*, and *Pravda*, now a more a right-wing organ, also occasionally voiced doubts about Soviet-Israeli policy.

Despite such articles, Soviet-Israeli relations continued to improve. Meeting with Israel's new foreign minister, David Levy, at the United Nations in late September, Shevardnadze agreed both to establish consulates general with Israel (a formalization of the previously existing quasi-consular arrangement) and to create regular consultations between the two foreign ministers at the ministerial level. An *Izvestia* correspondent noted that this development "provides legal grounds as it were, for the rather extensive contacts between our countries and creates a stable mechanism for maintaining these contacts."[40] *Izvestia* reported that Levy had spoken highly of the Soviet contribution to the transformation of international relations, "including the USSR's role in efforts to resolve Near East problems."[41]

Emigration to Israel continued to soar, despite the looming threat of an Iraqi attack on Israel. By early January 1991, the world's attention shifted to the Persian Gulf confrontation, which became a shooting war soon after the passing of the January 15 UN deadline for Iraq to withdraw from Kuwait. The war began with a massive allied bombing of Iraqi command and control installations, to which Iraq responded with a series of SCUD missile attacks against Israel, hoping to get Israel to retaliate and thus break apart the allied coalition. Gorbachev appealed to Israel to refrain from retaliating: in a message to Israeli consul general Aryeh Levin in Moscow, Gorbachev urged the Israeli government "to show the utmost circumspection and restraint and not yield to provocation."[42] He later praised Israel for its restraint. When the war ended with a massive U.S. military victory, however, Moscow had another concern—that the United States in cooperation with Saudi Arabia, Egypt, and Syria would dominate Middle East diplomacy.

Consequently, Moscow, whose cooperation with the allied coalition had been minimal, sought to demonstrate its continued relevance in the Middle East by arranging a meeting in London in mid-April 1991 between Soviet prime minister Valentin Pavlov and Shamir. Shamir restated the Israeli position that no Soviet participation in an international conference would be acceptable until the Soviet Union reestablished full diplomatic relations with Israel. Pavlov reportedly replied that the USSR would consider the Israeli position on a Middle East peace settlement, and the TASS report of the discussion noted only that "the participants in the conversation displayed understanding of the necessity to coordinate the efforts of the Soviet Union and Israel in the matter of a Middle East settlement."[43]

Shevardnadze, who had resigned as foreign minister in December 1990, warning of a coming dictatorship, had been replaced by Alexander Bessmertnykh, who toured the Middle East in May in an attempt to demonstrate continued Soviet influence in the region. Bessmertnykh's itinerary included Israel, along with Syria, Jordan, Egypt, Saudi Arabia, and Switzerland, where he met Arafat, thereby aiding in the Palestinian leader's postwar political rehabilitation (Arafat had backed Saddam Hussein in the war). As in the past, the question of Israel's building of settlements in the occupied territories and the possibility that Soviet Jewish immigrants might settle there arose. Angering both the United States and the Arab countries, Ariel Sharon announced that 13,000 housing units would be constructed in the West Bank and Gaza, out of a total of 250,000 to be constructed over the next two years. In an effort to reassure Moscow, however, Sharon stated: "We are building for Israelis. We are not providing housing for immigrants because we don't want to endanger Soviet emigration."[44] Nonetheless, neither U.S. secretary of state Baker, who condemned the settlement construction, nor the Arab states were reassured by Sharon's statement. Bessmertnykh strongly condemned the settlements and threatened a possible cutoff of emigration. In a statement in Amman he asserted: "I cannot foresee, conceive, or accept a situation when a peace conference is in session while the settlements are going to be built. The Soviet Union and other countries who are interested in arranging such a conference are going to deal with that problem straightforwardly and directly as one of the things to be solved before the conference starts." When asked whether the

Soviet Union planned to restrict Soviet Jewish immigration because of the settlements, Bessmertnykh stated: "I do not exclude anything when we talk about the necessity to stop the construction of these settlements."[45]

Nonetheless, in talks with Shamir and Levy in Israel, Bessmertnykh stated: "We have agreed that one country will not try to exert artificial pressure on another. Regarding immigration, this process is a result of [the] democratization of our society, of the new thinking in foreign and domestic affairs." David Levy was upbeat: "I must say the atmosphere was more than correct—it was friendly. There were no hints, no pressure, no threats, nothing like that."[46]

Three major problems continued to cloud Soviet-Israeli relations: Moscow's unwillingness to join the United States in repudiating the UN General Assembly's "Zionism Is Racism" resolution; its unwillingness, despite urging by the United States and Israel, to allow direct flights of emigrants from Soviet cities to Israel; and, most important, Moscow's reluctance to establish full diplomatic relations with Israel. It took the abortive coup in Moscow in August 1991 and the onset of the Middle East peace conference to prompt Gorbachev to move in all three areas.

Speaking at the UN on September 25, 1991, the new Soviet foreign minister Boris Pankin (Bessmertnykh had been replaced for not opposing the coup) strongly urged repeal of the "Zionism Is Racism" resolution: "The philosophy of new international solidarity signifies, as confirmed in practice, the deideologizing of the U.N. Our organization has been renewed and it is imperative that once and for all it rejects the legacy of the 'Ice Age' in which Zionism was compared with racism in an odious resolution."[47]

Three weeks later, Aeroflot signed an agreement with Israel's quasi-governmental Jewish Agency and El Al airlines to establish direct immigrant flights from Moscow and St. Petersburg to Tel Aviv.

Athough neither move was popular in Arab circles or among Soviet conservatives, the most controversial issue was the reestablishment of full diplomatic relations. Liberal circles in the USSR had long been campaigning for the move while conservatives strongly opposed it. *Pravda*, on October 15, came out strongly against restoration of relations. By contrast, a September 25 *Izvestia* editorial reflecting the liberal opinion, pointedly noted:

> After M. S. Gorbachev, swayed by his ambitious advisers, tried unsuccessfully to snatch the initiative in ending the war in the Persian Gulf, the invitation extended to the USSR to take part in an Arab-Jewish reconciliation looked more like an act of kindness on the part of the White House than a calculation. . . . Former USSR Foreign Minister Bessmertnykh [in his Middle East tour] saw for himself that [these countries] were able to manage very well without us. . . .

We will not end up in the absurd role of a dummy co-chairman [of the peace talks] if we remain honest and fair and that means we cannot go to the conference retaining full diplomatic relations with despotic Iraq while refusing to restore such relations with the democratic state of Israel.[48]

All these cross pressures caused Gorbachev to delay the reestablishment of full diplomatic relations with Israel—Israel's price for agreeing to Moscow's co-chairmanship of the peace talks—until literally the last minute. Nonetheless, after two rounds of talks between Pankin and Levy in Jerusalem, on October 18 Moscow agreed to reestablish full diplomatic relations. Immediately thereafter, Pankin and Baker, in a joint statement issued in Jerusalem, invited Israel, the Arab states, and the Palestinians to attend the Middle East peace conference that was to convene in Madrid on October 30. In mid-October, *Izvestia* reported that two hundred Soviet-Israeli joint ventures were already at work in the USSR. A TASS report of Gorbachev's earlier meeting with Shoshana Cardin, president of the National Conference on Soviet Jewry (an organization once anathema in the USSR), in which the issue of diplomatic relations with Israel had been raised, noted that her organization "enjoys wide support of state figures and business circles."[49] It appeared that the Soviet media reports about reestablishing diplomatic relations with Israel were aimed, at least in part, at convincing otherwise reluctant members of the Soviet elite and population that this policy would aid the USSR's increasingly faltering economy as well as satisfy the United States, which had long called for the reestablishment of full diplomatic relations between Israel and the USSR.

Following the establishment of diplomatic relations, the Middle East peace conference opened in Madrid, with Moscow serving as cosponsor—long a coveted Soviet goal. Unfortunately for Gorbachev, the dynamics of the peace conference demonstrated that he represented only the shell of a once great power, and less than two months later the Soviet Union collapsed and Gorbachev lost his job. The collapse of the USSR provides a useful point of departure for analyzing Soviet-Israeli relations in the Gorbachev era.

Conclusion

Three main conclusions can be drawn from this analysis of Soviet-Israeli relations in the Gorbachev era. First, after a slow start, there was an increasingly rapid improvement in all spheres (cultural, economic, and political), culminating with the reestablishment of full diplomatic relations in October 1991. Second, Gorbachev's primary motivation for improving relations with Israel appears to have been the hope of playing a significant role in the Arab-Israeli peace process and favorably influencing the United States from which he increasingly sought major trade and arms control agreements. Finally, Gorbachev throughout seemed to follow a "minimax" policy toward Israel, that is, making the minimal political concessions necessary to Israel to enable Moscow to gain entry to the Middle East peace process and favorably influence the United States, while at the same time trying to retain the maximum amount of influence in the Arab world. This was a difficult policy to manage, and it was not until after the abortive August 1991 coup d'état (endorsed by Moscow's erstwhile Arab allies Libya and Iraq) had failed and a Middle East peace conference was finally on the horizon that Gorbachev agreed to the restoration of full diplomatic relations with Israel and the revocation of the "Zionism Is Racism" resolution at the UN.

By late 1986, faced with mounting economic problems and needing an improved relationship with the United States, Gorbachev began to make substantive moves toward Israel. These included public talks in Helsinki on the establishment of consular relations (August 1986); increased emigration of Soviet Jews (beginning in February 1987); statements to Israeli leaders that a Middle East peace conference would not impose a settlement (April 1987); urging Israel's main foe, Syrian leader Hafiz Assad, to settle his country's conflict with Israel politically and not by war (April 1987); dispatching a consular delegation to Israel (July 1987) and accepting an Israeli consular mission in return (July 1988); and telling PLO leader Yasser Arafat that Israel's security had to be part of any Middle East settlement (April 1988).

By 1989, Gorbachev permitted a rapid increase in Soviet Jewish emigration and a flowering of cultural relations between the Soviet Union and Israel, moves calculated to win favor in the United States at a time when both the domestic and foreign positions of the USSR were rapidly deteriorating and the successful drive for independence in Eastern Europe was occurring. These moves, however, angered the Arabs, who were particularly upset at the rapid increase in emigration. Gorbachev publicly warned Israel in June 1990 not to allow the emigrants to settle in the occupied territories, but it soon became clear that Gorbachev's warnings (and those of Bessmertnykh one year later) were little more than lip service to Arab concerns because emigration continued to increase and the Israelis continued to build additional settlements in the occupied territories.

The Gulf War, during which Moscow was on the diplomatic sidelines, accelerated the decline of Soviet influence in the Middle East, and the abortive coup against Gorbachev in August 1991 made things even worse. In a weakened political position and far more desirous of American support than ever before, Gorbachev finally agreed not only to support repeal of the "Zionism Is Racism" resolution but also to allow direct flights to Israel and to restore full

diplomatic relations with Israel, which enabled the USSR formally to cosponsor the Madrid Middle East Peace Conference. Unfortunately for Gorbachev,
he would not be in power long enough to benefit from these two political
moves; less than two months after the Madrid conference, the Soviet Union
disintegrated and he resigned as president.

NOTES

1. Soviet-Israeli relations in the pre-Gorbachev era are discussed in detail in Robert O. Freedman, *Soviet Policy toward the Middle East since 1970* (New York: Praeger,
1975, 1978, 1982), and Freedman, *Moscow and the Middle East: Soviet Policy since
the Invasion of Afghanistan* (New York: Cambridge University Press, 1991).

2. See William Korey, "The Soviet Anti-Zionist Committee," in *Soviet Jewry in
the 1980s*, ed. Robert O. Freedman (Durham, N.C.: Duke University Press, 1989), 26–
50.

3. For the text of Sofer's comments, see *Jerusalem Domestic Service*, in Hebrew,
July 19, 1985 (Foreign Broadcast International Service Daily Report: the Soviet Union
[hereafter FBIS:USSR], July 19, 1985, H1, H2).

4. Quoted in *Jerusalem Post*, October 6, 1985.

5. See Moscow Radio International Service in Arabic, November 17, 1985
(FBIS:USSR, November 19, 1985, *Reportage on the Reagan-Gorbachev Summit*, 3).

6. For a description of the Soviet response to the U.S. bombing of Libya, see Freedman, *Moscow and the Middle East*, 237–40.

7. For the Soviet view of the talks, see the Tass report, in English, August 19, 1986
(FBIS:USSR, August 20, 1986, CC1). For the Israeli view, see Helsinki Domestic Ser-
vice, in Finnish, August 18, 1986 (FBIS:ME, August 19, 1986, I1) and Tel Aviv, IDF
Radio in Hebrew, August 18, 1986 (FBIS:ME, August 19, 1986, I1, I2).

8. Translated in FBIS:USSR, February 18, 1987, H8–H11.

9. Cited in Reuters report, *New York Times*, March 20, 1987. In fact, 8,155 Soviet
Jews were to emigrate in 1987.

10. For the text of the assurances, see National Conference on Soviet Jewry Report
(National Conference on Soviet Jewry, New York City), April 1, 1987.

11. This information, reported by "sources close to Peres," was discussed in the
Jerusalem Post, April 19, 1987 in the report coauthored by Wolf Blitzer, David
Horowitz, Jonathan Karp, and Robert Rosenberg.

12. For a detailed description of the Assad visit, see Freedman, *Moscow and the
Middle East*, 263–65.

13. Quoted in report by Neil Lewis, *New York Times*, July 17, 1987. See also the
report by Mary Curtius, *Christian Science Monitor*, July 16, 1987, and the report in
the *Jerusalem Post*, July 14, 1987. In interviews with Israeli Foreign Office officials in
Jerusalem in July 1988, I was told that Moscow had three to six months of consular
work in Israel.

14. For a detailed evaluation of the Soviet response to the Intifada, see Robert O.

Freedman, "The Soviet Union and the Intifada," in *The Intifada: Its Impact on Israel, the Arab World and the Superpowers*, ed. Robert O. Freedman (Gainesville: Florida International University Press, 1991), 136–90.

15. Ibid., 144–45.

16. *Al-Siyasah* (Kuwait), April 26, 1988 (FBIS:USSR, May 2, 1988, 35).

17. *Pravda*, June 3, 1988 (FBIS:USSR, June 3, 1988, 9).

18. See report by Menahem Shalev, *Jerusalem Post*, June 12, 1988.

19. Author's interview with Aryeh Levin, head of the Israeli Consular Mission in the USSR, Jerusalem, January 4, 1989.

20. Cited in report by Walter Ruby, *Jerusalem Post*, December 9, 1988.

21. Moscow Domestic Service, in Russian, January 4, 1989 (FBIS:USSR, January 5, 1989, 3).

22. Indeed, in an *Izvestia* article one year later (February 19, 1990) Konstantin Geyvandov, in discussing his impression of Soviet Jews who had emigrated to Israel, predicted that some of them would establish joint ventures with the USSR.

23. See article by Michel Zlatowski and Menahem Shalev, *Jerusalem Post*, January 9, 1989.

24. TASS International Service, in Russian, January 8, 1989 (FBIS:USSR, January 9, 1989, 11).

25. *Al-Anba* (Kuwait), January 7, 1989 (FBIS:USSR, January 10, 1989, 34).

26. TASS, February 20, 1989 (FBIS:USSR, February 21, 1989, 30).

27. Cited in report by Kenneth Kaplan, *Jerusalem Post*, June 18, 1989.

28. *Jerusalem Post*, December 4, 1989.

29. TASS, January 10, 1990 (FBIS:USSR, January 11, 1990, p. 31).

30. Quoted in Reuters report, *Jerusalem Post*, January 21, 1990.

31. See report by Caryle Murphy, *Washington Post*, November 20, 1989.

32. TASS, December 29, 1989 (FBIS:USSR, January 2, 1990, 4).

33. Quoted in report by Alan Cowell, *New York Times*, March 9, 1990. The full text of Assad's speech at the anniversary rally may be found in FBIS:NESA, March 9, 1990, 28–34.

34. The text of Gorbachev's comments may be found in the *New York Times*, June 4, 1990.

35. Quoted in report by Youssef Ibrahim, *New York Times*, June 4, 1990.

36. Quoted in report by Youssef Ibrahim, *New York Times*, June 5, 1990.

37. See the report by John Goshko, *Washington Post*, June 7, 1990.

38. For an analysis of the Soviet reaction to the invasion, see Robert O. Freedman, "Moscow and the Gulf War," *Problems of Communism* 40 (July–August, 1991), 1–17.

39. Author's interview with Yuval Ne'eman, Washington, D.C., April 16, 1991.

40. *Izvestia*, October 1, 1990 (*Current Digest of the Soviet Press [CDSP]* 42 [1990], 17).

41. Moscow Radio, in English, September 12, 1990 (FBIS:USSR, September 13, 1990, 26).

42. TASS, January 18, 1991 (FBIS:USSR, January 18, 1991, 5).

43. TASS, April 16, 1991 (FBIS:USSR, April 17, 1991, 3).
44. Quoted in *Jerusalem Post*, April 9, 1991.
45. Reuters report, quoted by Dan Izenberg, *Jerusalem Post*, May 10, 1991.
46. Quoted in report by Dan Izenberg, *Jerusalem Post*, May 10, 1991.
47. *Interfax*, September 30, 1991, (FBIS:USSR, October 2, 1991, 19).
48. *Izvestia*, September 25, 1991 (FBIS:USSR, October 2, 1991, 19).
49. TASS, October 2, 1991 (FBIS:USSR, October 3, 1991, 4).

13

Marxist Regimes in Developing Areas and Changes in the Soviet Union and Eastern Europe

David E. Albright

By the early 1980s, there had emerged in the developing areas a circle of eighteen states that at least loosely linked themselves ideologically with the Soviet Union and its Warsaw Pact allies in Eastern Europe. Moscow recognized the governments of only six of these states—Cambodia, Cuba, the Democratic People's Republic of Korea (DPRK), Laos, Mongolia, and Vietnam—as truly "socialist," but the regimes of the remaining twelve countries professed to be Marxist-Leninist or Marxist in outlook and qualified as "socialist-oriented" from Moscow's standpoint. This group included Afghanistan, Angola, Benin, Cape Verde, Congo, Ethiopia, Guinea-Bissau, Mozambique, Nicaragua, Sao Tome and Principe, the People's Democratic Republic of Yemen (PDRY), and Zimbabwe.

Inevitably, therefore, the profound changes in the Soviet Union and Eastern Europe since the mid-1980s have had a significant impact on these eighteen states. To a certain extent the changes have affected the governments of all of them in a common manner. That is, the events have tended to discredit Marxism-Leninism and even Marxism more broadly. Yet the precise meaning of the changes for Marxist regimes in developing areas, the responses of the regimes to the new circumstances confronting them, and the effectiveness of these responses have varied considerably. Furthermore, the variations have not depended on the precise standing of the regimes in Soviet eyes; rather, they have reflected essentially local situations. This chapter will explore these matters and assess their general implications with respect to constellations of states formed because of shared ideological premises.

EFFECTS

Developments in the Soviet Union and Eastern Europe have had three types of impact on the eighteen regimes. For some governments, the events delivered the final blow in a long process of disillusionment with Soviet political and economic prescriptions. For others, they resulted in the loss of key economic and/or military support. And for still others, they sparked serious challenges from local opposition elements.

The "Last Straw"

To the regimes in Mozambique and the PDRY, the collapse of communist rule in Eastern Europe and the Soviet Union merely confirmed their growing sense that traditional Soviet Marxist prescriptions were inappropriate for dealing with the local conditions facing them. The evolution in thinking on this score had been more sporadic for the PDRY government than for the Mozambique government, but it had still been plain in both instances.

The disenchantment of the Front for the Liberation of Mozambique (FRELIMO) with orthodox Soviet Marxist policies began as early as 1983.[1] By then a combination of efforts to install a centrally planned economy, escalating civil war by the Mozambique National Resistance (MNR) with the aid of the South African government, and several years of devastating drought had brought Mozambique's economy to the point of collapse. Consequently, the government resorted to a number of measures of an un-Marxist nature. It opened negotiations to join the International Monetary Fund (IMF) and the European Economic Community's Lome III group. It seriously encouraged foreign private investment. It committed itself to major changes in economic policy, including an expansion of the free market and the phasing out of price subsidies. And it struck a quid pro quo with South Africa's apartheid government in March 1984. In return for Pretoria's promise to cease assisting the MNR rebels, the Maputo authorities pledged to prevent the outlawed African National Congress of South Africa from using Mozambican territory as a base or transit point for conducting military operations against South Africa.

In 1987, confronted with an unending and economically costly military challenge from the MNR, FRELIMO decided to take further steps in an un-Marxist, pragmatic direction. It adopted a stringent Economic Recovery Program (ERP) drawn up by the IMF and the World Bank. Despite the hardships that this program imposed on the poorer sections of the country's population, its outcome was by and large positive. Although Mozambique's economy continued to be weak and dependent on foreign aid, economic growth resumed, there was a strengthening of public finances, and inflation dropped.

By the onset of the unraveling of communist power in Eastern Europe in 1989, then, the FRELIMO regime had already traveled a significant distance from standard Marxist positions. Indeed, in July 1989—when the transition to noncommunist rule had barely gotten under way in Poland, the first East European country to experience such a transformation—FRELIMO's Fifth

Congress opted to abandon Marxism-Leninism and the class struggle altogether. It opened the party's membership to all citizens and endorsed President Joaquim Chissano's plan to negotiate a settlement with the MNR.

Factions of differing ideological stripes existed in the PDRY from the time of independence in 1967, and these had given rise to severe power struggles and periodic shifts in leadership.[2] Up to the mid-1980s, drastic swings in policy accompanied the shifts in leadership, with hard-liners pursuing efforts to impose socialism internally and revolutionary tactics abroad and more moderate elements seeking to limit both. But this pattern changed in the mid-1980s.

In January 1986, another major turnover in PDRY leadership took place. Since 1980, Ali Nasir Muhammad, a pragmatist, had held the reins of power in Aden, and he had followed a largely nonsocialist economic course at home and had cooperated with nonrevolutionary states in the international arena, especially in the Arab world. After a complex armed confrontation with his opponents at the beginning of 1986, however, he fled the country. Shortly thereafter, a new government was formed.

Yet unlike previous instances when pragmatists lost power, extreme radicals did not control this regime; nonideological elements dominated it. Furthermore, the government did not repudiate Ali Nasir's policies. In internal matters, it stressed gradual movement along the path of socialist orientation and indicated that full-fledged communism in the PDRY might be centuries away. On the international front, it sought Arab acceptance and financial aid and pledged to adhere to the principles of mutual respect for and noninterference in the domestic affairs of other states.

Even more striking was the revised approach toward unification with the nonsocialist Republic of Yemen. Yemeni unification had figured in the articulated goals of PDRY leaders since independence, but the ways in which the leaders had pursued this objective had rendered its attainment highly improbable. During periods of rule by extreme radicals, the PDRY had opted for subversion and revolutionary takeover of its northern neighbor; however, the PDRY had lacked the base of support there and the military means to make such a policy work. At times when more moderate forces had held sway in Aden, the PDRY had often engaged in talks with the government in Sanaa about unification, but because of Moscow's desire not to lose its military-strategic assets in the PDRY, the latter had tended to set unrealistic conditions for unification.

A summit meeting between the heads of the PDRY and the Republic of Yemen in early May 1988 signaled a new willingness to compromise on outstanding differences between the two countries so as to facilitate unification. Not only did the communiqué issued by the two officials endorse the revitalization of institutions to discuss and prepare the way for unification, but it also addressed disputes in a fresh manner. For example, the two leaders agreed to resolve their border dispute by withdrawing military forces from the area in question and establishing a joint petroleum-investment corporation. Developments over the next year confirmed the shift in the PDRY approach.

Thus, by mid-1989 the PDRY had departed significantly from a Marxist course. Although it remained verbally dedicated to building socialism, its practice gave that goal a far different content than the goal had had during the rule of extreme radicals.

Evaporation of Soviet–East European Support

For nine Marxist governments, what really mattered about events in Eastern Europe and the former Soviet Union was the drastic cutbacks in military and economic assistance that these events produced. Afghanistan, Angola, Cambodia, Cuba, Ethiopia, the DPRK, Laos, Nicaragua, and Vietnam fell into this category. The extent and nature of the problems caused by reduction or cessation of such aid, however, differed greatly from regime to regime.

In the 1980s, all nine governments received substantial arms deliveries from the Soviet Union and Eastern Europe, and most also got major economic help from there. Arms deliveries in 1985–89 totaled $9.73 billion for Afghanistan, $5.65 billion for Angola, $3.66 billion for Ethiopia, $1.4 billion for Cambodia, $8.6 billion for Cuba, $2.7 billion for the DPRK, $575 million for Laos, $2.37 billion for Nicaragua, and $8.23 billion for Vietnam.[3] During 1981–89, Moscow's net development aid and trade subsidies to Cambodia reached $980 million; to Cuba, $38.2 billion; to the DPRK, $380 million; to Laos, $740 million; and to Vietnam, $10.7 billion. The Soviet Union in 1985–89 extended $780 million in economic credits to Afghanistan, $50 million to Angola, $165 million to Ethiopia, and $1.9 billion to Nicaragua. During 1984–88, other Warsaw Pact members offered $5 million in economic assistance to Afghanistan, $105 million to Angola, $180 million to Ethiopia, and $410 million to Nicaragua.[4]

But events in Eastern Europe and the Soviet Union from 1989 on caused the flow of material help from there to ebb and in many instances to dry up entirely. With the demise of communist rule in Eastern Europe in 1989–90, the ideological basis of their previous cooperation and assistance to Marxist countries in the developing areas vanished, and the new East European governments made clear that henceforth their own self-interests would dictate the depth of their military and economic relations with all governments in the world community.[5] Well before his departure from office in December 1991, Mikhail Gorbachev moved the Soviet Union far in the same direction, and the end of communist rule in the Soviet Union and the disintegration of the country resulted in completion of the shift.[6]

None of the nine Marxist regimes under discussion here fit the revised profile of a desirable candidate for economic aid or arms deliveries. All had built up substantial debts to the Soviet Union and its East European allies. Moreover, all had had to ask that their debt repayments be rescheduled in the latter half of the 1980s, and all seemed unlikely to meet even these revised schedules. Finally, all lacked the hard currency necessary to pay for imports for economic development or military use and had little to sell to either Eastern Europe or the Soviet Union to finance purchases of such items.[7]

Thus the nine governments soon found their access to East European and Soviet resources greatly curtailed. That access continued to shrink as the economies of the East European countries and the Soviet Union went into precipitous decline.[8]

The consequences of this dwindling of material support from the Soviet Union and Eastern Europe were serious for all nine regimes, yet they varied. In the cases of Afghanistan, Angola, Cambodia, Ethiopia, and Nicaragua, such a development deprived the regimes of crucial military means to stay in power. The governments in Afghanistan,[9] Ethiopia,[10] and Nicaragua[11] had assumed authority as the result of local revolutions, but they had never succeeded in eliminating armed opposition to their rule. The regime of the Popular Movement for the Liberation of Angola (MPLA) in Angola had emerged during an armed struggle among groups competing to replace Portugal's departing colonial rulers, and although the MPLA had managed to install itself in office in Luanda with Soviet, Cuban, and East European help, it had not destroyed its rivals. Indeed, the National Union for the Total Liberation of Angola (UNITA) had retreated to the bush and had continued to wage guerrilla warfare against it for more than a decade.[12] The Cambodian government had originally been the creation of communist Vietnam, which had invaded Cambodia in 1978 to oust the murderous and xenophobic regime of the communist Khmer Rouge; however, the Vietnamese had not managed to eradicate the Khmer Rouge, which had withdrawn to the hinterlands and had carried on military activities from there against the combined forces of Vietnam and the Cambodian government. Subsequently, noncommunist Cambodian elements had organized military forces of their own and had mounted operations as well against the Vietnamese and the Cambodian government. With Vietnam's withdrawal of its troops from Cambodia in 1989, antigovernment military undertakings had stepped up sharply.[13] To maintain at least the semblance of control in the face of these varied challenges, all five regimes depended heavily on arms from the Soviet Union and Eastern Europe.[14]

During the late 1980s and early 1990s, to be sure, Soviet negotiating efforts reduced the military risks confronted by the regimes in Afghanistan, Angola, Cambodia, and Nicaragua, for Moscow persuaded the suppliers of arms to the regimes' opponents to cut off shipments to them as a condition for ending its own arms deliveries to the four governments. But it was clear that none of the five regimes could any longer safely stake its survival on military instruments alone.

For the regimes in Cuba, the DPRK, and Vietnam, the declining assistance from the Soviet Union and Eastern Europe had both military and economic ramifications. None of the three governments had to cope with domestic military challenges, for they had long ago suppressed any that existed. Each, however, faced what it perceived to be a formidable security threat in the international realm—the United States for Cuba, the Republic of Korea (ROK)–United States alliance for the DPRK, and China for Vietnam. The cutbacks in Soviet and East European military aid left the three regimes increasingly vulnerable to these discerned challenges.

Economically, all three regimes had already encountered severe problems, and the drastic reductions in Soviet and East European help greatly exacerbated these. In 1990–91, Cuba experienced its most austere conditions since 1959.[15] The most damaging shortage was that of oil. As of October 1990, the state sector began to receive 50 percent less oil than before. Every family was also ordered to decrease its consumption of electricity (the output of which required heavy energy inputs) by 10 percent and was warned that its electricity would be cut off for a month if it failed to do so.

The DPRK, which had conducted more than 50 percent of its total annual trade with the USSR up to 1991, could not come up with the hard currency that Moscow now demanded for exchanges; as a result, its imports from the Soviet Union during the first half of 1991 fell to just $11 million, as compared with $587 million during the same period in 1990. Particularly significant was the drop in imports of oil, which caused a decline in the average operating rate of industries to 40 percent of capacity.[16]

In mid-1990, Vietnam found itself with an inflation rate that had jumped from a single-digit figure in 1989 to 30 percent a year, and its trade and budget deficits were climbing as well. Unemployment was on the rise, too, with about 20 percent of the labor force now out of work. Spot food shortages were again reappearing.[17]

The implications of diminishing Soviet and East European aid for the Laotian regime lay essentially in the economic sphere.[18] In the late 1980s, Laos, which is one of the least developed countries in the world and the most backward of the once centrally planned states, had relied on foreign aid and loans for an average of 51 percent of its budget, and the Soviet Union and Eastern Europe had provided the lion's share of this sum.

Encouragement of Opposition Challenges

For the remaining regimes, the primary impact of the Eastern European and Soviet upheavals was strong pressure from local opposition elements for revisions in the governments' political and, in some cases, economic policies. The regimes in Benin, Congo, Cape Verde, Guinea-Bissau, Mongolia, Sao Tome and Principe, and Zimbabwe all experienced such pressure; however, it flowed from diverse sources and emerged in varying contexts.

In Benin, Cape Verde, and Congo, the push came from individuals and groups unhappy with the existing situations in their homelands but unorganized in any formal political sense; events in Eastern Europe in 1989–90 helped to embolden them to seek political and economic change in their own states. Serious pressure from such forces originated in Benin in June 1989, when a coalition of legislators and concerned citizens informed President Mathieu Kerekou, head of the Revolutionary Party of the People of Benin (PRPB), that they wanted political and economic reforms in the country. It reached its zenith in February 1990 with the convening of a national conference for reconstruction involving nearly 500 people drawn from all sectors of society.[19]

Prodding to revamp Cape Verde's political system began in muted fashion about mid-1989. It stemmed from influential sectors of society—notably intellectuals, Roman Catholics, and the large Cape Verdean community overseas—who believed that the regime's 1985 concession allowing persons not affiliated with the ruling African Party for the Independence of Cape Verde (PAICV) to appear on the party-approved list in elections had not gone far enough. By February 1990, pressure had mounted to the point that President Aristides Maria Pereira told the PAICV's National Council that Cape Verde could not ignore current changes in the world.[20]

In Congo, prominent citizens issued an open letter to President Denis Sassou-Nguesso in July 1990 demanding a multiparty democracy. Within just a few months thereafter, trade unions and student organizations had moved to shake off the domination of the ruling Congolese Party of Labor (PCT), and the Ecumenical Council of Christian Churches of Congo had publicly deplored the PCT's attempt to decide unilaterally the speed and nature of democratization.[21]

Calls for new political and economic policies in Mongolia cropped up initially in the wake of the founding of opposition political bodies there, but reformist elements within the governing Mongolian People's Revolutionary Party (MPRP) soon added their voices. The first opposition political group in the country, the Mongolian Democratic Union, was formed in December 1989 by intellectuals influenced by developments in Eastern Europe; by early 1990 it had been joined by other organizations. These groups demanded a multi-party system, free elections with universal suffrage, replacement of the cen-trally planned economy with a market system, private property, reorganiza-tion of the government, and protection of human rights (including freedom of religion). As 1990 progressed, there were increasing signs of sympathy for these demands in some quarters of the MPRP. By the end of the year, a group within the MPRP styling itself the For Democracy Club had circulated an open letter to party members urging those favoring reform to unite to wrest con-trol of the MPRP from the opponents of democracy currently running the party.[22]

In Guinea-Bissau and Sao Tome and Principe, the push for far-reaching political change was largely the work of organized political groups based in the country or in exile. Guinea-Bissau president Joao Bernardo Vieira, head of the ruling African Party for the Independence of Guinea and Cape Verde (PAIGC), had already embarked on a new economic course well before the collapse of communist rule in Eastern Europe, and he had even agreed to un-dertake political reforms to satisfy the requirements of the World Bank and the IMF for assistance, as well as to attract foreign investment. But it was the exile Bafata Resistance Movement, headquartered in Lisbon, that sparked de-mands for immediate political reform in April 1990 with a public challenge to the government and PAIGC leadership to open talks in a "neutral" state about national reconciliation and the establishment of a multiparty system. Inter-nally, an opposition Social Democratic Front (FDS) formed in 1990, and pres-sure for revisions in the political order rose significantly during the year.[23]

President Manuel Pinto de Costa of Sao Tome and Principe, secretary-gen-eral of the governing Movement for the Liberation of Sao Tome and Principe (MLSTP), had also launched an economic liberalization program long before 1989, and he had eased political constraints to permit independent candidates to stand in legislative elections and to allow legislators to be chosen on the basis of direct and universal suffrage. In January 1989, he had even announced that a new constitution to be submitted for popular approval by referendum during the year would sanction the existence of factions in the MLSTP. None-theless, encouraged by the course of events in Eastern Europe, an underground group coordinated by Major Daniel dos Santos Daio (which in the fall of 1990 surfaced as the Party of Convergence-Reflection Group), the Lisbon-based Opposition Democratic Coalition, and prominent exiles such as former prime minister Miguel Travoada prodded him to go farther. In particular, they wanted a multiparty system and contested elections, not only for the legislature but also for the presidency.[24]

After 1989, individuals and groups in Zimbabwean society as well as elements within the ruling Zimbabwe African National Union-Patriotic Front (ZANU-PF) pressed Zimbabwe's president, Robert Mugabe, leader of ZANU-PF, to alter his basic political policies; however, the nature of the policies that these critics sought to overturn and the manner in which they pursued this goal reflected the country's distinctive situation. As a result of the 1979 accord that had laid the groundwork for Zimbabwe's independence in early 1980, the country's constitution provided for a pluralistic, multiparty political system, and there was a prohibition against constitutional revisions until at least 1990. Throughout the 1980s, Mugabe had made clear his intention to create a Marxist-Leninist one-party state as soon as this restriction lapsed. Yet the disintegration of Marxist-Leninist one-party states in Eastern Europe drove home to many in the populace and in ZANU-PF the utter folly of Mugabe's declared intentions. During the March 1990 general elections, opposition politicians, the churches, students, labor leaders, and many prominent persons spoke out against a one-party state, and the public accorded an opposition black party— Edgar Tekere's Zimbabwe United Movement (ZUM)—15 percent of the vote. Moreover, both the Politburo and Central Committee of ZANU-PF rejected Mugabe's call for a constitutional amendment to establish a one-party state. There was widespread feeling within these bodies that attempting to institutionalize ZANU-PF's de facto dominance of the country would invite trouble.[25]

RESPONSES AND EFFECTIVENESS

In trying to cope with the new circumstances growing out of events in Eastern Europe and the Soviet Union, the eighteen Marxist regimes in developing areas adopted one of four basic strategies. For shorthand purposes, these can be labeled "local legitimation," "distancing," "economic liberalization," and "military self-reliance/diversification of foreign economic ties." None of them has proved wholly successful, and local legitimation has failed entirely in specific instances.

Local Legitimation

Highly concerned about their domestic vulnerabilities, the regimes in Afghanistan, Angola, Benin, Cambodia, Cape Verde, Congo, Ethiopia, Guinea-Bissau, Mongolia, Mozambique, Nicaragua, the PDRY, and Sao Tome and Principe chose to attempt to enhance their local legitimacy. But the precise measures that these governments embraced differed substantially.

A number of regimes decided to abandon what remained of their commitments to Marxism-Leninism, especially a one-party state, and to seek a popular mandate in free and open elections. During 1990, the MPLA government in Angola formally discarded Marxism-Leninism as the basis for its policies and endorsed a multiparty system; it also moved to restructure the economy along nonsocialist lines. By May 1991, after lengthy and tortuous negotiations, it had concluded an agreement with UNITA to end the civil war and hold free elections in September 1992.

The National Council of Cape Verde's PAICV announced in April 1990 that henceforth other parties would be allowed to put forth candidates to the People's Assembly and the president would be directly elected. In September of that year, the People's Assembly enacted constitutional amendments to this effect. Legislative elections and a presidential election took place under these new arrangements in January and February 1991, respectively.

In September 1990, the government of Hun Sen, along with the three opposition factions, accepted a framework that had been worked out by the five permanent members of the UN Security Council to settle the civil war in Cambodia. Not until October 1991, however, did the warring parties reach a formal agreement fleshing out the framework. This called for a cease-fire, the disarming of the troops of all four factions, cessation of the supply of arms from outside the country, and the holding of elections under the supervision of UN personnel. Although the forces of both the Khmer Rouge and the Hun Sen government failed to surrender many of their weapons over subsequent months and there were periodic breaches of the cease-fire, the elections under UN auspices ultimately were carried out in May 1993.

President Vieira of Guinea-Bissau instructed the PAIGC in May 1990 to begin preparations to introduce a multiparty system in the country. The following July, the party's Central Committee proposed the adoption of "integral multipartyism," and by March 1992 multiparty elections had been set for November 1992 for president and for December 1992 for parliament. But in November 1992 President Vieira announced that he was postponing both elections until March 1993. Still further delays ensued before the elections finally took place in July–August 1994.

In March 1990, the MPRP regime in Mongolia promised that the party would give up its constitutionally mandated role as the "leader" of the country and there would be contested elections to the Great People's Hural, Mongolia's main legislative body. At the same time, the general secretary and the entire Politburo of the MPRP resigned and reform-oriented individuals replaced them. Two months later, an amendment to the state's constitution made the Great People's Hural a freely elected supervisory body, but it left selection of the president with the Hural. Under a new electoral law allowing the participation of non-MPRP candidates, balloting for the 430 seats in the Hural took place in July–August 1990 in two stages—primary elections and general elections. This body then chose a president in September 1990. During the course of 1991, however, a new national constitution was drafted that not only guaranteed human rights and a mixed economy with private property but also provided for direct election of both parliament and the president. Another election for the Hural was conducted in June 1992, and a president was chosen separately by popular vote in June 1993.

The FRELIMO government in Mozambique had already discarded major features of Marxist-Leninist rule by July 1989, and it subsequently entered into talks with the MNR about ending the conflict in the country. Then in August 1990 President Joaquim Chissano announced that the FRELIMO Politburo had approved establishment of a multiparty democracy in Mozambique. A new constitution incorporating this innovation was declared adopted by President Chissano in December 1990, after the FRELIMO Politburo reversed a decision by the Central Committee to reject the document. Over ensuing months, the FRELIMO government carried on protracted negotiations with the MNR that led in October 1992 to the conclusion of a general peace accord halting the country's sixteen-year civil war. The agreement called for demobilization of the forces of both, the formation of a new, integrated national army, and the holding of free elections—all under UN supervision. The peace process was originally supposed to be completed by October 1993, but the deliberate speed with which the United Nations acted (its military forces were not fully in place in Mozambique until May 1993) necessitated pushing back the elections until October 1994.

In December 1989, the first national conference of the ruling MLSTP of Sao Tome and Principe proposed the introduction of a multiparty system there, the elimination of the party's leading role in society, and popular election of the president on a freely contested basis for a maximum of two terms. President Pinto da Costa endorsed these proposals, and they were embodied in a new constitution promulgated in early 1990. This constitution was approved in a popular referendum in August 1990. Elections for the National Assembly and for president took place under the revised constitution in January and March 1991, respectively.

Several other governments in this group also cast aside what was left of their professed Marxism-Leninism, yet they opted to rely primarily on means other than popular elections to improve their local standings. The approach of the PDRY regime was the most unusual. In late September to early October 1989, the YSP Central Committee indicated that it intended to move toward marketization of the country's economy, and it highlighted the participation for the first time of independent candidates in recent local government elections. In December 1989, it declared itself in favor of a multiparty system and instructed the party's Politburo to draw up guidelines for a law allowing other parties to form. During the same few months, the PDRY government stepped up its efforts at unification with the Republic of Yemen. By late November, the presidents of the two countries had announced a merger agreement and had referred a draft constitution for the new entity to their respective legislative bodies. The first joint meeting of the two cabinets took place in January 1990. On May 22, 1990, the PDRY ceased to exist when the two states formally merged.

The regimes in Benin and Congo elected to pursue similar courses. After his meeting with concerned legislators and citizens in June 1989, President Kerekou appointed their spokesman, Robert Dossou, dean of the law faculty at the University of Benin, as his new minister of planning and asked that he come up with a program of reforms. Kerekou then agreed to a proposal that the country organize for change through a national conference for reconstruction, and he allowed Minister of Planning Dossou to designate groups to be represented and the number of persons that each constituency could send. This gathering of nearly 500 persons convened in February 1990. Two months before it assembled, Kerekou and the PRPB formally renounced Marxism-Leninism as the official ideology of the state.

The PCT government in Congo proclaimed in July 1990 that it was forsaking Marxism-Leninism as the state ideology and would end the one-party system under new legislation to be crafted at an extraordinary PCT conference sometime in 1991, but the PCT continued to be the country's sole legal party. After the Congolese Trade Union Confederation staged a general strike in September 1990 in support of an acceleration of democratization, however, President Sassou-Nguesso announced that parties could register immediately and would acquire legal status as of January 1991. No less important, he promised to convoke shortly thereafter a national conference to debate draft legislation on a multiparty system and to establish a timetable for elections. This conference opened in late February with 1,100 delegates drawn from political parties, religious bodies, nongovernmental organizations, and associations recognized by the Ministry of Interior, Information, and Sports.

In Afghanistan and Ethiopia, the regimes endeavored to bring about national reconciliation through negotiations with their military opponents but to retain a key role in any new political order by presenting themselves as defenders of national unity. President Najibullah of Afghanistan made many proposals for peace with the mujaheddin rebels during 1989–90. To underscore his seriousness, he pushed through amendments to the state's constitution in May 1990 that excised all references to the People's Democratic Party of Afghanistan (PDPA) and its main subordinate arm, the National Front, and laid down procedures for other parties to become active. In addition, the Second PDPA Congress in June 1990 changed the party's name to the Party of the Homeland and endorsed political pluralism, dialogue with opponents, and private enterprise. Yet none of Najibullah's proposals contemplated that he would yield power, at least immediately. Indeed, his incorporation of some ostensibly non-PDPA people into the Kabul regime in May 1990 allowed him to depict it as the nucleus of a truly national government.

In June 1989, Ethiopia's parliament, dominated by the ruling Workers' Party of Ethiopia (WPE), sanctioned unconditional peace talks with the state's Eritrean and Tigrean insurgents, and talks of this character began in September 1989. After these produced no meaningful results, President Mengistu Haile Mariam tried to create a climate conducive to an accord. In March 1990, he announced that Ethiopia's centrally planned economic system would be replaced with a mixed economy. He also said that he was abandoning Marxism-Leninism and transforming the WPE into the Democratic Unity Party of Ethiopia, which would be open to non-Marxists, and he even invited opposition groups to participate in national politics. At no time, however, did he imply that he would accept any settlement that involved secession of a portion of Ethiopia or his own removal from office.

One regime—that in Nicaragua—sought to preserve its essential commitment to Marxism-Leninism but to bolster its political position by conducting new presidential and legislative elections. In January 1989, after extensive public debate, the government decided to retain Marxism-Leninism as part of the required school curriculum, and shortly thereafter it extended ideological indoctrination and political training to all levels of the Sandinista Popular Army. During the same period, however, President Daniel Ortega promised the other Central American presidents that his Sandinista Front of National Liberation (FSLN) regime would move up Nicaragua's next elections to February 1990 and open them to all comers. (Contested elections for both president and the National Assembly had been held in November 1984, and a third of the Assembly seats had been won by opposition parties. But these elections had been widely regarded as rigged and undemocratic.) After lengthy negotiations with the opposition, arrangements for presidential and legislative elections were worked out. Despite some FSLN efforts at intimidation during the ensuing electoral campaign, elections were carried out in February 1990 in what international observers deemed a reasonably open and honest fashion.

None of these methods of trying to enhance local legitimacy has proved highly efficacious. Of the regimes that opted for multiparty elections, that in Mongolia initially had the greatest success in strengthening its popular standing, but this success sparked a resurgence of conservative elements within the MPRP that fractured the party and greatly weakened public confidence in it. The MPRP received 60 percent of the votes in the July–August 1990 legislative elections and wound up with 86 percent of the seats, and a MPRP member, Punsalmaagiya Ochirbat, was elected president by the Hural the following September. In the June 1992 parliamentary elections, the MPRP continued to attract about the same percentage of the votes; moreover, because the non-MPRP votes were split among several parties, the MPRP obtained seventy of the seventy-six seats in the new Hural. Nonetheless, such showings had sparked a revival of the assertiveness of conservatives within the party that was already causing disquiet. During the early months of 1992, some reformers had even split from the MPRP and formed the Mongolian Party of Renaissance to contest the elections. Disillusionment with the MPRP reached new heights during the run-up to the 1993 presidential balloting. At the instigation of its conservative members, the party declined to back President Ochirbat, a reformer, for reelection and endorsed a conservative. Ochirbat then agreed to stand as the candidate of a small two-party opposition coalition of National Democrats and Social Democrats. He won the contest handily. Subsequently, in the July 1996 parliamentary elections, the MPRP also suffered defeat at the hands of an opposition coalition of four parties, which won fifty of the seats in the Hural.

Guinea-Bissau's elections in July 1994 gave the PAIGC sixty-four of the 100 seats in the new parliament, but President Vieira obtained only a plurality of the ballots for president. The ensuing presidential runoff in August 1994 resulted in a narrow victory for Vieira, 52 to 48 percent.

In the Angolan elections under UN supervision in late September 1992, the MPLA captured 53.7 percent of the aggregate legislative vote as against 34.1 percent for UNITA, thereby gaining a parliamentary majority of 129 out of 220 seats. The MPLA's Jose Eduardo dos Santos also bested UNITA's Jonas Savimbi in the contest for president, although not by a sufficient margin to avoid a runoff with the UNITA leader. To the MPLA's great chagrin, however, Savimbi refused to recognize its victory, charging fraud. He withdrew UNITA elements from the integrated national army still being formed, retreated to his old base in the south, and resumed military operations. Not until late 1994, after UNITA had suffered a series of military setbacks and had failed to obtain significant international support, did he evince a willingness to work out a political compromise.

In Mozambique's elections in late October 1994, President Chissano won the presidential contest easily (54 percent to 35 percent) over his chief opponent, MNR leader Afonso Dhlakama. In the legislative voting, however, FRELIMO garnered only 44 percent of the ballots, while the MNR received 38 percent.

The Cambodian People's Party (CPP), the political backbone of the Hun Sen regime, won 38 percent of the vote and fifty-one legislative seats in the May 1993 parliamentary elections in Cambodia, but the party's performance did not match the more than 45 percent of the vote and fifty-eight seats captured by Funcinpec, the pro-royalist party headed by Prince Norodom Ranariddh. By claiming fraud and threatening to intervene with its still powerful military, however, the CPP did salvage something from the situation. Under the auspices of Prince Norodom Sihanouk, the restored head of state, an interim coalition government consisting of Funcinpec, the CPP, and the small Buddhist Liberal Democratic Party was formed in June 1993, and Prince Ranariddh and Hun Sen were designated co–prime ministers. In September 1993, when a more lasting government was set up under a new constitution approved by the legislative assembly, this coalition was preserved, but in line with a compromise proposed by Sihanouk, now officially king, and agreed to by the CPP, Prince Ranariddh was named first prime minister and Hun Sen became second prime minister.

All of the other regimes that chose to submit themselves to popular judgment in multiparty elections fared even less well than these five. The FSLN in Nicaragua lost both the legislative and presidential elections there in February 1990, although it managed to retain control of the armed forces when it turned over the reins of power to Violeta Chamorra and her coalition in April 1990. In Cape Verde, the PAICV suffered defeat in the parliamentary elections of January 1991 and the presidential election of February 1991. The MLSTP in Sao Tome and Principe met the same fate in the local legislative elections in January 1991 and the presidential election of March 1991, although President da Costa announced his retirement from public life in February after his party's defeat in the January balloting.

The governments in both Benin and Congo found themselves unable to control the national conferences that they convoked to enhance their legitimacy. When President Kerekou of Benin sanctioned the calling of a national conference for reconstruction, he plainly envisioned that it would simply discuss problems and offer recommendations to deal with them, and he anticipated that he and his PCPB would retain the power to determine which, if any, recommendations would be implemented. Yet once the assembly began in February 1990, it declared that its decisions must be accepted and put into practice. Then it proceeded to write a new constitution creating a multiparty democracy, providing for a transitional government, and setting up a schedule of elections from the local level to the presidency. Kerekou, allowed to stay on as president during the transitional period, finally acceded to the changes and opted to run for president again, but he went down to defeat in the second round of balloting for the post in March 1991.

President Sassou-Nguesso and the PCT confronted much the same situation with the national conference that opened in Congo in late February 1991. The assembly was adamant that its decisions would be binding and not subject to government veto. It drafted a new democratic constitution (approved by an acting parliament in December 1991 and by popular referendum in March 1992), called for multiparty elections during 1992, and installed a transitional government to rule until such elections took place. President Sassou-Nguesso reluctantly accepted these initiatives and agreed to stay on as president through the transition. In the two-stage elections for the lower house of parliament in June–July 1992, the PCT wound up third, winning only 18 of 120 seats. Then in the August 1992 presidential election, Sassou-Nguesso finished third in the first round of balloting, thus failing even to qualify for the runoff.

Neither the Najibullah regime in Afghanistan nor the Mengistu regime in Ethiopia ever managed to attract important elements of the local opposition into a coalition government of national unity, and the military position of each deteriorated quickly. In a few months, each fell in the face of escalating attacks by rebel forces. The denouement came in May 1991 in Ethiopia and in April 1992 in Afghanistan.

Ironically, the YSP government in the PDRY seems to have had the greatest degree of success in increasing its local legitimacy. The price that it paid for this achievement, however, was to pass out of existence as a separate entity.

Distancing

The ZANU-PF regime in Zimbabwe reacted in idiosyncratic fashion to the altered situation facing it. It strove to dissociate itself as much as possible from the crumbling communist governments in Eastern Europe and the Soviet Union and to stress its indigenous roots, although it did not cast aside all Marxist-Leninist precepts.

In pursuing this course, the regime benefited from several factors. First, it had gained power without Moscow's blessing. When Zimbabwe won its sovereignty in 1980, Soviet leaders would clearly have preferred that authority pass into the hands of the Zimbabwe African People's Union (ZAPU), the chief competitor of ZANU-PF. Second, thanks to the terms of Zimbabwe's independence constitution, ZANU-PF had never functioned as the sole party in the state; it had retained power only by defeating other parties in contested elections. Third, President Mugabe had from the outset endorsed a mixed economy, eschewing nationalization of private industries and farms. Such a policy had saved the country from the drastic drops in per capita GNP experienced in the 1980s by many other self-styled Marxist/Marxist-Leninist states in Africa.[26]

To differentiate itself still further from the discredited East European and Soviet regimes, the ZANU-PF government took a number of steps. It lifted the country's long-standing state of emergency, which had allowed the government to imprison individuals indefinitely without trial. It also undertook far-reaching economic reforms that, when fully implemented, would move the economy decisively toward a market-driven system. Finally, it attempted to show its sensitivity to the growing demands of the country's blacks for land, the bulk of which still remained in the hands of the local white minority. By March 1992, it had pushed through parliament a law permitting it to buy up nearly half of the 11.5 million hectares of farmland currently in commercial use and redistribute them to master communal farmers. In May 1993, it published a list of seventy commercial farms that it proposed to purchase under this act.

The government, however, did not fomally renounce the idea of a one-party state. In a face-saving measure for President Mugabe, the ZANU-PF Central Committee, in September 1990, professed an ongoing commitment to this goal but called for its achievement by political mobilization and organization, not by coercion or legislation.

Despite the efforts of the ZANU-PF government to sharpen the distinction between it and the old regimes in Eastern Europe and the Soviet Union, the persistence of many features of a de facto one-party state significantly eroded the government's support, especially in urban areas. Harassment of political dissidents by the Central Intelligence Organization, tight control of the news media, a bloated bureaucracy, and rampant official corruption proved particularly damaging. Nonetheless, through political intimidation and in some cases even rigged voting, ZANU-PF managed to capture 147 of 150 seats in the April 1995 parliamentary elections.

Economic Liberalization

The regimes in Vietnam, Laos, and eventually Cuba opted for a two-pronged approach to the new problems they confronted. On the one hand, they have stoutly upheld Marxism-Leninism and especially rule by a single, "vanguard" party. In March 1990, for example, Tran Xuan Bach was expelled from the Political Bureau of the Vietnam Communist Party (VCP) merely for implying that a one-party system might not be best for Vietnam. Kaysone Phomvihane, then general secretary of the governing Lao People's Revolutionary Party (LPRP), told an interviewer in January 1990 that "our Laotian party does not yet see any need for establishing other political parties."[27] Furthermore, when a group of mid-level government officials in Laos attempted later in the year to set up a movement to campaign for a multiparty democracy, the LPRP leadership did not hesitate to suppress this undertaking and imprison many of its instigators. Throughout the early 1990s, Fidel Castro referred to the Communist Party of Cuba (PCC) as "an indispensable instrument of the Revolution," and the PCC-controlled media described him as the only Cuban who could lead the country out of its present predicament. In addition, the Cuban government reversed a political opening of the 1980s and once again began to arrest Cuban citizens who spoke out in favor of human rights and broader democratization.

On the other hand, the three regimes have moved away from a centrally planned economy to attract investors and lenders from abroad. Both the VCP and LPRP governments have sought to entrench a market economy in their states, but the Castro government has been less decisive in this respect thus far.

In mid-1991, the VCP leadership unveiled a plan to construct a "market mechanism economy" in Vietnam. Over ensuing months, the government took a variety of steps that advanced the country a substantial way toward a market economy. Among the most striking was the adoption in May 1992 of a new constitution that allows private citizens to engage in business and to own the means of production. Although the provision on private ownership does not apply to land, long-term use of land and the right to transfer—but not inherit—land are sanctioned.

The LPRP government in Laos acted even more swiftly than the regime in Vietnam to demonstrate an irrevocable intention to build a market economy. By the end of the 1980s, the Vientiane authorities had already recorded fairly significant progress along the path of economic restructuring. Then in August 1990 the LPRP leadership took a major additional step toward a market economy by passing a set of laws on property ownership, contracts, inheritance, banking, and court fees. Further improvement of weak legal structures came in August 1991 when the National Assembly adopted the country's first constitution.

At the outset, the CPP government in Cuba sought merely to expand the state's roster of key trading partners and to entice foreign firms to invest on the island through joint ventures. Castro still doggedly proclaimed the need for progressive socialization of the country and emphatically refused to permit the reintroduction of free farmers' markets, which he denounced as "corrupt."

But as the severity of Cuba's economic situation increased, Castro approved several measures that altered the domestic economy in a capitalist direction as well. In July 1993, the president himself told Cuban citizens that, for the first time in three decades, they could legally possess U.S. dollars. Two months later, the Cuban government opened up more than 100 kinds of jobs to private enterprise. In October 1994, it allowed the reestablishment of free farmers' markets. Yet Castro took these steps reluctantly, and since December 1995 he has shown mounting determination to keep them from leading to the emergence of a broad market mechanism in the economy.

This two-pronged response permitted both the Hanoi and Vientiane regimes to register some noteworthy gains in their attempts to meet the new challenges before them. There has been a substantial warming of the relations of each government with the government of China. For the LPRP regime, this development has meant a welcome expansion of economic ties. As for the government in Vietnam, the rapprochement has lessened the key military threat to its security, thereby reducing the need for defense expenditures. At the same time, the approach opened up new opportunities for each regime to forge economic links with the developed states of the West. By mid-1996, for example, Laos had obtained Australian financing to build the first bridge across the Mekong River, which—when completed—will connect Vientiane to the Thai road and rail system at Nong Khai. Some American companies, among them Hunt Oil, had also invested in Laos. Vietnam had attracted large-scale investment from the United States after the lifting of the U.S. trade embargo against it in 1993. Indeed, U.S. investment rose from just $3.3 million in 1993 to $1.2 billion at the end of 1995.

By mid-1996, Cuba had also realized some major benefits from its approach. It had signed 212 agreements with foreign investors by the close of 1995, and these had brought $2.1 billion into 34 areas of the economy, especially tourism. This influx had had a positive impact on the economy's overall performance. The government claimed that the country's gross domestic product had risen 9.6 percent in the first six months of 1996. But the continuing U.S. embargo on trade with the island and Washington's ban on third-country U.S. subsidiary trade had limited the positive effects of the new approach.

Whether any of these three regimes will be able to sustain its existing response over the long haul is a moot issue. In Vietnam, domestic pressures for the VCP leadership to accept political pluralism have reached significant levels because of growing official corruption, and increasing economic liberalization could intensify these. The lack of an educated and/or technocratic class in Laos makes the base for a push for a multiparty system there exceedingly narrow, so the LPRP rulers may not feel great internal imperatives to abandon single-party rule in the foreseeable future. Nonetheless, as a highly backward and dependent state, Laos could find itself subject to compulsions from external sources. Much will depend in this regard on events in Vietnam and China. Few observers doubt that the CCP government in Cuba will have to embrace market economics more fully than it has to date if it is to survive, but its ability to maintain a political monopoly or even to retain power if it follows such a course stirs heated debate.[28]

Military Self-Reliance/Diversification of Foreign Economic Ties

Like the Zimbabwe regime, the DPRK government reacted in idiosyncratic fashion to the challenge posed by developments in Eastern Europe and the Soviet Union. It vigorously rejected any basic departures from either one-party rule or central economic planning. According to Kim Chong-il, the son of DPRK founder Kim Il-song and Kim Il-song's apparent successor in 1994, the Korean Workers' Party (KWP) must not tolerate "pagan elements" in its ranks; indeed, it must consolidate its organization and strengthen the ideological education not only of party members but of all "working people" to thwart the "ideological and cultural infiltration of the imperialists."[29] The 1990 New Year's message of Kim Il-song stressed that the DPRK needed not economic restructuring but successful completion of socialist construction; moreover, the ruling hierarchy's concrete measures to ease the country's economic plight reflected a distinct bias in favor of central planning.

However, the authorities in Pyongyang conceded that they could no longer count on help from the Soviet Union and its Warsaw Pact allies to keep the DPRK afloat militarily and economically. In the military realm, they decided to build sufficient capabilities of their own to deter an assault from outside the country and to maintain order within. Acquisition of at least a small number of nuclear weapons and the capacity to deliver them played a key role in this strategy. During the 1990s, the DPRK government accelerated the nuclear program that it had begun in the early 1980s, and by 1994 the U.S. Central Intelligency Agency had concluded that the DPRK possessed enough plutonium for five nuclear weapons and had probably already developed a nuclear device. In June 1993, DPRK engineers also successfully tested a medium-range missile capable of carrying nuclear, chemical, and biological payloads and of hitting the ROK and most of Japan.

In the economic sphere, the Pyongyang regime began a new drive to diversify the DPRK's external trade and to obtain Western technology and capital. It declared a "special economic zone" in the Tumen River region, where the DPRK, China, and Russia meet, and it proposed joint development of the river basin by a regional group of states including Japan and the ROK. It designated three of its northeastern seaports as economic and free trade zones. It applied for membership in the Asian Development Bank. And it launched an undertaking with the UN Development Program to find overseas business partners and to learn modern management.

The results of this approach have been mixed. On the positive side, mounting evidence of the Pyongyang government's advances in the nuclear weapons field has rendered the United States, the ROK, and Japan more conciliatory in dealing with it. Indeed, U.S. and DPRK officials signed an accord in October 1994 that called for a massive aid effort by the United States, the ROK, and Japan to supply the DPRK with new sources of energy in return for the complete dismantling of the DPRK's nuclear program over roughly ten years. Furthermore, the big Tumen development project has gotten under way, with participation by Russia, China, Mongolia, Japan, and the ROK as well as the DPRK. On the negative side, the DPRK's trade with Western states has remained essentially stagnant, and Pyongyang authorities have found little enthusiasm among foreign businessmen for long-term investment. International controversy over the Pyongyang's nuclear program has reinforced this leeriness of the DPRK.

Across the long run, however, it seems doubtful that the DPRK will prove economically viable without much larger infusions of foreign capital and technical know-how than it had received up to the mid-1990s. Growing evidence in 1995–96 that large segments of the population were facing famine or near-famine conditions reinforces such a judgment. Yet the Pyongyang regime persists with domestic economic policies that drive away most potential foreign investors.

IMPLICATIONS

The foregoing analysis suggests some broad conclusions regarding state groupings founded on common ideological viewpoints. To begin with, membership in such a constellation of states clearly entails significant dangers for regimes destined to play a peripheral role in it. If the government(s) forming the core of the grouping should collapse—a possibility not to be lightly dismissed—peripheral regimes could find their continued existence in jeopardy, for demise of the key proponent(s) of the ideology tends to undermine the legitimacy of the peripheral regimes.

The challenge to the survival of the constellation's peripheral regimes by the disintegration of the ideological center becomes more severe the greater the degree to which the regimes have alienated their local populations. This is true no matter how much local support a regime may have enjoyed at the outset of its rule because of its emergence in the wake of a revolution, at a country's independence, and so on.

Furthermore, the severity of the threat is affected by the extent to which peripheral regimes have allowed themselves to grow militarily and/or economically dependent on the primary government(s) of the grouping. If there is a heavy dependency, disappearance of the constellation's key government(s) creates a major challenge for a peripheral regime.

The worst threat to peripheral regimes arises in instances when alienation of the local populace and concrete dependence on the chief government(s) of the constellation have both been present in the recent past. Indeed, regimes that have to cope with such situations may have an exceedingly hard time surviving.

In dealing with the consequences of the collapse of the main government(s) of an ideological grouping to which it belongs, a peripheral regime whose claim to legitimacy has rested essentially on ideological grounds may have little choice but to forsake the ideology and hunt for alternative sources of legitimacy. This is especially the case if the regime has been militarily dependent on the core government(s), for the decrease or cutoff of arms supplies that the demise of the core government(s) typically triggers forecloses any possibility of the regime's holding on to power by means of force. Yet searching for alternative sources of legitimacy poses grave risks for peripheral regimes that have seriously alienated their local populations.

If a peripheral regime has bases of legitimacy besides ideological ones, it may manage to retain its ideological commitments, at least in part. But military or especially economic dependence on the former principal government(s) of the grouping reduces the chances that it will be able to do so. At minimum, abandoning all economic aspects of the ideology may prove crucial for survival.

NOTES

1. The discussion of Mozambique in this chapter draws on Colin Legum, ed., *Africa Contemporary Record, 1983–1984* (New York: Africana, 1985), B670–77; Colin Legum and Marion E. Doro, eds., *Africa Contemporary Record, 1987–1988* (New York: Africana, 1989), B621, B643–46; *Africa Research Bulletin: Political Series* 27 (August 15, 1989), 9343–44; Richard F. Staar, ed., *1990 Yearbook on International Communist Affairs* (Stanford: Hoover Institution Press, 1990), 17–21; Ruth Ansah Ayisi and Karl Maier, "Interview with President Joaquim Chissano: Creating Conditions for Peace," *Africa Report* 35 (May–June 1990), 53–57; "Update," *Africa Report* 35 (September–October 1990), 7; Witney W. Schneidman, "Conflict Resolution in Mozambique: A Status Report," *CSIS Africa Notes*, no. 122 (February 28, 1991), 1–8; Virginia Curtin Knight, "Mozambique's Search for Stability," *Current History* 90 (May 1991), 217–20; Shawn H. McCormick, "Mozambique's Cautious Steps toward Lasting Peace," *Current History* 92 (May 1993), 224–28; Andrew Meldrum, "Avoiding Another Angola," *Africa Report* 38 (September–October 1993), 46–49; information from the International Foundation for Electoral Systems, November 22, 1994; coverage of Mozambique in Foreign Broadcast Information Service, *Daily Report: Sub-Saharan Africa* (hereafter FBIS-AFR).

2. For the bases of the analysis of the PDRY here and elsewhere, see Robert W. Stookey, *South Yemen: A Marxist Republic in Arabia* (Boulder: Westview Press, 1982); Robin Bidwell, *The Two Yemens* (Singapore: Longman Company/Westview Press, 1983), 219–337; B. R. Pridham, ed., *Contemporary Yemen: Politics and Historical Background* (New York: St. Martin's Press, 1984); David Pollock, "Moscow and Aden: Coping with a Coup," *Problems of Communism* 35 (May–June 1986), 50–70; entries on the PDRY in the annual volumes from 1987 through 1990 of Staar, ed., *Yearbook on International Communist Affairs*; F. G. Cause III, "Yemeni Unity: Past and Future," *Middle East Journal* 42 (Winter 1988), 33–47; R. D. Burrowes, "Oil Strike and Leadership Struggle in South Yemen," *Middle East Journal* 43 (Summer 1989), 437–54; Fred Halliday, *Revolution and Foreign Policy: The Case of South Yemen, 1967–1987* (Cambridge: Cambridge University Press, 1990); Alan George, "Perestroika

Comes to Aden," *The Middle East,* January 1990, 21, and "This Time It's Really Happening," ibid., July 1990, 5–8; John King, "The New Republic of Yemen: The Pitfalls Ahead," *Middle East International,* June 8, 1990, 17–18.

3. U.S. Arms Control and Disarmament Agency, *World Military Expenditures and Arms Transfers, 1990* (Washington, D.C., November 1991), 131–34.

4. U.S. Department of State, *Warsaw Pact Economic Aid Programs in Non-Communist LDCs: Holding Their Own in 1986* (Washington, D.C., August 1988), 8–11; U.S. Central Intelligence Agency, *Handbook of Economic Statistics, 1989,* CPAS 89–10002 (Washington, D.C., September 1989), 175–76 and 178, and *Handbook of Economic Statistics, 1991,* CPAS 91–10001 (Washington, D.C., September 1991), 156, 160.

5. The statements of President Vaclav Havel and other top officials of Czechoslovakia were typical. Concerning these, see Jan Oberman, "Arms Trading Continues," *Report on Eastern Europe* 1 (October 26, 1990), 15–17; *New York Times,* April 3, May 3, 1991.

6. See Gorbachev's decree "Changes in the Soviet Union's Foreign Economic Practice," issued on July 24, 1990, and published in *Pravda,* July 25, 1990; interview with Russian president Boris Yeltsin by Nikolai Burbyga, *Izvestiia,* February 24, 1992.

7. Data on debts as of 1989 appear in *Izvestiia,* March 1, 1990. Statistics on the performance of the economies of the nine countries may be found in U.S. Arms Control and Disarmament Agency, *World Military Expenditures and Arms Transfers, 1990,* 52–88 (passim); Rhee Sang-Woo, "North Korea in 1990: Lonesome Struggle to Keep Chuch'e," Douglas Pike, "Vietnam in 1990: The Last Picture Show," Geoffrey C. Gunn, "Laos in 1990: Winds of Change," Justus M. van der Kroef, "Cambodia in 1990: The Elusive Peace," all in *Asian Survey,* 31 (January 1991), 72–74, 82–83, 87–89, and 98–99, respectively; Rhee Sang-Woo, "North Korea in 1991: Struggle to Save Chuch'e Amid Signs of Change," Douglas Pike, "Vietnam in 1991: The Turning Point," and Stephen T. Johnson, "Laos in 1991: Year of the Constitution," all ibid. 32 (January 1992), 57–60, 77–78, and 85–86, respectively. On the nature of the commodities that the nine had available for export, see United Nations, *1989 International Trade Statistics Yearbook* (New York, 1991), vol. 1, passim; United Nations Conference on Trade and Development, *Handbook of International Trade and Development Statistics, 1990* (New York, 1991), 194–217, passim.

8. By way of illustration, see the statement by Soviet foreign minister Eduard Shevardnadze in Nicaragua on October 5, 1989, in *Pravda,* October 6, 1989; Susan Kaufman Purcell, "Cuba's Cloudy Future," *Foreign Affairs* 69 (Summer 1990), 118; U.S. Department of Defense, *Soviet Military Power 1990* (Washington, D.C., September 1990), 19; *New York Times,* September 17, 1990, September 12, 14, 1991; Radio Seoul Domestic Service in Korean, September 28, 1990, in Foreign Broadcast Information Service, *Daily Report: East Asia* (hereafter FBIS-EA), September 28, 1990, 28; Hong Kong AFP in English, November 30, 1990, ibid., November 30, 1990, 44–45; Justus M. van der Kroef, "Cambodia in 1990: The Elusive Peace," *Asian Survey* 31 (January 1991), 94–102; entries on Ethiopia, Cuba, and Nicaragua in Staar, ed., *1991 Yearbook on International Communist Affairs,* 17, 73, 107; U.S. Central Intelligence Agency, *Handbook of Economic Statistics, 1991,* 158–60; *Financial Times* (London), September 14, 1991; *Keesing's Record of World Events* 37 (September 1991), 38430–

31; Cole Blasier, "Moscow's Retreat from Cuba," *Problems of Communism* 40 (November–December 1991), 96–97; Gilliam Gunn, "Cuba's Search for Alternatives," *Current History* 91 (February 1992), 59.

9. Regarding the treatment of Afghanistan here and throughout the chapter, see Henry S. Bradsher, *Afghanistan and the Soviet Union* (Durham: Duke University Press, 1983); Zalmay Khalizad, "Moscow's Afghan War," *Problems of Communism* 35 (January–February 1986), 1–20; Rosanne Klass, "Afghanistan: The Accords," *Foreign Affairs* 66 (Summer 1988), 922–43; Barnett R. Rubin, "The Fragmentation of Afghanistan," *Foreign Affairs* 68 (Winter 1989–90), 150–68; Staar, ed., *1991 Yearbook on International Communist Affairs*, 465–73; Rasul Bakhsh Rais, "Afghanistan after the Soviet Withdrawal," *Current History* 91 (March 1992), 123–27; coverage of Afghanistan in Foreign Broadcast Information Service, *Near East and South Asia*.

10. The discussion of Ethiopia in this chapter is based on Paul B. Henze, "Communism and Ethiopia," *Problems of Communism* 30 (May–June 1981), 55–74, and "Marxist Disaster and Cultural Survival in Ethiopia," ibid. 39 (November–December 1990), 66–80; Staar, ed., *1990 Yearbook on International Communist Affairs*, 14–15, and *1991 Yearbook*, 15–17; "Ethiopia: New Party, Same President," *Africa Confidential* 31 (March 23, 1990), 6–7; "Ethiopia: The Peasants Revolt," ibid. (May 18, 1990), 6–7; Terrence Lyons, "The Transition in Ethiopia," *CSIS Africa Notes* no. 127 (August 27, 1991), 2; coverage of Ethiopia in FBIS-AFR.

11. For data on Nicaragua relevant to the analysis here and elsewhere, see Jiri Valenta and Virginia Valenta, "Sandinistas in Power," *Problems of Communism* 34 (September–October 1985), 1–28; Staar, ed., *1990 Yearbook on International Communist Affairs*, 107–8 and 110–18, and *1991 Yearbook*, 103–6; International Institute for Strategic Studies, *Strategic Survey, 1989–1990*, 186–90, and *Strategic Survey, 1990–1991*, 122–26 (London: Brassey's, May 1990 and 1991, respectively); Richard L. Millett, "Nicaragua: A Glimmer of Hope," *Current History* 89 (January 1990), 21–24; 35–37; Paul Berman, "Why the Sandinistas Lost," *Dissent*, Summer 1990, 307–14; coverage of Nicaragua in Foreign Broadcast Information Service, *Daily Report: Latin America* (hereafter FBIS-LAT).

12. The treatment of Angola in this chapter draws upon John A. Marcum, "Angola: A Quarter Century of War," *CSIS Africa Notes*, no. 37 (December 21, 1984), 1–7; Chas. W. Freeman, Jr., "The Angola/Namibia Accords," *Foreign Affairs* 68 (Summer 1989), 126–41; Colleen Lowe Morna, "Ready for Peace," *Africa Report* 35 (July–August 1990), 39–41; Starr, ed., *1991 Yearbook on International Communist Affairs*, 4–7; Karl Maier, "Blueprint for Peace," *Africa Report* 36 (March–April 1991), 19–22; Anita Coulson, "Politics after Peace," *Africa Report* 36 (July–August 1991), 49–52, and "Constructing Capitalism," ibid. (November–December 1991), 61–65; Vicki Finkel, "Savimbi's Sour Grapes," *Africa Report* 38 (January–February 1993), 25–28; John A. Marcum, "Angola: War Again," *Current History* 92 (May 1993), 218–23; *New York Times*, February 9, 14, 1995; coverage of Angola in FBIS-AFR.

13. For the foundations of the discussion of Cambodia here and later in the chapter, see Kishore Mahbubani, "The Kampuchean Problem: A Southeast Asian Perception," *Foreign Affairs* 62 (Winter 1983–84), 407–25; Gareth Porter, "Cambodia: Sihanouk's Initiative," *Foreign Affairs* 66 (Spring 1988), 808–26; Stephen J. Solarz,

"Cambodia and the International Community," *Foreign Affairs* 69 (Spring 1990), 99–115; *New York Times*, September 11, 1990; Staar, ed., *1991 Yearbook on International Communist Affairs*, 145–55; Frederick Z. Brown, "Cambodia in 1991: An Uncertain Peace," *Asian Survey* 32 (January 1992), 88–96, and "Cambodia in 1992: Peace at Peril," ibid. 33 (January 1993), 83–90; reports on Cambodia in *Far Eastern Economic Review* from January to December 1993; coverage of Cambodia in FBIS-EA.

14. See the breakdowns of the sources of their arms imports in U.S. Arms Control and Disarmament Agency, *World Military Expenditures and Arms Transfers, 1990*, 131–34.

15. The analysis of Cuba here and elsewhere is based on Staar, ed., *1991 Yearbook on International Communist Affairs*, 72–76; Gunn, "Cuba's Search for Alternatives," 59–64; Susan Kaufman Purcell, "Collapsing Cuba," *Foreign Affairs* 71 (America and the World 1991–92), 130–45; Howard J. Wiarda, "Is Cuba Next? Crises of the Castro Regime," *Problems of Communism* 40 (January–April 1991), 91; Jeremy Main, "Cuba: Pushing for Change," *Fortune*, August 26, 1991, 90–97; Jorge I. Dominguez, "The Secrets of Castro's Staying Power," *Foreign Affairs* 72 (Spring 1993), 97–107; Jo Thomas, "The Last Days of Castro's Cuba," *New York Times Magazine*, March 14, 1993, 34–39, 62–64, 68; Andrew Zimbalist, "Dateline Cuba: Hanging On in Havana," *Foreign Policy* 92 (Fall 1993), 151–67; *New York Times*, September 26, 1994, February 29, July 25, 1996; coverage of Cuba in FBIS-LAT.

16. For data underpinning the treatment of the DPRK in this chapter, see Rhee, "North Korea in 1990," 73–78, and "North Korea in 1991," 57–63; Clark Sorensen, "North Korea's Search for Legitimacy in a Multipolar World," *Problems of Communism* 39 (July–August 1990), 96–97; Staar, ed., *1991 Yearbook on International Communist Affairs*, 184–91; reports on the DPRK in *Far East Economic Review* from August 1991 to July 1996; John Merrill, "North Korea in 1992: Steering Away from the Shoals," *Asian Survey* 33 (January 1993), 43–53; *New York Times*, October 20, 21, 22, 1994, May 14, 1996; coverage of the DPRK in FBIS-EA.

17. These and other details regarding Vietnam in this chapter come from Pike, "Vietnam in 1990," 80–83, and "Vietnam in 1991," 74–81; reports on Vietnam in *Far Eastern Economic Review* from February 1990 through June 1996; Staar, ed., *1991 Yearbook on International Communist Affairs*, 241–56; Douglas Pike, "Change and Continuity in Vietnam," *Current History* 89 (March 1990), 117–20; Gareth Porter, "The Politics of 'Renovation' in Vietnam," *Problems of Communism* 39 (May–June 1990), 75–88; Charles A. Joiner, "The Vietnam Communist Party Strives to Remain the 'Only Force,'" *Asian Survey* 30 (November 1990), 1053–65; Dorothy R. Avery, "Vietnam in 1992: Win Some; Lose Some," *Asian Survey* 33 (January 1993), 67–74; *New York Times*, July 25, 1996; coverage of Vietnam in FBIS-EA.

18. The discussion of Laos in this chapter draws upon U.S. Arms Control and Disarmament Agency, *World Military Expenditures and Arms Transfers, 1990*, 132; *New York Times*, January 27, 1990, May 17, 1992; Gunn, "Laos in 1990," 87–93; Staar, ed., *1991 Yearbook on International Communist Affairs*, 193–96; Johnson, "Laos in 1991," 82–87; Stephen T. Johnson, "Laos in 1992: Succession and Consolidation," *Asian Survey* 33 (January 1993), 75–82; coverage of Laos in FBIS-EA.

19. For data concerning Benin throughout this chapter, see Staar, *1990 Yearbook*

on *International Communist Affairs,* 10–11, and *1991 Yearbook,* 10–12; "Benin," *Africa Demos* 1 (November 1990), 2–3; Vivian Lowery Derryck, "The Velvet Revolution," *Africa Report* 36 (January–February 1991), 24–26; George Neavoll, "A Victory for Democracy," and Margaret A. Novicki, "Interview with Msgr. Isidore de Sousz: Building a New Benin," both in *Africa Report* 36 (May–June 1991), 39–42 and 43–45, respectively; coverage of Benin in FBIS-AFR.

20. The analysis of Cape Verde here and later in the chapter rests on Daphne Topouzis, "Determined to Develop," *Africa Report* 35 (September–October 1989), 54; *Keesing's Record of World Events* 36 (February 1990), 37239; 37 (January 1991), 37948, and (February 1991), 37994–95, 38030; "Update," *Africa Report* 36 (March–April 1991), 8; "Cape Verde," *Africa Demos* 1 (July–August 1991), 2–4; Arthur S. Banks, ed., *Political Handbook of the World, 1991* (Binghamton, N.Y.: CSA Publications, 1991), 116–17; "Interview with Prime Minister Carlos Veiga," *Africa Report* 36 (May–June 1992), 9; coverage of Cape Verde in FBIS-AFR.

21. For these and other details about Congo in this chapter, see *Keesing's Record of World Events* 36 (February 1990), 37239; 37 (January 1991), 37948, and (February 1991), 37994–95, 38030; "Update," *Africa Report* 36 (July–August 1991), 7; "Congo," *Africa Demos* 2 (November 1991), 3; Starr, ed., *1991 Yearbook on International Communist Affairs,* 12–14; Banks, *Political Handbook of the World, 1991,* 152–54; "Congo: Characteristic Ambiguity," *Africa Confidential* 33 (March 6, 1992), 5–6; coverage of Congo in FBIS-AFR.

22. The treatment of Mongolia in this chapter is based on William R. Heaton, "Mongolia in 1990: Upheaval, Reform, But No Revolution Yet," *Asian Survey* 31 (January 1991), 50–54; Staar, ed., *1991 Yearbook on International Communist Affairs,* 202–4; William R. Heaton, "Mongolia in 1991: The Uneasy Transition," *Asian Survey* 32 (January 1992), 50–52; Tsedendambyn Batbayar, "Mongolia in 1992: Back to One-Party Rule," *Asian Survey* 33 (January 1993), 61–66; reports on Mongolia in *Far Eastern Economic Review* from April 1993 to June 1996; *Keesing's Record of World Events* 39 (June 1993), 39510–11; *New York Times,* July 3, 1996; coverage of Mongolia in FBIS-EA.

23. Information about Guinea-Bissau here and elsewhere comes from Daphne Topouzis, "Guinea-Bissau: Shifting Course," *Africa Report* 35 (September–October 1989), 49–51; Banks, *Political Handbook of the World, 1991,* 274–75; *Keesing's Record of World Events* 36 (October 1990), 37802; 37 (February 1991), 37948, 38003; 38 (March 1992), 38801; 38 (July 1992), 38993; and 39 (May 1993), 39452; "Guinea-Bissau: Pluralism Comes Home to Roost," *Africa Confidential* 34 (June 11, 1993): 8; "Guinea-Bissau: An Uneasy Honeymoon," *Africa Confidential* 35 (July 15, 1994), 7; "Election Watch," *Journal of Democracy* 5 (October 1994), 181; coverage of Guinea-Bissau in FBIS-AFR.

24. The sources on which the discussion of Sao Tome and Principe in this chapter relies include *Keesing's Record of World Events* 35 (October 1989), 56995; 36 (May 1990), 37479, and (August 1990), 37645; 37 (January 1991), 37949, and (February 1991), 38040; "Update," *Africa Report* 35 (May–June 1990), 7; "Sao Tome e Principe:

Trovoada's Return," *Africa Confidential* 31 (August 24, 1990), 7; Banks, *Political Handbook of the World, 1991,* 578–79; coverage of Sao Tome and Principe in FBIS-AFR.

25. For the foundations of the analysis of Zimbabwe in this chapter, see the chapters on "The USSR and Africa" in the volumes of Legum, *Africa Contemporary Record,* for the first half of the 1980s; Staar, ed., *1990 Yearbook on International Communist Affairs,* 34–36, and *1991 Yearbook,* 40–42; Andrew Meldrum, "Mugabe's Folly," *Africa Report* 35 (March–April 1990), 54–57; Meldrum, "The One-Party Debate," ibid. (July–August 1990), 53–56; Meldrum, "The Land Question," ibid. 36 (March–April 1991, 26–30; Meldrum, "The Kaunda Option?" ibid. 37 (July–August 1992), 13–16; Meldrum, "The Poor Pay the Price," ibid. 38 (July–August 1993), 63–67; Meldrum, "Zimbawe: Rubber-Stamp Parliament," ibid. 40 (May–June 1995), 60–63; Virginia Curtin Knight, "Zimbabwe: The Politics of Economic Reform," *Current History* 91 (May 1992), 220–21; *New York Times,* May 13, 1996; coverage of Zimbabwe in FBIS-AFR.

26. See the various states' yearly GNPs per capita in the 1980s, in U.S. Arms Control and Disarmament Agency, *World Military Expenditures and Arms Transfers, 1990,* table 1.

27. *New York Times,* January 27, 1990.

28. Compare, for example, Dominguez, "The Secrets of Castro's Staying Power," and Zimbalist, "Dateline Cuba," with the views of Cuban dissidents such as Elizardo Sanchez Santa Cruz and Gustavo Cano Escobar and of many Cuban-Americans, as reported in the *New York Times,* September 29, October 6, 1993.

29. Speech of June 9, 1990, as carried by the Korea Central News Agency the same day, and article in *Kulloja,* October 1990, both quoted in Staar, ed., *1991 Yearbook on International Communist Affairs,* 183.

Contributors

DAVID E. ALBRIGHT is visiting scholar, Russian and East European Institute, Indiana University, Bloomington.

HENRY E. BRADY is professor of political science and public policy, University of California, Berkeley.

LUCJA SWIATKOWSKI CANNON is adjunct fellow, Center for Strategic and International Studies, Washington, D.C.

BARBARA ANN CHOTINER is professor of political science, University of Alabama, Tuscaloosa.

LENARD J. COHEN is professor of political science, Simon Fraser University, British Columbia, Canada.

ROBERT O. FREEDMAN is acting president and professor of political science, Baltimore Hebrew University.

CYNTHIA KAPLAN is associate professor of political science, University of California, Santa Barbara.

ILPYONG J. KIM is professor of political science, University of Connecticut, Storrs.

ANDRZEJ KORBONSKI is professor of political science, University of California, Los Angeles.

LT. GEN. WILLIAM E. ODOM, USA (ret.), is director of national security studies, Hudson Institute, Washington, D.C.

THOMAS W. ROBINSON is president of American Asian Research Enterprises and professor of national security, Georgetown University.

ZENOVIA A. SOCHOR is associate professor of government, Clark University.

NILS H. WESSELL is head of the Department of Humanities, U.S. Coast Guard Academy, New Haven.

JANE SHAPIRO ZACEK is director, Office of Grant Support, and adjunct professor of political science, Union College, Schenectady.

Index